GOING TO THE PEOPLE

Going to the People

Jews and the Ethnographic Impulse

Edited by Jeffrey Veidlinger

INDIANA UNIVERSITY PRESS

Bloomington & Indianapolis

This book is a publication of

INDIANA UNIVERSITY PRESS
Office of Scholarly Publishing
Herman B Wells Library 350
1320 East 10th Street
Bloomington, Indiana 47405 USA

iupress.indiana.edu

*Manufactured in the
United States of America*

*Library of Congress
Cataloging-in-Publication Data*

Names: Veidlinger, Jeffrey, [date], editor.
Title: Going to the people : Jews and the
ethnographic impulse / edited by
Jeffrey Veidlinger.
Description: Bloomington ; Indianapolis :
Indiana University Press, [2016] |
Selected papers presented at a conference
held at Indiana University in
February 2013. | Includes index.
Identifiers: LCCN 2015023878 | ISBN
9780253019080 (cloth : alk. paper) | ISBN
9780253019141 (pbk. : alk. paper) | ISBN
9780253019165 (ebook)
Subjects: LCSH: Jews—Europe, Eastern—
Social life and customs—Congresses. |
Jews—Social life and customs—
Congresses. | Jewish folklorists—Europe,
Eastern—Congresses. | Folk literature,
Yiddish—Congresses. | Jewish folk
literature—Congresses. | Ethnology—
Europe, Eastern—Congresses. |
Europe, Eastern—Ethnic
relations—Congresses.
Classification: LCC DS135.E83 G654 2016 |
DDC 305.892/4047—dc23 LC record avail-
able at http://lccn.loc.gov/2015023878

1 2 3 4 5   21 20 19 18 17 16

Go out and see what the people do.

—BT ERUVIN 14B

CONTENTS

ACKNOWLEDGMENTS

THIS BOOK EMERGED out of a conference held at Indiana University in February 2013. First and foremost I would like to thank the conference co-organizers, Dov-Ber Kerler, Haya Bar-Itzhak, and Anya Quilitzsch, who worked with me in putting together the event. I would also like to thank Melissa Deckard for coordinating and administering the event, as well as the other staff at the Borns Jewish Studies Program for their assistance: Janice Hurtuk, Tracy Richardson, and the Borns program's own folklorist and assistant director, Carolyn Lipson-Walker. In addition to those whose papers appear in this volume, there were several others who participated in the conference as paper presenters, commentators, or chairs: Michael Alpert, Alan Bern, Valery Dymshits, Itzik Gottesman, Sarah Imhoff, Jason Jackson, Dov-Ber Kerler, Marija Krupoves, Moisei Lemster, Shaul Magid, Anya Quilitzsch, David Ransel, Ilana Rosen, Boris Sandler, Dmitri Slepovitch, and Yuri Vedenyapin. Their input and ideas are also reflected in these papers. I would particularly like to thank Dmitri Slepovitch and Michael Alpert for also providing evening entertainment and enlightenment at the conference with the "Traveling the Yiddishland" show. Both Dov-Ber and I express our heartfelt thanks to Dr. Alice Ginott Cohn z"l, who was a longtime supporter of Yiddish studies at Indiana University; without her generosity the conference would not have been possible.

Former director of Indiana University Press Janet Rabinowitch attended the conference and solicited the book manuscript. I thank her for helping envision how the ideas we discussed at the conference could be formulated into a book. At Indiana University Press, I also thank Robert Sloan and Jenna Whittaker for seeing the project through. Thanks, as well, to Eric Levy for his patient and precise copyediting, my undergraduate research assistants Jacqueline Khutorsky and Terra Schroeder for their assistance, and Paula Durbin-Westby for compiling the index. I am grateful to Eugene Avrutin and the other peer reviewer who remained anonymous for providing helpful and insightful critiques of the manuscript. I completed the final edits while on fellowship at the Frankel Institute for Advanced Judaic Studies at the University of Michigan, and am grateful for the opportunity to have had time to work on this manuscript while simultaneously embarking upon a new project of my own.

Finally, I extend my deepest thanks to the contributors of the volume for taking the time to develop their conference papers into coherent chapters, for their patience as the publication process wore on, and for providing me with the opportunity to learn more about Jewish folklore, ethnography, anthropology, and oral history. It has been a pleasure to work with each of them.

GOING TO THE PEOPLE

Introduction

JEFFREY VEIDLINGER

In the spring of 1873 a manifesto written by an ad hoc group of populists based in St. Petersburg began circulating among Russian university students: "Go to the people and tell it the whole truth to the very last word. Tell it that man must live according to the law of nature. According to this law all men are equal; all men are born naked, all men are born equally small and weak."[1] The following summer, the summer of 1874, hundreds, perhaps thousands, of students abandoned their universities and went into the countryside "to the people." These urban students and alienated nobility had come to believe that the future lay in the revolutionary power of the Russian peasantry, the simple folk, the *narod* or the *muzhik*.

This compulsion to "go to the people" was infectious: it not only played an important role in the growth of the Russian revolutionary movement, but it also encouraged intellectuals, amateur scholars, and aspiring artists to draw inspiration from their roots, to return to "their people." The Jews of the Russian Empire took part in this movement of "return" with enthusiasm. The most celebrated spokesperson for the movement to the people among Jewish activists was probably Shloyme Zaynvl Rapoport, known more commonly by his pseudonym, S. An-sky.[2] An-sky's manifesto, "Jewish Folk Creativity," published in the short-lived journal *Perezhitoe* (The past) in 1908, began with an epigraph from the Talmudic tractate Eruvin 14b, "Go out and see what the people do," that paralleled the populists' rallying cry and linked the modern cause to the Jewish past.[3] "Our task today," he wrote in that seminal manifesto, "is to organize without delay the systematic collection of the works of folk art, of the monuments of the Jewish past, and to describe Jewish lifestyles over the generations. This task is not partisan, but national and cultural, and the best forces of our people must be mobilized and unified for it. The time has come to create Jewish ethnography!"[4] Between 1912 and 1914, An-sky would try to put his ideas into action by leading a series of ethnographic expeditions to the Pale of Jewish Settlement.

In the winter of 2013, marking one hundred years since this now famed expedition, a group of artists and scholars—linguists, ethnomusicologists, historians, practicing musicians, folklorists, literary scholars, sociologists, and anthropologists—met at Indiana University in Bloomington to discuss the past, present, and future of the Jewish ethnographic impulse. This book is derived from those discussions. The contributions included in this volume are divided into three broad sections, the first of which comprises historical analyses of particular Eastern European Jewish ethnographic traditions or individual ethnographers. These chapters include Nathaniel Deutsch's exploration of the idea of return in Jewish ethnography; Marina Mogilner's analysis of the influence of race theory in Russian Jewish anthropology; Sergei Kan's biography of the prominent ethnographer Lev Shternberg; Elissa Bemporad's examination of the Jewish ethnographic tradition in Belorussia; Mikhail Krutikov's survey of Soviet Jewish folkloristics; Deborah Yalen's exploration of the museum exhibit that Isaiah Pul'ner mounted on the eve of World War II; Sarah Ellen Zarrow's piece on the YIVO *zamlers* (collectors) of Poland; and David E. Fishman's writing on the Paper Brigade in the aftermath of World War II Vilna.

The second section presents some findings from scholars who have conducted their own fieldwork research among Eastern European Jews. Haya Bar-Itzhak shows how Polish Jewish immigrants to Israel understood and explained their new predicaments through folklore; Alexandra Polyan looks at the role language plays in shaping the identity of Jews in Bessarabia and Bukovina; I examine the relationship between food and religious identity among Jews in small-town Ukraine; and Sebastian Z. Schulman analyzes the legends of the Ribnitser Rebbe.

The third section presents some personal reflections of scholars who have themselves "gone to the people," inspired by the "ethnographic impulse." This section includes Larisa Fialkova and Maria Yelenevskaya's reflections on autoethnography as applied to their own fieldwork among ex-Soviets in Israel; Halina Goldberg's personal thoughts on the museum exhibit she established about her own family's history in Łódź, and Asya Vaisman Schulman's reflections on her experiences as an observant Jew from the former Soviet Union conducting research among American Hasidim. Simon J. Bronner's chapter, which concludes the volume, offers a retrospective on Jewish ethnography with a focus on the American context.

The populists who went "to the people" in 1874 were divided on why exactly they were going to the people. Was it to learn from them? Or was it to teach them? And what exactly were they to be teaching or learning? Some, like the anarchists Mikhail Bakunin and Petr Kropotkin, saw great revolutionary potential within the peasantry and urged city dwellers to go among them to soak in that spirit. Others ascribed great wisdom to the masses, imagining them as uncorrupted keepers of tradition who could remind the city folk of their origins and restore balance to the Russian nation.

Perhaps the most influential advocate of the "going to the people" movement was Petr Lavrov, who inspired the students from his exile in Paris and Zurich. Lavrov believed that intellectuals, or "critically thinking individuals" in his terminology, owed a "moral responsibility" to teach the toiling masses so that they could share in the intellectual and moral progress that the critically thinking few had been able to enjoy at the expense of the majority population. In the end, the much-celebrated summer of 1874 did little to advance either mutual understanding or revolutionary fervor, but was remembered as a formative experience not only by those who participated, but also by those who only wished they had. Like the "Summer of Love" nearly one hundred years later, many more claimed to have participated in and been influenced by the movement than were actually involved in any concrete manner.

There were particularly few Jews among the students of 1874. University admissions discriminated against Jews, and the few Jewish students enrolled had trouble tracing their ancestry to the Russian village. Certainly some students, like O. V. Aptekman, had had themselves baptized, in order, they claimed, to draw nearer to the peasantry. But, generally speaking, Russia's Jewish revolutionaries tended not to place their faith in the Russian peasantry, preferring a more strictly—and urban—Marxist interpretation. But many Russian Jewish intellectuals were touched by the idea of returning to their own people, of gleaning wisdom from the common folk from whom they believed their rabbinical and political leadership had become alienated.[5]

The connection between An-sky's ethnographic impulse and the "going to the people" movement was more than just symbolic. When Lavrov became ill and bedridden in Paris in 1895, he hired An-sky, who was then a young aspiring Jewish writer, to be his personal secretary. An-sky had previously been active in the Russian Populist movement, and had published a few articles on the Russian peasantry. While working in the salt mines of Donetsk he had also collected Russian miner songs. Influenced by Lavrov's personality and passion for the people, An-sky decided to make it his life's work to go back to *his* people, to the Jews of the Pale of Jewish Settlement. He would later write in his memoirs that Lavrov had shown him the importance of loyalty to one's own people.[6]

The Russian Jewish ethnographers who went to the people in the late nineteenth and early twentieth centuries were also partaking in a rich tradition within the Russian Empire, a tradition that was itself heavily influenced by German *Kulturwissenschaft*. Russian ethnographers adapted Johann Gottfried Herder's notion of culture, with its emphasis on geography and philology, and, beginning in the eighteenth century, learned from the Germans the discipline of academic fieldwork. Throughout the nineteenth century, the imperial Russian state sought to learn more about the empire it ruled and established societies of learned scholars to study the terrain. The Russian Geographic Society was the most important of these, and served to extend imperial power to the empire's peripheries by allowing the state to rule through knowledge. Some in the society, like Karl von Baer and Nikolai Nadezhdin, thought it made sense to study not only the lands ruled from St. Petersburg, but also the peoples who inhabited those lands. In 1845–1846, they established the Ethnographic Division of the Russian Geographic Society. Baer, who was himself an ethnic German from Estonia, and Nadezhdin, the son of a village priest, differed in their views of the society: Nadezhdin envisioned it as an arena for studying ethnic Russians, and Baer as a venue in which to study the different peoples of the Russian Empire. Although both showed some interest in physical anthropology, the Ethnographic Division emphasized the material culture, daily life, beliefs, and rituals of the peoples it studied more than their physical traits. By the late nineteenth century, Germanic "race science" was relegated to the field of anthropology in Russia, whereas ethnography became a humanistic discipline focused on descriptive fieldwork and cultural practices. The ethnographic impulse was contagious in Russia: writers, musicians, and artists came to embrace the *narod*, and made careers for themselves based on thick descriptions of the everyday life and folklore of the common folk.[7]

The ethnography of Russian Jews was similarly divided between those who adopted anthropological approaches, studying the skulls and measuring the girth of Jewish bodies, and those who preferred to observe and analyze Jewish daily life. As was the case with general Russian ethnography, the Jewish ethnographic impulse was highly influential in creating a literary image of the Jew. Yiddish writers of the Russian Haskalah (Jewish Enlightenment), like Sholem Yankev Abramovitsh, better known by his pseudonym Mendele Moykher-Sforim, adopted the language of ethnography to critique what they saw as the backward culture of the Jewish shtetl. Other writers like Yitkhok Leybush Peretz in Poland or Martin Buber in Germany celebrated the quaintness of traditional (and usually Hasidic) Jewish life, which they saw as embodying an authenticity that was absent in their own urban milieus.[8]

As the study of Jews in the Russian Empire developed in the nineteenth century, it became intertwined with politics, history, ethnography, and folklore. In contrast to the German *Wissenschaft des Judentums* (Science of Judaism) movement, which imagined history as a science divorced from contemporary politics and external influences, the study of Jewish history in the Russian Empire was from its beginnings a political gesture, intertwined with defenses of the legal rights of Jews in the empire.[9] The empire's most celebrated Jewish historian, Simon Dubnow, doubled as a political advocate for diaspora nationalism, and in 1907 helped establish the *Folkspartey* (Folkist party). Dubnow had long regarded history as a collective and public effort rather than just the scholarly work of an elite cadre of intellectuals: in 1891 he issued a pamphlet urging the general

public to collect and preserve historical artifacts from their own neighborhoods, including specifically folk sayings, gravestone rubbings, and
community minute books, as well as official government documents.[10]

Dubnow's vision to construct a historical narrative of Jewish life in
Eastern Europe from the bottom up was finally implemented in 1908 with
the establishment of the Jewish Historical- Ethnographic Society (JHES)
in St. Petersburg, which he helped oversee. Dubnow laid much of the
groundwork for the eventual realization of the society during his time in
Odessa, where he befriended among others Yehoshua Hana Ravnitski,
who together with Hayim Nahman Bialik would later embark upon their
own project of *kinus,* or cultural ingathering, to collect Jewish folklore and
texts of national significance.[11] The *Sefer ha-agadah* (Book of legends) that
Bialik and Ravnitski published in 1908 presented a compendium of legends from written rabbinical sources, and served as a parallel project to
Dubnow's own ingathering. Outside of the Russian Empire, Martin Buber
was engaged in a similar project, as had been Max Grunvald and Louis
Ginsburg, reminding us that collecting Jewish folklore was not exclusively
an Eastern European compulsion. But it did take on a particularly populist
agenda in the East, where—Bialik and Ravnitski notwithstanding—collectors were more inclined to look toward contemporary stories told by
common folk than to mine Judaic texts for instances of *aggadah* (fables
from rabbinic literature). It was, as An-sky envisioned it, an effort to revive
the oral tradition that he believed had since become ossified in its written
form. In this sense, the JHES explicitly combined the study of history,
folklore, and ethnography, conflating Dubnow's vision with An-sky's.

Indeed, not long after An-sky returned to Russia in late 1905, he conceived of the idea of an ethnographic expedition through the Pale of Jewish Settlement. In 1909, he began petitioning the newly established JHES
to sponsor an expedition he would lead to record Jewish "traditions, legends, tales, parables, songs, proverbs, bywords, sayings, riddles, the peculiarities of local dialects, and so on" in Russia's western provinces, to
record "customs, beliefs, charms, superstitions, remedies," and to gather
"historical materials relating to each location—communal record books,
documents, old papers, memoirs, stories of eye-witnesses."[12] The JHES
embraced An-sky's proposal, and in 1910 urged the collection of "every
type of material (original manuscripts, copies of correspondence, memo-

rial material, etc.) related to the history and ethnography of the Jews in Poland and Russia."[13]

With the help of Baron Vladimir Gintsburg, An-sky gathered together a team of researchers that included the photographer Solomon Iudovin and the musician Yo'el Engel to explore the region during the summer of 1912. In two additional expeditions, with an expanded team of students from the Higher Courses on Oriental Studies and the folklorist and musicologist Zinovii Kiselgof, An-sky and his teams would collect about two thousand photographs; take down 1,800 folk stories, legends, sayings, and parables; transcribe 1,500 Jewish folk songs; and record one thousand folk motifs and instrumental songs on over five hundred wax cylinders. They would also write what An-sky called "pure ethnographic material descriptions" of ceremonies, beliefs, tokens, and sayings. Finally, the team collected more than one hundred historical documents, fifty old manuscripts and minute books, and some seven hundred objects and artifacts.[14] As part of his project, An-sky also prepared a two-thousand-question survey about all aspects of Jewish life from cradle to grave. Perhaps the most famous product of his ethnographic work, though, was the play *The Dybbuk*, inspired in part from the folkloric material he came across during these expeditions.

By fusing together history and ethnography, the JHES also set a precedent that would remain relevant for years to come. It regarded history as part of ethnography. In the words of Lev Shternberg, the renowned ethnographer who would succeed Dubnow as director of the society and who edited An-sky's ethnographic questionnaire, "An ethnographer is also a historian. The sole difference is that historians study more or less the distant past, whereas ethnographers study the recent past and the present, both of which will become subjects of history in the future."[15]

Shternberg, for his part, was one of several scholars of Jewish heritage who played formative roles in the establishment of ethnography as a field of research in general.[16] Perhaps the most famous of these internationally was Franz Boas, a German-Jewish immigrant to New York, who helped reorient anthropology away from the study of indelible racial characteristics and toward the study of a more mutable culture. Boas would make his mark in Russia through the Jessup North Pacific Expedition, on which he collaborated with Shternberg, who was then an expert on the Nivkh people of Sakhalin Island, and Vladimir Bogoraz, also known by the pseudonym N. A. Tan, who had been studying the Chukchi people of the Arctic. These scholars engaged in "salvage ethnography," a project designed to document minority cultures that were perceived as being remote and threatened by the expanding official state or imperial culture. Eventually, Shternberg and Bogoraz would both come to the same conclusion as An-sky: that their "own culture" was also being threatened. Later in life, both would turn their gazes from the peoples of remote Siberian outposts to their own Jewish communities.

In the first chapter of this volume, Nathaniel Deutsch explores what it meant for these Jewish ethnographers to return to their own people. Building on M. N. Srinivas's idea of the thrice reborn, he argues that An-sky's return to his own people presaged the post–World War II and twenty-first-century trends among anthropologists to study their own cultures rather than only seek out remote and foreign cultures. Yet, Deutsch points out that conceiving of such a turn as only a "return" is to miss much of the nuance in gazing at the other. An-sky and his subjects may have shared a religion, Deutsch reminds us, but the distances between them remained rather large. Deutsch asks what it means for the ethnographer to return to a home that he or she never knew.

While most Russian-Jewish ethnographers focused their attention on the culture of the Jews as opposed to their physical traits, there were also those who engaged in racial anthropology. As Marina Mogilner demonstrates in her contribution, early twentieth-century scholars like Aron El'kind subjected the Jewish body to the gaze of race science, joining other anthropologists in identifying specific physical characteristics shared by Ashkenazic Jews. El'kind maintained a delicate balance in his scholarship, on the one hand implying that the "Jewish physiognomy" he uncovered justified claims of Jewish distinctness and nationhood, while on the other hand explaining Jewish physical characteristics as products of their environment rather than inborn racial traits.

As Lev Shternberg's biographer Sergei Kan demonstrates in his contribution, Shternberg was instrumental in continuing the tradition of Jewish ethnography established by An-sky, a tradition that largely eschewed the type of racial anthropology becoming popular in Central Europe in favor of scholarship closer to what Claude Lévi-Strauss would later popularize as "cultural anthropology." Working after the Russian Revolution, Shternberg also helped adapt Jewish ethnography to the new realities of Soviet life: the old ways of the shtetl could no longer be romanticized, and instead ethnography, like all scholarship, had to serve the cause of the revolution. Shternberg developed what he called "a new ethnography of the present" that would focus on change and not just tradition. He sought to study not only the remnants of religious life and folk customs, but also the socioeconomic impact of the modern era. It was this mode of collection that his student Isaac Vinnikov would continue and that would manifest itself in much Soviet ethnography of the 1920s and 1930s.

Ethnography and folkloristics, though, were relatively unaffected by Marxist tendencies in the first decade of Soviet power. In general, aspiring Marxist scholars preferred more social-scientific approaches to the study of human relations, such as sociology, anthropology, and history, rather than the humanism and thick descriptions of ethnography and folkloristics. Bogoraz and Shternberg, both of whom had achieved their preeminence in the field in the prerevolutionary era, remained dominant figures throughout the 1920s, a period during which many of their colleagues in the social sciences fell from favor. During this time the field was torn between those who promoted universalist notions of culture, which elided ethnic or tribal differences, and those whose fieldwork demonstrated the distinct cultural traditions of different peoples. Marxist ethnography, as it was developing in the 1920s, favored the former in the belief that national cultures and ethnos were merely bourgeois fabrications.[17]

In addition to emphasizing universal traits, Soviet folkloristics could combat national and ethnic identity by highlighting regional differences within the culture of an ethnic group. In her contribution, Elissa Bemporad demonstrates how Jewish ethnographers and historians in 1920s Belorussia sought to "territorialize" Jewish ethnography by rejecting models that portrayed Jews as a uniform and homogenous entity, and instead highlighting customs specific to the territory of Belorussia. In 1921, amateur ethnographers, collectors, and students set out to Belorussian provincial towns in search of a local Belorussian Jewish folklore. Under the auspices of the Jewish Department of the Institute for Belorussian Culture, they collected and translated a vast array of stories, songs, jokes, proverbs, and other folkloric material, much of which was sent to them by amateur collectors. These songs, Bemporad argues, reflect a genuine pride in the achievements of the revolution. The display these ethnographers sponsored at the Jewish Department of the Belorussian State Museum in 1925 highlighted some of their findings and served to reinforce the new political geography of the USSR.

By the 1930s, even humanistic fields like ethnography and folklore were not immune to Sovietization. As traditional Jewish practices declined under the pressures of Sovietization, the study of Yiddish folklore retained its legitimacy, and even attained a respected position in the academy. As Mikhail Krutikov notes, Yiddish folklorists and writers, like Meir Wiener, were able to study Jewish folklore by reframing it as a "Marxist reconstruction of the culture of the oppressed classes." The folkloric practices of YIVO and the German *Volkskunde,* with their emphasis on the national spirit of the folk, were repressed as bourgeois and reactionary. Instead, Soviet Yiddish folklorists emphasized the universal folk motifs of the working class. Wiener's Marxist Yiddish folkloristics was subsequently taken up by Moyshe Beregovski and Zalmen Skuditski in Kiev, who focused on the musical traditions of Eastern European Jews, privileging songs of social protest and revolution and disseminating a genuinely popular new Soviet folklore.[18]

Indeed, ethnomusicological work in the former Pale of Jewish Settlement, begun by Yo'el Engel and the Jewish Folk Music Society, among others, continued in the Soviet Union through the 1930s under the leadership of Beregovski, who worked with Engel at the Malakhovsky orphanage outside Moscow.[19] Beregovski devoted himself to the collection of Jewish folk music in 1927 under the auspices of the Commission for the Study of Jewish Folk Music, which was part of the Faculty of Jewish Culture at the Academy of Sciences, and then as head of the Institute of Jewish Proletarian Culture, which later became the Cabinet of Jewish Culture. Under the auspices of these organizations, Beregovski traveled around the former Pale every summer, notating and recording local musical traditions with a phonograph. He collected some 4,000 musical samples in all, recorded on 1,200 phonographic cylinders. Only portions of Beregovski's planned five-volume work on Jewish musical folklore were published in his lifetime, but his contributions continue to influence new generations of musicians and his findings continue to be published today.

Beregovski may be the most celebrated collector of Soviet Jewish folk material in the 1930s, but he was by no means the only one. In her contribution to this volume, Deborah Yalen looks at the writings of Isaiah Pul'ner and the exhibit "Jews in Tsarist Russia and the USSR" that he mounted on the eve of World War II. Yalen discusses how Pul'ner balanced his theoretical rejection of the premise that Jews constitute an indivisible ethnographic whole with the reality that commonalities of tradition and religious practice united Jews from around the world and the Soviet Union. She argues that when Pul'ner established his exhibit in 1939, the practical benefits of presenting Russian Jewry as a unified whole trumped the ideological impediments. As a result, the exhibit was able to remain on display at the State Museum of Ethnography until 1941. Pul'ner, she shows, inherited An-sky's urge to collect as an act of salvage, but he combined it with Bogoraz's embrace of the changes the revolution wrought.

While folkloristics and ethnography in the Soviet Union were focused on deconstructing the notion of a united Jewish nation, across the border in Poland, the YIVO (Yiddish Scientific) Institute in Vilna was engaged in a massive campaign to employ scholarship and ethnography in the process of Jewish nation building.[20] YIVO's folklore commission was inspired in large part by the circle of folklorists that emerged in Warsaw around the Yiddish philologist and public activist Noah Pryłucki, who imagined a rejuvenation of Jewish national life inspired by the promotion and dissemination of Yiddish folklore.[21] Sarah Ellen Zarrow examines how YIVO encouraged Polish youth to collect folklore, sayings, and customs within their own communities. YIVO's project of encouraging ordinary folk to "go to the people and collect" represented the fulfillment of Dubnow's dream of turning the general public into amateur historians and ethnographers in order to forge a national mission through public history. Zarrow argues that in fostering *zamlers*, or amateur collectors, in the 1920s, the Ethnographic Commission of YIVO hoped to reconnect young people with their Jewish heritage. *Zamlung*, the act of collection, was supposed to be generative, not preservationist. Zarrow assesses the success of the YIVO project in creating Yiddish scholars out of common hobbyists. Most zamlers, she argues, had little interest or connection with YIVO and resisted the Ethnographic Commission's exhortations to conduct themselves as professional scholars. Rather, they were collecting for their own amateur interest and for the camaraderie of being with other collectors, not to service the Jewish nation. Ultimately, the act of collection became an end in and of itself, rather than the first stage of data collection for scholarly purposes.

There were some important attempts during and in the immediate aftermath of the war to continue the zamler tradition by collecting materials on Jewish daily life in the ghettos of Nazi-occupied Europe. The most famous of these is probably Emanuel Ringelblum's Oyneg Shabes archive, which clandestinely collected artifacts of ghetto life. Hidden in milk cans and buried in the ghetto, caches of these archives were discovered after the war.[22] Even before the war, Ringelblum's approach to history shared the ethnographic and historical bent of Dubnow, Shternberg, An-sky, and others. Long before the social turn in history, Ringelblum, along with other Polish Jewish historians like Majer Bałaban, was writing about the social interaction between peoples and encouraging the construction of a type of public history. The Oyneg Shabes's counterpart in the Vilna ghetto was the Paper Brigade, led by the Yiddish writers Avrom Sutzkever and Shmerke Kaczerginski. As slave laborers for the Einsatzstab Reichsleiter Rosenberg, the Nazi agency responsible for looting cultural treasures, Sutzkever and Kaczerginski clandestinely saved Jewish cultural treasures, hiding them in underground bunkers. In his contribution to this volume, David E. Fishman explores how members of the Paper Brigade established a Jewish Museum after the war in order to display and preserve the cultural heritage of Jewish Vilna. As evidence of the importance of the collection, Fishman points out that the museum was established even before the first synagogue, orphanage, and boarding school began to function. Once again, in the aftermath of war, the collection and preservation of the Jewish cultural heritage became an essential aspect of Jewish life.

Both Sutzkever and Kaczerginski remained influential intellectuals after the war, but from abroad—Sutzkever moved to Tel Aviv in 1947 and Kaczerginski settled in Argentina in 1950 after a sojourn in Paris. Indeed, after the destruction of Eastern European Jewish communities in the Holocaust and the onset of Communism throughout the region, zamlung was no longer possible in situ. Instead, scholars resorted to conducting ethnography in absentia. Influenced by Ruth Benedict (Boas's student) and Margaret Mead's Research in Contemporary Cultures project, Mark

Zborowski and Elizabeth Herzog began to study Jewish culture "at a distance." Their ethnographically inspired study of the Shtetl—then commonly rendered with a capital "S"—was based more on nostalgia and trauma than on observation or collection. The product of their work, *Life Is with People,* remained an important book in creating an image of the Eastern European Jew that helped fuel further interest in the subject.[23]

Other scholars recognized that the type of immersive field research and participant observation that ethnography demands could simply not be recreated in absentia. Instead of seeking to paint comprehensive landscapes of Eastern European Jewish life, they produced more focused studies that shed new light on specific aspects of Ashkenazic culture and experience, particularly those parts that could be carried away—oral traditions, folklore, music, and language.

Some of the first such studies were actually surveys conducted by relief agencies or by volunteers in displaced-persons camps. In 1946 David Boder conducted some of the earliest, if not the earliest, oral history work among Jewish survivors. Boder, who was born into a Jewish family in 1886 in Courland, spent much of his youth on the move. In the summer of 1946, he secured passage to Europe in order to interview displaced persons. He would eventually interview about 130 displaced persons in France, Switzerland, Italy, and Germany, utilizing the nine languages he had acquired during his own travels. These oral histories are among the first Holocaust testimonies and include extensive detail on everyday Jewish life in Eastern Europe before and during the Holocaust.[24]

To this day, the Jewish ethnographic impulse is often interconnected with oral history. Indeed, many oral historians trace the origins of their discipline to those like Barbara Myerhoff, who in her landmark study of Jewish clients at a senior center in Venice, California, encouraged scholars to listen to life stories in order to rescue the voices of ordinary folks.[25] Like An-sky, Shternberg, and Bogoraz, Myerhoff came to study the Jewish community only after establishing a reputation examining other ethnic groups, in her case investigating the pilgrimage practices of the Huichol Indians of Mexico.

Disciplinary distinctions exist between oral historians and ethnographers: historians tend to emphasize the particularities of individual experiences for the purpose of establishing a public record, whereas ethnographers tend to highlight more generalized experiences; and oral historians also tend to triangulate the life story with a wider range of primary sources, whereas field research, including behavior and narrative, remains the primary focus of study for ethnographers.[26] But, as Lev Shternberg suggested decades ago, the two methodologies share important commonalities, including a mutual emphasis on memory and its relationship to narrative. Like salvage ethnography, oral history has often been part of a project to bring marginal and otherwise silent groups into the historical narrative, and remains largely committed to the goal of "giving voice to the voiceless." In this sense, the practice of oral history is a natural development of the type of participatory and public history that Simon Dubnow had advocated.

It was not just oral historians who sought to preserve the voices of Eastern European Jews at a distance. As early as 1912, Yehudah Leib Cahan, who had immigrated to America from Vilna in 1904, published two volumes of Yiddish folk songs with melodies, and became a leader in the study of Jewish folk music. The project of collecting and preserving the folk music of Ashkenazic Jews became even more urgent during and immediately after the Holocaust. Ben Stonehill, an amateur zamler who made his living selling carpet and linoleum, recorded over one thousand songs from displaced peoples in New York City during the summer of 1948. The field recordings he deposited at the YIVO Institute for Jewish Research and the Library of Congress have only recently begun to attract scholarly attention.[27] Beginning around the same time, Ruth Rubin conducted pioneering ethnomusicological work collecting Yiddish songs from predominantly Eastern European Jewish immigrants in America. Through her recordings with Smithsonian Folkways, she raised awareness among broad American audiences not only of Yiddish folk song traditions but also of the plight of Jewish survivors. "My focus from the beginning," she declared, "was examining the songs as they reflect the life of the people. I found that, in the Yiddish folksong, the people had poured out their feelings, which had no other place to go at that time."[28]

Other scholars of Jewish life in the early postwar period continued the ethnographic impulse by collecting and studying the folk traditions that survived in emigration and were now being disseminated in the Americas and Israel. Dov Noy, who was born in Polish Kolomyia and in 1939 immigrated to Palestine, where he studied at Hebrew University, was one of the most influential scholars of Jewish folklore in the immediate postwar period. Like Boder, he encountered Jewish refugees in displaced-persons camps, working at a camp in Cyprus until 1948. He then continued his studies in the United States, completing his doctorate at Indiana University in 1954. Upon his return to Israel, he taught at Hebrew University, Ben-Gurion University, and Haifa University, where he directed the Haifa Ethnological Museum and founded the Israel Folktale Archives. He was also among the first folklorists to conduct ethnographic expeditions in post-Soviet Eastern Europe, and was awarded the Israel Prize in 2004. Noy looked toward folk tales as a means of memorializing a lost culture.

A new generation of scholars, most of whom were now born in the United States, Canada, and Israel to immigrant parents, were able to straddle the old and the new and question the salvage motivations of the earlier generation. Dan Ben-Amos and Barbara Kirshenblatt-Gimblett, who received their doctorates from Indiana University in 1967 and 1972 respectively, expanded upon Noy's work and led the next generation of folklore research. In his influential 1971 article, "Toward a Definition of Folklore in Context," Ben-Amos argued against what he saw as the prevailing view that folklore could be conceived of as "a collection of things," including "either narratives, melodies, beliefs, or material objects," all of which, he continued, "are completed products of formulated ideas; it is possible to collect them." Instead, he argued, "in its cultural context, folklore is not an aggregate of things, but a process—a communicative process," which takes place in small groups of peers.[29] Kirshenblatt-Gimblett, for her part, has played an important role in presenting Eastern European traditions to the general public through her work as a consultant for films and museum exhibitions, and most recently as designer of the Core Exhibition of Polin: Museum of the History of Polish Jews. These scholars were increasingly aware of the myriad of ways in which folklore is constantly changing, even by the process of observation itself. Writing of museum installations, for instance, Kirshenblatt-Gimblett warned that "in-situ installations, no matter how mimetic, are not neutral. They are not a slice of life lifted from the everyday world and inserted into the museum gallery,"[30] a caution equally applicable to ethnographic collection or oral history. Contemporary ethnographers, folklorists, oral historians, and sociolinguists have become acutely aware that they are not studying stationary and unchanging objects, but rather are engaging in fluid processes of verbal and performative interactions.[31]

In Israel, the folklorists Haya Bar-Itzhak, Galit Hasan-Rokem, Aliza Shenhar, and their students were running ethnographic projects to collect and study the folklore of new immigrants, much of which they deposited in the Israel Folktale Archive.[32] Introducing the second part of this volume, Haya Bar-Itzhak, who succeeded Noy and Aliza Shenhar as director of the Israel Folktale Archive, presents some findings from her own ethnographic work among Jews who migrated to Israel from Poland in the late 1950s. Bar-Itzhak's chapter is representative of the new scholarship being conducted by those who study Jewish folklore through ethnographic fieldwork. Rather than just attempt to retrieve and salvage folkloric traditions from the old world, many scholars now appreciate how the experience of migration created a genuinely new folklore. Bar-Itzhak uses the tools of folklore analysis to see what these newly created texts can tell us about the immigrant experience, and to examine how the struggles and victories of immigrants came to be expressed in the language of folklore.

The field of sociolinguistics, which draws upon the philological bent of many early ethnographers, has moved in a parallel direction. In 1954, the Vilna-born linguist Uriel Weinreich, the son of the linguist and YIVO founder Max Weinreich, began collecting samples of Yiddish-language speech in America, both to preserve the culture of Eastern European Jews in the aftermath of the Holocaust and to study what he called "language-in-contact,"[33] the interactions between coterritorial languages and dialects. The Language and Culture Atlas of Ashkenazic Jewry he established was the culmination of his practical work collecting and mapping Yiddish dialects. In his 1954 landmark article "Is a Structural Dialectology Possible?" Weinreich sought a reconciliation between structural and dialectological studies by comparing language varieties and urging that languages be studied as part of a larger social system.[34] This work influenced the development of sociolinguistics, a field largely established by Weinreich's student William Labov and further popularized by the work of Joshua Fishman, who, like Weinreich, focused his studies on Yiddish. The prominence of Yiddish in the development of sociolinguistics is not purely coincidental; as a hybrid language, the study of Yiddish had long necessitated the realization that languages develop not as closed systems but in relationship to social interactions. Indeed, ever since Dubnow's publication on the spoken language of Eastern European Jews, the role of language has been crucial in the attempt to understand how Eastern European Jews interacted with their neighbors and with each other.[35] The Language and Culture Atlas of Ashkenazic Jewry that Weinreich created was continued after Weinreich's death in 1967 by Marvin Herzog. More recently, the German-based EYDES (Evidence of Yiddish Documented in European Societies) project has begun digitizing, cataloguing, and transcribing these voice interviews, and making them available to scholars on the internet.[36]

Alexandra Polyan's contribution, based on research she has conducted in Bessarabia and Bukovina as part of the Russian State University for the Humanities expedition, looks at the role that language plays today in defining and contributing to Jewish identity in the region. In particular, she explores the way her informants perceive of the distinctions between *loshn-koydesh* (prayerbook Hebrew), contemporary Israeli Hebrew, and Yiddish, as well as the persistent role that Yiddish plays in ways that contemporary Eastern European Jews think about Jewish rituals and customs. Ultimately, she argues that these two languages, once viewed in opposition, have become closely related and even conflated in public perceptions.

My own involvement in the collection of oral history and linguistics began in 2002, when Dov-Ber Kerler and I joined with Dovid Katz to conduct field research among Yiddish speakers in Ukraine. Katz, the son of the Yiddish poet Menke Katz, had already been traveling through his own ancestral Lite, or Jewish Lithuania (including much of present-day Belarus), since the late 1980s, where he was conducting Yiddish-language dialectological and life-story interviews for his Atlas of Northeastern Yiddish, modeled on Weinreich's Language and Culture Atlas. Kerler, a former student of Katz's and the son of the Soviet Yiddish poet Joseph Kerler, brought his expertise on Ukrainian Yiddish dialects and Soviet Jewish culture to the project. Our Ukrainian expeditions led to the establishment of the Archives of Historical and Ethnographic Yiddish Memories (AHEYM; http://www.aheym.org), which Kerler and I established with Katz's assistance. Our own work, as my contribution to the volume explains, began largely as a linguistic project, but has since expanded to

include oral history. AHEYM is by no means the only major project to interview Eastern European Jews: the Blavatnik Archive interviews Soviet
Jewish combatants in World War II, while the USC Shoah Foundation
Visual History Archive interviewed tens of thousands of survivors of the
Holocaust, many of whom were still living in Eastern Europe at the time
of their interview. Valery Dymshits, Alla Sokolova, Alexander L'vov, and
other scholars associated with the Petersburg Judaica Center of the European University in St. Petersburg have also been conducting ethnographic
expeditions to the former Pale of Jewish Settlement since the early 1990s,
and Maria Kaspina has been leading similar expeditions under the auspices of the Russian State University for the Humanities and the Sefer
Institute. The findings from these expeditions have greatly enriched our
understanding of Jewish folk practices in the shtetl.[37] Similarly, social
scientists and scholars of Jewish culture have studied Jews and Jewish
identity in the former Soviet Union, conducting hundreds of face-to-face
interviews.[38]

Each of these new oral history collections, ethnographic studies, and
social scientific surveys present opportunities to study the different ways
that individuals remember the past, experience the present, and imagine
the future. In my contribution to this volume, I look at how contemporary memories of religious life center overwhelmingly on food traditions,
which serve as stimulants to memory. I argue, as well, that in many cases
food served as a stand-in for families and lifestyles that were lost with
the war.

In his contribution to this volume, Sebastian Z. Schulman investigates
the myth and reality of the Ribnitser Rebbe (Khayim-Zanvl Abramovitsh), a charismatic religious leader who insisted on maintaining aspects
of Jewish religious life in the Soviet Union during World War II and the
postwar period. The influence of the Ribnitser Rebbe was widespread
within the southeastern parts of Ukraine and Moldova, where stories
of his miracles and kindness spread far and wide. Followers flocked to
him to study and be blessed, during a time in which such religious devo-
tion posed a serious risk of arrest and imprisonment. Abramovitsh served
as a model of support for survivors of the Holocaust in the Soviet Union
as well as a symbol of renewal for those Jews seeking to rebuild in the
aftermath of the war.

For other scholars, particularly those who had fled the Soviet Union since the late 1980s, the sense of return was facilitated by their newfound scholarly freedom and the ability to openly study subjects that had previously been considered taboo. Finding that their cultural practices were suddenly rendered "strange" by American and Israeli Jews, many ex-Soviet Jews were motivated to document these differences. Established Jewish communities in America and Israel—many of which had valiantly fought for the rights of their Soviet co-religionists—were now confronted with the task of actually absorbing new Jewish immigrants from the former Soviet Union. American, Canadian, and Israeli Jews often found that the values and religious practices of their Soviet "cousins" contrasted, and even conflicted, with what they had previously imagined. Not every Jewish emigrant from the Soviet Union turned out to be an Anatoly (Natan) Sharansky, a dissident intellectual committed to Jewish renewal and the future of Israel. In part as an effort to educate Westerners about the particular cultural mores of ex-Soviet Jews, a few scholars, many of whom hailed from the Soviet realm themselves, sought to interview and study Eastern European émigrés as ethnographic subjects.[39] In their introduction to the third part of this volume, Larisa Fialkova and Maria Yelenevskaya reflect on how this type of "autoethnography" helped new immigrants to Israel articulate their own distinct customs and negotiate coexistence and mutual understanding in their new homeland.

Halina Goldberg, a musicologist and expert on Chopin who grew up in Łódź and now teaches at Indiana University's Jacobs School of Music, returned to the study of her own culture soon after her parents passed away. In her chapter, she explains how she was able to present the history and culture of interwar Jewish life in the working-class district of Bałuty in the exhibit "Mrs. Goldberg's Kitchen," which she mounted at the Łódź Museum of Textiles. The exhibit weaves together period audio recordings, photos, and artifacts to render a recreation of Goldberg's childhood home. Goldberg's sensitivity to sound and music, in particular, helped craft an aural landscape, which aimed to correct stereotyped preconceptions of Jewish life in Eastern Europe for the predominantly Polish audiences who would visit the exhibit. Goldberg recounts the reactions of visitors to the museum, many of whom responded by donating artifacts from their own families' pasts. The exhibit itself is becoming a communal collection, as museum-goers channel the exhortations issued a century earlier by Dubnow and An-sky to record and collect.

In her chapter, Asya Vaisman Schulman reflects on her experiences conducting ethnographic work among the Hasidim of Williamsburg in order to collect and study Hasidic women's songs. Schulman describes the processes she undertook in order to convince women in these closed communities that she was a trustworthy listener, and to convince them to share with her their songs and singing. In contrast to most of the other contributors to this volume, Schulman did not conduct her work in Eastern Europe or with Eastern European émigrés. Yet, she notes that it was in part her own background as a Jew from the former Soviet Union that helped gain her access. In this case, she—the researcher—was the one admired for her direct connection to the old world. Through the researcher, the research subjects may have sought a return to their people, their Eastern European ancestors.

In his concluding contribution, Simon J. Bronner contrasts An-sky's nation-building project, geared toward salvaging the relics of a civilization located in a specific locale, with more modern American folkloristics, which focuses on the portability and transmutability of culture as it helps guide individuals toward personal fulfillment. Bronner argues that American folklorists, following Boas and Joseph Jacobs, were motivated in part to counter anthropological hierarchies of nations, which invariably placed the Jews at the lowest level of development. These folklorists, like their Soviet counterparts, were concerned with the role of folklore in a modernizing society. They celebrated a variety of Jewish folk traditions, viewing each as an attempt to adapt and grapple with the modern world and the new locales in which Jews were settling, rather than mourn the loss of an imagined ur-folklore as An-sky was wont to do.

The Jewish "ethnographic impulse" has continued through the twentieth century and into the twenty-first. The initial motivations of salvage, recovery, and return remain important themes among those who have "gone to the people." Indeed, the impulse to collect and study fragments of Eastern European Jewish culture—language, music, folklore, customs, and history—remains today very much intertwined with the zamler tradition that originated some one hundred years ago. But these themes have been supplemented with new scholarly traditions that recognize and appreciate that memory, language, beliefs, folklore, and other cultural expressions are not static artifacts that can be collected and mounted for display, but rather are vibrant, ever-changing systems that are in flux even as we come into contact with them. By writing, collecting, learning, and yearning, scholars have themselves contributed to a new folklore. The quest to "go to the people" has, in the century since An-sky, been transformed from a salvage operation into a participatory project. Communities once imagined as static and in need of salvage are now broadly understood and appreciated as vibrant communities in perpetual states of transformation.

NOTES

1. Franco Venturi, *Roots of Revolution: A History of the Populist and Socialist Movements in Nineteenth Century Russia* (New York: Alfred A. Knopf, 1960), 398.

2. For more on An-sky see Gabriella Safran, *Wandering Soul: The Dybbuk's Creator, S. An-sky* (Cambridge, MA: Belknap Press of Harvard University Press, 2010); Gabriella Safran and Steven J. Zipperstein, eds., *The Worlds of S. An-sky: A Russian Jewish Intellectual at the Turn of the Century* (Stanford, CA: Stanford University Press, 2006).

3. S. A. An-sky, "Evreiskoe narodnoe tvorchestvo," *Perezhitoe: Sbornik, posviashchennyi obshchestvennoi i kul'turnoi istorii evreev v Rossii* 1 (1908): 276–314. For an English translation see Haya Bar-Itzhak, *Pioneers of Jewish Ethnography and Folkloristics in Eastern Europe* (Ljubljana: Scientific Research Center of the Slovenian Academy of Sciences and Arts, 2010), 27–74.

4. Translation from Bar-Itzhak, *Pioneers*, 35.

5. See Simon Rabinovitch, "Positivism, Populism and Politics: The Intellectual Foundations of Jewish Ethnography in Late Imperial Russia," *Ab Imperio* 3 (2005): 227–256.

6. S. An-sky, *Gezamelte shriften in fuftsehn bender* (Warsaw: Tsentral, 1922), 10:76.

7. For the origins of the Russian Geographic Society see Alexei Elfimov, "Russian Ethnography as a Science: Truths Claimed, Trails Followed," in *An Empire of Others: Creating Ethnographic Knowledge in Imperial Russia and the USSR*, ed. Roland Cvetkovski and Alexis Hofmeister (Budapest: Central European University Press, 2014), 51–79; and Nathaniel Knight, "Science, Empire, and Nationality: Ethnography in the Russian Geographic Society, 1845–1855," in *Imperial Russia: New Histories for the Empire*, ed. Jane Burbank and David L. Ransel (Bloomington: Indiana University Press, 1998), 108–141. On the introduction of field research in the eighteenth century see Yuri Slezkine, "Naturalists versus Nations: Eighteenth-Century Russian Scholars Confront Ethnic Diversity," *Representations* 47 (1994): 170–195.

8. For more on literary adaptations of Jewish ethnography see Samuel Jacob Spinner, "Jews behind Glass: The Ethnographic Impulse in German-Jewish and Yiddish Literature, 1900–1948" (PhD diss., Columbia University, 2012).

9. See Benjamin Nathans, "On Russian-Jewish Historiography," in *Historiography of Imperial Russia: The Profession and Writing of History in a Multinational State*, ed. Thomas Sanders (Armonk, NY: M. E. Sharpe, 1999), 397–432.

10. For more on Dubnow's conception of history see Jeffrey Veidlinger, "The Historical and Ethnographic Construction of Russian Jewry," *Ab Imperio* 4 (2003): 165–184; and Robert M. Seltzer, *Simon Dubnow's "New Judaism": Diaspora, Nationalism and the World History of the Jews* (Leiden: Brill, 2014).

11. See Mark William Kiel, "A Twice Lost Legacy: Ideology, Culture and the Pursuit of Jewish Folklore in Russia until Stalinization: 1930–1931" (PhD diss., Jewish Theological Seminary, 1991).

12. Safran, *Wandering Soul*, 189.

13. Jeffrey Veidlinger, *Jewish Public Culture in the Late Russian Empire* (Bloomington: Indiana University Press, 2009), 250–251. For more on the An-sky expedition see, in addition to sources previously cited, Nathaniel Deutsch, *The Jewish Dark Continent: Life and Death in the Russian Pale of Settlement* (Cambridge, MA: Harvard University Press, 2011); Eugene M. Avrutin et al., eds., *Photographing the Jewish Nation: Pictures from S. An-sky's Ethnographic Expeditions* (Waltham, MA: Brandeis University Press, 2014); Rivka Gonen, ed., *Back to the Shtetl: An-sky and the Jewish Ethnographic Expedition, 1912–1914* (Jerusalem: Israel Museum, 1994); and Abram Efros and Alexander Kantsedikas, *Semyon An-sky: The Jewish Artistic Heritage; An Album* (Moscow: RA, 1994).

14. S. An-sky, "Pis'mo v redaktsiiu. (O rabotakh etnograficheskoi ekspeditsii)," *Evreiskaia starina* 8 (1915): 239–240.

15. Veidlinger, *Jewish Public Culture*, 256.

16. For more on Shternberg see Sergei Kan, *Lev Shternberg: Anthropologist, Russian Socialist, Jewish Activist* (Lincoln: University of Nebraska Press, 2009).

17. Yuri Slezkine, "The Fall of Soviet Ethnography, 1928–38," *Current Anthropology* 32, no. 4 (August–October 1991): 476–484.

18. For more on Beregovski see Mark Slobin, Robert Rothstein, and Michael Alpert, eds., *Jewish Instrumental Folk Music: The Collections and Writings of Moshe Beregovski* (Syracuse, NY: Syracuse University Press, 2001); Mark Slobin, ed., *Old Jewish Folk Music: The Collections and Writings of Moshe Beregovski* (Syracuse, NY: Syracuse University Press, 2000); and M. Beregovskii and E. M. Beregovskaia, *Arfy na verbakh: Prizvanie i sud'ba Moiseiia Beregovskogo* (Moscow: Evreiskii Universitet v Moskve; Jerusalem: Gesharim, 1994).

19. For more on the Jewish Folk Music Society see James Loeffler, *The Most Musical Nation: Jews and Culture in the Late Russian Empire* (New Haven, CT: Yale University Press, 2010).

20. For more on YIVO see Cecile Esther Kuznitz, *YIVO and the Making of Modern Jewish Culture: Scholarship for the Yiddish Nation* (New York: Cambridge University Press, 2014).

21. For more on Prylucki see Kalman Weiser, *Jewish People, Yiddish Nation: Noah Prylucki and the Folkists in Poland* (Toronto: University of Toronto Press, 2011). See also Itzik Nakhmen Gottesman, *Defining the Yiddish Nation: The Jewish Folklorists of Poland* (Detroit: Wayne State University Press, 2003), and Bar-Itzhak, *Pioneers*.

22. Samuel Kassow, *Who Will Write Our History? Emanuel Ringelblum, the Warsaw Ghetto, and the Oyneg Shabes Archive* (Bloomington: Indiana University Press, 2007).

23. Barbara Kirshenblatt-Gimblett, introduction to *Life Is with People: The Culture of the Shtetl*, by Mark Zborowski and Elizabeth Herzog (New York: Schocken Books, 1995), ix–xlviii.

24. Alan Rosen, *The Wonder of Their Voices: The 1946 Holocaust Interviews of David Boder* (New York: Oxford University Press, 2010); Jeffrey Veidlinger, "One Doesn't Make

Out Much with Furs in Palestine: The Migration of Jewish Displaced Persons, 1945–7," *East European Jewish Affairs* 44, no. 2–3 (2014): 241–252.

25. Barbara G. Myerhoff, *Number Our Days: A Triumph of Continuity and Culture among Jewish Old People in an Urban Ghetto* (New York: Dutton, 1979).

26. Micaela Di Leonardo, "Oral History as Ethnographic Encounter," *Oral History Review* 15, no. 1 (Spring 1987): 1–20. See also Alistair Thomson, "Four Paradigm Transformations in Oral History," *Oral History Review* 34, no. 1 (Winter–Spring 2007): 49–70.

27. See Janina Wurbs, "A Treasure Trove in a Hotel Lobby—Songs of the Ben Stonehill Collection at the Y I V O Sound Archives," *European Journal of Jewish Studies* 8 (2014): 127–136; and Ravenna Koenig, "1,000 Songs from Holocaust Survivors Archived," N P R Weekend Edition Saturday, May 16, 2015, http://www.npr.org/2015/05/16/406967291 /1-000-songs-from-holocaust-survivors-archived.

28. Hankus Netzky, "Ruth Rubin: A Life in Song," *Pakn Treger* 57 (Summer 2008): http://www.yiddishbookcenter.org/pakn-treger/12-09/ruth-rubin-a-life-song.

29. Dan Ben-Amos, "Toward a Definition of Folklore in Context," *Journal of American Folklore* 84, no. 331 (January 1971): 9.

30. Barbara Kirshenblatt-Gimblett, "Objects of Ethnography," in *Exhibiting Cultures: The Poetics and Politics of Museum Display,* ed. Ivan Karp and Steven D. Lavine (Washington, DC: Smithsonian Institution, 1991), 389.

31. In addition to the works cited above, see Jack Kugelmass, ed., *Between Two Worlds: Ethnographic Essays on American Jewry* (Ithaca, NY: Cornell University Press, 1988).

32. See, for instance, Haya Bar-Itzhak and Aliza Shenhar, *Jewish Moroccan Folk Narratives from Israel* (Detroit: Wayne State University Press, 1993).

33. Uriel Weinreich, *Languages in Contact: Findings and Problems* (New York: Linguistic Circle of New York, 1953).

34. Uriel Weinreich, "Is a Structural Dialectology Possible?," *Word* 10 (1954): 388–400.

35. S. Dubnov, "Razgovornyi iazyk i narodnaia literature pol'sko-litovskikh evreev v XVI i pervoi polovine XVII veka," *Evreiskaia starina* 1 (1909): 7–40.

36. See the website of the Language and Culture Atlas of Ashkenazic Jewry at http://www.eydes.de.

37. Some of the many important works by these researchers have been published in V. A. Dymshits, A. L. L'vov, and A. M. Sokolova, eds., *Shtetl, XXI vek: Polevye issledovaniia* (St. Petersburg: European University in St. Petersburg, 2008).

38. Zvi Y. Gitelman, *Jewish Identities in Postcommunist Russia and Ukraine: An Uncertain Ethnicity* (Cambridge: Cambridge University Press, 2012); and Anna Shternshis, *Soviet and Kosher: Jewish Popular Culture in the Soviet Union, 1923–1939* (Bloomington: Indiana University Press, 2006).

39. Larisa Fialkova and Maria N. Yelenevskaya, *Ex-Soviets in Israel: From Personal Narratives to a Group Portrait* (Detroit: Wayne State University Press, 2007); Larisa Fialkova and Maria Yelenevskaya, *In Search of the Self: Reconciling the Past and the Present in Immigrants' Experience* (Tartu: ELM Scholarly Press, 2013); Ilana Rosen, "Matchmaking and Marriage Narratives of Israelis of Carpatho-Rusyn Origin," *Electronic Journal of Folklore* 59 (2014): 45–66.

Part I

History of the Ethnographic Impulse

Thrice Born; or, Between Two Worlds

REFLEXIVITY AND PERFORMANCE
IN AN-SKY'S JEWISH ETHNOGRAPHIC
EXPEDITION AND BEYOND

NATHANIEL DEUTSCH

In his foreword to *Number Our Days,* Barbara Myerhoff's now classic work of Jewish ethnography, Victor Turner invoked the Indian anthropologist M. N. Srinivas's concept of the "thrice-born" to explain—and praise—Myerhoff's approach to her fieldwork in a community of elderly Jews of Eastern European origin now transplanted to a senior center in Los Angeles. Srinivas, a Brahmin and therefore "twice born" according to traditional Hindu belief, "urged anthropologists . . . to go one stage further. We were to seek to be 'thrice-born.' The first birth is our natal origin in a particular culture. The second is our move from this familiar to a far place to do fieldwork there. . . . The third birth occurs when we have become comfortable within the other culture—and found the clue to grasping many like it—and turn our gaze again toward our native land. We find that the familiar has become exoticized; we see it with new eyes."[1] Remarking on Myerhoff's transition from her fieldwork among the Huichol Indians of the Sierra Madre Occidental of Mexico, which resulted in her award-winning book *Peyote Hunt,* to her work at the Aliyah Senior Citizens' Center of Venice Beach, Turner asserted, "'Thrice-born' anthropologists are perhaps in the best position to become the 'reflexivity' of a culture. Dr. Barbara Myerhoff is one of the few anthropologists whose work attests to this double cultural rebirth."[2]

Since the publication of *Number Our Days,* the phenomenon of the anthropologist who conducts fieldwork in a place far from home and then returns to study their own "native land" has become commonplace (Vincent Crapanzano, Paul Rabinow, and others).[3] Indeed, many anthropologists now move back and forth between research sites at home and abroad, inspired by changing intellectual interests or shifting life circumstances and facilitated by easy air travel and modern technologies. At the same time, the line between native and nonnative ethnographers in a postcolonial, globalized world has become increasingly blurred, as Kirin Narayan has written in her provocative essay "How Native Is a 'Native' Anthropologist?": "I argue against the fixity of a distinction between 'native' and 'non-native' anthropologists. Instead of the paradigm emphasizing a dichotomy between outsider/insider or observer/observed, I propose that at this historical moment we might more profitably view each anthropologist in terms of shifting identifications amid a field of interpenetrating communities and power relations."[4] In this chapter, I will demonstrate, in turn, that the complex issues of identity articulated by Srinivas, Narayan, and others have been present—indeed have animated—Jewish ethnographic fieldwork from its earliest days, including one of its touchstone events, the Jewish Ethnographic Expedition conducted by the Russian Jewish ethnographer, playwright, and revolutionary S. An-sky between 1912 and 1914. Phrased differently, we might say that "How native is a 'native' Jewish anthropologist?" has always been one of the key—if for a long time, only implicit—questions of Jewish ethnography.

THE JEWISH ETHNOGRAPHIC EXPEDITION:
GOING NATIVE OR GOING HOME?

On June 30, 1912, a day before the Jewish Ethnographic Expedition departed from Kiev for Ruzhin, the first stop of what would become three summers of traveling to nearly seventy communities in the Pale of Jewish Settlement, An-sky wrote to his wealthy patron, Baron Naftali Hertz Gintsburg, "I am very nervous, as if standing before the great unknown. How will this all turn out? Will I be able to gain the trust of the poor and primitive people from whose ranks I myself have come but whom I left so far behind over these past years? . . . And yet, at the same time, I have a great feeling of joy in my soul, that the most treasured dream of my life is beginning to come to fruition."[5] What had An-sky been doing in "these past years" that caused him to feel that he had left the "primitive" residents of the Pale of Jewish Settlement "so far behind"? Several decades earlier, in the mid-1880s, An-sky, then known by his given name, Shloyme Zaynvl Rapoport, had abandoned the Pale, where he was raised in the town of Vitebsk, and relocated to the rough-and-tumble southern district of Slavianoserbskii. There, inspired by the ideology of *narodniche-stvo,* or Russian populism, which had taken the young intelligentsia by storm during the 1870s, he labored in the region's salt and coal mines and read literature to fellow workers and the local peasants, while trying to publish his own writings, albeit without much luck. A decade later, and now known as An-sky, he achieved greater success as a writer, publishing essays on Russian workers, peasants, and their folklore in *Russkoe bogats-vto* (Russian wealth), *Vestnik Evropy* (The herald of Europe), and other journals and newspapers.[6]

By 1894, An-sky was living in Paris and had become deeply involved in the radical Russian émigré community, ultimately joining the Socialist Revolutionary Party. An-sky remained in Western Europe until 1905, when the revolution brought him back to Russia. Within a few years of his return, An-sky had become one of the central figures in a circle of Russian Jewish intellectuals and cultural activists rooted—although this term must be used with more than a bit of irony, since many did not have official residency permits, including An-sky—in St. Petersburg and anchored by Simon Dubnow, the founder of the Jewish Historical-Ethnographic Society (JHES) and cofounder of *Evreiskaia starina* (Jewish antiquity), as well as other organs of the Jewish cultural renaissance then unfolding. On January 9, 1910, at a banquet organized in his honor by fellow Jewish journalists, An-sky explicitly linked his rebirth as a Jew to the cultural and political rebirth of the Jewish people in the Russian Empire:

> When I first entered literature twenty-five years ago I wanted to labor on behalf of the oppressed, the working masses, and it appeared to me, mistakenly, that I would not find them among the Jews.... Possessing an eternal longing for Jewishness, I [nevertheless] threw myself in all directions and left to work for another people. My life was broken, split, torn.... I lived among the Russian folk for a long time, among their lowest classes. Things

are different for us now than when I wrote my first story. We have cultural,
political and literary movements. . . . I believe in a better future and in the
survival of the Jews![7]

By 1912, An-sky had come to believe that ethnography would serve as
the chief vehicle for his own personal redemption as well as the cultural
redemption of the Jewish people. Drawing on an earlier call by Simon
Dubnow in which the great historian told his readers, "Not every learned
or literary person can be a great writer or historian. But every one of
you can be a collector of material, and aid in the building of our history,"
An-sky—along with Y. L. Peretz and Jacob Dinezon—issued a public appeal exhorting "all members of our people, men and women, young and
old. . . . Don't depend on the hands of strangers! Record, take it down,
and collect!"[8] By transforming as many Jewish residents of the Pale as
possible into amateur ethnographers, or *zamlers,* An-sky hoped to inspire
one of the greatest, if not *the* greatest, projects of autoethnography in history, one that would help produce a grand cultural rebirth or, as An-sky
put in Yiddish, *oyflebn,* or "revival."[9] At the head of this project, An-sky
imagined, would be a vanguard of what Srinivas would later call thrice-
born ethnographers—Jewish individuals, like An-sky, who had spent
years among other people(s) but who would now turn their gazes to their
own "native land," the Pale of Settlement, and its residents.

Indeed, as early as 1908, An-sky had published an essay in *Perezhitoe*
(The past) entitled "Evreiskoe narodnoe tvorchestvo" (Jewish folk creativity) in which he lamented, "There is no people like the Jewish people,
that talks about itself so much, but knows itself so little," despite the fact
that there were many prominent Russian Jewish ethnographers, including
Lev Shternberg, Vladimir Bogoraz, Moisei Krol, and Vladimir Jochelson,
who had spent years—often while exiled for political reasons—studying
the "savage and semi-savage" tribes of the Russian Empire in Central Asia
and Siberia.[10] During the planning sessions for the Jewish Ethnographic
Expedition in St. Petersburg in March 1912, An-sky attempted to enlist
the participation of some of these individuals as well as other Jewish figures in the field of anthropology, with only varying degrees of success,
since many considered An-sky's ethnographic approach to be naive at
best and foolhardy at worst. Nevertheless, he did manage to get the official imprimatur of Lev Shternberg, who was listed as the editor of *Dos*

Yidishe etnografishe program (The Jewish ethnographic program), the massive, Yiddish-language life-cycle questionnaire An-sky printed but never distributed in 1914, though unpublished correspondence suggests that Shternberg had serious reservations about the questionnaire and may not have contributed much to its creation beyond his name.

As the Jewish Ethnographic Expedition prepared for its first season exploring and documenting life in the Pale, An-sky was well aware that time had not stood still in the decades since his youth in Vitebsk, where he attended a traditional *kheyder* (religious institution of higher learning) and was probably exposed to the traditions of local Lubavitcher Hasidim, before embracing the ideals of the Haskalah. Indeed, it was precisely the dramatic changes that had taken place in the past few years in the shtetls of the Pale of Settlement that convinced An-sky that preserving the traditions of its residents was an absolutely urgent matter, for as he put it in the foreword to the *Jewish Ethnographic Program*, "The great upheaval in Jewish life that has occurred in the last fifty to sixty years has above all devastated our folk traditions, a great many of which have already vanished. With every old man who dies, with every small-town fire, with every exile, a piece of our past is lost, and the most beautiful expressions of traditional life, with its customs, traditions, and beliefs, disappear."[11]

Despite these losses, enough traditional Jewish life still survived in the hundreds if not thousands of shtetls that dotted the Pale of Settlement that An-sky could unself-consciously refer to Jewish residents—in a nod to Simon Dubnow's earlier description of the Pale as a kind of Jewish "Dark Continent"—as "primitive." Dubnow had first applied the Russian translation *temnaia materika,* as well as the original English phrase, to the Pale in 1891, writing, "When Burton, Speke or Stanley undertook their bold expeditions into then uncharted Central Africa, they could not predetermine in advance exactly all the great discoveries—geographic, ethnographic, naturalistic—that would subsequently give us a completely new idea of that part of the world. . . . We also have before us our own kind of dark continent ('the dark continent')—as the English called the interior of Africa—that lies ahead to be explored and illuminated."[12] Nearly twenty years later, in 1908, Dubnow would return to the theme at the inauguration of the JHES in St. Petersburg, lamenting that "the greatest [Jewish] center after Babylonia and Spain in the history of the diaspora—Poland-Russia—remains the least explored, remains a 'dark continent.'"[13]

Dubnow's characterization of the Pale reflected a contemporary tendency to stereotype Jews, especially those of Eastern European origin, or *Ostjuden* in German, as Orientals, savages, "white negroes," and so on.[14] As Gabriella Safran has noted, within the Russian imperial context in particular, there was a legal basis for identifying Jews with the supposedly "savage and semi-savage tribes" of the empire, "since Jews and Siberians both belonged to the legal category of *inorodtsy*, non-Christian and seemingly unassailable foreigners."[15] Of course, a major difference between Richard Burton, John Hanning Speke, and Henry Morton Stanley, and figures like An-sky and Dubnow, is that the former were explorers of supposedly more uncivilized lands far from their places of origin, whereas the latter were themselves sons of the Pale of Settlement, which is to say, they were at once explorers and natives of their own Dark Continent.

Like the thrice-born anthropologists later imagined by Srinivas, who, upon turning their gaze to their own native land, "find that the familiar has become exoticized," An-sky characterized the residents of the Pale as primitive, thereby implicitly placing himself on the side of civilization. On the one hand, this usage indicated that An-sky had internalized the kind of pejorative stereotypes applied to traditional Eastern European Jews, en masse, as less civilized than more secular, Westernized Jews. On the other hand, An-sky's use of the term suggested a positive reevaluation of the Jews of the Pale, at least from the point of view of their ethnographic value. Rather than dismissing them as political and economic reactionaries, even parasites, as he had during his early days as a *narodnik*, or populist, An-sky now saw the traditional Jews of the Pale as primitive in a fin-de-siècle ethnographic sense, which is to say, he now viewed—and valued—them as a real "folk" whose culture was worthy of anthropological study.

PERFORMING ETHNOGRAPHY AND PERFORMING JEWISHNESS

Reflecting the wider phenomenon of *kinus*, or "ingathering," that characterized turn-of-the-century Jewish intellectuals across a broad ideological spectrum, An-sky hoped that the kind of large-scale autoethnography he envisioned, with local Jewish ethnographic societies established in communities throughout the Pale and individual zamlers in contact with a central bureau in St. Petersburg, would become a meaningful way of performing Jewishness that would cut across class, age, gender, and other lines, in an era in which many young Jews, in particular, were turning away from traditional practices.[16] In this regard, An-sky's vision of the public role of ethnography fits within a broader pattern in late imperial Russian Jewish society in which public cultural institutions took on ever-increasing importance. As Jeffrey Veidlinger has argued, "Jews in the early-twentieth-century Russian Empire tended to enact, express, and debate their public culture through everyday rituals and marked performances within the realm of the new public institutions that were being established on voluntary bases throughout the empire."[17] Concerning An-sky, in particular, Veidlinger has noted, "This impetus to find new ways of collecting folk culture and presenting it in accessible forms united An-sky's approach to ethnography to Dubnow's approach to history and defined the people's perception of their own culture."[18]

At the core of An-sky's redemptive view of ethnography was that Jewishness itself was a kind of performance consisting of certain types of music, rituals, customs, and other traditional practices, that together constituted Jewish folk culture. Ethnography, in turn, was the best means for recording and documenting these traditional cultural performances, thereby producing the raw material for new Jewish cultural forms, such as theater (including An-sky's play *The Dybbuk*), museums, and so on. Barbara Kirshenblatt-Gimblett has described this process of cultural transformation as the creation of "heritage," or, as she puts it, "Heritage, for the sake of my argument, is the transvaluation of the obsolete, the mistaken, the outmoded, the dead, and the defunct. Heritage is created through a process of exhibition (as knowledge, as performance, as museum display). Exhibition endows heritage thus conceived with a second life."[19] Significantly, we can see the same logic at work in the observations of a local zamler in Kremenits, one of the towns visited by the Jewish Ethnographic Expedition: "All the customs and ways of life, stories, legends, expressions about the evil eye, placing garlic on gravestones, throwing a pebble when one meets a priest on the road, the hymns one sings over one's bed during

childbirth ... and so on—everything the Jews of Kremenits used to do in
their lives was perceived by the youth as a higher cultural word."[20]

For An-sky, Hasidism was an especially important source for Jewish
performance, both because Hasidim had long valued the production
and transmission of melodies, dances, tales, and customs—indeed, they
applied mystical significance to these forms—and also because An-sky
viewed Hasidim as having long functioned as indigenous zamlers inso-
far as they collected, interpreted, and preserved precisely those features
of Jewish and, in some cases, non-Jewish folk culture that An-sky himself was interested in. Thus, on at least one occasion during the Jewish
Ethnographic Expedition, An-sky had to compete with a Hasidic collector who wanted to acquire the same manuscript of *zgules* (folk methods
for bringing about good fortune) attributed to Levi Yitshak of Berdichev,
an important Hasidic master.[21] On another occasion recorded by Chana
Schneerson, the mother of Menachem Mendel Schneerson, the seventh
Lubavitcher Rebbe, An-sky swapped Hasidic tales with her husband, Levi
Yitzhak Schneerson, in what became a performance for other passengers
on a train:

> On our journey back from abroad, the writer S. Ansky joined our train in
> Warsaw. He sat down in our compartment, and a conversation ensued as
> we traveled. The conversation was mainly between my husband and the
> writer, and the topics included many stories about Chasidic Rebbes, Cha-
> sidim of previous times, renowned personalities and Jewish spiritual life
> in general. Many Jewish passengers, young and old, from the neighboring
> train-cars, came into our compartment to listen to the conversation. At
> night they didn't return to their compartments to sleep but stayed to
> listen to the conversation with great interest, for it was an exceptionally
> rich and wide-ranging discussion.[22]

An-sky's emphasis on the performative dimension(s) of Hasidism was
a radical departure from then regnant scholarly approaches to the movement, which emphasized either historical accounts (e.g., Simon Dubnow)
or anthologies of its tales, many of them highly edited to appeal to a wider
audience (e.g., Martin Buber). Neither of these approaches, however, paid
significant attention to the cultural context of Hasidic gatherings, rituals,
and storytelling. Nor did they attempt to record such performances in
situ. By contrast, An-sky and the Jewish Ethnographic Expedition de-

voted many hours to observing and documenting a wide range of Hasidic cultural performances, including storytelling, singing, petitionary prayer, healing, and so on, in their original settings. As such, An-sky's ethnographic work anticipated a later expansion of the scope of Jewish studies, in general, away from the overwhelmingly literary focus that had dominated the field since the emergence of the Wissenschaft des Judentums in nineteenth-century Germany.

To gain access to these performances, however, An-sky soon discovered that he would have to modify his own behavior and that of his fellow researchers on the expedition, or, as a resident of Kremenits succinctly put it, to "act Jewish."[23] In practice, this meant speaking Yiddish rather than Russian (a challenge for Yoel Engel, a musicologist whose Yiddish was rudimentary), not smoking cigarettes on the Sabbath, and participating in a variety of religious rituals—praying, Torah reading, etc.—in local synagogues and elsewhere. For An-sky in particular, who had already achieved a significant reputation among the intelligentsia for his writings and activism, it meant downplaying or even covering up his real identity and instead modifying his behavior and his cover stories to fit the situation at hand. As Shmuel Shrayer, who accompanied the Jewish Ethnographic Expedition during its second season, later recalled, "We needed to gain the trust of Hasidim. It was impossible, therefore, for An-sky to appear in Jewish towns as An-sky the writer . . . and yet over the course of many years An-sky had forgotten all the Jewish customs! I therefore acquired for him a tallis and tefillin, and taught him how to use them."[24] It was a performance that An-sky, the Socialist Revolutionary who had turned his back on religion decades before in Vitebsk, apparently relished, or as Shrayer put it, "Our phonograph stood in the corner and recorded the Hasidic melodies. . . . Sometimes An-sky would get into the groove and he would sing along like one of them."[25]

NOTES ON THE NATIVE LAND(S)
OF JEWISH ETHNOGRAPHY

More than half a century after An-sky journeyed to the towns of the Pale of Settlement, Barbara Myerhoff arrived at the Aliyah Senior Citizens' Center of Venice Beach, where she would engage in fieldwork among Jews old enough to have been present during the Jewish Ethnographic Expedition. In an essay on An-sky entitled "The Father of Jewish Ethnography," Jack Kugelmass, whose own *Miracle on Intervale Avenue* has become another classic in the field, observed, "It is commonplace to consider S. An-sky the father of Jewish ethnography. Yet, when asked to discuss the impact of An-sky on Jewish anthropology, I was hard pressed to come up with a solid genealogical connection between so ostensive a progenitor and the field as it exists today."[26] Significantly, the one notable exception, according to Kugelmass, was Barbara Myerhoff's *Number Our Days*. He argued, "Although apparently not inspired by him ... [it] closely parallels An-sky's—in its formulation as 'return,' its concern for salvage, and its transmission to us via the rhetoric of ethnographic realism albeit through dramaturgical techniques that make the work as much one of fiction as it is ethnographic."[27] As I will suggest below, while An-sky may not have directly influenced later generations of Jewish ethnographers, many of them, at least, have grappled with similar questions concerning their intersecting identities as ethnographers and as Jews.

In the case of Barbara Myerhoff, it is worth asking whether, like An-sky, she had in fact "turned her gaze again to her native land" when she embarked on the fieldwork that resulted in *Number Our Days,* as Victor Turner assumed she had. Was a middle-aged American Jewish woman raised in Cleveland really from the same place as a group of elderly, Yiddish-speaking Jews from Eastern Europe, and her fieldwork therefore a kind of return to her "natal origin"? There is no easy answer to these questions, or perhaps the only easy—and accurate—answer is "yes and no."

On the one hand, Myerhoff acknowledged the cultural distance between her and the members of the senior center, as when a particularly—and, in the context of the Leftist background of most members, unusually—religious informant jokingly referred to her as "'my dear little shiksa,'" employing a Yiddish term for a non-Jewish woman and prompting Myerhoff to observe, "I winced at the term he used to underscore my ignorance of Jewish law, though I knew he used it affectionately."[28] Yet, in other settings, Myerhoff stressed her closeness to the same elderly Jews, even the inevitability of becoming one herself. As an article in the *Los Angeles Times* put it, "She had chosen the Jewish community of Venice to study with a true anthropologist's thoroughness because, as she said, being an old Jew was something possible to her. She would never be a South American Indian, she said, facing the camera almost jauntily, "but I will be old."[29] Rather than invoking the image of return, Myerhoff employed the language of *becoming*, suggesting yet another way to understand Srinivas's concept of being "thrice-born," here connected to the human life cycle instead of the anthropological endeavor.

In all its senses, the phrase "thrice-born" implies personal transformation and transition from one mode of being to another. But does the native/nonnative ethnographer's journey necessarily end in rebirth, return, or even becoming? Rather than achieving this kind of resolution, however dialectical, many Jewish ethnographers engaged in fieldwork of other Jews have represented their own journeys as more open-ended, unresolved, and, to borrow another term made popular by Victor Turner, liminal. Thus, for example, in an important collection of essays entitled *Between Two Worlds: Ethnographic Essays on American Jewry*, Jack Kugelmass, its editor, noted, "There are many stories within this volume. Although some are presented in a more self-reflexive way than others, there is everywhere here a sense of quest, an interest in learning more about Judaism (Belcove-Shalin; Myerhoff; Prell), of rediscovering one's personal past (Boyarin), or of trying to understand personal identity by looking, as Richard Schechner suggests, at people who are simultaneously 'me' and 'not me.'"[30] Indeed, despite—or, perhaps, precisely because of—her profound sense of identification with her elderly Jewish subjects and even her acknowledgment that she would eventually become one of them, Barbara Myerhoff also admitted that she felt "betwixt and between" the anthropological and personal quests throughout her fieldwork on *Number Our Days*: "In the beginning, I spent a great deal of time agonizing about how to label what I was doing—was it anthropology or a personal quest? I never fully resolved the question."[31]

The phrase "between two worlds" stems from the title of An-sky's play *The Dybbuk*, or, as it was originally called in Yiddish, *Der dibek: Tsvishn tsvey veltn* (The Dybbuk: Between Two Worlds), which was based in part on the voluminous folkloric material collected during the Jewish Ethnographic Expedition and was first performed in Warsaw on December 9, 1920, soon after An-sky's death. For the Jewish ethnographer doing fieldwork among Jewish research subjects, being at once a native and a nonnative, studying people "who are simultaneously 'me' and 'not me,'" oscillating between the personal and the anthropological quests, means constantly moving between two—or more—worlds both physically and imaginatively, as Kugelmass himself does when, in his own contribution to the volume, he describes the effects of traveling by subway between the worlds of Hasidic Williamsburg, the Intervale Jewish Center of the South Bronx, and the YIVO Institute in Manhattan.[32]

As we have already seen with An-sky, navigating these worlds often means performing, or at least approximating, different Jewish identities, depending on the context. Indeed, one of the most frequently repeated— and fraught—scenes in the history of Jewish ethnography is that of the secular Jewish ethnographer who literally dons the hat—or the yarmulke or the modest dress, etc.—of the more orthodox Jews among whom he or she is conducting fieldwork. To dismiss such performances as solely pragmatic attempts to better fit in or avoid friction misses the impact that these masquerades, however transient, can have on the ethnographer.[33] What is made possible through such performances, if only momentarily and incompletely, is the feeling of belonging to a community that is other- wise inaccessible and may even be personally unappealing in many of its aspects. At the same time—and perhaps somewhat paradoxically—pre- cisely the same experience may also confirm the ethnographer's sense of otherness vis-à-vis the community being studied.

In his essay "Between Two Worlds: Notes on the Celebration of Purim among New York Jews, March 1985," Kugelmass describes the ambivalent emotions he experiences when he puts on a yarmulke and attends a *sude* (festive meal) in Hasidic Williamsburg. Kugelmass writes, "I would like to see a *sude,* not take part in one. . . . For me the anthropologist, there is a great sense of risk here. I feel less secure about the nature of the enterprise because anthropology does not lend itself to casual encounters. Besides, I am worried that my ruse will be exposed, that the Hasid will see who I am behind the yarmulke mask."[34] A few pages later, he finds himself ac- cepting the role that he has chosen to perform and its implications for his own complicated sense of self: "Tonight, despite my questions, I cannot turn the occasion into an ethnographic interview. . . . Content to listen and accept my lot as their Purim *mitzvah,* I think: here we are, Jews from Canada, from Holland, from Hungary, from Rumania and Israel, celebrating together in America the holiday of Purim. We are as different from each other as night is from day and yet I, the non-Jewish Jew, feel perfectly entitled to sit here with them."[35]

Here we come to yet another recurring theme in the history of Jewish ethnography. The secular Jewish ethnographer's masquerade, whatever it may come to mean for him or her, signifies something different to the more traditional Jews for whom it is intended. Now they, rather than the ethnographer, are the observers. And what they see, what they want to see, is either a Jew who has fallen off the *derekh,* that is, the right path of observant Judaism, or one who is a *tinoq shenishba* (literally, "captured infant"), a Jew who has never had the opportunity to learn the commandments and therefore is unaware of his or her transgressions, nevertheless performing a mitzvah in the course of performing ethnography, and, hopefully, starting on the path of becoming *frum* (devout). Or, as Janice Belcove-Shalin records in her essay "Becoming More of an Eskimo: Fieldwork among the Hasidim of Boro Park," "This is the essence of my predicament. I was a stranger, an intruder, a potential threat to the community, yet I was tolerated, even welcomed, as someone who could be shown the right way of living—the Hasidic way. The context of my fieldwork, then, is best characterized as a struggle for dominance between my secular and religious selves; as the Hasidim tried to enflame my religious passions, I, the curious ethnographer and unobservant Jew, plumbed the mysterious depths of their faith."[36] Rather than simply the ethnographer's symbolic rebirth, it is the community claiming one of its own—or at least attempting to do so—which characterizes this kind of ethnographic return. As Kugelmass puts it,

> Herein lies the great dilemma of Jewish ethnography: the problematic nature of encountering the Other cannot be transcended, no matter how close the observer feels himself to be to the subject of study.... We are looking for a more authentic self and who more so than those who would study our own? But if making subjects into historical relics is our way of making sense out of otherness, they, that is, our subjects, are not bound by such formulations, except when we have subjugated them politically. So they respond to us not as relics but as equals or as our betters, determined to define in ways that suit them the nature of our interaction.[37]

Jack Kugelmass's evocative description in the same essay of working "amid the documentary remains of Eastern European Jewry," at the

YIVO Institute, alludes to a different dimension of Jewish ethnography, one less anchored in place than in time, although the two can never be fully untangled.[38] Accordingly, the ethnographer's return to his or her "native land" may take place, as it were, in the form of vicarious memory or imagination, rather than a physical journey. In particular, the Jewish ethnographer doing fieldwork in one of the various outposts of the Eastern European Jewish diaspora—Hasidic communities, senior centers, synagogues, the YIVO Institute, and so on—is constantly presented with reminders of Jewish worlds lost: the Eastern European shtetls visited by the Jewish Ethnographic Expedition, the old Jewish neighborhood, the yeshiva, the socialist Jewish chicken farms of New Jersey (in the case of Jonathan Boyarin), and so on. Moreover, as Boyarin indicates in his essay "Waiting for a Jew: Marginal Redemption at the Eighth Street Shul," these worlds are themselves interconnected in a complex web of memory and representation, both for their current denizens—if any remain—and for the ethnographer, whose own fieldwork may involve tracing the links between various sites, some actually visited in person and others only imagined and, in the process, memorialized, in a kind of ethnographic *recherche du temps perdu*.[39]

ETHNOGRAPHERS AS PRIESTS

In 1948, M. N. Srinivas, newly returned from his doctoral studies at the University of Oxford, embarked on the fieldwork that would lead, three decades later, to the publication of his classic book *The Remembered Village*—remembered, because in the intervening years his original field notes had been destroyed in a fire, and Srinivas had been forced to reconstruct his time in the South Indian village of Rampura largely from memory, a process which Srinivas later came to appreciate as liberating. Srinivas had grown up in the nearby city of Mysore, where his Brahmin family had earlier migrated from a multicaste village not unlike Rampura. Thus, Srinivas was himself a thrice-born anthropologist in the kind of complicated way that characterizes the Jewish ethnographers I have examined in this chapter. Like Barbara Myerhoff, Srinivas returned to a "home" that he personally never knew but one that nevertheless existed in his familial imagination, if not his memory.

What Srinivas encountered in the village of Rampura confirms Kugel-mass's observation that it is not only the anthropologist who shapes the ethnographic encounter but also the research subjects who are "deter-mined to define in ways that suit them the nature of our interaction." Indeed, the villagers expected Srinivas, the thrice-born ethnographer of the priestly caste, to act according to local norms of proper Brahmanical behavior:

> My daily shave also drew comment from the villagers. . . . Contact with the Barber rendered a Brahmin or other high caste men impure, and this resulted in shaving being associated with impurity. . . . It was only in the village that I realized how far I (and my family) had travelled from tradi-tion. The morning shave had been a habit with me for several years, and I generally shaved before my bath. One morning, however, I had to reverse the order though I cannot recall why. . . . Anyway, I was shaving when the Headman [of the village] walked in. He asked me at once why I was shav-ing after my bath. I do not remember what I told him but he told me firmly that it was better that I finished shaving every day before my bath. The fact that I was a Brahmin made my disregard for the rules more culpable. I took care never again to shave after a bath. I had gone to Rampura to study and I did not want to do anything to jeopardize that.[40]

I have chosen this particular episode because it recalls in striking fash-ion an experience of that other thrice-born ethnographer, An-sky, him-self a kohen, or member of the Jewish priestly caste. Like the villagers of Rampura, the residents of the shtetls that An-sky visited during the Jew-ish Ethnographic Expedition had their own clear ideas of what a "priest" should act like, thrice born or not. As Shmuel Shrayer recalled in his mem-oir of the expedition,

> As is known, the name "Rapoport" is the name of an ancient family of Kohanim, and indeed An-sky was a Kohen and was related to the two sons of Rabbi Shlomo Rofeh of Aporto. . . . In one town there was a rabbi well-informed in these matters and he asked me: "How does Reb Shloyme Rapoport allow himself to visit cemeteries?" The question took me by sur-prise, but I immediately came up with a suitable excuse: I explained that in truth, An-sky was a descendent of the well-known Rapoport family only on his mother's side and that only in order to escape from military service did he take on the name of his mother's family. The rabbi accepted this expla-nation since in almost every city and town it was possible to find brothers

with the same father who each had a different surname—as a protection against military service. And from that point on it immediately made the rounds in the town that he [An-sky] was a counterfeit "Rapoport," and thus we avoided yet another potential disaster.[41]

In the end, I would argue, both Srinivas and An-sky discovered that despite having returned "home" with new eyes—and having experienced their third birth as ethnographers—they were nevertheless fated to remain between two worlds.

NOTES

1. Victor Turner, foreword to *Number Our Days: A Triumph of Continuity and Culture among Jewish Old People in an Urban Ghetto,* by Barbara G. Myerhoff (New York: Simon & Schuster, 1980), xiii.

2. Ibid., xiv.

3. On this issue, see, for example, Harry Wolcott, "Home and Away: Personal Contrasts in Ethnographic Style," in *Anthropologists at Home in North America: Methods and Issues in the Study of One's Own Society,* ed. Donald Messerschmidt (Cambridge: Cambridge University Press, 1981), 255–266.

4. Kirin Narayan, "How Native Is a 'Native' Anthropologist?," *American Anthropologist* 95, no. 3 (1993): 671.

5. An-sky to Gintsburg, June 30, 1912, Vernadsky National Library of Ukraine Manuscript Division (Jewish Section), Kiev, 6/30(7/13)/1912, IR NBUV. For discussions of this quote, see Nathaniel Deutsch, *The Jewish Dark Continent: Life and Death in the Russian Pale of Settlement* (Cambridge, MA: Harvard University Press, 2011), 11; Gabriella Safran, *Wandering Soul: The Dybbuk's Creator, S. An-sky* (Cambridge, MA: Belknap Press of Harvard University Press, 2010), 196–197.

6. For a chronological synopsis of An-sky's life, see Gabriella Safran, "Timeline: Semyon Akimovich An-sky/Shloyme-Zanvl Rappoport," in *The Worlds of S. An-sky: A Russian Jewish Intellectual at the Turn of the Century,* ed. Gabriella Safran and Steven Zipperstein (Stanford, CA: Stanford University Press, 2006), xv–xxix.

7. Moshe Shalit, "Sh. An-ski loyt zayn bukh fun di tsaytungs oysshnitn," *Fun noyentn ever* 1 (1937): 231. See also Deutsch, *The Jewish Dark Continent,* 6–7.

8. Dubnow's call is from a Hebrew version of the Russian original, "Ob izuchenii istorii ruskikh evreev," quoted in Adam Rubin, "Hebrew Folklore and the Problem of Exile," *Modern Judaism* 25 (2005): 70; An-sky's exhortation is quoted in David G. Roskies, *The Jewish Search for a Usable Past* (Bloomington: Indiana University Press, 1999), 18. On these calls, see Deutsch, *The Jewish Dark Continent,* 38.

9. S. An-sky, *Dos yidishe etnografishe program: Ershter teyl; Der mentsh,* ed. I. L. Shterberg (St. Petersburg: Yosef Luria, 1914), as translated in Deutsch, *The Jewish Dark Continent,* 105.

10. S. An-sky, "Evreiskoe narodnoe tvorchestvo," *Perezhitoe* 1 (1908): 276–314. See Deutsch, *The Jewish Dark Continent,* 28.

11. Full translation in Deutsch, *The Jewish Dark Continent,* 104.

12. Simon Dubnow, *Ob izuchenii istorii russkikh evreev i ob uchrezhdenii russkoevrei-skogo istoricheskogo obshchestva* (St. Petersburg: A. E. Landau, 1891), 36–37; Deutsch, *The Jewish Dark Continent,* 7.

13. Simon Dubnow, *Evreiskaia Starina* 1, no. 1 (1909): 154; Deutsch, *The Jewish Dark Continent,* 8. See also Benjamin Nathans, *Beyond the Pale: The Jewish Encounter with Late Imperial Russia* (Berkeley: University of California Press, 2002), 378.

14. On this phenomenon, see Deutsch, *The Jewish Dark Continent,* 8.

15. Gabriella Safran, "Jews as Siberian Natives: Primitivism and S. An-sky's *Dybbuk,*" *Modernism/Modernity* 13, no. 4 (2006): 635.

16. On *kinnus,* see Israel Bartal, "The *Kinnus* Project: *Wissenschaft des Judentums* and the Fashioning of a 'National Culture' in Palestine," in *Transmitting Jewish Traditions: Orality, Textuality, and Cultural Diffusion,* ed. Yaakov Elman and Israel Gershoni (New Haven, CT: Yale University Press, 2000), 310–323.

17. Jeffrey Veidlinger, *Jewish Public Culture in the Late Russian Empire* (Bloomington: Indiana University Press, 2009), xii.

18. Veidlinger, *Jewish Public Culture,* 260.

19. Barbara Kirshenblatt-Gimblett, "Theorizing Heritage," *Ethnomusicology* 39, no. 3 (1995): 369.

20. Quoted in Veidlinger, *Jewish Public Culture,* 260.

21. On this episode, see Deutsch, *The Jewish Dark Continent,* 52.

22. Chana Schneerson, "Memoirs of Rebbetzin Chana—Part 28," accessed April 4, 2015, http://www.chabad.org/library/article_cdo/aid/1844542/jewish/Memoirs-of-Rebbetzin-Chana-Part-28.htm.

23. Deutsch, *The Jewish Dark Continent,* 25.

24. Shmuel Shrayer (a.k.a. Shrira), unpublished memoir (unpaginated). My thanks to Eilat Gurfinkel, his granddaughter, for providing me with this document. Quoted in Deutsch, *The Jewish Dark Continent,* 46.

25. Shrayer, unpublished memoir, quoted in Deutsch, *The Jewish Dark Continent,* 47.

26. Jack Kugelmass, "The Father of Jewish Ethnography?," in Safran and Zipperstein, *The Worlds of S. An-sky,* 346.

27. Ibid., 356.

28. Myerhoff, *Number Our Days,* 129.

29. Sheila Benson, "'Time' Offers Look into Hasidic Life," review of *In Her Own Time,* directed by Lynne Littman, *Los Angeles Times,* December 7, 1985, http://articles.latimes.com/1985-12-07/entertainment/ca-14272_1_barbara-myerhoff.

30. Jack Kugelmass, ed., *Between Two Worlds: Ethnographic Essays on American Jewry* (Ithaca, NY: Cornell University Press, 1988), 23.

31. Myerhoff, *Number Our Days,* 12.

32. Jack Kugelmass, "Between Two Worlds: Notes on the Celebration of Purim among New York Jews, March 1985," in Kugelmass, *Between Two Worlds,* 33–51.

33. Concerning this issue, Janet Belcove-Shalin writes, "Participant observation, I discovered, was not mere method, unreflexively applied to achieve entrée into community life. It was rather an intricate process of interpretation and role playing . . . what Erving Goffman has variably referred to as 'face-work,' 'presentation of self,' and 'impression management.'" Janet Belcove-Shalin, "Becoming More of an Eskimo: Fieldwork among the Hasidim of Boro Park," in Kugelmass, *Between Two Worlds,* 79,

34. Kugelmass, "Between Two Worlds," 44.

35. Ibid., 46–47.

36. Belcove-Shalin, "Becoming More of an Eskimo," 79.

37. Kugelmass, "Between Two Worlds," 47–48.

38. Ibid., 33.

39. Jonathan Boyarin, "Waiting for a Jew: Marginal Redemption at the Eighth Street Shul," in Kugelmass, *Between Two Worlds,* 52–76.

40. M. N. Srinivas, *The Remembered Village* (Berkeley: University of California Press, 1980), 17–18. For another ethnographic encounter that raises some of the same issues, see Triloki Pandey, "The Anthropologist-Informant Relationship: The Navajo and Zuni in America and the Tharu in India," in *The Fieldworker and the Field: Problems and Challenges in Sociological Investigation,* ed. M. N. Srinivas, A. M. Shah, and E. A. Ramaswamy (Delhi: Oxford University Press, 1979), 260: "My first fieldwork introduced me to people who were not much different from the lower caste members I had known in my natal village as a child. Whenever I asked my Tharu friends questions about their religion, their response was: 'What sort of a Brahmin are you that you are asking us questions about religion? You should know all this and tell us about them.'"

41. Shrayer, unpublished memoir.

2

———— ✑ ————

Between Scientific and Political

JEWISH SCHOLARS AND RUSSIAN-JEWISH PHYSICAL ANTHROPOLOGY IN THE FIN-DE-SIÈCLE RUSSIAN EMPIRE

MARINA MOGILNER

Recent and burgeoning scholarship on Jewish ethnographic self-fashioning in the Russian Empire and the Soviet Union has focused primarily on those who "went to the people" to discover, catalogue, salvage, invent, interpret, learn from, normalize, nationalize, territorialize, or revolutionize their culture.[1] Culture was the central category of humanist scholarship focused on the phenomenon of "the people," which explains its paradoxical persistence during the epoch of rising nationalisms and collapsing empires, revolutions and world wars. Even "cultural revolutions" could not question the centrality of "culture" in its essentialist rendering because culture was perceived as a projection of "peoples" (or nations) in the sphere of "spiritual life." In the case of Russian Jewish ethnography, rooted in the Russian populist tradition and intimately connected to the political and historical project of Russian-Jewish identity, this fixation on "culture" seems inevitable and obvious to this day—indeed, so obvious that it has resulted in a peculiar historiographical blindness toward another effect of the late imperial "ethnographic impulse"—the concern with Russian Jews as a race, a category fundamental to the fin-de-siècle cultural moment worldwide.

In fact, in Russia this concern generated its own version of a "going to the people" story, in which the collective Jewish body, the Jewish race, was discovered as an "objective" and "scientific" answer to the challenges of the particular Jewish cultural hybridity (multilingualism, localized traditions) and political deficiency (of a diaspora people), not to mention antisemitic invectives. Even more importantly, the focus on the holistically imagined Jewish body promised to overcome the most disturbing problem of Russian-Jewish identity—its coexistence in two distinct cultural norms/traditions. Russian-Jewish race scientists and amateurs of physical anthropology went to the Jewish people as experts who possessed the scientific language and authority required to study and read the Jewish body as a "text" containing information on the natural history of their nation and blueprints for its future development.

Late imperial Russia provided an ideal setting for developing a fixation on the collective Jewish body: this body was locked within the Pale of Jewish Settlement, suffered from pogrom violence, and was symbolically marked as "traditional" and "degenerate." The symbolic visibility of the Jewish body facilitated the popularity of Jewish race science, and this popularity, in turn, promoted broad social support for the racialized vision of modern Jewishness—a trend that eventually culminated in the creation of the all-Russian OZE (Obshchestvo Okhraneniia Zdorov'ia Evreiskogo Naseleniia, the Society for the Preservation of the Health of the Jewish Population) movement led by medical professionals.[2] Jewish medical doctors, disproportionately overrepresented among educated Russian Jews, partook in the international professional culture that in many respects had been centered on the concept of race since the end of the nineteenth century.[3] Due to the *numerus clausus* for Jews in Russian universities, many of them graduated from European universities, mostly German and Austrian, where they were directly exposed to racialized medical and anthropological theories.[4]

The race paradigm had the potential to overcome the parochialism and particularism reinforced by an ethnographic scholarship that sought to reconstruct unique traditions and specific national "cultures." In the Russian context of the late imperial period, it was precisely this universalistic, emancipatory, and democratizing quality of race science that attracted intellectuals, regardless of their ethnic origin, who shared anti-imperial and anti–ancien régime sentiments. Those politically subversive implications made the Russian imperial state even more reluctant to embrace the discourse of race consistently as a language of political legitimacy. Different agents and institutions inside and outside the government and official academia claimed racial anthropology as their sphere of authority.

Academically, the leading position in this discursive competition belonged to the Moscow school of liberal anthropology represented by the empire-wide network of scientists and professionals coordinated by the Anthropological Division affiliated with the Imperial Moscow University Society of the Lovers of Natural Sciences, Anthropology, and Ethnography (IOLEAE) and based in Moscow. The Moscow school kept a safe distance from the imperial state (and this estrangement was rather mutual), successfully tamed various nationalizing anthropological projects of its members, and equally successfully derailed attempts at imposing "classical" colonial hierarchies of power-knowledge in the empire. The Moscow school of liberal anthropology differentiated between race and culture, advanced the concept of the "mixed physical type," and calculated degrees of racial kinship among all major imperial physical types. It studied Russian and non-Russian population groups, integrated scholars regardless of their ethnoconfessional background (including Jews), and offered a broad and inclusive liberal epistemological and ideological framework for their projects.[5] Theoretically, this created a unique, welcoming, and inspiring situation for Russian-Jewish anthropological projects, and indeed Jewish intellectuals actively partook in the network.[6] In what follows, I attempt to understand how and why an endeavor that had every chance of becoming a truly unique case of emancipatory and universalizing science lost its universalizing potential and came to reinforce a particularistic ethnographic "cultural" paradigm of Jewishness. Here I consider the case of only one physical anthropologist—albeit a quite central one for Russian-Jewish race science—in his multiple Jewish and non-Jewish contexts. The resulting "thick description" should (hopefully) prevent this narrative from becoming a reductionist plot of triumphant success or equally wholesale failure.

AN EXEMPLARY JEWISH SCHOLAR AND
A PERFECT JEWISH PROJECT

Among the early twentieth-century Russian physical anthropologists, Aron Girsh Donov (Arkadii Danilovich in the Russified version) El'kind occupied a special place. He was among the few who actually defended dissertations in physical anthropology—a rare achievement for a science semi-institutionalized everywhere, not only in Russia. Moreover, this Jewish scholar got his academic degree from one of the oldest imperial universities, and, moreover, for a study in Jewish anthropology: "The Jews: A Comparative Anthropological Study Based Primarily on Observations of Polish Jews." The initial research was completed and published in 1903, but for the defense in 1912 it was supplemented by an extended discussion of recent anthropological literature: "Anthropological Studies of Jews Written in the Course of the Past Ten Years."[7] On December 12, 1912, the day of El'kind's public defense, Moscow University's Anatomic Theater was packed with listeners who "welcomed El'kind with loud applause."[8] The atmosphere in the theater was more appropriate for a public rally than for a regular dissertation defense, which was only understandable given the topic of the dissertation and the timing of the event (amid the controversy of the Mendel Beilis case).

It is striking how poorly the candidate suited the role of Jewish public activist or political hero. A graduate of the Medical Department of Moscow University,[9] and a longtime member of the IOLEAE Anthropological Division, El'kind was virtually unknown in Russian-Jewish political or public contexts, except for his presence in the pages of the professional Russian-language magazine of Jewish physicians, the Odessa *Evreiiskii meditsinskii golos* (Jewish medical voice).[10] El'kind's reputation as a Russian race scientist was much more solid, but he never attempted to convert his work in this field into an official career in state service. He was not baptized and thus could not apply for a university position. Instead, he made a successful career in the liberal anthropological network and rose to its very top: in 1914 El'kind became secretary of the IOLEAE Anthropological Division and editor of the *Russian Anthropological Journal.*

His mentor at the university was the dean of Russian physical anthropology, leader of the Moscow school, and the first Russian anthropology professor, Dmitry Anuchin,[11] who published on Jewish anthropology only once—the article "Jews" in the *Brockhaus and Efron Encyclopedic Dictionary*[12] (although he used data on the height of Jewish conscripts in his famous work on height as a race indicator, based on the anthropometric data of Bavarian, Hungarian, and Russian conscripts).[13] El'kind's fundamental *The Jews* (1903) contained references to all of the leading world specialists on Jewish race, but he dedicated the work to Anuchin.[14] In his work El'kind strictly followed the rules of the Moscow school: no articulated political or national agenda, or "cultural arguments"; acceptance of the existing borders of the Russian Empire as the "natural" limits for field research; and a reliance on the methodology of measurements and classification approved by the Moscow school. *The Jews* seemed to prove that Jewish anthropology did not require any special methods or concepts, and was indifferent to the anthropologist's own ethnicity or national agenda. Anuchin appreciated this universalist and normative aspect of his student's research when he presented it at the defense as a work "dedicated to an anthropological study of one of the peoples [*narodnostei*] living in the Russian Empire," and supported its nomination for a special distinction.[15] Indeed, IOLEAE awarded El'kind its most prestigious anthropological prize, named after Great Prince Sergei Aleksandrovich[16]—the highest Russian anthropological prize instituted by a representative of the family of a tsar known for his notorious antisemitism. Definitely, the liberal anthropologists administering the prize did not miss this opportunity to show their political independence and scientific objectivity, and also to confirm the normality of Jewish race science in the context of their anthropological project.

Concurring with this understanding of academic normality, El'kind remained demonstratively apolitical even in 1912, when any public discussion of Jewish specificity evoked politics. He amassed and presented multiple anthropometric data that, according to him, proved the existence of a special and pure Jewish racial type dating back to the prediaspora period.[17] Otherwise El'kind tended to avoid precise conclusions. His colleagues endorsed his approach, and were especially impressed by how, in order "to determine the dynamics of specific measurements and their correlations, the author arranges them in rows, builds curves, and in general applies all methods available in anthropology."[18] Even if they were capable of spotting a hidden "Jewish text" in the content of this objective and scientific dissertation, they probably would have preferred to close their eyes to it.

JEWISHNESS AS A HIDDEN AGENDA

It is amazing to see how successful El'kind was in concealing from his many colleagues the hidden Jewish agenda of his dissertation. To uncover it, one has to read between the lines, or rather between the tables and graphs of *The Jews,* and, most importantly, to approach with suspicion the very object of El'kind's analysis—the collective Russian-Jewish body that he constructed and presented as something self-evident. This was the body of the Jews of Russian Poland who were introduced from the outset as "European," while the Jews of Russian Central Asia and the Caucasus were characterized as "allotypical." In the dissertation, they literally embodied racial anomaly. Without using civilizational terms, El'kind effectively orientalized the Jews of non-European parts of the Russian Empire by questioning their role even as passive objects of Jewish racial self-description. El'kind, like many other Jewish anthropologists, insisted on the cultural (and thus temporary and curable) causes of "racial" deficiencies of the collective European Jewish body, such as a narrow chest or feeble constitution, as well as of characteristically "Jewish" physical illnesses,[19] inverted gender markers of their bodies, and even the universal "recognizability" of the "Jewish physiognomy," which betrayed an imagined racial degradation or, at best, an absence of the healthy development of the archaic "Jewish race." At the same time, the racial otherness of the "allotypical" Jews of Central Asia and the Caucasus was of a different (physical) nature, and thus they were destined to stagnate along with the civilizational "Orient." By sacrificing discursively one part of the scientifically constructed racial whole, El'kind elevated the other part, avoiding debates over the very feasibility of the Jewish degeneration theory, and without revealing his hidden ideological agenda.

Contrary to the accepted pattern of ethnographic research requiring scholars to "go to the people" and observe them in their "natural environment," that is, in their rustic shtetls or *auls* (in the case of the Caucasian and Central Asian Jews), El'kind constructed his "people" as factory workers in a modern city. He measured 200 Jewish men, ages twenty to sixty, and 125 Jewish women, ages fifteen to thirty-seven, at two Warsaw factories. The resulting collective Jewish body exhibited no ethnographic peculiarity. It was quintessentially modern, suffering from the negative influences of urbanization and industrialization and easily imaginable in any other industrial center of the Russian Empire or of Europe. As El'kind's dissertation reveals, he was well aware of the possible implications of his findings: Jews were not a race; removed from their traditional cultural nests, they quickly assimilated.

Some prominent Jewish race scientists, such as Maurice Fishberg, advanced precisely this argument in Jewish academic and political debates of the time. Fishberg, who in 1889 emigrated from Russia to the United States, where he established himself as the chief medical expert of the United Hebrew Charities and as a race scientist specializing in "comparative Jewish pathology" and anthropology, was well known in Russia mostly due to El'kind's reviews of his works.[20] Fishberg's anthropological statistics showed the great transformative power of the American soil, which attracted the healthiest and strongest among Eastern European Jews and exposed their self-modernizing potential. Naturally, Fishberg, not unlike the Eurocentric El'kind, polemicized with Zionist race science, which posited an intimate connection between Palestinian soil and the collective Jewish body. One year before El'kind's defense, in 1911, Fishberg summarized the results of his own long-term studies in the monograph *The Jews: A Study of Race and Environment.*[21] This monograph contained suggestive visual material. A portrait of a skinny and stooped "Polish Jew in Jerusalem," with beard and earlocks, wearing a traditional Jewish caftan, demonstrated that the Holy Land had not improved his physical condition. At the same time, American Jews were represented by men and women in modern fancy dresses and suits, all of the men shaven and bareheaded, and all of the women displaying fashionable hairstyles, looking particularly healthy and harmonious. Only a subtle "imprint" on their faces, expressed through hardly verifiable manifestations, exposed them as Jews. They were not a race, only a cultural/religious community destined to dissolve in the American nation. When applied to the Eastern European context, Fishberg's approval of Jewish assimilation into the American "melting pot" meant the disappearance of Jews from the scene of modern European history, where nations were major actors.

El'kind's hidden agenda was to reestablish Jews on the European historical scene as a distinct, though definitely not "degenerate," race with the potential to resist assimilation and develop into a modern nation.

This explains why he asked his younger brother, then a student at Warsaw University, to photograph for the dissertation the Jews of the traditional small town of Kholm (Chełm; Yiddish, Khelem) of Lublin province—a prominent target of Jewish jokes. Alongside illustrations from the collection of the Moscow University Museum and the Moscow Rumiantsev Museum, El'kind included these pictures of Kholm Jews in the 1903 edition of *The Jews*. Unlike Fishberg, whose images juxtaposed "degenerating" traditional Jewry with healthy and assimilated modern Jews, El'kind did not want any visual contrasts. He needed recognizably Jewish faces to compensate for the ethnographic neutrality of the "European" Jewish physical type that he constructed. And he wanted these faces to represent eternal Jewishness, as imprinted in Abyssinian and Egyptian images, Rembrandt's rabbis, and twentieth-century photographs of Jews from Eastern Ukrainian lands and Kholm.

Formally speaking, El'kind's visual text had little to do with the rest of the dissertation, and during his defense Anuchin expressed his justified perplexity: why did El'kind miss a chance to elaborate scientifically on the enigma of "Jewish physiognomy? . . . The very fact of assembling such a great number of Jewish portraits in the dissertation invites such an analysis."[22] Anuchin personally believed firmly in the "amazing resemblance between the types from the Ancient Egyptian memorials and characteristic types of contemporary Jews,"[23] and he expected his student to verify and explain this impression in the language of science. But how was El'kind to spell out his idiosyncratic Jewish concerns in this "neutral" and universalistic language? Instead, he left the visual anthropology to speak for itself (to those who were able to decipher the message), whereas his general conclusion stated that "modern European Jews, in terms of their anatomic structure, produce a quite homogeneous ethnological group whose basic characteristics (hair and eye color, head index, height) everywhere demonstrate more or less similar divergence from the same characteristics of the local Christian population. On the other hand, some facts suggest that the Polish Jews had better-preserved national anthropological peculiarities, compared to the Jews of other countries."[24] This passage also provoked Anuchin's comments. In particular, he criticized El'kind's use of the term "ethnological" here and in other parts of the dissertation:

"Ethnos can be applied to a people only if we understand it in a spiritual and cultural sense, but not as a physical type."[25]

It is highly doubtful that having completed Anuchin's university courses in anthropology and ethnography, El'kind did not know this basic distinction. Most likely, this was one of the rare moments when the suppressed Jewish text of the dissertation revealed itself explicitly. For El'kind, being a normal "European" race was a necessary precondition for developing a national—"spiritual and cultural"—life, not only in the past but also at present and in the future. His colleague, and in a sense ideological antipode, another leading Russian-Jewish anthropologist, member of the Moscow liberal network, and winner of its highest distinction,[26] Samuel Weissenberg—who sympathized with Simon Dubnow's political autonomist program, supported the Jewish ethnography project of S. An-sky, and was inclined to view Russian Jewry as a single yet internally heterogeneous cultural and national entity—was equally concerned with the "Europeanness" of his object of research. Unlike El'kind, Weissenberg constructed the Russian-Jewish race as a combination of European and Asian elements. This model had little in common with the conventional "Semitic type," was racially mixed, and thus was also quintessentially European.[27] As John Efron pointedly wrote, for Weissenberg, "European Jews were merely intimately linked to Europeans by having been racially transformed by the intermixture that had taken place in the Caucasus; it was not West European but Eastern European Jews, with their noble past and culturally vital present, who were the authentic creators and bearers of the European Jewish tradition."[28]

Hence the task of anthropology as understood by El'kind and many other Jewish scientists was to undermine "the older view that assigned Jews a specific physical organization that differed from that of other cultured peoples."[29] This particular line from the dissertation alarmed Anuchin as yet another characteristic instance of letting the cat out of the bag: "The author claims that Jewish physical organization follows the same developmental rhythm as that of 'other cultural people,' while 'some somatic peculiarities' characteristic of the Jews have developed under the influence of 'environment.' The expression of 'other cultural people' is not quite clear: first, the level of our knowledge about developmental rhythms of different cultured peoples varies, and second—what does culture have to do with it anyway?"[30]

For El'kind this was not a rhetorical question, and to answer it he would have to compromise the scientific neutrality of his discourse with explicit references to different constructions of Jewish otherness, to the theme of Jewish degeneration, to antisemitic clichés about Jews' incapacity for valuable cultural productivity, their lacking a "national" culture, and so on. But these were not legitimate topics in the eyes of representatives of the Moscow school. They did not share antisemitic stereotypes and believed that any attempt to use the objective method of their science in ideological polemics (even with "affirmative action" purposes) exposed the clear political bias of a scholar and compromised his or her arguments. In exchange for the complete normalization of Jewish race science in the imperial intellectual community, El'kind (unlike the more controversial and also scientifically independent Weissenberg) consciously and honestly embraced the normalizing paradigm and attempted to give up his national subaltern agenda.

SEEING LIKE A RUSSIAN ANTHROPOLOGIST

Sacrificing his Jewish (cultural and political) agenda in order to normalize Jewish anthropology as an academic subfield required El'kind to exercise serious self-censorship. We can grasp the pressure of this self-imposed muteness (compromised only by slips of the tongue or ambivalent messages of the assorted imagery) by comparing El'kind's anthropology of Jews to his studies of non-Jewish peoples. There, his analysis loses any ambiguity and closely sticks to the methodological orthodoxy of the Moscow anthropological school. For example, soon after his successful dissertation defense, El'kind published an article titled "On Negro Anthropology: Dahomeans (with Six Pictures)," featuring the results of anthropometric measurements of twenty-two men and three women from the traveling show of Dahomeans—Africa's natives performing at the Moscow Zoological Garden. Before Moscow, the black artists had been measured in Berlin, London, and Zurich. El'kind applied to them the standard Moscow-school program of measurements that did not differ from the one he used in his Jewish project.[31] He found that the body proportions of Dahomeans were not so different from those of Europeans and that "their abdominal circumference is too low; it is much lower than the abdominal circumference of the Jews—the most narrow-chested people of Europe."[32]

As in the Jewish case, El'kind explained Dahomean narrow-chestedness and small stature as being due to unfavorable living conditions (as well as the colonial policies of Europeans). Indeed, in his account, Dahomeans in many ways resembled Jews, but in regard to them El'kind did not experience any complicated and contradictory feelings of simultaneous belonging and estrangement. He had no problem placing the black artists who had abandoned Africa decades before into their proper "natural environment." To this end, he studied all of the available literature on Dahomey climate and biological history. The author of "On Negro Anthropology" was a benevolent European scientist who possessed universal methodology and produced objective knowledge. El'kind's racial conceptualization of Dahomeans did not need any special visual subtext. He did not have to differentiate them into "allotypical" and "cultured" groups or exercise strict self-censorship. In this project, the language of anthropological science did not cover for anything else, and El'kind used it to convey everything he wanted to say.

Only the well-intended normalizing discourse of El'kind's colleagues could have prevented them from noticing the liberating effect that the absence of a Jewish agenda had on El'kind. Their drive to "normalize" Jewishness had an unintended side effect: a peculiar blindness toward the profound irregularity of diversity characteristic of the Russian imperial situation in general and the Jews as a typical imperial minority in particular. Accepting the existence of a separate "European" Jewish racial type in the version presented by El'kind, members of the Moscow school ignored the actual internal heterogeneity of Russian Jewry, their controversial status vis-à-vis Jews of Western Europe and the discourse of modernity, and the conflict that existed between the ideals of social integration and the preservation of national identity. This suppressed complexity had troubling epistemological (and political) consequences: whereas in the works of representatives of the Moscow school all imperial peoples, including Russians, existed as local and always mixed and interrelated racial types (Great Russians of a particular district, Little Russians of a particular region . . .), Jews, even when studied on a territorial basis, presented pure parts of one organic whole—the Jewish race—isolated from the rest of the imperial family.

The vision of the imperial family of racial relatives received its fullest embodiment in the classification of racial types of the Russian Empire produced by Aleksei Arsen'evich Ivanovskii (1866–1934), a Moscow professor and a longtime secretary of the Anthropological Division and editor of the *Russian Anthropological Journal*. Except for his academic position (Ivanovskii received a full professorship at Khar'kiv University and moved there from Moscow after his dissertation defense), Ivanovskii was, institutionally speaking, El'kind's direct non-Jewish "analogue" and predecessor. His degree from Moscow University was in geography, but as in the case of El'kind, his actual dissertation was in physical anthropology: "On the Anthropological Composition of the Population of Russia" (1904).[33] It is in this dissertation that Ivanovskii developed his method of racial classification based on calculating degrees of racial kinship between imperial racial types and on the acceptance of a mixed racial type as the only scientifically observable reality in the empire. His methodology remained the same for the "titular" and "subaltern" population groups alike, whereas the term "Russians" (without the necessary predicates, such as "Great," "Little," "of a given district," etc.) was demonstratively absent from this classification that took account of all kinds of "Russian" groups of the empire. The only race that was set apart from this family of racial relatives, the only pure race that did not mix with the surrounding population, was the Jewish race. This is the table of racial kinship for Jews composed by Ivanovskii:

Jews of Warsaw province
I. Jews
II. Jews of Mogilev and Odessa
III. Jews of Kovno and Courland
Jews of Mogilev province
I. Jews
II. Jews of Warsaw and Odessa
III. Jews of Courland
Jews of Kovno province
I. Jews of Courland
II. Jews of Odessa, Jews

  III. Jews of Warsaw and Vitebsk
       Jew of Vitebsk province
  III. Jews of Kovno
       Jews of Lifland province
  III. Great Russians of Yerevan province
       Jews of Courland province
   II. Jews of Kovno province
       Jews of Odessa
    I. *Jews*
   II. Jews of Warsaw, Mogilev, and Kovno
       Jews
    I. Jews of Warsaw, Mogilev, and Odessa
   II. Jews of Courland[34]

Only a negligible number of Jews of Lifland province (Latvia and Estonia), eleven people, showed the lowest (III) degree of kinship with Great Russians of Yerevan province (Armenia) in the Caucasus (apparently, the exiled Russian Orthodox sectarians). Statistically, this fact was truly insignificant, and Ivanovskii concluded with confidence that the "accumulated Jews" represented "a single and quite isolated anthropological group that is not connected with any other people."[35] He had no apparent reasons to interpret his results as being politically biased (personally Ivanovskii was quite philosemitic) or scientifically invalid. As early as 1900 Ivanovskii offered his own Lamarckian explanation of this "evident" fact of Jewish uniqueness—internal wholeness and external otherness—as being reflected on the level of the most observable physical features (proverbial "Jewish physiognomy"): "Generally speaking, the fact of the particular Jewish physiognomy's existence is beyond doubt. The question is: is it determined by a number of known characteristics, or also in addition by some special [facial] expression? In the first case, we could explain it by heredity, in the latter—by the "Ghetto expression," to quote Jacobs's words. If we accept that lasting oppressions, persecution, and the struggle for survival with surrounding peoples and conditions marked Jewish physical organization, why should we deny that these factors also influenced their facial expression?"[36]

Ivanovskii, along with the majority of Russian anthropologists, was well acquainted with the famous anthropological survey of German schoolchildren initiated and administered in the 1870s by Rudolf Virchow. In

Virchow's mass-scale project, German Jews were studied separately from the rest of the German population: the teachers who conducted the survey, following the instructions of professional anthropologists, from the outset had to separate Jewish pupils from all the rest and collect their racial statistics in a special section.[37] Nevertheless, no one used this survey to accuse Virchow of trying to exclude Jews from the nation of united Germany.[38] The analytical "segregation" of Jews was justified by strictly scientific considerations: as "Semites," by definition they represented a racial group of non-Germanic origin. At the same time, Virchow interpreted the results of his survey as having proved the success of Jewish-Christian integration in Europe. He understood the story of racial evolution as beginning with pure "types" that, in the course of intermixing, evolved into mixed "types." The survey of German schoolchildren revealed the presence of racial mixture among Germans as well as among German Jews (more than 10 percent of Jewish schoolchildren were classified as "blonds" and conceptualized as mixed).[39] Russian liberal anthropologists accepted this as a congenial approach corresponding to their understanding of the empire as a space of racial interactions and mixing. Neither Virchow nor Ivanovskii meant to exclude Jews from this "natural" biological process and from the complex political communities emerging on its basis. However, outside of the proper scientific context, neutral anthropological classifications could easily transform into a formula of absolute racial estrangement. This had eventually happened in Germany, and it was a possibility in Russia as well. In the same way, although within the domain of hegemonic control of the Moscow school the ambivalent normalization/estrangement of Jews remained "scientific" and politically neutral, outside this domain it could serve as a basis for the scientific justification of different versions of modern Jewish nationalism (which seems to be the case with the hidden Jewish text of El'kind's dissertation).

The earliest versions of Ivanovskii's classification did not feature data on Caucasian and Central Asian Jews, but it gradually expanded due to new studies by Russian anthropologists who embraced Ivanovskii's method of calculating racial kinship. Still, both the classical and new updated versions of this classification reserved a special role for the anthropology of Jews: having been formally integrated into the larger project of imperial race science, and thus into Ivanovskii's classification, it could legitimately develop in relative isolation. The imperial comparative framework was not a sine qua non for studies of the Jews, as they were seen a priori as a race apart, rather than a population unit in the empire of racial relatives. In other words, not unlike German Jews in Virchow's survey, Russian Jews could be symbolically, and practically, separated from the rest of the population and studied independently of the taxonomy of other imperial racial types. This explains the "narrow" specialization of Russian-Jewish anthropologists, most of whom studied only Jews, which was otherwise almost unthinkable for anthropologists belonging to the Moscow-oriented network. An exclusive fixation on one particular ethnic group raised suspicions of nationalist partisanship and caused critical comments from colleagues. Jewish anthropologists alone were exempt from this rule. Their ambivalent subaltern position (equal members of the community of scholars developing an influential language of imperial modernity, who nevertheless spoke in a voice that was not quite theirs) simultaneously empowered them and encouraged self-alienation.

It seems that everyone in the liberal anthropological network was satisfied with this situation. Jewish anthropologists such as El'kind could achieve the highest level of scholarly recognition in the multiethnic community of race scientists and academically legitimize their projects. Their non-Jewish colleagues—liberal opponents of the oppressive imperial regime—successfully solved the "Jewish question" in their ranks and in their common academic research project. Their political correctness in regard to racial antisemitism and internal Jewish diversity and cultural and ideological splits created a situation in which Jewish anthropologists could pursue—partially concealed and partially using the available scholarly opportunities—their specific Jewish agenda, thus contributing to projects of Jewish particularism. The epistemological singling out of the Jews as an object of study facilitated the creation of a distinctive Jewish social and political public discourse. Despite their ideals of positivist objectivity, and the absence of discrimination within the generally philosemitic and multiethnic liberal anthropological network, Jewish scientists were turning into Jewish activists, which partly explains the unprecedented success of mass Jewish medical-sanitation self-mobilization in the Russian Empire. In the early twentieth century, thousands of educated Jews joined the movement pursuing the agenda of normalizing the Jewish national body as a repository of the Jewish soul. They created a wide public sphere for scientifically driven Jewish national politics. This sphere was capable of absorbing Zionist, autonomist, socialist, and liberal political ideals and was not limited to any of them. A Russian-Jewish physical anthropologist such as Arkadii El'kind did not have to be a member of any established Jewish political party in order to influence an understanding of modern Jewishness in the Russian Empire and the goals and methods of struggle for it.

NOTES

1. Other chapters in this book illustrate most of these strategies and contain references to the works that illustrate the rest.

2. My version of the story of this medical mobilization in the Jewish medical societies, scholarly and professional press, and then in the OZE movement is presented in Marina Mogilner, "Toward a History of Russian-Jewish 'Medical Materialism': Russian-Jewish Physicians and the Politics of Jewish Biological Normalization," *Jewish Social Studies* 19, no. 1 (2012): 70–106.

3. On this culture, see John M. Efron, *Defenders of the Race: Jewish Doctors and Race Science in Fin-de-Siècle Europe* (New Haven, CT: Yale University Press, 1994); Pierre Birnbaum, "French Jewish Sociologists between Reason and Faith: The Impact of the Dreyfus Affair," *Jewish Social Studies* 2, no. 2 (1995): 1–35; Bryan Cheyette and Laura Marcus, eds., *Modernity, Culture and "the Jew"* (Cambridge: Polity, 1998); Sander Gilman, *The Jew's Body* (New York: Routledge, 1996); Michael Stanislawski, *Zionism and the Fin de Siècle: Cosmopolitanism and Nationalism from Nordau to Jabotinsky* (Berkeley: University of California Press, 2001); Todd Samuel Presner, "'Clear Heads, Solid Stomachs, and Hard Muscles': Max Nordau and the Aesthetics of Jewish Regeneration," *Modernism/modernity* 10, no. 2 (2003): 269–296; and many others.

4. Lisa Rae Epstein, "Caring for the Soul's House: The Jews of Russia and Health Care, 1860–1914" (PhD diss., Yale University, 1995).

5. For a detailed history of physical anthropology in the Russian Empire and especially of the liberal anthropology of imperial diversity (Moscow school), see Marina Mogilner, *Homo Imperii: A History of Physical Anthropology in Russia* (Lincoln: University of Nebraska Press, 2013).

6. For an overview of Russian-Jewish anthropology as a part of the liberal school of imperial anthropology, see the chapter "'Jewish Physiognomy,' the 'Jewish Question,' and the Russian Race Science between Inclusion and Exclusion," in Mogilner, *Homo Imperii*, 217–250.

7. A. D. El'kind, "Evrei (Sravnitel'no-antropologicheskoe issledovanie, preimushchestvenno po nabliudeniiam nad pol'skimi evreiami)," *Izvestiia IOLEAE* 104 (1903): 1–458.

8. "Ob'iavlenie dlia napechataniia v gazetakh," December 10, 1913, Tsentral'nyi Istoricheskii Arkhiv Goroda Moskvy (TsIAM), f. 418, op. 90, d. 709, l. 3. On the defense, see ibid., ll. 4–4 rev.; "Antropologicheskoe izuchenie evreev i disput A. D. El'kinda," *Zemlevedenie* 1–2 (1913): 230.

9. See his university medical diploma, "Diplom Moskovskogo Universiteta o pris-voenii A. D. El'kindu zvaniia lekaria," 1894, TsIAM, f. 418, op. 90, d. 709, l. 8.

10. As an example, see his article "On the Social Struggle against Degeneration": D-r A. D. El'kind, "K sotsial'noi bor'be s vyrozhdeniem," *Evreiskii meditsinskii golos* 2–4 (1908): 141–156.

11. For more on Anuchin and his role in Russian physical anthropology, see Mogilner, *Homo Imperii*, 133–166.

12. D. A. (Dmitrii Anuchin), "Evrei (v antropologicheskom otnoshenii)," in *Entsiklope-dicheskii slovar'*, ed. F. A. Brokgaus and I. E. Efron (St. Petersburg, 1893), 11:21:426–428.

13. D. N. Anuchin, "O geograficheskom raspredelenii rosta muzhskogo naseleniia Ros-sii (po dannym o vseobshchei voinskoi povinnosti v Imperii za 1874–1883 gg.) sravnitel'no s raspredeleniem rosta v drugikh stranakh," *Zapiski geograficheskogo obshchestva* 8 (1889): 1–184.

14. El'kind, "Evrei, (Sravnitel'no-antropologicheskoe issledovanie, preimushche-stvenno po nabliudeniiam nad pol'skimi evreiami)," iii.

15. "Antropologicheskoe izuchenie," 230.

16. "Prisuzhdenie premii po antropologii imeni Ego Imperatoskogo Vysochestva Velikogo Kniazia Sergeia Aleksandrovicha A. D. El'kindu za ego issledovanie 'Evrei,'" *Russkii antropologicheskii zhurnal* 11, no. 3 (1902): 117–119. The decision was made even before the complete text of *The Jews* was published, on the basis of El'kind's presentations in the Anthropological Division of IOLEAE and his earlier publication: El'kind, "Evrei (Sravnitel'no-antropologicheskii ocherk)," *Russkii antropologicheskii zhurnal* 11, no. 3 (1902): 1–44.

17. El'kind, "Evrei (Sravnitel'no-antropologicheskoe issledovanie, preimushche-stvenno po nabliudeniiam nad pol'skimi evreiami)," 457.

18. "Prisuzhdenie," 117. The announcement that El'kind was to be granted the Doctor of Medicine degree was met with applause. See "V sovete imperatorskogo Moskovskogo universiteta," December 15, 1912, TsIAM, f. 418, op. 90, d. 709, ll. 5–5 rev. Arkadii Danilov-ich El'kind received his doctoral diploma, signed by the rector of Moscow University and the dean of the Medical Department, Professor Dmitrii Nikolaevich Zernov, on Decem-ber 29, 1912. See "V sovete imperatorskogo Moskovskogo universiteta," l. 7. The archival file contains El'kind's handwriting: "The certified diploma was accepted" ("Podlinnyi diplom poluchil").

19. These aspects were discussed by El'kind in his other anthropological and medical-sanitation works as well: El'kind, "N. R. Botvinnikov. Materialy k voprosu o blizorukosti u evreev. 'Vrach.' 1899. # 42," *Russkii antropologicheskii zhurnal* 2, no. 2 (1900): 105–106; El'kind, "I. Kovarskii. Fizicheskoe razvitie drevnikh evreev v sravnenii s sovremennymi. 'Budushchnost' 1900. Nos. 20, 21, 22," *Russkii antropologicheskii zhurnal* 2, no. 3 (1900): 135–136; El'kind, "M. Fishberg. The Comparative Pathology of the Jews. 'N.Y. Med. Jour.' 1901. March-April," *Russkii antropologicheskii zhurnal* 11, no. 3 (1902): 107–111; El'kind, "M. Fish-berg. The Relative Infrequency of Tuberculosis among Jews ('American Medicine,' 1901, November)," *Russkii antropologicheskii zhurnal* 11, no. 3 (1902): 111; El'kind, "K sotsial'noi bor'be s vyrozhdeniem," *Evreiiskii meditsinskii golos* 2–4 (1908): 141–156; and others.

20. El'kind, "M. Fishberg. The Comparative Pathology of the Jews"; El'kind, "M. Fish-berg. The Relative Infrequency of Tuberculosis among Jews"; El'kind, "M. Fishberg. Phys-ical Anthropology of the Jews. Washington, 1902," *Russkii antropologicheskii zhurnal* 13, no. 1 (1903): 154–155; El'kind, "M. Fishberg. Physical Anthropology of the Jews. II. Pig-

mentation. Washington, 1903," *Russkii antropologicheskii zhurnal* 14, no. 2 (1903): 90–91.
Here El'kind provided incorrect information; both parts of Fishberg's *Physical Anthropology of the Jews* appeared in the journal *American Anthropologist* 4 (1902): 684–706; and 5 (1903): 89–106.

21. Maurice Fishberg, *The Jews: A Study of Race and Environment* (London: Walter Scott, 1911).

22. "Antropologicheskoe izuchenie evreev i disput A. D. El'kinda," 232.

23. "Protokol publichnogo zasedaniia 25-go oktiabria 1895," *Izvestiia* IOLEAE: *Trudy antropologicheskogo otdela* 8, no. 1–3 (1897): 492.

24. El'kind, "Evrei (Sravnitel'no-antropologicheskii ocherk)," 42.

25. "Antropologicheskoe izuchenie evreev i disput A. D. El'kinda," 232.

26. "Prisuzhdenie premii po antropologii imeni Velikogo Kniazia Sergeiia Aleksandrovicha d-ru S. A. Vaisenbergu," *Russkii antropologicheskii zhurnal* 30–31, no. 2–3 (1912): 187–189.

27. For more about Weissenberg in his Russian and Russian-Jewish contexts, see Mogilner, *Homo Imperii*, 217–250. On liberal discourses in European turn-of-the-century race science and racial mixture, see "Forum AI: Anthropological Knowledge and the Politics of Difference in Empire and Nation," *Ab Imperio* 1 (2007): 113–239. See esp. Andre Gingrich, "Liberalism in Imperial Anthropology: Notes on an Implicit Paradigm in Continental European Anthropology before World War I," 224–239; Andrew D. Evans, "A Liberal Paradigm? Race and Ideology in Late-Nineteenth-Century German Physical Anthropology," 113–138; and other contributions.

28. Efron, *Defenders of the Race*, 107.

29. El'kind, "Evrei (Sravnitel'no-antropologicheskii ocherk)," 42.

30. "Antropologicheskoe izuchenie evreev i disput A. D. El'kinda," 232.

31. The program included descriptive indicators and measurements of body height, head index, height longitudinal index, nasal index, head horizontal circumference, head size in a vertical projection, skull height, dolichocrania, transverse head diameter, ear and forehead diameters, facial length, body measurements and proportions, and so on.

32. El'kind, "K antropologii negrov: Dagomeitsy (s 6 ris.)," *Russkii antropologicheskii zhurnal* 29, no. 1 (1912): 34–35.

33. For biographical information on Ivanovskii, see L. P. Nikolaev, "A. A. Ivanovskii (Nekrolog)," *Antropologicheskii zhurnal* 1–2 (1934): 16–18. See also his curriculum vitae composed for his dissertation defense: "Opyt novoi antropologicheskoi klassifikatsii i disput A. A. Ivanovskogo," *Zemlevedenie* 1–2 (1913): 335–336. On the defense of his first dissertation on April 22, 1904, see "Predstavlenie fiziko-matematicheskogo fakul'teta o utverzhdenii A. A. Ivanovskogo v stepeni magistra geografii," April 25, 1904, TsIAM, f. 418, op. 82, d. 178, l. 4; "Svidetel'stvo o prisvoenii A. A. Ivanovskomu stepeni Magistra geografii," April 25, 1904, TsIAM, f. 418, op. 82, d. 178, l. 7. The full text of the dissertation was published as A. A. Ivanovskii, "Ob antropologicheskom sostave naseleniia Rossii," *Izvestiia* IOLEAE: *Trudy antropologicheskogo otdela* 22 (1904): 1–287. For more on Ivanovskii, see Mogilner, *Homo Imperii*, 101–120.

34. Ivanovskii, "Ob antropologicheskom sostave naseleniia Rossii," 142–143. This means that, according to Ivanovskii's classification, the Jewish population of Warsaw province, for example, demonstrated the highest correlation with the average indicators built on the basis of all the available measurements of Jews in different regions, provided by different scholars. They were in a "second degree of kinship" with Jews in Mogilev

(in Belarus) and in the biggest center of Jewish migration, Odessa. The Jews of Baltic provinces (now Latvia and Lithuania) demonstrated just "a third degree of kinship" with Warsaw Jews.

35. Ibid., 152.

36. A. A. Ivanovskii, "Evrei (Ripley über die Anthropologie der Juden. 'Globus,' Bd. 76, No. 2)," *Russkii antropologicheskii zhurnal* 2, no. 2 (1900): 87.

37. Rudolf Virchow, "Gesammtbericht über die von der deutschen anthropologischen Gesellschaft veranlassten Erhebungen über die Farbe der Haut, der Haare und der Augen der Schulkinder in Deutchland," *Archiv für Anthropologie* 16 (1886): 275–475. For an analysis of Virchow's survey of schoolchildren, see Andrew Zimmerman, *Anthropology and Antihumanism in Imperial Germany* (Chicago: University of Chicago Press, 2001), 136–141.

38. On Virchow's actual and perceived liberalism, universalism, and humanism, see George Mosse, *Toward the Final Solution: A History of European Racism* (Madison: University of Wisconsin Press, 1985), 90. On Virchow's political and anthropological liberalism, see Evans, "A Liberal Paradigm?," 113–138.

39. Virchow, "Gesammtbericht über die von der deutschen anthropologischen," 385.

3

"To Study Our Past, Make Sense of Our Present and Develop Our National Consciousness"

LEV SHTERNBERG'S COMPREHENSIVE PROGRAM FOR JEWISH ETHNOGRAPHY IN THE USSR

SERGEI KAN

L ike Jewish scholarship in general, Jewish ethnography in the Soviet Union had a rather short life span. It enjoyed a brief period of
relative freedom for about a decade after the Bolshevik coup, persisted for
two decades within rigid ideological boundaries, and then came almost
to a standstill after World War II in an atmosphere of state-sponsored antisemitism.[1] In the 1920s the ideology of *korenizatsiia,* with its promotion of
the use of the local minority languages in education, "cultural construction," and local administration, which dominated the new regime's policy
on nationalities during that time, created a favorable climate for the study
of local Jewish culture, at least in its secular manifestations. However, the
country did not have a tradition of Jewish ethnography and lacked specialists in it. The only serious study of Jewish ethnography undertaken
before 1917 was the famous ethnographic expedition led by S. An-sky
in 1912–1914.[2] Its leader, however, left the country during the Civil War,
while its findings remained scattered and unpublished.[3] Moreover, with
the Jews of the Soviet Union not having their own ethnic-based administrative units larger than small settlements, it was more difficult to secure
government funding for an ethnographic expedition to study the Jews
than to study larger ethnic groups and peoples.[4]

Nonetheless, there did exist one prominent ethnographer of the old school who developed an outline of a comprehensive program for the study of Jewish ethnography in the USSR. He was Lev Iakovlevich (Khayim Leyb) Shternberg (1861–1927), one of the leading figures in late imperial Russian ethnology, and despite his political disagreements with the Bolsheviks, he chose to remain in Soviet Russia after their coup and soon became the dean of the Ethnology Faculty of the Geography Institute in Petrograd (Leningrad), which in the mid-1920s was transferred to Leningrad University.[5] Shternberg's plans for the study of the culture of Soviet Jews are not well known, mainly due to the fact that he did not publish much on the subject except for a very brief 1922 article in *Evreiskii vestnik* (Jewish herald) on the revival of the Jewish Historical-Ethnographic Society and a somewhat longer piece based on a talk he gave to the same society in the mid-1920s, published posthumously in its journal *Evreiskaia starina* (Jewish antiquity).[6] Fortunately, thanks to recently discovered notes taken by his student(s?) on his "Instruction for the Study of the Ethnography, Economy, and Social Relations of the Jewish Population," delivered as part of a lecture course on Jewish ethnography he offered in 1923–1924 at the Leningrad Institute of Jewish Literature and History (LIEIL), we now have a much better idea of what his plans entailed. The goal of this chapter is to explore Shternberg's post-1917 vision for Jewish ethnography and explain the reasons his views on the subject changed significantly compared to the prerevolutionary era.

SHTERNBERG AND JEWISH ETHNOGRAPHY
IN LATE TSARIST RUSSIA

Most scholars familiar with the history of Russian anthropology identify Lev Shternberg as a prominent ethnographer of the indigenous peoples of the Russian Far East, such as the Nivkhi of Sakhalin Island and the adjacent mainland, the Ainu, and several others. However, as my research has demonstrated, he also played a major role in the development of Jewish ethnography in late imperial Russia.[7] Although Shternberg himself never conducted ethnographic research among the empire's Jewish residents, he was keenly interested in the culture of the shtetl as well as in using the

FIGURE 3.1

Lev Shternberg. From the personal collection of the author.

Hebrew Bible and other Jewish religious texts as sources of ethnographic data. In fact, being well versed in Judaism, he frequently incorporated these texts into his lectures and scholarly publications.[8]

At the same time, as a Jewish *intelligent* and liberal activist of the late imperial period who had also been a *Narodovolets* (a member of the "People's Will" party) in the 1880s and a Socialist-Revolutionary (SR) throughout the first two decades of the twentieth century, Shternberg viewed Judaism primarily as a highly advanced spiritual and moral teaching rather than as a system of rituals. The latter for him was worth preserving only as a reminder of the heroic and inspirational history of the Jews as well as a way to bring the Jewish masses and the intelligentsia closer together. Thus he encouraged assimilated urban Jews to continue celebrating the holidays of Passover and Hanukkah, but as an opportunity to celebrate and teach the heroic history of the Jewish people rather than as religious ritual. He also felt a strong nostalgic attachment to these and other domestic Jewish rituals, which reminded him of the world of his childhood and linked him to the world of his parents. As for the various "old-fashioned" beliefs and practices of the shtetl Jews, these in his opinion were worth studying only as the "survivals" of earlier stages of the evolution of Jewish and world religion. Thus, as I have argued, Shternberg's views of Judaism were a peculiar mix of classical evolutionism of an Edward Burnett Tylor and Herbert Spencer variety and a kind of romantic Jewish populism and nationalism similar to those of S. An-sky.[9]

Given Shternberg's interests as well as his prominent stature as the senior curator of the Museum of Anthropology and Ethnography (Kunstkamera), St. Petersburg's oldest and one of its only two ethnographic museums, it is not surprising that he came to play an active role in the Jewish Historical-Ethnographic Society (JHES), which was established by members of the St. Petersburg Jewish intelligentsia in 1908.[10] While another ethnologist by the name of Mikhail Kulisher served as one of the society's two vice presidents, Shternberg was its only officer who had actually done any ethnographic field research. Through the JHES's prerevolutionary years, Shternberg fought to maintain a balance between its historical and ethnological foci, even though, given the predominance of historians (many of them amateur) among its members and the fact that the leading historian of Russian Jewry, Simon Dubnow, served as its journal's editor, the society's focus was clearly on history rather than ethnography.

The one opportunity the Kunstkamera curator had to articulate his vision of a comprehensive ethnography of the empire's Jewish population was during major discussions that took place in 1912 among the JHES members about the direction and the focus of the An-sky expedition. Unlike An-sky himself, who emphasized the collection of folklore as the expedition's main thrust, Shternberg called for a comprehensive and multifaceted scholarly endeavor that would gather ethnographic data on both material and spiritual culture, and even undertake measurements of human subjects typically done by physical anthropologists. Shternberg's views prevailed to a degree: the expedition did cast a broader net than its leader had originally planned.[11] In recognition of Shternberg's contribution to the debate, he was appointed editor of the expedition's detailed ethnographic program, which An-sky prepared with the help of his several young assistants.[12]

Despite their significant differences, An-sky, Shternberg, and the rest of the JHES members agreed on one important matter: the study of Jewish ethnography had to focus exclusively on those aspects of Jewish life that were distinctively "Jewish" and could be identified with the past. Prerevolutionary Jewish ethnographers were interested primarily in the Jewish heritage, or those aspects of contemporary Jewish life that they saw as remnants of the past. After all, the official journal of the JHES was called *Evreiskaia starina* (Jewish antiquity).

JEWISH ETHNOGRAPHY AFTER THE "CATASTROPHE"

Like other cultural institutions maintained by Petrograd's Jewish intelligentsia, the JHES suffered a great deal from the emigration of many of its members and leaders as well as the devastation caused by the Russian Civil War. Thus for several years *Evreiskaia starina* stopped being published, and in 1922 the society lost its longtime chairman, Simon Dubnow, who left Russia forever. Not surprisingly, however, a year later, when it revived its activities and resumed publishing its journal, the JHES chose Shternberg as Dubnow's replacement. After all, Shternberg was one of the JHES's leaders from prerevolutionary days, as an old *Narodovolets* he enjoyed a good deal of respect from the authorities, and he was also the highly respected dean of Petrograd's ethnologists.

Since Shternberg never abandoned his evolutionist anthropological views, he remained committed to the study of traditional Jewish culture (both as written in sacred texts and as expressed in its less formal manifestations in the shtetl) as a rich source of data for the reconstruction of the evolution of the social and spiritual culture of humanity as a whole. A perfect example of this type of research is his own brief article "The Role of the Preservation of the Name in the Jewish Levirate," published in *Evreiskaia starina*.[13] In it, Shternberg speculated that the belief of the ancient Israelites that the person's soul (identified with his blood) continued to exist after his death served as the foundation of the subsequent notion of the eternal existence of the Jewish people. In fact, as he argued in his lectures and publications of the early 1920s, the upheavals (which he referred to as the "catastrophe") in the life of traditional Jewish communities caused by the World War, the revolution, and the Civil War, and the radical transformations brought about by their subsequent Sovietization, made this kind of study more urgent than ever before.[14] Having become particularly interested in the evolution of religion in the last decade of his life, Shternberg was concerned about the disappearance of "traditional folk beliefs and superstitions" caused by the rapid secularization and urbanization of Soviet Jewish life.[15]

At the same time, he strongly criticized the notion that ethnographic research among the Jews of the USSR had to be limited to the study of traditional beliefs and practices.[16] On the contrary, he argued, precisely because "such colossal" changes had been taking place in Jewish economic, social, and spiritual life since 1917, "the present moment in the life of the Jewish people is a uniquely interesting one for an ethnographer."[17] Thus the old evolutionist was clearly moving away from some of his own deeply held scholarly views. For the first time Shternberg drew a parallel between the work of an ethnographer and that of a sociologist (or a social anthropologist in the British structural-functionalist understanding of the term): "Ethnography is no longer understood as only a study of the curious phenomena from the life of primitive peoples. Most importantly ethnography is a sociological discipline, which studies both the static and the dynamic aspects of a people's life. It studies both the manifestations of the traditional culture and the processes of the creation of a new one such as present-day social and economic relations."[18] And in his 1923–1924 lectures to the students of the Institute of Jewish History and Literature he defined the new ethnography of the Jews of Russia, stating, "The goal of ethnographic expeditions is a study of daily life as well as the socio-cultural [kul'turno-sotsial'nykh] conditions of the life of the Jewish popu-lation, both as far as their experience of the disappearing old order and the growing new one are concerned. More specifically the changes in the social life of the Jews that have occurred since 1914, 1917, 1923, and 1924 must be recorded."[19]

Several factors made this die-hard evolutionist modify his views so dramatically. To begin with, as I have argued in my study of his work, Shternberg was never dogmatic but was open to new developments in his discipline. Thus by the 1920s he was well aware of the new developments in Western ethnography (such as the research of British anthropologist Bronislaw Malinowski in New Guinea), which emphasized field research focused on the present-day life of the "natives" rather than a study of the "survivals" of some ancient "primitive customs."[20] Second, despite being a unilinear evolutionist, Shternberg had always been open to the possi-bility of temporary devolution and regress rather than progress. Having been deeply shocked by the economic and social devastation experienced by Russia (and much of the rest of Europe) in the decade after 1914, he could not ignore the fact that in some areas of life a serious decline had occurred. Although as a citizen and a firm believer in progress Shternberg was deeply troubled by this, as an ethnographer he was fascinated by it.[21] Third, in the 1920s he developed a very strong interest in the relationship between culture and individual psychology, and hence viewed those radi-cal changes in the lives of Soviet Jews as a golden opportunity to study the reaction of individuals to change and the psychological significance the changes had for the individuals. As he put it, "A whole set of psycho-logical shifts have also been taking place, which say something about not only human psychology in general but the unique national [Jewish] psychology."[22]

Finally, Shternberg never abandoned his commitment to using Jewish ethnography and history as a cornerstone of his own people's national identity or self-consciousness. On this issue he sided with An-sky, both of them being *narodniks* (populists) of the old school. In fact, Shternberg argued that the "catastrophe" experienced by the Jews of Russia between 1914 and the early 1920s, as well as the radical changes to their way of life under the Soviet regime, made consciousness-raising a major priority. As he put it passionately to his fellow members of the JHES,

> In spite of it all, the Jewish population [of Russia] does not wish to and cannot die. But in order to live, one needs to know what to live for, what the purpose of life is. An individual can live without a purpose, day to day, but only as a miserable animal-like creature. But a people cannot live without an ideal, without a national goal. A people must have clear self-consciousness resulting from an understanding of its own past, which gives it the only right key to its present life. It is toward this understanding of the past, of everything we have lived through as a people, that all active members of Russian Jewry should apply their energy.[23]

At a time when all of the other peoples of the USSR were engaged in nation building, the Jewish population, he argued, also had to develop its own powerful "national idea and national ideal."[24] Like the other ethnicities of the country, the Jews were being "called upon to create their own life, and were eager, first and foremost, to know themselves, learn about their own past, to make sense of their present, identify their own intellectual and psychological strengths, and [thus] formulate their own national consciousness."[25]

Unfortunately, as he pointed out, Jewish ethnography in the Soviet Union was seriously lagging behind that of many of the other peoples of the country. As Deborah Yalen has noted, "Shternberg attributed this state of affairs not only to the economic and social dislocation of the Jews, but also to their lack of 'primitiveness.'"[26] What he meant by this was that among many of the other Soviet peoples, the layers of "primitiveness" or traditional culture were so "thick" that a beginning ethnographer could easily identify and begin collecting information on them. In his words, "The Jews are a cultured population, almost completely urban, and even that which could be called 'primitive' about them is a bookish provenance, or else borrowed from the surrounding peoples."[27] The idea that "primitive" (*primitivnye*) Jewish customs were not at the core of the culture but instead were borrowings from their neighbors was an idea that Shternberg had first articulated in his "Conversations with the Reader" published in

Novyi voskhod (New sunrise) in the 1910s and further elaborated in his 1924 article "Issues in Jewish National Psychology." As I have argued before, it was clearly influenced by his general philosemitism as well as his view of Judaism as a superior religion, one which he argued emphasized belief and moral teaching rather than ritual.[28] However, he asserted, it would be a serious mistake to assume that because of this special characteristic of Jewish culture no ethnographic work among Soviet Jews was necessary. As he put it, "There is not one single people, regardless of what level it occupies, which does not have its own distinct ethnography, if only we understand ethnography in the current meaning of the word."[29]

Of course, as an old narodnik, Shternberg believed that this national idea had to be constructed and cultivated by the progressive Jewish intelligentsia, whose job it was to collect and preserve the Jewish cultural heritage and disseminate it among the Jewish masses. Hence a Jewish ethnographer had to wear two hats: that of a social scientist and that of a *Kulturträger* (culture-bearer).[30] In other words, in one respect Shternberg's vision of Jewish ethnography did not change in the post-1917 era: he continued to view it as *both* a social science *and* an important instrument of national consciousness building among his own people.

ASPECTS OF MODERN-DAY JEWISH CULTURE WORTH STUDYING

Having made a strong argument for the need to study Jewish culture in both its old and new manifestations, the Kunstkamera curator had to offer a set of guidelines for the future fieldworkers being trained to practice Jewish ethnography. And this he did in his lectures to the students of the Leningrad Institute of Jewish History and Literature. According to Mikhail Beizer, some of the LIEIL's students were being trained as ethnographers, and in the summer of 1924 joined a group of ethnography students from the Geography Institute (also trained by Shternberg as well as his colleague Vladimir Bogoraz) to document the culture of their hometowns during their winter and summer vacations.[31] LIEIL was the successor to the Institute of Higher Jewish Knowledge, established in 1920. Despite the establishment of Communist Party and Komsomol (Young Communist) sections within it, LIEIL employed a number of faculty of the old school whose views were far from Marxism. After all, this was the era of the New Economic Policy (NEP), when one could say rather unorthodox things from a university podium. LIEIL existed between 1923 and 1925, at which point it was closed down for good. Some of Shternberg's students from it must have transferred to the Ethnography Division of the Geography Institute, over which he presided.

The document preserved in the Russian State Archive of Sociopolitical History is a detailed and comprehensive instruction covering every aspect of Jewish life from economic activities to religious ones and from sexual life to criminality. In terms of their respective weight, the occupational pursuits and material culture of the Jews are given less attention than their social and spiritual culture, education, women's status, and other elements of social life and ideology.[32] This is understandable. As Shternberg explained in his abovementioned JHES lecture, the task of Jewish ethnography was not to focus on those aspects of Jewish material culture and economic pursuits that were the same as those of their Gentile neighbors, but rather to identify what the innovations in these areas of Jewish life meant to the Jewish people and what role they came to play in their lives.[33] Thus his Instruction encouraged the budding ethnographers to pay particular attention to new developments, such as the Jewish *kolkhozes* (collective farms) as well as the fate of the classic shtetl figure of the *luftmentsh* (an impractical person without any definite business or income), in the new Soviet-dominated Jewish society. He also instructed his students to focus on a completely new and very important social phenomenon: the unprecedented influx of Jews into the state apparatus and the use of (or refusal to use) Yiddish in that new work environment.

A lengthy section under the heading "Social Culture" was subdivided into separate sections dealing with "the forms of prerevolutionary Jewish social life and organization" and postrevolutionary ones. The former included such typical communal organizations and institutions such as the *gemilut hesed* (benevolence society) and *hekdesh* (poorhouse). Shternberg also encouraged the future ethnographers to inquire about the existence of any local branches of nationalist organizations, such as various Zionist ones, and whether tsarist authorities had persecuted them. He then proceeded to discuss the need to inquire about the fate of these communal and political organizations during and after the 1917 revolution, as well as about the establishment of new ones, including the Jewish Sections of the Communist Party and the Komsomol. He also advised the students to inquire about the relationship these young local activists had with their parents and the older generation in general. At the same time, he insisted on gathering information on the charitable activities of the ORT (Society for Trades and Agricultural Labor) and the Jewish Colonization Society, which were still operating in Soviet Russia in the early 1920s. The section on education contained questions about the decline as well as survival of the old *kheyders* and *yeshivas* as well as the religious homeschooling of boys and girls. It also directed student ethnographers to collect information on the struggle between the religious and secular forces in Jewish education by focusing on various local attempts to introduce nonreligious Jewish education before and after the establishment of the Soviet schools (e.g., Hebrew-based Zionist education).

Detailed instructions listed under the rubric "Spiritual Culture" advised the young ethnographers to collect detailed information on the religious moods and attitudes of the older and the younger generations, including biographical data on typical representatives of each one. The degree to which the holy days, the Sabbath, fasts, and so forth were still observed also had to be recorded. The functioning of the synagogue and the fate of its staff had to be documented in detail as well. Special attention had to be paid to the local *tsadikim* as well as the status of the various so-called "sects": the Hasidim, the Misnagdim, and the Karaites. The subsection entitled "Religious Customs and Traditions" instructed the future ethnographers to learn about the degree of observance among the social classes, age groups, and genders of the shtetl. It also suggested that whenever possible ritual objects should be brought back from the expedition. As far as life-cycle rituals were concerned, the Instruction referred the students to An-sky's "Mentsh" program. Mindful of the new developments in the religious life of Soviet Jews, Shternberg also asked his students to collect information on antireligious propaganda and its degree of success, such as whether cases of confiscation of synagogues had occurred. The "Folklore" section also reflected the new era in which the Jews of Russia were living: "It is desirable to collect not only the old folk tales, songs, riddles, jokes, sayings, etc., but also new verbal phenomena reflecting the revolutionary times, such as new words, jokes, stories, etc."

It also directed the researchers to collect data on any local young authors whose writing might or might not have been connected to the culture of the "working masses."[34]

Shternberg's strong interest in new developments in Jewish life after 1917 was reflected in separate detailed sections devoted to the life of children and young people. His section on Jewish youth divided them into "bourgeois," "petty bourgeois" (*meshchanskii*), and "proletarian" groups, as well as into urban, rural, and shtetl ones. Once again he instructed his audience to collect data on each of these groups, their social life, views, and opinions, and how these had been changing since the revolution. Reflecting the relatively liberal political climate of the early 1920s, Shternberg told his students to inquire about the involvement of Jewish youth in all of the existing (legal) political organizations, from the Communist-affiliated to the Bund and Poalei Zion, and from Kadimah to the Maccabees.

Well aware of the major changes introduced into Jewish family life and gender relations, Shternberg devoted entire separate sections of the Instruction to sexual life, family life, and the status of the woman. He also encouraged his students to pay serious attention to the health status of the Jewish population and the measures undertaken by the state to improve it. Mindful of the long-established Jewish institution of pauperism, he also devoted a separate section to it, encouraging future ethnographers to examine whether the status of Jewish paupers and attitudes toward them were changing and whether the local Soviet authorities were fighting pauperism. The next section of the Instruction was devoted to crime among the Jews, with a particular focus on prostitution as well as the effect of the revolution and the new regime on the disappearance of some types of crime and the development of new ones. Shternberg was also concerned with gathering data on local manifestations of antisemitism and anti-Jewish violence. Here he spoke as a Jew whose own immediate and extended family suffered from the devastating Zhytomir pogrom of 1905 as well as from the subsequent violence of the revolution and especially the Civil War. He wanted detailed information not only on local victimization of Jews and various manifestations of antisemitism, but also on any acts of Jewish self-defense and the Soviet state's attitudes toward and prosecution of antisemites and *pogromshchiks*.

The very last brief section of Shternberg's Instruction reflected his growing interest in a phenomenon I have already alluded to. It might be called "collective psychology," or, borrowing from the name of an important simultaneous development in American anthropology, "culture and personality." The kinds of psychological phenomena the old ethnographer was telling his students to pay attention to included attitudes toward important recent events and the development of Jewish humor. It also advised them to collect data on both outstanding and typical representatives of all the social categories and classes of the Jewish populations, such as merchants, clergy, and the working class. Unable or unwilling to refrain from some wishful thinking when it came to his own beloved people, Shternberg closed the Instruction with a call to collect information on the "spirit of the Jewish people's optimism."[35]

FROM INSTRUCTIONS TO FIELD ETHNOGRAPHY

A major question still in need of discussion is whether any of these detailed instructions were actually followed by the handful of young Jewish ethnographers who headed for the shtetls and larger towns of the former Pale of Settlement in the summers of the mid-to-late 1920s. Unfortunately the existing data is rather scant, so that a definitive answer to this question cannot be offered. However, a few pertinent sources that do exist suggest that several major logistical and political problems, combined with Shternberg's own preference for the study of the "old" rather than the "new," inhibited those few Jewish ethnographers who ventured to study Jewish life in the 1920s, let alone 1930s, from faithfully following his Instruction.

The major extant publication on the subject is a collection of ethnographic sketches that several students of Shternberg and Bogoraz prepared on the basis of ethnographic research they conducted during the summer of 1924 in two small shtetls, a Jewish agricultural colony, and the town of Gomel. The collection was edited by Bogoraz and published as a two-hundred-page book under the title *Evreiskoe mestechko v revoliutsii* (The Jewish shtetl in revolution).[36] The publication reveals that only some of Shternberg's guidelines were indeed followed. Thus there is plenty of information on the economic, social, and religious life of the communities in question prior to 1917 as well as on the anti-Jewish violence and dislocations of World War I and the Civil War. Detailed coverage of new developments in the local economy is also provided, especially the gradual replacement of small-scale private businesses and enterprise of the early New Economic Policy (NEP) by state enterprises or the state-supervised cooperatives of the late NEP, as well as the alleged enthusiastic embrace by a large number of Jews of the new agricultural colonies. Finally there is a fair amount of information on the younger and even the middle-aged generations' rejection of religion and the rise of such new rituals as the "red seders." The young Jews' hunger for secular education and Komsomol membership and activities, as well as their desire to move to the cities, are also documented in some detail.

However, many of the more sensitive topics discussed in Shternberg's Instruction are not mentioned at all, such as crime committed by and against Jews, prostitution, sexual life of the young, and the existence of any political and cultural organizations other than those affiliated with the new regime. No folklore, old or new, was collected, and neither was any information on the survival of specific local folk religious customs and beliefs, the kind that the An-sky expedition had focused on.

There were a number of reasons for this one-sided coverage of Jewish life. The most obvious one was also the simplest: it was just not possible for a single budding ethnographer spending a few months in a Jewish community to collect ethnographic data on every or even many of the subjects highlighted in Shternberg's Instruction. Politics also must have played a major role. After all, some of the topics Shternberg instructed his students to explore were too dangerous to touch. Thus, for example, no one in his right mind would go around a shtetl asking its residents about their involvement with nationalist organizations.[37] However, the most important cause of the collection's bias was its editor's own agenda, that is, his focus on "the passing of the old and the birth of the new" way of life in the shtetl and his lack of interest in traditional culture and its preservation, even its most "innocent" aspects. Unlike Shternberg, who always maintained a certain degree of nostalgic affection for the Jewish way of life of his childhood, and who believed that certain core values of Judaism and Jewish culture were worth preserving as the foundation of the new Jewish national ideology, Bogoraz hated the shtetl which he had been

happy to escape as a youngster, and identified with fellow Jews only when
they were victimized and discriminated against.[38] Consequently it is not
surprising that it was Bogoraz and not Shternberg who served as the editor of the four other collections of essays based on the data collected by
Leningrad ethnography students in the mid-1920s. The titles of these publications speak for themselves: *The Old and the New Life* (1924), *Revolution
in the Countryside* (two volumes, 1924 and 1925), *The Renewed Countryside*
(1925), and *Komsomol in the Countryside* (1925). The only volume of student
ethnographies that Shternberg edited presented data on weddings, with
most of it reflecting traditional customs rather than any postrevolutionary innovations.[39]

Despite a very ambitious vision of a "new ethnography of the present"
that Shternberg outlined in his Instruction, one should not conclude that
his long-held interest in what in the American context has been called
"salvage ethnography" declined after 1917. As a matter of fact, I believe
that he was particularly concerned that the traditional customs and beliefs
of Soviet Jews were in danger of rapidly disappearing before being recorded by competent ethnographers. Moreover, Shternberg never lost his
fascination with identifying the "survivals" (*perezhitki*) of some ancient
cultural elements in a modern-day tradition. Hence, despite his proclama-
tion about the need to study Jewish culture in its totality, when he came
across a student well-versed in Judaism, he encouraged him to explore
those aspects of shtetl culture that the An-sky expedition had focused on
but in a much more professional manner.

During Shternberg's short career as a Soviet ethnologist he only had
one such student. His name was Isaac Natanovich Vinnikov (1897–1972).[40]
Unlike some of the other Jewish students of Shternberg and Bogoraz who
conducted ethnographic research among Soviet Jews, Vinnikov, the son
of a *melamed* (teacher) from the small Belorussian shtetl of Khotimsk,
received a very solid traditional Jewish education beyond the *kheyder* and
was actually supposed to follow in his father's footsteps as far as his occupation was concerned.[41] In 1922, having taught Yiddish in several schools
in Khotimsk and Vitebsk and having done some literary and journalistic
work in that language, he was sent by the Commissariat of Enlightenment
to Petrograd to study ethnolinguistics at the Faculty of Social Sciences at
Leningrad University. There, he specialized in general ethnography and

linguistics as well as Semitic languages and literatures (Arabic, Syrian, Assyro-Babylonian, and ancient Hebrew), studying with prominent linguists and Orientalists as well as Shternberg. According to a letter from one of Vinnikov's former students to Valerii Gessen, cited in Gessen's article, "It was his teacher L. Ia. Shternberg, who turned Vinnikov in the direction of ethnography; Vinnikov loved him dearly, literally worshipping him. . . . It was Shternberg who decided that Vinnikov was the one to specialize in general Semitic ethnography, since he was the student best versed in Judaic literature."[42]

Inspired by his teacher, Vinnikov, while still a student, prepared a forty-page paper on eighteenth- and nineteenth-century Jewish beliefs concerning the *dybbuk* and other phenomena involving the transmigration of souls from one body to another. He also taught a course at the LIEIL on the ethnography of nineteenth-century Jews. Upon graduating from LGU, he was appointed a "junior *assistant*" (lecturer) at the Ethnography Division of the Geography Faculty, where he taught seminars on the evolution of social organization and Islam, and also researched topics in biblical and Jewish ethnography. Prompted by Shternberg, he began preparing an index of ethnographic data gleaned from the Babylonian Talmud.[43] The influence of his mentor was also present in Vinnikov's unpublished paper on the cult of the cedar tree in Talmudic literature as well as in a published article on secondary burial among the ancient Hebrews, which appeared in an Austrian anthropological journal (undoubtedly with Shternberg's help).[44]

As far as ethnographic field research was concerned, it is clear that Vinnikov followed his mentor's Instruction. In the summer of 1925 he collected ethnographic data in his hometown of Khotimsk and the neighboring Jewish community of Kalin. A presentation he made to the Society for the Dissemination of Education among the Jews of Russia (OPE) covered the following topics: "1. The shtetl and its population; 2. The economic condition of the population; 3. Occupations; 4. The youth of the shtetl; 5. Literacy and education; and 6. Local religious beliefs, customs, and institutions."[45] In 1929 he conducted ethnographic research among the Bukharan Jews and returned to Belorussia as part of an ethnographic expedition, during which he and Solomon Yudovin (one of the An-sky expedition participants) collected ethnographic data and recorded traditional Jewish songs. This particular expedition had been underwritten by the JHES and it is for the society's museum that the two ethnographers collected Jewish religious objects, including some that had come from a decommissioned synagogue.[46]

Nonetheless Vinnikov's heart seems to have been in his big Talmud project. Thus, while spending his summer vacations in Khotimsk, he was working on the Talmud project rather than interviewing local Jewish residents. As he wrote to his mentor from Khotimsk, "My wife claims that I do not know how to enjoy a vacation, hinting that I am spending too much time with my Talmud studies; she might actually be right."[47]

In conclusion I would like to consider briefly the following question: did Lev Shternberg's program for the study of Jewish ethnography, with its focus on both the old culture of the shtetl and the post-1917 developments within it, have any future in the Soviet Union? As the chapters by Elissa Bemporad and Deborah Yalen in this volume, as well as a number of previous works, clearly indicate, the answer to this question is definitely a negative one.[48] To begin with, by the late 1920s, a number of topics Shternberg had proposed as subjects of ethnographic research, such as those having to do with any political organizations other than the Communist Party, would have been dangerous to pursue. As the Soviet state began its radical antireligious campaign in the late 1920s and early 1930s and as Hebrew came to be branded the language of religion and bourgeois Zionism, any research on traditional Jewish religious education and synagogue life also had to be curtailed. As a result, in the 1930s, as Yalen's contribution to this volume demonstrates, while ethnographers like Isaiah Pul'ner were still allowed to collect artifacts representing the Jewish "religious cult," their focus had to shift increasingly toward Yiddish-language folklore and the present-day life of the Soviet "working-class Jewish masses."

There is no better illustration of Soviet Jewish ethnography's turning away from its An-skyan and Shternbergian roots than a 1931 article by Pul'ner (himself a student of Shternberg and Bogoraz), discussed by Yalen, in which he severely criticized the so-called "populist ethnographers" for treating Jewish culture as a single whole and not differentiating between its bourgeois and proletarian versions, that is, for not being Marxist. Paradoxically, as Yalen also points out, underneath all of Pul'ner's Marxist rhetoric and the repeated contrasts he drew between the harsh life of the Jews under the tsars and the flourishing of Jewish culture in the USSR, he still conducted his research and organized his exhibits with a good deal of old-fashioned prerevolutionary ethnographic methodology and thinking. Nonetheless, I cannot imagine Shternberg, a man of great integrity, changing his scholarly views to satisfy the changing ideological and political demands of the authorities.

Bemporad's chapter in this volume also shows that Shternberg's project of doing Jewish ethnography in Soviet Russia was doomed. As she demonstrates convincingly, starting in the late 1920s a good deal of research on Jewish folk culture in Ukraine and Belorussia was aimed at helping establish and nurture distinct local identities for Ukrainian and Belorussian Jews, respectively. Consequently, Shternberg's notion of one single Jewish culture of the entire Pale of Settlement could not possibly fit this new ideology.

If this ambitious program for ethnographic research was doomed in Stalinist Russia, so was its author. As one of his students in the 1920s, the prominent linguist Nikolai Poppe, who escaped from the Soviet Union during World War II, wrote in his memoirs, "Shternberg was a revolutionary of the old school, which held freedom to be the most important tenet of all, and he was suffering in spirit under the Soviets. He died in 1927. Had he lived longer he would probably have been arrested and left to die in a concentration camp."[49]

NOTES

Some of the arguments presented in this chapter first appeared in my book *Lev Shternberg: Anthropologist, Russian Socialist, Jewish Activist*. I would like to thank Jeffrey Veidlinger and Dov-Ber Kerler for inviting me to take part in the 2013 conference on Jewish ethnography, where an earlier version of this chapter was presented. I would also like to thank Deborah Yalen and Jeffrey Veidlinger for their thoughtful comments on an earlier draft.

    1. Abraham Greenbaum, *Evreiskaia nauka i nauchnye uchrezhdeniia v Sovetskom Soiuze, 1918–1953* [translated from English] (Moscow: Evreiskii Universitet v Moskve, 1994).

    2. Eugene M. Avrutin et al., eds., *Photographing the Jewish Nation: Pictures from S. Ansky's Ethnographic Expeditions* (Waltham, MA: Brandeis University Press, 2014); Nathaniel Deutsch, *The Jewish Dark Continent: Life and Death in the Russian Pale of Settlement* (Cambridge, MA: Harvard University Press, 2011); Gabriella Safran, *Wandering Soul: The Dybbuk's Creator, S. An-sky* (Cambridge, MA: Belknap Press of Harvard University Press, 2010).

3. Deutsch, *The Jewish Dark Continent*; and Safran, *Wandering Soul*.

4. The Jewish Autonomous Region (*oblast*) was not established until 1934 and its creation did not give a boost to Jewish ethnography.

5. Kan, *Lev Shternberg*, 277–282.

6. Lev Shternberg, "Problema evreiskoi etnografii," *Evreiskaia starina* 12 (1928): 11–16.

7. Kan, *Lev Shternberg*.

8. See, for example, Lev Shternberg, "Rol' sokhraneniia imion v evreiskom levirate," *Evreiskaia starina* 11 (1924): 177–179. Since the mid-1880s, when he spent three years in solitary confinement, and throughout his 1890s exile on Sakhalin, Shternberg also wrote short stories in the style of Valentin Korolenko and other Russian realists. A number of them had Jewish themes, although only one, an autobiographical story entitled "A Forgotten Cemetery," was ever published. See Lev Shternberg, "Zabytoe kladbishche," *Kolos'ia* Book 3 (1913): 1–45.

9. Sergei Kan, "An Evolutionist Ethnologist Confronts Post-Revolutionary Russia: Lev Shternberg's 'Anthropological Suggestions and Perspectives during the Revolutionary Years in Russia' [Introduction to an unpublished Russian-language essay by Lev Shternberg, edited and reproduced here]," *Ab Imperio* 1 (2009): 259–277. See also Safran, *Wandering Soul*.

10. For more on the JHES see Kan, *Lev Shternberg*, 212–218; and Jeffrey Veidlinger, *Jewish Public Culture in the Late Russian Empire* (Bloomington: Indiana University Press, 2009), 229–260.

11. Kan, *Lev Shternberg*, 217; Deutsch, *The Jewish Dark Continent*, 58–62. No physical anthropology data were collected by the An-sky expedition.

12. According to Deutsch (*The Jewish Dark Continent*, 70–71), Shternberg did not play as active a role in editing the expedition's program as he had originally been expected to, owing to Shternberg's disagreements with An-sky about the direction his expedition was supposed to follow (as well as various personal and professional troubles that occurred in 1913 and are described in my own biography of Shternberg). These conflicts, combined with the fact that the work of the expedition had been interrupted by World War I, resulted in the publication of only the first part of this program, entitled *Der Mentsh* (Man).

13. Shternberg, "Rol' sokhraneniia."

14. Shternberg, "Problema."

15. Ibid., 15.

16. Ibid., 12.

17. Ibid., 14. Among the most dramatic economic and social changes in Jewish life that he emphasized were the following:

A rearrangement of classes took place. New forms of labor developed. A whole series of sociological processes have been taking place, which are of such importance to a sociologist but which one so rarely observes . . . in the economic sphere, [such as] the reappearance of the new phenomenon of the Jewish [agricultural] colonies. . . . The youth has moved away from religion, the children have been parting ways with their parents, the institution of marriage and the patriarchal authority of life have been weakened. Instead not only civil marriages but also mixed ones have been appearing, phenomena that have been undermining the old foundation of national life more than anything else.

Ibid., 14–15.

18. Ibid., 12.

19. Lev Shternberg, "Instruktsiia dlia obsledovaniia evreiskogo naseleniia v etnogra-ficheskom i ekonomicheskom otnoshenii: Iz zapisei studentov na lektsiiakh, chitannykh v Leningradskom Institute Evreiskoi Istorii i Literatury Professorom L. Ia. Shternbergom v 1923–24 uchebnom godu," 1923–1924, Rossiiskii Gosudarstvennyi Arkhiv Sankt-Peter-burga (RGASPb), f. 272, op. 1, d. 532, l. 1, 1–2.

20. See Lev Shternberg, "Sovremennaia etnologiia," *Etnografiia* 1, no. 1–2 (1926): 15–43.

21. His fascination with this subject was articulated in an unpublished lecture given sometime during or immediately after the Civil War and entitled "Anthropological Suggestions and Perspectives during the Revolutionary Years in Russia." See Kan, "An Evolutionist."

22. Shternberg, "Problema," 15.

23. Ibid., 10.

24. Ibid.

25. Ibid., 11.

26. Deborah Yalen, "Documenting the 'New Red Kasrilevke': Shtetl Ethnography as Revolutionary Narrative," *East European Jewish Affairs* 37, no. 3 (2007): 355.

27. Shternberg, "Problema," 7.

28. Kan, "An Evolutionist," 259–277.

29. Shternberg, "Problema," 12. See also Yalen, "Documenting the 'New Red Kasri-levke,'" 355.

30. It should be pointed out that this new focus on present-day life and the recent history of the Jewish people of the former Russian Empire also manifested itself in the new directions in which the JHES was planning on expanding its work. Thus, while its new charter, voted on in 1923, included its earlier goals, it also featured some new ones, among them the establishment of a new commission for the study of the Jewish socialist and labor movements (Sankpeterbugskii Filial Arkhiva Rossiiskoi Akademii Nauk [SPF ARAN], f. 282, op. 1, d. 176, l. 362). Several publications that appeared in *Evreiskaia sta-rina*'s 1920s issues reflected these new directions.

31. Mikhail Beizer, *Evrei Leningrada* (Moscow: Mosty Kul'tury; Jerusalem: Gesharim, 1999), 300. See also Yalen, "Documenting the 'New Red Kasrilevke,'" 354.

32. Thus the subsection titled "Material Culture" simply referred the students to a generic instruction on this subject prepared by Vladimir Bogoraz for all ethnography stu-dents. See Shternberg, "Instruktsiia," 4.

33. Shternberg, "Problema," 13.

34. Shternberg, "Instruktsiia," 6.

35. Ibid., 9.

36. This publication as well as the broader issue of Soviet "shtetl ethnography" is dis-cussed in detail in Deborah Yalen's contribution to this volume.

37. One should also keep in mind that during the two years that passed between the time of the ethnographic research featured in *The Jewish Shtetl in Revolution* and the date of its publication, the regime's attitudes toward all of the non-Communist Jewish political organizations, even the leftist ones, had hardened significantly.

38. As a young man Bogoraz even converted to Orthodox Christianity, changing his name from Nathan to Vladimir. He later claimed that he had converted solely for the sake of facilitating his revolutionary activities.

39. Lev Shternberg, *Novye materialy po svad'be sredi narodov SSsr* (Leningrad: Nauka, 1926).

40. Biographical information on Vinnikov presented here comes from his file stored in the St. Petersburg Branch of the Archive of the Russian Academy of Sciences (SPF ARAN, f. 1045) and Valerii Gessen, "N. I. Vinnikov v 20-e gody XX veka: Evreiskaia tema," *Vestnik evreiskogo universitet v Moskve* 8 (1995): 186–198. Along with Erukhim Kreinovich, who conducted fieldwork among the Nivkhi just like Shternberg, Vinnikov was Shternberg's favorite student. It is no accident that he played a major role in organizing his teacher's funeral and designed his gravestone with its striking design and inscription, "All Humanity Is One!" See also Vinnikov's obituary for Shternberg, "Leo Shternberg," *Anthropos* 23 (1928): 135–140.

41. In addition to the more basic subjects taught in a *kheyder*, Vinnikov studied Talmud and rabbinic literature with a very well-educated local young man, Benzion M. Grande (1891–1974), who later became a well-known professor of Semitic studies at Moscow University. See Gessen, "N. I. Vinnikov," 187.

42. Gessen, "N. I. Vinnikov," 195.

43. Unfortunately this gigantic project was never completed.

44. See Vinnikov to Shternberg, July 20, 1926, SPF ARAN, f. 282, d. 2, l. 56, 2a.

45. Gessen, "N. I. Vinnikov," 190.

46. Gessen, "N. I. Vinnikov," 192–195.

47. Vinnikov to Shternberg, July 20, 1926, SPF ARAN, f. 1, d. 2, l. 56, 1. After the closing of the JHES and the OPE, Vinnikov was forced to abandon his research on Jewish/Talmudic ethnography. However, he became a prominent scholar of Oriental history and culture, including Semitic and Hebraic studies (within the limits established by the authorities).

48. See, for example, Alfred Greenbaum, *Jewish Scholarship and Scholarly Institutions in Soviet Russia, 1918–1953* (Jerusalem: Hebrew University, 1977); David Shneer, *Yiddish and the Creation of Soviet Jewish Culture* (Cambridge: Cambridge University Press, 2004); Anna Shternshis, *Soviet and Kosher: Jewish Popular Culture in the Soviet Union, 1923–1939* (Bloomington: Indiana University Press, 2006).

49. Nicholas Poppe, *Reminiscences,* ed. Henry G. Schwarz (Bellingham: Center for East Asian Studies, Western Washington University, 1983), 68.

"What Should We Collect?"

ETHNOGRAPHY, LOCAL STUDIES, AND THE FORMATION OF A BELORUSSIAN JEWISH IDENTITY

ELISSA BEMPORAD

I began to collect songs, stories, and jokes among the *bal-melokhes,* the artisans. . . . I passed through the neighborhood of Novokrasnaia, by the houses of ill repute, then by the cemetery, and between the Vilna and Brest train stations, where the *balegoles,* or carters, lived. I remember the streets that connected Nemiga to the High Market, with crowds of Jewish brush-makers, shoemakers, carpenters, tailors, chimney sweepers, bakers, glaziers . . . and the painters who had coated the [city's] roofs . . . in green or red; . . . this was the large *tkhum ha-bal-melokhes,* the "Pale of the Artisans." I went there to collect folklore. . . . There were so many songs, Jewish folk songs, I wrote down the text but I could never remember the melodies, so another young man came and collected the *nigunim,* the melodies. . . . You could hear them everywhere, the songs. . . . It wasn't hard to find them, as the *bal-melokhes* sang constantly. . . . It was harder to find the stories. . . . [I would approach] the *balegoles,* [but not on shabes,] for them shabes was shabes, but on *motsei shabes* when they would come together. . . . The best stories I found among the older shoemakers . . . and by Mume Reyze, a *zogerke* [a prayer-leader in the synagogue women's section], . . . who was a source of storytelling. . . . These places were somewhat strange for me, I discovered a world. . . . I even visited the *zogerke* on shabes, when many youngsters would gather to listen to her stories.[1]

These are not the words of a fieldworker from An-sky's ethnographic expedition collecting folklore through the "Dark Continent," as historian Simon Dubnow contemptibly labeled the Pale of Settlement. From 1912 to 1914, with a team of musicologists and photographers, the writer, revolutionary, and ethnographer S. An-sky embarked on an expedition to document the lives of the masses in the Pale. The fieldworkers traveled to more than sixty shtetls to uncover the people and their artifacts, folk tales, legends, proverbs, cemeteries, superstitions, incantations, and melodies.[2]

The aforementioned words, however, were those of a young *zamler*, a collector of folklore, who explored a city in the former "Dark Continent" following the 1917 Bolshevik rise to power. The city was Minsk, the new capital of the Belorussian Soviet Socialist Republic (BSSR), and the year was 1922. Enrolled in the Faculty of Medicine at Belorussian State University, the institution of higher education founded by the Soviets in the republic's capital in 1921, Leybush Rozenbaum, together with several other young Jewish students, was hired by members of the Jewish studies faculty at the city's university to collect the lore of the people through the streets of Minsk.

If the goal of An-sky's ethnographic project lay in the forging of a secular national Jewish identity that would guarantee the renaissance of Russian Jewish culture through the establishment of museums and the rebirth of theater, art, and literature, the ethnographic impulse in the Soviet context was informed by the Soviet nationality policy and the attempt to emphasize the rootedness of Jewish identity and culture in the region of the new Bolshevik creation, Soviet Belorussia. The study of the folklore, but also of the history, the culture, and the language, of "Belorussian Jews" would foster the emergence of a new Soviet Jewish identity grounded in the region of the Belorussian SSR. Therefore, if for An-sky the folk traditions of the Pale would help forge authentic Jewish cultural creations and strengthen Jewish national identity, the collection of folklore in the context of the Bolshevik experiment would support the legitimacy of a Soviet Jewish culture and identity, entrenched in and connected to the new Soviet geopolitical entity of the Belorussian Republic.

In the words of a Minsk Jewish activist who in 1924 emphasized the need to "territorialize" Jewish culture and identity, connecting it to the republic,

> The Jew in Belorussia feels himself a citizen ... of the USSR in general
> and not of Belorussia where he actually lives.... Our first task is to make
> ... [him] a citizen of Belorussia, so that he should feel that Belorussia is
> his own.... From this it follows that our culture should become "territo-
> rialized."... [It must] gain a local coloration, mesh with Belorussian cul-
> ture.... Belorussian culture is ... becoming a national-territorial culture,
> that is, not a culture of Belorussians as a people isolated in themselves but
> a culture of Belorussians as citizens living in the given territory.[3]

The author was probably also alluding to the embryonic and sui generis
status of a modern national Belorussian identity. Compared to the national consciousness of other national groups in Russia and Eastern Europe in the nineteenth century, a modern national Belorussian awareness
emerged rather late and therefore retained an element of ambiguity and
tenuousness, at least in its earlier stages. Unlike Ukrainian nationalism,
which was relatively well established and rooted before the birth of the
USSR, Belorussian nationalism was, in many ways, the outcome of the
Soviet experiment on the territories that in 1920 came to be known as
the BSSR.[4] Moreover, from the vantage point of Jewish cultural and historical traditions and perceptions, Belorussia did not represent a distinct
and well-defined entity, but rather belonged to the greater *Lita* (Hebrew;
Yiddish, *Lite*), which included the territories of present-day northeastern
Poland, northern and western Belarus, southern Latvia, and northeastern
Prussia.[5] Therefore, much more than its Ukrainian counterpart, Belorussian regional identity had to be constructed by scholars, instilled in the
intelligentsia, and then disseminated en masse.

This "territorialization" effort profoundly influenced the realm of Soviet Jewish culture, literature, theater, and scholarship, thus producing an
innovative focus on Belorussia. The emphasis on the Belorussian region
emerged in the themes explored by new Jewish literary groups founded
after the revolution. The Minsk Yiddish literary group Yunger Arbeter
(the Young Workers), established in December 1924, encouraged "the
emergence of Belorussian motifs in the work of the group." This would
consolidate the writers' relationship with the motherland, Soviet Belorussia, as well as "attract all revolutionary Yiddish writers, who were born
in Belorussia, but live elsewhere, both in the USSR and abroad."[6] The

same geographic and cultural boundaries were set for Jewish actors who wished to perform in the Jewish section of the Belorussian State Theater (Belgoset). Only those born in Belorussia could be part of the Jewish section of the Drama Studio of the Belorussian State Theater, established in 1921. The language of instruction of the three-year courses for actors in the Jewish section was Yiddish, and in order to apply, actors should "have knowledge of Belorussian and Yiddish, as well as come from the territory of ethnographic Belorussia." Besides studying Yiddish literature, the actors in the Jewish section had to take courses in Belorussian studies (*Belorussovedenie*) and become acquainted with the Belorussian village and way of life (*byt*).[7] While before the revolution the Jews who lived in Minsk and its environs saw themselves as culturally part of Lithuanian Jewry, or in some cases Russian Jewry, they were now encouraged to identify only with the geopolitical reality of Belorussia and see themselves as Belorussian Jews.

The attempt to territorialize Jewish scholarship and enclose it within the borders of the newly established Belorussian SSR, and thus forge a new "Belorussian-Jewish" identity, emerged through original historical studies in the 1920s and 1930s. In 1926, historian Israel Sosis published the opening article of the first volume of the Minsk-issued scholarly journal *Tsaytshrift*, entitled "On the Social History of the Jews of Lithuania and Belorussia." Regarded as one of the first Marxist historians to create a socioeconomic narrative of the Jewish past, Sosis emphasized the importance of a local/regional focus in Jewish historiography over a universal or all-Russian one. Rejecting Heinrich Graetz's *Leidensgeschichte,* Simon Dubnow's romantic nationalism, and Yulii Gessen's juridical approach, he criticized the tendency to study the past of the Jews of Russia as a uniform and homogeneous entity. "The need to research the history of the Jews of the Lithuanian-Belorussian area separately is not determined," argued Sosis, "by our national politics, but rather by the objective reality: the Jews of this region have always distinguished themselves through their specific dialect, culture, and socioeconomic traits."[8]

In a later essay, which appeared in 1929, Sosis added that "the history of the Jews in Lithuania, Belorussia, and Ukraine is usually not even mentioned by the Jewish historian: until the partitions of Poland these territories are imagined as an organic part of the Polish Kingdom; after Poland's collapse they are . . . imagined as Russia."[9] According to Sosis, then, not only had Russian-Jewish historiography removed from its narrative all socioeconomic dimensions of the Jewish past, but it had also overrated the "abstract notion of a universal Jewish history," invalidating the tangible historical conditions of time and place typical of regional history.[10] The progressive shift from a general all-Russian—or all-Soviet—focus to a local one transpired through the contents of *Tsaytshrift's* 1928 volume, which included seven different articles with a regional emphasis, ranging from a study of the Jewish guilds in Lithuania and Belorussia during the seventeenth and eighteenth centuries to a demographic study of the Jewish population in the cities and shtetls of Belorussia. This regional focus, and its ensuing emphasis on a specifically Belorussian nature of Jewish culture and identity, strove to create a long-standing notion of Belorussian Jewishness that predated the new reality of Soviet geopolitics.

The "territorialization" of Jewish literary works in Belorussia influenced, for example, Moyshe Kulbak, one of the most celebrated Yiddish writers in the USSR, who wrote two major works in Minsk. Both were profoundly rooted in the city's contemporary Jewish history and folklore. The novel *Zelmenyaner*, published in two volumes in 1931 and 1935, respectively, took place in the Belorussian capital and told the story of the Sovietization of a Jewish family of artisans, the Zelmenyaners, and the revolution in the ethnic space of the courtyard in which they lived.[11] Similarly, Kulbak's play *Boytre*, published and performed onstage in 1936, was based on the story of a Jewish Robin Hood who lived in Minsk in the nineteenth century—a Belorussian "Jewish Pugachev," wrote literary critic Max Erik, who stole from the rich to give to the poor.[12] A well-known legend in Jewish Minsk, the story of Boytre produced a local Yiddish saying to identify a courageous villain: *"Er iz a Boytre"* (He is a Boytre).[13] The interplay between Belorussianization and the creation of a new Soviet Yiddish culture possibly led Kulbak to focus on Minsk and Belorussian-Jewish motifs, both largely missing from his pre-Soviet literary career.[14] The tendency to territorialize the literary output (which by the second half of the 1930s might have been seen also as a way to justify the existence of the literature of a national minority) is echoed in the words of Yasha Bronshteyn and Izi Kharik, editors of the 1935 collection of poems and short stories *Sovetishe Vaysrusland* (Soviet Belorussia): "We should not forget that in

each Republic Soviet Yiddish literature conveys its specificities, its local republican uniqueness. . . . Yiddish literature in Belorussia brings to
the All-Union Soviet Yiddish literature the scent of the Belorussian landscape, the sound of the Belorussian folk song, the distinctiveness of the
socialist construction in Belorussia. . . . The goal [of the collection] is to
show how Soviet Belorussia is artistically embodied in our literature."[15]

The young Jewish student Leyzer Rozenbaum was only one of the
many zamlers who during the 1920s and 1930s engaged in ethnographic
explorations through the cities and shtetls of Belorussia, thereby promoting regional identity formation among the Jews of the BSSR. The students
of the Evpedtekhnikum, the pedagogical institution that trained a new
cadre of "Red Teachers" who served as instructors in Jewish preschool,
elementary, and adult educational institutions in Minsk and the surrounding shtetls, periodically returned to their city or shtetl of origin
as zamlers. They collected proverbs, riddles, and folk songs; they inves-
tigated local expressions typical of different social settings (both Soviet
and non-Soviet alike), such as the factory, the marketplace, and the *shul;*
and they organized expeditions through other cities and shtetls of Belorussia; the students would thereby "bond with the people, improve their
Yiddish—the sounds, the rhythm of the language—and [most impor-
tantly] maintain a focus on the region, on the land" (*krai* in Russian and
Belorussian; *kant* in Yiddish).[16]

The impulse to collect with a regional focus found expression in the
field of history in the different scholarly and educational institutions established by the Soviets in the Belorussian capital. Founded in Minsk in
1921, the Jewish Historical Commission of Belorussia sponsored public
lectures to spread knowledge about the history of the Jews of Belorussia.
It also issued a call to collect historical material about Belorussian Jews,
which was markedly reminiscent of Dubnow's 1891 plea, addressed to the
residents of the Pale of Settlement, to collect Jewish sources and study
the past of Russian Jews.[17] Entitled *Vos darf men zamlen* (What must be
collected), the commission's call appealed to local zamlers to gather a
variety of historical sources, including religious books, *pinkasim* (Jewish
communal records), and records on the Jewish workers' movement in

Belorussia, including, for example, information about the family, social background, and political activity of Hesia Helfman, the Jewish woman involved in the assassination of Alexander II, who was born and grew up in Mozyr (Mazyr), Minsk province.[18] While in his 1891 call, issued in Hebrew and Russian only, Dubnow had viewed the collection of historical material as the groundwork for the birth of a Russian-Jewish national and historical consciousness, in its Yiddish-language call the Minsk Commission saw the importance of collecting historical documents on the Jews of Belorussia, as well as building archives to preserve them, as the first stage in the creation of a new Jewish regional identity closely intertwined with Soviet Belorussia.

The wealth of artifacts, books, and documents collected during the ethnographic expeditions in different areas of the Belorussian SSR were put on display in the Jewish Department of the Belorussian State Museum, opened in Minsk, in 1925. The museum displayed antiques, manuscripts, some of the first Jewish books printed in Belorussia, a model of a typical Jewish home from the 1880s, Jewish religious and household objects, and photographs of Jewish tombstones. Its permanent exhibitions included one on Jewish arts and crafts produced in Dubrovno (Dubrouna), Minsk province, in particular *talitot* (prayer shawls) and parchment for *seforim* (holy books); and one on the work and life of Yiddish writer Mendele Moykher-Sforim (Sholem Yankev Abramovitsh)—who after all was born in the Belorussian shtetl of Kapulye (Kapyl), Minsk province. The special exhibits installed by the museum staff in 1928 included one titled "Ancient Jewish Silver—The Work of Jewish Artisans from the Seventeenth Century" and one titled "The History of the Jews of Minsk."[19]

Throughout the 1920s, the main commissions of the Jewish Department of the Institute for Belorussian Culture, founded in 1921 as the leading research institution in the BSSR, relied on the help of approximately 1,650 correspondents and zamlers from across Belorussia (including the former rabbi of Bykhov [Bykhaw], I. Manes, who upon renouncing his rabbinical title in 1925 decided to devote himself to the scholarly cause of the Jewish Department).[20] The department collected, translated, and published a vast array of documents, including rabbinical responsa, *musar-seforim*, Hasidic stories, folk songs, jokes, proverbs, and the jargon of tailors, *katsovim* (butchers), and *klezmorim* (klezmer musicians), as well as information about the regional variations of the Yiddish dialects spoken in Belorussia. This was amassed in response to the appeal *Forsht yidishe dialektn!* (Study Yiddish dialects!), which was sent to zamlers, students, activists, and teachers throughout the shtetls and cities of Belorussia. Underlining the Belorussian nature of the ethnographic project and rooting it in the Soviet Belorussian geopolitical entity, one of the activists in the Jewish Department noted about the nature of the Institute for Belorussian Culture that it was "an institute of and for Belorussia [*fun un far Vaysrusland*]," and not an all-Soviet Jewish academic institution.[21]

An important area of focus for the scholars and activists in the Jewish Department was the field of "regional or local studies" (*kraevedenie* in Russian; *kraiaznaustva* in Belorussian; *kantkentenish* in Yiddish).[22] Through a microscale approach, the Jewish version of "regional studies" focused on the socioeconomics, culture, ethnography, and everyday life of Jews living in one city or shtetl of contemporary Soviet Belorussia. Also referred to as a *kraeved* (student of *kraevedenie*) or *kraiaznavets* (student of *kraiaznaustva*), the zamler would collect, for example, the lore produced by the inhabitants of one shtetl in the post-1917 era, which might include revolutionary folk songs performed there at the time of the revolution. In 1928, the Jewish Department of the Institute for Belorussian Culture issued another appeal, entitled *Forsht ayer shtetl!* (Research your shtetl!). It called upon potential zamlers/kraevedy to study their shtetl: "We hope that our local leaders—teachers, agronomists, . . . students . . . —will support the task of researching the shtetl, thus helping the State, as well as our social and scholarly institutions."[23] Researching and collecting information on the culture and life of the Belorussian shtetl assisted the state not only in carrying out its social engineering project but also in adjusting the socioeconomic structure of the Jewish population to the needs of collectivization and industrialization, thus building a new Soviet society. The research of the life and culture of one place or region also served the purpose of connecting Jewish identity to Soviet Belorussia. It is therefore not surprising that in 1924 the Jewish studies program at Belorussian State University announced that the subject "Local Jewish Studies" (*Evrevedenie* in Russian and Belorussian; *Yidkentenish* in Yiddish), which covered the history, the culture, the language, and the ethnography of the Jews of the Belorussian SSR, would be mandatory for all students enrolled in the Jewish studies program. Along the same lines of *Research Your Shtetl!*, in 1929 the Jewish Department of the Institute for Belorussian Culture subsidized the publication of a textbook for the Jewish schools of Belorussia, entitled *Undzer kant* (Our region). Defined as "the first attempt to put together a *gegnt-bukh* [book about the region] for Jewish schools," the goal of the two-volume work was to promote knowledge of the history, geography, economy, and climate of the Belorussian SSR among generations of young Jews. Through the study of this textbook Jewish children were being exposed to a new regional identity, the core principle of which lay in the axiom "The city or shtetl in which we live belongs to the land called the Belorussian Soviet Socialist Republic."[24] The new emphasis on the Belorussian region in the classroom thus resulted in the attempt to recast (and confine) Jewish identity within Belorussian borders, thereby creating the new Jewish citizen of the BSSR.

Soviet nationality policy compelled Jewish ethnographers to define and celebrate a specifically Belorussian Jewishness. As they tried to come to terms with the complexities of political negotiations, at times reminiscent of colonial attempts to generate new identities and cultures that would fit the new borders, they engaged in changing, recreating, and recasting. In this Soviet context, therefore, the collection of folklore was aimed not necessarily at salvaging Jewish customs, beliefs, and culture on the verge of extinction, but rather at building up the foundation of Soviet Jewish life and identity, and "normalizing" it by virtue of connecting it to the territory, as well as by highlighting the revolutionary spirit of its workers and artisans and their "innate tendencies" to celebrate Lenin and the revolution through folk songs. This endeavor was not unique to the Jews, but seems very similar to the one carried out by the second-largest extraterritorial national minority in Soviet Belorussia, namely, the Poles. The head of the Polish Section of the Belorussian Academy of Sciences—the academic institution that in 1929 replaced the Institute for Belorussian Culture—stated that the goal of Polish scholars and ethnographers was to research Polish themes in Belorussian culture, and specifically collect Polish folk songs, legends, and proverbs, study the Belorussian influence on the Polish language, and record the history of the revolutionary movement among the Polish population of Belorussia.[25]

Compared to the ethnographic impulse experienced by Russian Jews at the end of the nineteenth and beginning of the twentieth century, the urge to collect information about the history and lore of the people in the context of the Bolshevik experiment increased. This was not determined only by the unprecedented availability of state funds, the support of scholarly and educational institutions, and the number of newspapers in Yiddish with rubrics on folklore that provided detailed guidelines to the enthusiastic zamler. The momentum was also due to a sense of urgency that grew into anxiety in the 1930s: the local emphasis on the Belorussian region and the "territorialization" of the ethnographic impulse grew out of the Soviet nationality policy, as the Jews had to provide a territorial justification for their existence as a national group. But by the second part of the 1930s especially, in order to remain a full-fledged Soviet national group immune to dangerous suspicions of "bourgeois nationalism," the Jewish *folk* had to produce acceptable forms of lore, namely, Soviet folklore embedded in the great Stalinist era of Stakhanovite heroes, epic struggles against fascism, and the fame of the Red Army. If An-sky's collecting endeavor had been all-encompassing and had imposed no qualitative restrictions on the work of the zamlers who partook in the expeditions, the Soviet Jewish enterprise of the 1930s was much more restrictive, its contents being curtailed by the political culture and socioeconomic reality of contemporary Soviet society.

The calls to collect and produce folklore continued in the second half of the 1930s. In late 1936, a brigade in Minsk was active in writing down and inscribing on gramophone records folk songs performed by the Jewish State Vocal Ensemble (established in 1931 and acclaimed as a center for the best Yiddish musical culture in the USSR); these included *chastushki* (two-line poems or ditties) performed by the workers of the Soviet collective farm of Parichi, Minsk province.[26] That same year, ethnographers M. Grinblat and L. Dushman, employed by the Folklore Commission of the Jewish Division of the Belorussian Academy of Sciences, renewed the call to potential zamlers through the central Jewish organ in Minsk, *Oktyabr*. In the section entitled "*Folklor-vinkl*" (The folklore corner), they asked readers to "send [them] folk songs, stories, legends, *chastushki* about the struggle against tsarism or about the happiness of contemporary life," hinting here at Stalin's slogan of the time, "Life Has Become Better, Life

Has Become More Joyous!"[27] When in mid-1937 the Folklore Commission launched a contest for the best folklore zamler, 183 participants responded to the call from throughout Belorussia—including from Mozyr (Mazyr), Klimovich, and Homel—collecting the folklore produced in the Soviet factories and capturing the greatness of Stalin's era.[28]

According to the official party narrative, the Stalinist epoch infused new life into the Jews, "emancipating" them from their past and transforming them into modern Soviet citizens. The works included in the 1938 collection of folk songs entitled *Yidishe folks-lider vegn der Royter Armey* (Yiddish folk songs about the Red Army), put together by the Folklore Commission of the Belorussian Academy of Sciences to mark the twentieth anniversary of the establishment of the Red Army, and which never appeared in print, echoed this transformation and celebrated the new ideal Soviet Jew as mighty, heroic, and patriotic. In one of the folk songs, transcribed in Bobruisk (Babruysk) by a twenty-six-year-old Red Army soldier, both the soldier's fiancée and his mother encourage, rejoice in, and take pride in the new Soviet Jewish heroes of the day:

S'hot mayn khaverte in feld	My girlfriend in the field
af der rakhves breyter	In the broad expanses
mir gezogt: zolst zayn a held	Said to me: be a hero
in armey der royter.	In the Red Army.
Mayn zun iz a held	My son is a hero
Er rayt af a gutn ferd	He rides a good horse
Az es vet zayn neytik	If need be
vet er farhitn undzer frayer erd.[29]	He will protect our free land.

This song is an example of authentic Soviet Jewish folklore, produced "from below," about the Soviet Jewish hero who defends the motherland and hastens the bright future of Communism. It indicates that the dissemination of official ideology gave birth to popular culture in the hinterland that replicated its ideas and themes. The image of the heroic Jewish Red Army soldier as an object of admiration was embedded in many such songs recorded throughout the Belorussian SSR.

From the 1920s through the second part of the 1930s, the content of Soviet Jewish patriotism was grounded in a temporal focus of "better now than then." The temporal comparison emphasized, on the one hand, the miseries of Jewish life before the Bolshevik Revolution (highlighting tsarist antisemitism, pogroms, the existence of the Pale of Settlement, and the quotas for Jewish university students), and, on the other hand, the infinite joys of Jewish life after 1917, characterized by the absence of anti-Jewish legislation. This kind of pro-Soviet patriotism grounded in a temporal focus was also expressed in Soviet Jewish folklore, in a sort of guided response to the party line from below. A folk song transcribed in 1937, and also included in the collection *Yiddish Folk Songs about the Red Army,* celebrated the new Soviet Jewish people liberated from the tsarist yoke.

Biter iz geven in shtot,	Life in our city was bitter,
Fun derfer hot men getribn	Jews were expelled from the villages
Umetum in yedn ort	Everywhere and everywhere
Flegt men zayn batribn.	Jews were despondent.
Az Nikolaike flegt pogromen	When Little Nicholas used to
Af zey blutike makhn,	make bloody pogroms against them,
Flegt shteyn zhandarmen bay	the gendarmes used to stand at the
der zayt	side
Kveln nor un lakhn.	enjoy and laugh.
Iz uf a shtern af der velt,	And then a star arose in the world,
Un farshvundn iz di nakht	and the night was gone
Farshvundn iz di nakht	and the night was over
Di fintsternish un kelt.	the darkness and the cold.
Rusn un yidn zaynen itsts	Russians and Jews are now together
Komandirn in eyn folk,	the commanders of one people,
Gliklekh, ibergliklekh	happy, overjoyed
Iz itsts dos yidishe folk.	is now the Jewish people.
Vi ale felker hobn mir	Like all peoples we have
Itst di fulste rekht	full rights,
Mir zaynen itsts fray, fray,	we are now free, free,
Oys knekht! Oys knekht![30]	Slaves no more! Slaves no more!

At the end of the 1930s, the tsarist-Soviet dichotomy was complemented by a new comparison with a geographic focus on "better here than there." This focus distinguished between the social and legal discrimination against Jews in Poland and Germany and the countless successes of the Jews in Soviet territory. The awareness—or rather conviction—that life under the Soviets had overall significantly improved was testified to most sharply by the comparison with nearby "fascist" Poland and Germany. The knowledge of intensifying antisemitism in Poland and Nazi Germany, weighed against the absence of official antisemitism in the Soviet Union, informed Jewish identity in the late 1930s and produced expressions of patriotism in folklore. A Yiddish children's counting rhyme, collected in Bobruisk (Babruysk) in 1938, reads as follows:

Di fashistn viln a milkhome—	The fascists want war—
Zol zey aroys di neshome	May their souls expire
Di trotskistn tantsn nokh nokh zey—	The Trotskyites are their lackeys—
Zol zey zayn vind un vey	May they have endless woes
Bolshevikes viln sholem zol zayn,	Bolsheviks want there to be peace,
A gezunt zol in zey arayn,	May they be healthy,
Eyns, tsvey, dray,	One, two, three,
Geyt aroys fray![31]	You are free!

Whether in their effort to emphasize a connection to the territory of Soviet Belorussia or to underline the greatness of Stalin's heroic era, the selectively collected Jewish folklore in Soviet times served the same purpose as An-sky's and Dubnow's endeavors in national identity formation, namely, to demonstrate the "normality" and legitimacy of Jews as a national group. In Soviet Belorussia, Jews could become a "normal" national group by virtue of their lore, so intrinsically intertwined with the Belorussian reality; similarly, in the second half of the 1930s, Jews could become a "normal" and trustworthy national group because they celebrated—perhaps even more than other groups—the "father" of the Soviet peoples and his greatness.

NOTES

1. Leybush Rozenbaum (Arye Ram), March 23, 1969, Oral History Division of the Hebrew University Institute for Contemporary Jewry, Jerusalem, OHD (58) 11, 22–25.

2. On S. An-sky's ethnographic endeavors, see Nathaniel Deutsch, *The Jewish Dark Continent: Life and Death in the Russian Pale of Settlement* (Cambridge, MA: Harvard University Press, 2011). See also Gabriella Safran and Steven J. Zipperstein, eds., *The Worlds of S. An-sky: A Russian Jewish Intellectual at the Turn of the Century* (Stanford, CA: Stanford University Press, 2006); and Eugene M. Avrutin et al., eds., *Photographing the Jewish Nation: Pictures from S. An-sky's Ethnographic Expeditions* (Waltham, MA: Brandeis University Press, 2014).

3. Quoted in Zvi Y. Gitelman, *Jewish Nationality and Soviet Politics: The Jewish Sections of the CPSU, 1917–1930* (Princeton, NJ: Princeton University Press, 1972), 397.

4. Francine Hirsch, *Empire of Nations: Ethnographic Knowledge and the Making of the Soviet Union* (Ithaca, NY: Cornell University Press, 2005), 149–155. On the emergence of modern Belorussian nationalism in the early twentieth century, see Per Anders Rudling, *The Rise and Fall of Belarusian Nationalism, 1906–1931* (Pittsburgh: University of Pittsburgh Press, 2014).

5. See Dovid Katz, *Lithuanian Jewish Culture* (Vilnius: Baltos Lankos, 2004), 53–54; and Allan Nadler, "Litvak," in *The YIVO Encyclopedia of Jews in Eastern Europe,* ed. Gershon David Hundert (New Haven, CT: Yale University Press, 2008), 1:1077–1078.

6. "Resolution on Jewish Culture," 1923, Natsionalniy Arkhiv Respubliki Belarus (NARB), Minsk, f. 63, op. 2, d. 276, ll. 29–30.

7. "Resolution on Jewish Cultural Work," 1921, NARB, f. 42, op. 1, d. 1600, ll. 4, 47–48, 56–58.

8. Israel Sosis, "Tsu der sotsyaler geshikhte fun yidn in Lite un Vaysrusland," *Tsaytshrift* 1 (1926): 1–4; in particular, see 1.

9. I. Sosis, "Tsu der antviklung fun der yidisher historiografye," *Shriftn fun Vaysrusishn melukhe-universitet* 1 (1929): 8.

10. Ibid., 12. On the perception of Belorussia as a region with a history, an identity, and a culture that predated the establishment of the Soviet Union, see, for example, Israel Sosis, "Der yidisher seym in Lite un Vaysrusland in zayn gezetsgeberisher tetikayt (1623–1761), loyt zayne protokoln," *Tsaytshrift* 2–3 (1928): 76–79.

11. See Moshe Kulbak, *The Zelmenyaners: A Family Saga,* trans. Hillel Halkin (New Haven, CT: Yale University Press, 2013).

12. Notes by Max Erik, 1932, YIVO Institute for Jewish Research, New York, Pomeranz Collection, RG 500, box 1, ff. 16–28.

13. Sh. Eynhorn, "Mishlei-am be-idish be-Minsk," in *Minsk 'ir va-'em: Korot, ma'asim, ishim, havi,* ed. Shlomoh Even-Shoshan (Tel Aviv: Irgun Yots'e Minsk u-Venoteha be-Yisra'el), 2:639. *Boytre* was first published in the literary journal *Shtern* in 1936 (nos. 7, 9, 11). For the play's original text with the author's proofreading, see Belorusskii Gosudarstvennyi Arkhiv-Muzei Literatury i Iskusstva (BGAMLI), Minsk, f. 182, op. 1, d. 1, *Boytre.*

14. The one exception in Kulbak's work which predates his Soviet years is the epic poem on Belorussia entitled *Raysn* and published in Vilna in 1922.

15. Y. Bronshteyn and I. Kharik, eds., introduction to *Sovetishe Vaysrusland: Literarishe zamlung* (Minsk: Melukhe Farlag fun Vaysrusland, 1935).

16. "Kabinet far shprakh baym yidishn pedagogishn tekhnikum in Minsk," *Af di vegn tsu der nayer shul,* no. 2 (1924): 81–82. From 1925 to 1930, the Central Bureau for Local Studies (Kraiaznaustva) at the Institute for Belorussian Culture (Institut Belorusskoi Kultury, or Inbelkult) in Minsk issued a monthly publication devoted to local studies, by the title of *Nash krai* (Our land). The journal was renamed *Savetskaia kraina* (Soviet country) in 1930, and issued by the Belorussian Academy of Sciences until 1933.

17. Simon Dubnow, *Ob izuchenii istorii russkikh evreev i ob uchrezhdenii russko-evreiskogo istoricheskogo obshchestva* (St. Petersburg: A. E. Landau, 1891).

18. Minutes of the meetings of the Jewish Historical Commission of Belorussia, October 1923, NARB, f. 42, op. 1, d. 1614, ll. 4, 9.

19. "Muzey oyshtelungen," *Oktyabr,* January 8, 1928, 4.

20. B. Orshanski, "Di yidishe opteylung fun 'Invayskult,'" *Af di vegn tsu der nayer shul*, no. 7–8 (1927): 72.

21. Ibid., 66.

22. On regionalism, local studies, and museum culture, see, for example, Catherine Evtuhov, *Portrait of a Russian Province: Economy, Society, and Civilization in Nineteenth-Century Nizhnii Novgorod* (Pittsburgh: Pittsburgh University Press, 2011). See in particular chapter 11, in which Evtuhov explores the provincial identity that emerged through the understanding of the local environment and the construction of a local past in the Nizhnii Novgorod region. See also Donald Raleigh, *Provincial Landscapes: Local Dimensions of Soviet Power, 1917–1953* (Pittsburgh: University of Pittsburgh Press, 2001); and Susan Smith-Peter, "Bringing the Provinces into Focus: Subnational Spaces in the Recent Historiography of Russia," *Kritika: Explorations in Russian and Eurasian History* 12, no. 4 (Fall 2011): 835–848.

23. Hillel Alexandrov, *Forsht ayer shtetl!* (Minsk: Institut far Vaysruslendisher Kultur, 1928), 9.

24. H. Alexandrov and I. Roznhoyz, *Undzer kant: Bashraybungen fun der Vaysrusisher Sotsyalistisher Sovetn-Republik* (Minsk: Institut far Vaysruslendisher Kultur, 1929), 1:3–4, 25.

25. Minutes of the meetings of the Polish Section, 1929, Tsentralniy Nauchnyi Arkhiv Natsionalnoi Akademii Nauk Belarusi (TSNANANB), Minsk, f. 67, op. 1, d. 8, l. 69.

26. *Oktyabr*, September 23, 1936, 4.

27. M. Grinblat and L. Dushman, "Folklor-vinkl," *Oktyabr*, June 3, 1937, 3.

28. L. Dushman, "Di arbet fun der folklor komisye fun der visnshaftlekher akademye fun VSsR," *Oktyabr*, February 9, 1937, 3. On folklore and Stalinism, see, for example, Frank J. Miller, *Folklore for Stalin: Russian Folklore and Pseudofolklore of the Stalin Era* (Armonk, NY: M. E. Sharpe, 1991); and Anna Shternshis, *Soviet and Kosher: Jewish Popular Culture in the Soviet Union, 1923–1939* (Bloomington: Indiana University Press, 2006).

29. *Yidishe folks-lider vegn der Royter Armey*, 1938, TSNANANB, f. 72, op. 1, d. 2, 12–13.

30. *Yidishe folks-lider vegn der Royter Armey*, 17–18.

31. *Yidishe folks-lider vegn der Royter Armey*, 22.

Yiddish Folklore and Soviet Ideology during the 1930s

MIKHAIL KRUTIKOV

In the conclusion of his comprehensive history of Jewish folklore studies in Russia, Mark Kiel states, "Jewish folkloristics was born out of ideology, not nostalgia. In the Soviet Union it died because of an ideology which could not make room for it, though not before demonstrating some remarkable instances of creativity in scholarship, literature, art and music."[1] Kiel ends his story in 1931, which he correctly identifies as the beginning of the Stalinist "Sovietization" of Jewish folkloristics, a period when Soviet Jewish folklorists "were forced to speak with masks" if they "desired to say more than what was permitted."[2] The present chapter is an attempt both to examine the meaning of "masks" and to recover what Soviet Yiddish folklorists "desired to say" from behind them. Indeed, by the late 1930s most of the institutions that were dedicated to practical work among the Jewish population outside of Birobidzhan, such as education, vocational training, social welfare, and agricultural colonization, were closed down, and most of their leaders perished in the Stalinist purges. The largest and most productive of these institutions, the Kiev Institute for Yiddish Proletarian Culture, was downgraded to the Cabinet of Yiddish Literature, Folklore and Language. While the sphere of the official and public usage of Yiddish was shrinking, it retained its formal status as the language of Soviet Jewish "nationality," which entitled it to certain cultural agencies, such as periodicals, presses, and theaters, which were integrated into the larger, all-Soviet cultural institutions. Yiddish literature was published and promoted by the state, Yiddish theater enjoyed high prestige, Yiddish folk songs were arranged for symphonic orchestras, performed in prestigious venues, and recorded by the major labels, but the teaching of the Yiddish language was drastically reduced. Yiddish was losing its practical utility but retained its symbolic significance as a recognized minority language. How did this evolution of Yiddish fit the trends in Soviet culture in general, and in folklore studies in particular, and was the Jewish case in any way special?

In her study of Soviet folkloristics Dana Prescott Howell described its trajectory during the 1930s as a shift from the "sociology of folklore" in the early 1930s to the reclaiming of "popular culture" by the end of that decade. This shift was in turn a result of the shift in ideological emphasis from social conflict to the unity of the multinational Soviet people: "In these years, the definition of folklore by ideological content, combined with the general assertion of Soviet ideological unity across national boundaries, supported a reintroduction of the concept of 'popular' with regard to folkloric materials. . . . By the second half of the 1930s, the fact of social differentiation in culture, including folklore, was eclipsed by an insistence upon unity."[3] The new political function of folklore as an ideological resource for the fostering of Soviet patriotism raised the prestige of folklore as a "high" genre as well as the public status of folklore studies as an academic discipline. On the "Jewish street" this shift coincided with a rolling back of the practical work of Sovietizing the Jewish population, which by the late 1930s was mostly successfully completed. While Jews abandoned Jewish traditional customs and folkways under the impact of intensive policies of industrialization, urbanization, secularization, and acculturation, Yiddish culture, and especially Yiddish folklore, came to occupy a respected place in the newly constructed multinational Soviet socialist culture. Instead of disappearing in the process of modernization, as some theorists had predicted in the late 1920s, folklore acquired a high status in the Soviet cultural hierarchy. Yiddish followed the general trend that the contemporary Russian scholar Konstantin A. Bogdanov described as the emergence of "folklorizing discourse of Soviet ideology,"[4] but its position was more precarious than other languages. In a way, Yiddish folklore became a symbolic substitute for the disappearing vernacular.

As Kiel suggests, "Until 1928, the study of folklore apparently was not overtly restricted by official party doctrines and a more broadly national outlook seemed to prevail."[5] A radical change occurred at the turn of the 1930s as part of the general ideological "great break," which imposed strict ideological control over the entire field of humanities and social sciences. The new situation also implied a reformulation of the goals and methodology of folklore studies and their place in the new Soviet academic structure. The new Marxist agenda for Jewish ethnography and folkloristics was outlined by the scholar and writer Meir Wiener,[6] the newly appointed head of the Section of Ethnography and Folklore at the Kiev Institute for Jewish Proletarian Culture, in an article in the leading Soviet Yiddish newspaper *Der emes* on November 24, 1931. In the combative spirit of the time, the article opened with an attack against "bourgeois scholars" who "deliberately exaggerate the significance of ethnographic science for other socioeconomic disciplines."[7] However, as Wiener cautioned in a dialectic twist, one must not dismiss ethnography as entirely useless for the practice of socialist construction. The issue with bourgeois ethnography and folkloristics had to do with the essentialist concept of *folksgayst* (national spirit), which, according to Wiener, was the methodological foundation of research at the YIVO Institute in Vilna as well as among the Ukrainian and Polish scholars, all of whom followed the German nationalist model of ethnography as *Volkskunde* (study of the people). In the Soviet Union, this kind of methodology was dangerous because it easily lent itself to use by "class enemy forces" who "smuggled their nationalist petty-bourgeois and even counterrevolutionary trends" into socialist cultural construction.[8] Wiener identified signs of bourgeois nationalism in folkloric and ethnographic references in works of contemporary Jewish and Ukrainian modernist art, such as religious elements in the visual imagery of Issachar Ber Ryback and El Lissitzky, allusions to the Ukrainian Baroque style of the seventeenth and eighteenth centuries in the architectural designs of new railway stations and to Byzantine icons in the portraits of Soviet leaders and historical personalities, and echoes of church music in Soviet songs. The mission of the Section of Ethnography and the Cabinet of Musical Folklore was to combat these reactionary trends in both foreign and Soviet scholarship on ethnography and folklore.

The first task of the section was to "revise and clarify" the methodological foundations of ethnography as a "historical category" in accordance with Marxist-Leninist teaching, and its role in the practice of Soviet
cultural construction. The second task was to define the "field of Jewish
ethnography," which encompassed oral and musical folklore and material culture, and to start organizing and processing materials from the
archives and collections that were seized after the closure of the prerevolutionary institutions (some of those holdings were brought to Kiev from
An-sky's Jewish Museum and Jewish Historical-Ethnographic Society in
Leningrad), as well as those collected by the Kiev Institute during recent
fieldwork. Priority was to be given to folklore dealing with social issues,
in particular revolutionary and proletarian folklore. As the newest department at the institute, the section was at that time focusing on textual
and musical folklore, while other important directions, such as the study
of material culture and "beliefs" ("antireligious scholarship") were still
absent.

In a manuscript that has been preserved in his archive, Wiener further
specified the directions of research in the field of ethnography and folklore.[9] In these guidelines Wiener declared that the task of Soviet ethnography should be a Marxist reconstruction of the culture of the oppressed
classes. He did not consider folkloristics an independent discipline but
rather an important "auxiliary research instrument" (*hilfsvisnshaftlekh
mitl*) for other disciplines, such as history, sociology, or philology.[10] He
also criticized the traditional descriptive and comparative methodology
of folklore studies, aimed at creating a universal classification of ethnographic phenomena across ethnic borders. The purpose of the new Marxist methodology, he argued, should be to extract a "historical reality"
from ethnographic materials. Contrary to "bourgeois scholarship," with
its claim to objectivity, Soviet scholarship had to be openly ideological in
its selection and interpretation of ethnographic material. The importance
of the ethnographic material for Soviet scholarship depended on its ability to represent the dominant trend of historical development. This did
not mean that certain kinds of materials, such as Hasidic folklore, were
to be disregarded completely. Everything was to be collected, but not
everything could be published. After all, it is not the ethnographic material per se but its interpretation that makes the material significant, and

the task of Soviet scholarship was to provide a new Marxist interpretation that would replace the previous readings by S. An-sky and Noah
Prylucki.

Wiener's engagement in ethnography and folklore was not driven entirely by his intellectual interest. A scholar and translator of medieval
Hebrew literature, a German literary critic, and a Yiddish novelist, he
immigrated to the Soviet Union from Vienna in 1926, attracted by the opportunity to publish his literary works in Yiddish and pursue an academic
career. His first academic appointment was at the Literary Section of the
Kiev Institute, but around 1931 he was assigned to the newly founded Section of Ethnography and Folklore as a result of an ideological campaign
launched against the leadership of the Literary Section by the champions
of "proletarian literature." This situation caused Wiener a great deal of an-
guish, and in 1932 he quit the institute and soon after moved to Moscow,
where he eventually got a job at the Department for Yiddish Language
and Literature at the Moscow State Pedagogical Institute and resumed his
work on literature, treating folklore as a literary genre rather than an ethnographic subfield. Wiener was fortunate to leave Kiev just in time before
the start of another ideological campaign against "bourgeois nationalists"
among Ukrainian and Belorussian ethnographers in the spring of 1933.

It is possible that Wiener's attack on "nationalist" and "bourgeois"
ethnography and his deliberate marginalization of folklore studies and
ethnography in the Soviet hierarchy of disciplines was a maneuver that
enabled him to step away from the ideological frontline. The rejection
of the "folkist" essentialism and the interpretation of folklore as a mere
reflection of social conflicts were in line with the ideas of the leading Soviet folklorists of that time, such as Yuri Sokolov and Evgenii Kagarov. In
his programmatic article "On the Present Tasks of the Study of Russian
Folklore," which opened the newly established academic annual *Khudozhestvennyi fol'klor* (Artistic folklore), Sokolov criticized his predecessors for their insufficient attention to the social aspects of folklore: "Class
differentiation in our time, the history of class relationships in the ancient
period, the sequential change of social groups which created folkloric
works or, at least, for which these works were created—all of this was in
most cases not taken into account properly. Researchers continued to
operate with such broad and vague terms as 'people' [*narod*] and 'national

character' [*narodnost'*]."[11] As a literary scholar, Wiener also shared Sokolov's view that "we must insist on a closer connection between the study
of folklore and written literature."[12] But in his rejection of the independent
disciplinary status of folklore studies, Wiener went further than Sokolov.
In this respect Wiener was closer to Kagarov, who believed that "philology and sociology are the two main axes, around which folklore studies
are bound to rotate."[13]

An additional ideological motive that was not yet part of mainstream
Soviet folkloristics of that time might have been behind Wiener's concept of folklore. Wiener's personal intellectual and artistic evolution that
led him from expressionism to Marxism and from Berlin and Vienna to
Kharkov, Kiev, and Moscow could make him highly sensitive to what he
perceived as dangerous trends in German intellectual life. In the long introduction to the first issue of *Problemes fun folkloristik* (Problems of folkloristics; 1932), the semiperiodical publication of the Section of Ethnography, Wiener offered a detailed critique of non-Marxist theories of folklore.
Rather than Yiddish or Hebrew *folkloristic*, the main target of his critique
was German Volkskunde. Wiener distinguished two kinds of *folklorizm*,
as he called the use of folklore in cultural practice: the liberating kind
(exemplified by the work of Herder), which helps raise the consciousness
of oppressed classes by highlighting elements of protest in folk creativity,
and the oppressive kind, which fetishizes conservative values and reflects
the class interests of the oppressing classes. The latter kind came to domi-
nate German Volkskunde in the nineteenth and twentieth centuries, turning folklore into an instrument of nationalist propaganda.

The next stage in the development of that oppressive kind of *folklorizm*
was the program of "pan-ethnographization" of all human knowledge,
which was proposed by the influential German folklorist Adolf Spamer
in his book *Wesen, Wege, und Ziele der Volkskunde* (Essence, ways, and
goals of Volkskunde; 1928). Wiener read Spamer's book as a call for transforming the entire set of disciplines of humanities and social sciences,
from law to psychology, into branches of a nationalist superdiscipline
of Volkskunde, which would endow them with a deeper meaning. Spamer
believed that such an all-embracing discipline, together with its practical applications in the areas of law, education, etc., was of great political
importance for state building and therefore had to be run by high-ranking

state officials and controlled by the police. In a covertly psychoanalytical fashion, Wiener interpreted Spamer's vision of ethnography as a main instrument of consolidation and control of the entire intellectual and political life of a nation in terms of a reaction to the trauma of World War I and the rise of Communism in Russia. Spamer and other German folklorists wanted to come up with an intellectual formula for a "Mission of Germany" (*Daytshlands shlikhes*) to help mobilize the German people for a new war. Another prominent German folklorist criticized by Wiener was Hans Naumann, the author of the theory of *gesunkenes Kulturgut* ("sunk cultural legacy"), according to which folk masses were incapable of producing their own culture and could only utilize elements of "high" culture that "sunk down" to them.[14] Opposing Naumann, Wiener argued that "in the broadest sense, 'folklore' is a certain complex of ideological expressions of the oppressed and exploited poor masses of the past (with some last remainders in the present)."[15] From Wiener's class-determined sociohistorical perspective folklore was an original product of the creativity of the working masses, rather than "sediment" of the high culture of their exploiters.

Wiener's sharp critique of German folkloristics was not typical for Soviet scholarship until the mid-1930s. As Dana Prescott Howell notes, "In the early 1930s, there was little Soviet criticism of German work. Soviet folklorists agreed with the general direction of German folkloristics and ethnography in the 1920s in terms of sociological study, regional studies, and analysis of individual performer."[16] In 1927, the Soviet folklorist Nadezhda Eliash concluded her positive review of current folklore studies in Germany on an optimistic note: "Let us hope that our further work will follow the path of united collaborative scholarly production, that common interests and problems will bring us even closer."[17] Sokolov "cited approvingly Naumann's concept of 'gesunkenes Kulturgut,'" although he disapproved of a certain "antidemocratic tendency" of underestimating the creativity of the rural masses.[18] It was not until 1934 that the Soviet attitude toward German scholarship began to change, and at the 1936 all-Union folklore conference Kagarov presented a report on the subject of "German folkloristics in the service of German fascism."[19] In 1937 Sokolov completely dissociated from Naumann's theory, which by then had been appropriated by Nazi ideology; in Sokolov's 1938 textbook on folklore, "the thesis of the aristocratic origins of epic was unequivocally regarded as 'fascist.'"[20] Wiener was among the first Soviet scholars to identify the fascist tendencies in German folkloristics, but his detailed critique had no impact at that time because it was written in Yiddish.

Wiener's critical attitude toward German Volkskunde can be regarded as the overzealous attempt of a recent newcomer from German-speaking culture to be more orthodox than the Soviet mainstream, but it could also be explained by his sensitivity to any intellectual forms of nationalism. His critique turned out to be prophetic in light of Spamer's later career under the Nazi regime and his postwar reemergence as one of the leading German folklorists. In 1934 Spamer was appointed the Reichsleiter für Volkskundeforschung (Imperial Head of Ethnographic Research), a position that suited his ambition to become a high-ranking state official in charge of ethnographic scholarship. Although not a National Socialist Party member himself, Spamer had close ties to the Nazi ideological establishment, which was keen on utilizing folklore scholarship for propaganda purposes. But Spamer's career under the Nazi regime was short. In 1937 he fell out of favor and was subjected to "psychic terror" and interrogations by the Gestapo, and in 1942 he suffered a complete nervous breakdown.[21] Ironically, it was his Jewish colleague Victor Klemperer, who became famous for his work on the language of the Nazi regime, who helped bring Spamer back to the Dresden Technical University after 1945, where Spamer began a new successful career in the German Democratic Republic.

Wiener's critique of the nationalist tendencies in German Volkskunde informed his negative attitude toward Yiddish and Hebrew folklore studies in Poland and Palestine. Well aware of the potentially dangerous political implications of intellectual theories in a totalitarian society, he was in a good position to observe how German folklorists made themselves useful to the emerging Nazi regime. From his Marxist perspective, Yiddish and Hebrew folklorists were following the same dangerous path toward servicing the needs of nationalist Jewish politics, which he overzealously identified as fascist. For him, the only valid ideological alternative to intellectual nationalism was Marxist materialism, which regarded culture as a product of the social superstructure and denied it any existence independent of the economic basis. For a short time, and probably against his wishes,

Wiener found himself in charge of creating a new Soviet Jewish ethnography. His task, as he saw it, was to place his discipline firmly under the control of Marxist ideology as an auxiliary branch of sociologically determined scholarship, in marked contrast to the nationalist "super-science" embraced in Germany and elsewhere. Wiener's own intellectual interest in folklore was not ethnographic but literary, which he was free to pursue after he left Kiev. In his studies of the literature of the Yiddish Haskalah he developed a concept of *shprakhfolklor,* according to which folkloric elements played a formative role in the development of the literary language at its early stages by way of creating close and fixed associations between metaphoric imagery on the one hand and emotions and ideas on the other hand. As a result of their frequent use, over time these images turned into idioms and acquired a whole set of different associations. These basic units gradually developed into more complex literary figures with a wider variety of symbolic and metaphorical meanings. Thus, according to this theory and contrary to Naumann's, high culture had its origins in folklore. In this way Wiener was able to salvage high culture for Marxist theory and eventually celebrate it as a "grandiose creative achievement of the people."[22]

While Wiener nominally remained in charge of Yiddish folklore studies through the 1930s, and served as the editor of several collections even after he left the institute, the bulk of work in collecting, researching, and publishing folklore materials was done by his Kiev colleagues, such as Zalmen Skuditski and Moyshe Beregovski. In the first volume (1933) of the series *Folklor lider,* Skuditski, in line with Wiener's sociological agenda, declared that the primary task of Marxist folkloristics was "to identify those products of folk creativity that are aimed against the exploiting classes,"[23] giving publication priority to the "song materials that are saturated with sharp and vibrant social content," thus drawing a clear line between folklore as the creativity of the exploited classes and the exploiters' "high culture." The content was dominated by proletarian songs, which were divided chronologically into prerevolutionary songs, songs about strikes, songs about the revolutionary struggle and its victims, and "folkloric revolutionary hymns." In contrast to the first group of songs, which reflected the pessimistic worldview of the oppressed working masses under capitalism, the revolutionary songs were "permeated with the social optimism of the bravely rising class which is confident in its struggle for a better future."[24] One of the logical implications of this theory was the importance of the collecting effort, because that kind of folklore was bound to disappear in the future classless socialist society: "Our folkloristics must urgently and immediately organize this work because with the victory of socialism in our Union all remains of all kinds of folklore will be lost."[25] A smaller section included songs that had little to do with class struggle but which had a certain sociohistorical value, such as songs of artisans and songs about the Russo-Japanese War and World War I. The collection concluded with so-called *shteygerishe lider* (songs about everyday life and customs). Skuditski justified their publication as follows: "From the large amount of unpublished materials we have selected a group of folk songs that are characterized by their petit-bourgeois and bourgeois content. We have included this group for the sake of contrast, in order to highlight social differentiation in folklore creativity."[26]

The problem of social differentiation in Yiddish folk songs was discussed by Ayzek Rozentsvayg in his study that was published by the Kiev Institute's Section of Ethnography in 1934 and edited by Wiener's chief rival, the literary scholar Max Erik, who came to Kiev in 1932 as the head of the Literary Section. In his brief introduction Rozentsvayg announced the beginning of a new research project on "social differentiation of folklore," which he presented as a "fact and factor of class struggle."[27] His methodological point of departure was the negation of the very concept of "folk creativity" because it presumed the existence of a uniform "folk" as an essentialist category. On these grounds, he was equally dismissive of An-sky's "clerical-Yiddishist" notion of a special spirituality of Jewish folk creativity, as well as of Oyslender's "national-democratic" conception of folklore as a pure expression of the realistic and materialistic imagination of the folk masses: "Whereas An-sky theologized folklore according to one nationalist model [*nusekh*], Oyslender radicalized it according to another one."[28] Both theorists operated on the presumption of the existence of a certain general national consciousness and style. Instead, Rozentsvayg set off to investigate different kinds of "folklore" as a product of different social groups. He identified three such groups in traditional Jewish society, each with its own kind of folklore according to its "psycho-ideology": the merchant bourgeoisie, the petty bourgeoisie, and artisans and women. The fourth and most historically recent group was the proletariat, which emerged among Jews at the turn of the twentieth century and created the most accomplished and progressive folklore.

For each group, Rozentsvayg argued, folklore served not only as a means for the expression of their psycho-ideology, but also as a weapon in class struggle. The ruling class of merchant bourgeoisie used folklore to impose a sense of national and religious unity upon the suppressed masses and keep them under control. The petty bourgeoisie, which was reduced to poverty by capitalist development, expressed its bitterness and complaints but was unable to see the real root of its troubles, let alone to protest. Elements of social protest and critique were more pronounced in the folklore of artisans and women, and became fully articulated in the folklore of the revolutionary proletariat. This does not mean that each group created its own folklore; rather, common formal and stylistic features were modified to reflect the respective class attitude. Folklore material was produced by all classes, but the lower, oppressed groups were more intensively engaged in that process because for them folklore creativity was almost the only means of self-expression.[29]

Rozentsvayg further proceeds to differentiate between "reactionary" and "progressive" stylistic features in folklore. He argues that the folklore of the ruling classes contains more archaic and Hebraic elements in its language, includes references to religious literature, and is assertive in its nationalist collectivist optimism. The folklore of the impoverished petty bourgeoisie, on the contrary, is more pessimistic and individualist, filled with "desperate sadness and hopelessness."[30] The oppressed masses, and particularly women, were able to raise their protest, but their voices remained "quiet and helpless."[31] Their folklore is completely free from religious references and "Hebrew ballast" (unless they are used subversively), and begins to use the device of *antiteze* (antithesis), contrasting imagery associated with opposite classes. This device will develop into a full "form of expression of the rising class consciousness" only in the folklore of the revolutionary proletariat.[32]

Another genre of folklore that was revolutionized by the oppressed classes was the love song as an expression of social protest against the oppressive custom of arranged marriage. At its most accomplished stage of social development, the folklore of the organized revolutionary proletariat practically merges with the literary genre of revolutionary poetry, because both draw their creative nourishment from the revolutionary consciousness of the proletariat and express its psycho-ideology. At this stage folklore acquires an epic quality, which, according to Rozentsvayg, is more advanced and accomplished artistically than the lyricism of the older folklore. Thus, in Rozentsvayg's theory of the social evolution of folklore from the archaic forms associated with the oppressive classes to the revolutionary epic of proletarian struggle, folklore eventually merges with literature and thus effectively disappears by fulfilling its historic role.

Applying this perspective to musical folklore in his 1934 article "Jewish Folk Music," which was part of the Russian collection *Evreiskii muzy-kal'nyi fol'klor* (edited by Wiener), Moyshe Beregovski accused his predecessors, the "bourgeois" composers and researchers, of unwillingness "to view musical (or any other) folklore in its historical development." Instead, they attempted to "create a definitive national musical grammar, to find the eternal national specificity, which will be obligatory once and for all for the composer of the given nationality."[33] As a result, they were deaf to the proletarian and revolutionary folklore with its historical topicality: "Mass gatherings, strikes, freedom, prison, arrest, exile, police, exploiters—all these new words and new concepts that infiltrate the working revolutionary creativity grate on the ears of these honorable folklorists."[34] Revolutionary folklore, Beregovski argued, following Wiener, "is a transitional stage from folklore to revolutionary literature, and precisely therein lies its great value." Thus by entering the historical process folklore gradually loses its ethnographic quality and "convert[s] into revolutionary art,"[35] and "in this case it is the last folklore, since it already serves the revolution, which annihilates every basis for a further development of folklore."[36] Beregovski saw a sign of the disappearance of folklore as the creativity of oppressed masses in the ongoing "significant penetration of the songs of proletarian composers into the mass repertoire" and "active and creative participation of the broader masses in immediate musical work."[37] Acknowledging the historical importance of folklore, particularly revolutionary songs, as a musical expression of the oppressed and exploited classes, he asked a practical question: "Can folk music be used for contemporary Soviet art?"[38] His answer was somewhat cautious and evasive: it can, "to the extent that we can use any musical tradition, or any musical heritage of the past, that is, through socialist reworking and dialectic resolution."[39]

Wiener's "Folklorizm un folkloristik" was positively reviewed in the leading Russian journal *Sovetskaia etnografia* (Soviet ethnography) by Sofia Magid, who was at that time working on her dissertation on the Yiddish ballad at the Leningrad Institute of Russian Literature (Pushkinskii Dom).[40] Magid mildly criticized Wiener for his "artificially narrow definition of folklore as the creativity of exclusively oppressed and backward masses,"[41] which led him to the conclusion that folklore was dying and would have no value for the proletariat once it was liberated from oppression under socialism. She also questioned Wiener's view of ethnography as an auxiliary instrument for other disciplines. Magid's critique reflected the emergence of the new trend in Soviet folkloristics, which was articulated at the first meeting of writers and folklorists in Moscow on December 15, 1933, under the auspices of the Organizational Committee of the Soviet Writers' Union. In his programmatic speech Yuri Sokolov declared folklore to be "one of the most important areas of poetic creativity" and folkloristics as "one of the most essential parts of literary scholarship."[42] He also called for an "active intervention into the folklore process" and the "guidance of oral poetic creativity" by means of "mobilization of all contemporary tools of ideological influence," such as the publication of "critically proven" songbooks for the masses, radio programming, mass production of gramophone records, "model" folklore performances, and the issuing of programs and instructions for local authorities.[43]

Two years later, in her review of the publications of Beregovski and Skuditski, Magid was more critical of Wiener's concept, to which she attributed the methodological shortcomings of both studies: "By accepting unreservedly Wiener's position that 'production and consumption of folklore is characteristic mainly of the oppressed classes, and that the ethnographic way of life [*byt*] is by no means the way of life of the ruling class,' . . . both authors constrain themselves in their articles to mere references to, and some development of, Wiener's scheme in purely theoretical terms, without elaborating it by using concrete live materials; as a result, both authors do not by any means validate Wiener's problematic concepts, but rather confirm its falsity [*porochnost'*; literally, perversity], namely: the absence of historicism."[44] By sticking to Wiener's concept,

YIDDISH FOLKLORE AND SOVIET IDEOLOGY

Magid continued, Skuditski and Beregovski were unable to see the "genesis of folkloric phenomena" and ignored the "complex way in which they are being rethought in the process of social development."[45] She criticized both publications for their lack of critical analysis, and offered her interpretation of a number of songs to prove that the authors often attributed to Yiddish songs "entirely wrong class equivalents."[46] The label of "vulgar sociologism," which Magid applied to Wiener's concept,[47] became operational in the 1934 theoretical debate around the issue of class determinism in culture. The official condemnation of "vulgar sociologism" was an indication of the turn from strict adherence to the internationalist Marxist dogma to a more flexible approach that enabled the consolidation of the Soviet people as a multiethnic socialist nation and eventually led to the rise of Russian nationalism.

Apart from Magid's reviews, studies of Yiddish folklore attracted little attention among mainstream Soviet scholars. It was probably on the basis of her reviews that Wiener was criticized in 1938 by Yuri Sokolov, at that time his colleague at the Moscow State Pedagogical Institute: "Wiener had an absolutely harmful view that folklore can only be ancient, that today it is outdated." Because of this attitude, students of the Yiddish Department had no interest in contemporary folklore. Sokolov complained, "I, a Russian man, have to convince and even plead with Jews to collect the most interesting Jewish folklore that characterizes our Soviet life!"[48] In his response Wiener said that he had long ago repudiated his mistaken view of folklore as a phenomenon of the presocialist past, but this did not save him from being fired from the institute and expelled from the Communist Party. One can add to this episode that Sokolov's interest in Yiddish folklore was not accidental, and he served as the editor of the Russian edition of Yiddish folk songs that was prepared by Yekhezkel Dobrushin and published in 1947.

The new approach to folklore was adopted by Skuditski in his introduction to the second volume of *Folklor-lider* (1936). Now folklore was treated not in opposition to high culture (presumably of the ruling classes) but as its hidden counterpart: "Until the most recent time, in every historical age of the class society, along with the official literature and arts, there existed an unofficial, as it were underground, culture, in which the talent and creativity of the broadest suppressed folk masses was concentrated."[49] Folklore possessed revolutionary potential as a driving force of renewal and development of the entire culture, high and low. But it would be a gross simplification, Skuditski warned, in line with Rozentsvayg's analysis, to think of all folklore as "progressive and rebellious," because "folklore reflected a whole broad spectrum of social interests of different classes" and not merely the oppressed poor.[50] Revolutionary folklore was still to be regarded as the most important part of folkloric creativity, but, Skuditski noted, "this does not in any way mean that the rest of folklore is not important for us."[51] As a result, proletarian songs occupied a more modest place in the second volume than in the first one because, Skuditski pointed out, the new material had little to add to what had already been published. A significant part of his introduction was devoted to love songs, and several new sections were added, among them songs about emigration (Skuditski even criticized the American folklorist Yehudah Leib Cahan for his lack of interest in this theme), maskilic anti-Hasidic songs, and Yiddish adaptations of Ukrainian songs. Those adaptations provided support for the Marxist concept of the primacy of class solidarity over ethnic and linguistic divisions, while the "anticlerical" songs served as a proof against S. Ansky's idea about the inherent religiosity of Jewish folklore. In conclusion, Skuditski promised to publish a new collection of Soviet folklore about the revolution, the Civil War, Lenin, Stalin, socialist construction, struggle against the class enemy, and the "new happy Socialist life in the USSR"[52] to mark the twentieth anniversary of the October Revolution in 1937.

Skuditski was unable to fulfill his promise because he was imprisoned in 1937 and after his release never returned to the study of Yiddish folklore. But Beregovski's career during the late 1930s was more successful. In the summer of 1936, when the Institute for Jewish Proletarian Culture was downgraded to the lower status of cabinet, Beregovski was for a while looking for another job as a Ukrainian folklorist, but was soon reinstated in the new institution. His new project was an "attempt at a more or less complete and comprehensive characterization of Jewish musical folklore in all of its variations (vocal, instrumental, etc.)."[53] In 1937 he was appointed head of the Cabinet of Musical Ethnography at the Kiev Conservatory, and in 1938 he organized a Jewish Section at the Union of Composers in Kiev.[54] He also proposed to create a Soviet Jewish Choral Society to promote Jewish musical folklore.[55] In 1937 he signed a contract for a new collection of Yiddish folk songs with the Ukrainian National Minorities Press: "The (material) conditions are not bad," he wrote, "but they forced on me Fefer as a collaborator (in the work that is nearly complete). I have been fighting long, tried to get rid of that revolting offer, but in the end had to give up."[56] Nonetheless, Beregovski felt satisfied: "The collected material is very good, and it seems that I have every reason to be happy about this collection."[57] Although Fefer apparently contributed nothing to the actual work, his name as the major Yiddish poet of Ukraine certainly added symbolic weight to the publication.

Published in 1938 in a print run of 2,700 copies, *Yidishe folks-lider* contained texts and notes of songs but no introduction or academic apparatus, as it was apparently intended for a popular audience, or perhaps newly established amateur Jewish choirs that would perform these songs on various public and private occasions.[58] The structure of the collection reflected the new position of folklore as a genre of Soviet "high culture." It appropriately opened with "The Internationale," which was followed by the section titled "Noyt, arbet un kamf" (Need, labor and struggle). The next section, "Rekrutchine—priziv" (Recruitment—conscription), included protest songs against the tsarist regime, but the rest of the collection celebrated the joys of ordinary life: "Love Songs," "Wedding and Festive Occasions," "Family Customs," "Lullabies," "Children's Songs," and "Humor and Satire." Most of the songs were taken from the previous *Folklor-lider* collections, but the final section, "Soviet Folk Songs," consisted of what folklore scholars call "fakelore," newly written folk-style Soviet propaganda songs. This type of production is usually dismissed by serious scholarship as opportunistic and inauthentic, perhaps justified as a necessary price to be paid for the opportunity of preserving and publishing "genuine" folklore under the totalitarian regime. From a different perspective, Bogdanov proposes treating these texts as "(self)representational practices of Soviet culture" which can reveal the folkloric foundations and the mechanisms of production of that culture: "By initiating and editing texts that were to be regarded as 'folklore,' Soviet folklorists eventually became authors of an experiment that had demonstrated on a large scale the practicability of the very theory by Hans Naumann that they trashed."[59]

Together with their colleagues in other Soviet minority cultures, Yiddish poets and folklorists were actively engaged in the process of "folklorizing" their culture. Although deeply ideological and politicized, that culture possessed a folkloric quality which made it recognizable and even appealing to Yiddish speakers, and some of its products, such as "Dzhankoe," became genuinely popular folk songs. Soviet Yiddish folklorists, composers, and poets were working on behalf of the new "ruling class" by producing an idealized, sterile, and conflict-free version of folklore, something that was strongly criticized by the scholarship of the early 1930s. Yet one could also argue that these songs are the most lasting and popular vestige of Soviet Yiddish culture because they were remembered and sung by people, most of whom could not read Yiddish and had little knowledge of Jewish culture.

NOTES

I would like to thank my colleagues Lauren Benjamin, Valeri Dymshits, Leonid Fliat, and Deborah Yalen for their helpful comments and suggestions.

1. Mark William Kiel, "A Twice Lost Legacy: Ideology, Culture and the Pursuit of Jewish Folklore in Russia until Stalinization: 1930–1931" (PhD diss., Jewish Theological Seminary, 1991), 580. On the meaning of the Yiddish term *folkloristik,* see Barbara Kirshenblatt-Gimblett, *"Di folkloristik:* A Good Yiddish Word," *Journal of American Folklore* 98, no. 389 (July–September 1985), 331–334.

2. Kiel, "A Twice Lost Legacy," 577.

3. Dana Prescott Howell, *The Development of Soviet Folkloristics* (New York: Garland, 1992), 366.

4. Konstantin A. Bogdanov, *Vox populi: Fol'klornye zhanry sovetskoi kul'tury* (Moscow: Novoe Literaturnoe Obozrenie, 2009), 27.

5. Kiel, "A Twice Lost Legacy," 484.

6. For a detailed account of Wiener's life and work, see Mikhail Krutikov, *From Kabbalah to Class Struggle: Expressionism, Marxism, and Yiddish Literature in the Life and Work of Meir Wiener* (Stanford, CA: Stanford University Press, 2011), in particular chap. 5, on his work on folklore.

7. Meir Wiener, "Di oyfgabes fun der etnografisher forshung: Vegn der arbet fun der etnografisher sektsie baym institut far yidisher forshung," *Der emes,* November 24, 1931. I am grateful to Leonid Fliat for providing me with this text.

8. Ibid.

9. Meir Wiener, "Proyekt tsu a[n] arbetsprogram far der etn[ografisher] sektsye," 1931, Meir Wiener Archive, Jewish National and University Library at Jerusalem, 4° 1763/25.

10. This position differed from the somewhat blurry "official" Soviet definition of folkloristics as a discipline in the "category [*razriad*] of historical sciences" on the one hand, and a "specific area of literary scholarship" on the other hand (A. N. Lozanova, "K blizhaishim zadacham sovetskoi fol'kloristiki," *Sovetskaia etnografiia* 2 [1932]: 5).

11. Iuri Sokolov, "Ocherednye zadachi izucheniia russkogo fol'klora," *Khudozhestvennyi fol'klor* 1 (1926): 11.

12. Ibid., 23.

13. Evgenii Kagarov, "Chto takoe fol'klor?," *Khudozhestvennyi fol'klor* 4–5 (1929): 8.

14. Meir Wiener, "Folklorizm un folkloristik," in *Problemes fun folkloristik*, vol. 1, ed. Meir Wiener (Kharkov: Melukhisher Natsmindfarlag, 1932), 90–91. On Spamer's critique of Naumann see Hermann Strobach, "'... but when does the prewar begin?': Folklore and Fascism before and around 1933," in *The Nazification of an Academic Discipline: Folklore in the Third Reich*, ed. James R. Dow and Hannjost Lixfeld (Bloomington: Indiana University Press, 1994), 61–63.

15. Wiener, "Folklorizm un folkloristik," 89.

16. Howell, *The Development of Soviet Folkloristics*, 370.

17. N[adezhda] Eliash, "Sovremennaia fol'kloristika v Germanii," *Khudozhestvennyi fol'klor* 2 (1927): 172.

18. Howell, *The Development of Soviet Folkloristics*, 204.

19. Ibid., 371.

20. Bogdanov, *Vox populi*, 110.

21. Ibid., 59.

22. Meir Wiener, "Di rol fun shablonisher frazeologye in der literatur fun der haskole," in *Tsu der geshikhte fun der yidisher literatur*, vol. 1 (New York: YKUF, 1945), 279.

23. Zalmen Skuditski, introduction to *Folklor-lider: Naye materialn-zamlung*, vol. 1, ed. Meir Wiener (Moscow: Emes, 1933), 5.

24. Ibid., 6.

25. Ibid., 9.

26. Ibid., 11.

27. Ayzek Rozentsvayg, *Sotsiale diferntsiatsie inem yidishn folklor-lid* (Kiev: Ukrainishe Visnshaftlekhe Akademie, 1934), 5.

28. Ibid., 10.

29. Ibid., 17.

30. Ibid., 27.

31. Ibid., 32.

32. Ibid., 34.

33. Moshe Beregovski, "Jewish Folk Music," in *Old Jewish Folk Music*, ed. and trans. Mark Slobin (Philadelphia: University of Pennsylvania Press, 1982), 20.

34. Ibid., 28–29.

35. Ibid., 29.

36. Ibid., 30.

37. Ibid.

38. Ibid., 36.

39. Ibid.

40. Sofia Magid, review of "Folklorizm un folkloristik," by Meir Wiener, *Sovetskaia etnografiia* 1–2 (1934): 276–278. On Sofia Magid, see N[atalia] Svetozarova, "Muzykoved and fol'klorist S. D. Magid," in *Iz istorii evreiskoi muzyki v Rossii*, issue 2, ed. Galina V. Kopytova and Aleksandr Frenkel (St. Petersburg: Evreiskii Obshchinnyi Tsentr Sankt-Peterburga, 2006), 309–334.

41. Magid, review of "Folklorizm un folkloristik," 277.

42. Quoted in "Fol'klor v SSSR: Pervoe soveshchanie pisatelei i folkloristov," *Sovetskaia etnografiia* 1–2 (1934): 204.

43. Ibid., 205.

44. S[ofia] D. Magid, "Evreiskii revoliutsionnyi fol'klor," *Sovetskii fol'klor* 2–3 (1936): 397.

45. Ibid.

46. Ibid., 405.

47. Ibid., 398.

48. Minutes of the meeting at the director's office, May 9, 1938, Archives of the Moscow State Pedagogical Institute, Tsentral'nyi Arkhiv Goroda Moskvy, f. 586, op. 1, d. 52, 156.

49. Zalmen Skuditski, introduction to *Folklor-lider: Naye materialn-zamlung*, vol. 2, ed. Meir Wiener (Moscow: Emes, 1936), 3.

50. Ibid., 13.

51. Ibid., 10.

52. Ibid., 81.

53. Beregovski to Isaak Rabinovich and Maria Poryvkina, September 21, 1936, in *Arfy na verbakh: Prizvanie i sud'ba Moiseia Beregovskogo*, ed. Eda Beregovskaya (Moscow: Evreiskii Universitet v Moskve; Jerusalem: Gesharim, 1994), 98.

54. Beregovski to Rabinovich and Poryvkina, November 14, 1937, and April 13, 1938, in Beregovskaya, *Arfy na verbakh*, 100–101.

55. Beregovski to Rabinovich and Poryvkina, April 15, 1937, in Beregovskaya, *Arfy na verbakh*, 100.

56. Ibid.

57. Ibid.

58. M. Beregovski and I. Fefer, eds., *Yidishe folks-lider* (Kiev: Melukhe-Farlag Far di Natsionale Minderhaytn in USSR, 1938).

59. Bogdanov, *Vox populi*, 19.

6

After An-sky

I. M. PUL'NER AND THE JEWISH
SECTION OF THE STATE MUSEUM
OF ETHNOGRAPHY IN LENINGRAD

DEBORAH YALEN

I n a memo dated June 4, 1941, Yehoshu'a (Isaiah Mendelevich) Pul'ner, the director of the Jewish Section of the State Museum of Ethnography in Leningrad (hereafter SME) outlined his plans to conduct ethnographic research among Jews in "Western Ukraine" and "Western Belorussia" later in the month. These territories constituted regions of Poland that had been forcibly annexed by the Soviet Union ("liberated," in Stalinist rhetoric) according to the secret terms of the Nazi-Soviet Nonaggression Pact concluded in August 1939. As a result of the Soviet invasion of eastern Poland, entire Jewish communities came under Soviet control.[1] In his memo to the SME administration, Pul'ner explained that his proposed research expedition would allow him to address serious shortcomings in the ethnographic inventory of the SME's Jewish Section. In particular, Pul'ner hoped to collect artifacts of traditional Jewish material culture that could be used in museum displays, such as clothing, ornamental objects, and domestic implements. This research, Pul'ner insisted, had to be carried out with the greatest urgency, before the inevitable process of Sovietization compromised the distinctive features of traditional Jewish life in the annexed territories.[2]

Pul'ner's plan to conduct research in "Western Ukraine" and "Western Belorussia" was preempted by the Nazi invasion of the Soviet Union on

June 22, 1941. Between June 1941 and his death by starvation in January 1942, Pul'ner remained on the premises of the SME together with his colleagues, protecting the museum collections from aerial bombardment during the Siege of Leningrad. In the antisemitic atmosphere of postwar Stalinism, the Jewish Section of the SME was not reinstated: its collections languished, and Pul'ner's contributions to Soviet ethnography faded into obscurity. Had Pul'ner survived the war, he may very well have fallen victim to the "anticosmopolitan" campaign that disproportionately targeted the Soviet Jewish cultural elite from the late 1940s to the early 1950s. Yet during its short-lived existence between 1937 and 1941, the Jewish Section of the SME enjoyed the support of the regime, and was slated for expansion under Pul'ner's leadership. In what seems like an apparent paradox, moreover, its establishment coincided with the Stalinist terror, when Soviet elites, including leaders of the Jewish Autonomous Region (JAR) in Birobidzhan, were purged by the regime.[3] The goal of this chapter is to explore what the brief history of the Jewish Section—and its director's unrealized research agenda on the eve of World War II—might tell us about the Jewish "ethnographic impulse" as it played itself out in this politically volatile period of Soviet history. An overview of Pul'ner's biography and early scholarship is an important first step in evaluating the complex interplay of intellectual, cultural, and ideological factors that informed the ethnographic study of Soviet Jews at this historical juncture.

THE MAKING OF AN ETHNOGRAPHER: FROM ZIONIST ACTIVISM TO MARXIST-LENINIST MUSEUM WORK

Born in 1900 in the shtetl Snovsk (Chernigov province), Pul'ner spent his formative years in Gomel and completed general studies at the A. E. Ratner gymnasium for Jewish young men in 1919.[4] When Pul'ner left Gomel in 1923 to pursue higher education in Leningrad, he was following a pattern typical of an entire generation of young Soviet Jews: following the collapse of the old regime, Jews had begun to migrate en masse to major urban centers in pursuit of educational and professional opportunities.[5] While the Provisional Government was the first to declare the equality of all nationalities, it was the Bolshevik regime that would institute a concerted "affirmative action" program for the educational, professional, and political advancement of non-Russians.[6] Among the innumerable national minorities targeted by these policies, the Jews stood out, by virtue of their literacy and lack of compromising connections to the old regime, as attractive candidates for a host of positions within the new regime, including those at higher levels of the state apparatus. Indeed, the demographic transformation of Jews in the early years of the Soviet Union was so dramatic that it would itself become a subject of study within the broader rubric of Soviet ethnography.

The new regime required its citizens to provide educational and workplace institutions with detailed information about their "social origins." Pul'ner's employment records therefore provide useful clues about how he fashioned his own identity. For example, he referred to his late father, who had worked as an accountant for various establishments in Gomel, as a *sluzhashchyi* (white-collar worker), and he categorized himself as a *meshchanin,* a term used in imperial Russia to designate "townsperson" but which in the Soviet context signaled that Pul'ner was of neither proletarian nor peasant background.[7] While biographical information published long after his death implies that Pul'ner came from a religiously literate family (his father is described elsewhere as a *lamdan,* a person with deep knowledge of Talmud), Pul'ner not surprisingly omitted any reference to traditional Judaism in his personnel records.[8] He also took pains to note that although he had been an active member of the Zionist sports organization Maccabees between 1918 and 1923, he had publicly resigned from this "nationalistic" institution in a letter to the Yiddish-language party newspaper *Der emes* (Truth).[9] Perhaps in an effort to demonstrate his break from Zionism, he subsequently became active in the Komsomol (Young Communist League) and in 1925 he co-authored a Yiddish-language guide to group sports and games for Jewish shtetl youth intended for use by local Communist Party activists.[10] Despite his public repudiation of Zionism, however, Pul'ner's employment files indicate that he remained without a Communist Party affiliation.[11]

From 1923 to 1925, Pul'ner studied at the Leningrad Institute of Jewish History and Literature, where he also served in an administrative position from 1924 to 1925. In 1926, he enrolled in the Ethnography Division of the Geography Department at Leningrad State University, where he earned a degree in 1930 as an ethnographer of the Caucasus region. At both institutions, Pul'ner worked under the supervision of the prominent ethnographers Vladimir Bogoraz and Lev Shternberg, who were also from Jewish backgrounds.[12] At Leningrad State University, his course work reflected the rigorous curricular standards set by his mentors for both theoretical and practical training.[13] Preparatory instruction included courses such as Evolution of Material Culture, Museum Studies, Comparative Folklore, Experimental Psychology, Prehistoric Culture, Economic Geography, General Geology, Introduction to Biology, Ethnography of the Caucasus, and Georgian and German language study. Practical training comprised instruction in drawing, statistics, field geology, and photography, and seminars in topics such as Evolution of Religious Beliefs, Islam, and Evolution of Social Culture. Beyond this, students were obligated to study "political subjects" including historical materialism, political economy, and the history of the Communist Party of Bolsheviks, along with military training (military administration, tactics, etc.).[14]

Pul'ner's early training and scholarship should be understood in light of not only the Bolshevik regime's overt politicization of ethnography, but also the extraordinary scale and pace of social transformation experienced by all Soviet citizens at this time, including ethnographers themselves. As Francine Hirsch has demonstrated, "ethnographic knowledge" was marshaled as a tool of Soviet state building. Ethnographers were given the task of "mapping" the peoples of the USSR according to Marxist class criteria, explicating the relationship of class and culture, and collecting data on the "productive forces," whether actual or latent, of the population.[15] These data not only informed Soviet economic planning, but were also utilized for so-called mass enlightenment: ethnographic museum displays became useful vehicles for Soviet propaganda, illustrating to the public the transition of previously oppressed peoples "from darkness to light."[16] The quest to capture the fleeting transition from the "old" to the "new" ways of life (*byt*) among the peoples of the USSR thus dominated Soviet ethnographic scholarship in the interwar years.

From a more personal point of view, it is important to bear in mind that ethnographers were themselves experiencing these cataclysmic changes in Soviet society. When young Jewish ethnographers such as Pul'ner chose to specialize in the study of their coethnics (as opposed to, say, peasants or nomads), they were in some sense embarking on a program of autoethnography, albeit one that was state-funded and heavily circumscribed in ideological terms. Given the fraught political position of Jews at this time as both upwardly mobile beneficiaries and victims of Bolshevik nationality policy (a disproportionate number of Jews were being "disenfranchised" as members of the bourgeoisie at the same time that they were equalized as a national minority),[17] the choice to study Jews ethnographically raises significant questions about identity. In a sense, Pul'ner was personally experiencing the very transition from old to new that he was being trained to observe and document with the detached eye of a professional. When Pul'ner, the self-described *meshchanin,* soon applied his ethnographic training to the study of Soviet Jews transitioning from old to new ways of life, the line dividing observer and observed had to have been slender indeed.

Although they each wrote occasional pieces on Jewish ethnography and played an influential role in mentoring young ethnographers who gravitated toward the study of Jews and Judaism, the ethnographic study of Jews never dominated the research agendas of either Shternberg or Bogoraz. As Sergei Kan observes in his contribution to this volume, the two scholars diverged significantly in their attitudes toward Jews and traditional Jewish beliefs and practices: Shternberg was interested in the evolutionary significance of Judaism, while Bogoraz seemed more intrigued by its dissolution under the impact of Soviet modernization. During the 1923–1924 academic year at the Leningrad Institute of Jewish History and Literature, Shternberg lectured on the need to conduct systematic ethnographic research among Soviet Jewish populations in former market towns, cities, and agricultural colonies. Shternberg clearly framed this task in terms of documenting the ephemeral transition from old to new ways of life, and urged his students to collect data on subjects as wide-ranging as child-rearing practices, occupational patterns, the official use of Yiddish in Soviet institutions, and changing sexual mores, to name just a few.[18] Shternberg's posthumously published 1928 article "Questions of Jewish Ethnography" further elaborated on the importance of such research for the cultivation of Jewish national consciousness in the Soviet Union, a concept he would likely have been compelled to retract had he lived longer.[19]

It was Bogoraz, however, who served as the driving force behind the funding and sponsorship of student ethnographic expeditions. In what was originally conceived as a study of "Western Jews,"[20] several students, including Pul'ner, conducted ethnographic studies of their own communities in the summer of 1924. In 1926, the results of these expeditions were featured in a volume edited by Bogoraz entitled *The Jewish Shtetl in Revolution: Essays.* This volume bore the distinct influence of Bogoraz in that its focus on the transition from the old to the new overwhelmingly emphasized the latter. Pul'ner's article "From the Life of Gomel," which he referred to in his employment records as an "ethnographic-economic sketch,"[21] described the socioeconomic transformations taking place among Jewish workers, artisans, and traders in what was by now a significant urban center. The article provided a lively sociological portrait of warring ideological camps—Bundists versus Zionists versus religious traditionalists—and how various groups of Jews coped with the economic crises of the Civil War era and the New Economic Policy (NEP). Pul'ner addressed intergenerational conflicts and the role of children in drawing their parents into revolutionary culture, and included extensive statistical data on Jewish artisans.[22]

While Pul'ner undoubtedly attended Shternberg's lectures on Jewish ethnography, his first significant publication would seem to align him more closely with Bogoraz and a focus on the new. To be sure, "From the Life of Gomel" reflects Shternberg's advice to explore intergenerational conflict and socioeconomic transformations, and its exhaustive statistical documentation displays the rigorous scholarly training that Shternberg imparted to his students. Still, Pul'ner very clearly emphasizes the dissolution of the old and the primacy of revolutionary consciousness. It is perhaps in other areas of Pul'ner's work that we can better discern the influence of Shternberg. In July 1927, for example, Pul'ner sent an affectionately worded letter to Shternberg from the village of Zaverezh'e (Mogilev district, Belorussia) where he was studying the local Jewish community. In this letter, Pul'ner reported on his research activities, asked for advice, and noted that some of the materials he was collecting would be appropriate for "the Jewish museum."[23] Pul'ner did not identify exactly which museum he was referring to, but at the time Lev Shternberg was directly involved in the operations of both the Museum of Anthropology and

Ethnography at the Academy of Sciences and the museum of the Jewish Historical-Ethnographic Society (JHES). While Shternberg, who died in the late summer of 1927, may have been too ill to reply by the time he received this letter, it nonetheless indicates that the two were clearly in contact regarding Jewish ethnographic research and museum work, and that Pul'ner considered the esteemed former populist to be both a mentor and a colleague.

This connection to Shternberg becomes more significant given that in 1926 Pul'ner was also assigned the task of cataloguing the collections that An-sky had temporarily left in the care of the Ethnographic Department of the State Russian Museum back in 1917–1918 (and which the museum of the JHES was hoping to retrieve).[24] Pul'ner's deep familiarity with the massive Yiddish-language questionnaire which Shternberg edited for the An-sky expedition is evident in his own unpublished field notes and dissertation manuscript, entitled "Marriage Rites among Jews," in which he replicated many of An-sky's questions and attempted to answer them based on his own field research.[25] Indeed, the working title of the revised manuscript based on his dissertation, "Birth, Marriage, and Death among Jews in Light of Ethnography," closely mirrored the structure of An-sky's questionnaire.[26]

Arguably, traces of An-sky's influence as well as Shternberg's can also be detected in two articles that Pul'ner published in 1929 regarding Jewish folk beliefs and rituals associated with pregnancy, labor, and the newborn child. "On the Folklore of Georgian Jews" was published in German in the Vienna-based *Mitteilungen zur Jüdischen Volkskunde* (Communications on Jewish folklore) and described the results of field expeditions sponsored by Leningrad State University in 1926 and 1928 to Georgia.[27] The other article, "Customs and Beliefs Related to Pregnancy, Birth, and the Newborn among Jews," was published in Ukrainian in the *Etnohrafichnyĭ visnyk* (Ethnographic herald) of the Ethnographic Commission of the Ukrainian Academy of Sciences, and offered a comparative approach to Jewish and Slavic cultures. For this article, Pul'ner drew on a range of prerevolutionary and contemporary sources, including the material he collected in Zaverezh'e, Belorussia, in 1927 and the work of his colleague Zalmen Amitin-Shapiro in Soviet Central Asia.[28] Pul'ner also made numerous references to the Old Testament and the Talmud, and

to Jewish literary sources on subjects such as the demon Lilith. Both
of these articles were chiefly descriptive and contained little in the way
of tendentious political rhetoric. That Pul'ner also participated in an ethnographic expedition to Georgia under the auspices of the JHES in 1929
and served officially as its consultant testifies to his close affiliations with
a "bourgeois" institution that would soon be shut down by the Bolshevik
authorities later that year. Throughout the 1920s, then, Pul'ner's academic
training and professional activity pointed to a multifaceted scholarly
agenda and a readiness to work on both independent and state-sponsored
ethnographic initiatives.

A MANIFESTO FOR A NEW ERA? PUL'NER'S DEBUT IN *SOVIET ETHNOGRAPHY*

Despite the forcible closure of the JHES in 1929, Pul'ner maintained a
busy schedule working on several projects. In 1930, he curated displays on
Judaism for the Leningrad State Central Antireligious Museum (located
in the former St. Isaac's Cathedral), as well as for an Antireligious Exhibition sponsored by the Academy of Sciences and held at the former Winter
Palace.[29] He would organize yet another "Jewish exhibit" at the Maxim
Gorky People's House in Leningrad in 1932. Also in 1930, he joined the
Jewish Working Group of the Saltykov-Shchedrin State Public Library
in Leningrad, a position he would maintain until 1937. In this capacity, he
worked on a major undertaking to catalogue scholarly materials on a range
of Jewish subjects, a task that reveals Pul'ner's grasp of both Yiddish and
Hebrew.[30] In 1931, he organized a conference that brought together representatives of the Jewish sections of libraries in the Russian, Ukrainian,
and Belorussian republics in Leningrad.[31]

   Of particular significance for Pul'ner's career in this era of the "Great
Break"[32] was his recruitment in 1931 by the Jewish Working Group of the
Institute for the Study of the *Narodnosti* of the USSR (IPIN).[33] As a member of IPIN, Pul'ner participated in additional ethnographic expeditions
to Belorussia, and served as secretary of the Jewish Working Group.[34]
In what could be interpreted as a sign of his growing visibility as an ethnographer, he was called upon by the Belorussian Sector of IPIN and

the Ethnographic Department of the State Russian Museum to outline a new program for Soviet Jewish ethnographic museum displays. Given the wider campaign against "bourgeois specialists" and the efforts of the State Russian Museum in the early 1930s to replace older personnel with a new generation of ideologically reliable ethnographers, this article appears to signal a conscious decision on Pul'ner's part, whether arising out of conviction or necessity, to align himself with the party's program of renewed "cultural revolution."[35] His article "Questions on the Organization of Jewish Ethnographic Museums and Jewish Sections of Ethnographic Museums," published in the journal *Sovetskaia etnografiia* (Soviet ethnography) in 1931, offers a radically different impression of the same author who, just two years earlier, had published seemingly apolitical scholarship on Jewish folk beliefs and customs associated with pregnancy and childbirth.[36]

Pul'ner began his article by announcing the collapse of the "old bourgeois museum structure." In its place, he wrote, "new Soviet ethnographic museums are being created, with new aims and a Marxist-Leninist methodology." While he repudiated the entire legacy of the old museum system, which had been established by "ethnographer-populists," he took Jewish ethnographers and ethnographic museums to task with particular vehemence: in the same spirit in which the tsarist regime had elevated the principle of Great Russian chauvinism, so too had Jewish scholars promoted the false notion of Jews as "singular, monolithic, and classless":

> Zionist nationalist theoreticians, on the one hand, and antisemitic ones, on the other hand, view world Jewry, living in separate groups in different countries, as a united, indivisible nation. The Jewish bourgeoisie constructed their museums according to the point of view that regarded the Jewish nation as the "People of the Book," as the chosen people, who bear a great divine mission to bring universal culture to all the peoples of the world, as the nation that gave humanity "world" religion out of which other "world" religions were born. In all Jewish museums, religion—*kult*—occupies the dominant position. In this way, Jewish museums lock Jewish culture into a narrow nationalistic framework, tearing it away from all its surroundings, idealizing and glorifying it. Of course, the exposure of class aspects and class conflicts had no place here. Everything was exhibited under the slogan "the brotherhood of Israel."[37]

Although Pul'ner refrained from naming names, it would not be difficult
to interpret his sweeping critique of "ethnographer-populists" as a calculated attempt to distance himself not only from the legacy of An-sky, but
also from his own populist mentors Shternberg and Bogoraz.[38] Indeed,
Pul'ner's derisive characterization of Jews' putative world-historical importance as the inventors of monotheism could even be seen as an implicit
attack on Shternberg's lengthy 1924 article "Problems of Jewish National
Psychology," which explored the interplay of "biological" and cultural
factors in the formation of Jewish national character.[39]

This theoretical discussion was followed by a practical program for
the organization of Jewish ethnographic exhibits in the Soviet Union.
Pul'ner's concrete proposals reflected a larger debate that had been taking
place among scholars and officials regarding the proper conceptualization
and function of Soviet ethnographic museums.[40] Specifically, he was tapping into a broader discussion about how Soviet minorities lacking their
own titular republics should be ethnographically represented: according
to ethnogeographic principles (i.e., as minorities identified with the republics in which they were located) or according to ethnic principles, with
their own sections or departments.[41] Pul'ner insisted that Jews should be
studied as integral members of their local geographic and socioeconomic
environments. Noting that "Jews living within the borders of the USSR,
like Jews of other countries, do not represent a unified national organ-
ism," Pul'ner divided the Jewish population into five distinct categories:
(1) Western Jews, (2) Georgian Jews, (3) Mountain (Dagestani) Jews,
(4) Crimean Jews, and (5) Central Asian or Bukharan Jews. "We must
never exhibit all Jewish ethnic groups living in the USSR together," he
wrote. "Georgian Jews should be exhibited together with Georgians,
Mountain Jews—in Dagestan, and so forth. It follows that Western Jews,
living in Ukraine, Belorussia, and Russia, should be exhibited in each
of their respective republics."[42] Having made this point, however, Pul'ner
proceeded to devote the core of his article to the ethnographic representation of so-called Western Jews. Indeed, of the various Jewish groups
enumerated by Pul'ner, only the Jews of the former Pale of Settlement
received a detailed historical discussion, beginning with their incorpora-
tion into the Russian Empire in 1772 and continuing through the present.
Despite the fact that Pul'ner was a specialist on the Caucasus region, then,

he implicitly placed Western Jews at the center of his reconceptualization of Soviet Jewish ethnography.

Pul'ner's article, thoroughly saturated with Marxist-Leninist rhetoric about class conflict and the colonialist legacy of bourgeois ethnography, would seem to perfectly fit the template of a cultural revolutionary manifesto. Viewed in light of his earlier training, however, his militant program for the reorganization of Jewish ethnographic museum exhibits arguably echoes many of the themes emphasized by the "ethnographer-populist" Shternberg in his 1923–1924 lectures at the Leningrad Institute of Jewish History and Literature. Pul'ner's historical exposition of Western Jews was methodical, beginning with the Polish annexations and continuing through the formation of the Pale, Nicholas I's military recruitment campaign, the emergence of the Haskalah, pogrom policies and mass emigration, the participation of Jews in the revolutionary movement, and the experiences of Jews during World War I, the February and October Revolutions, and the Civil War era. Although Pul'ner stressed the nature of Soviet Jewish identity as "national in form and socialist in content," he nonetheless placed great emphasis on the details of Jewish religion and tradition. Visitors to his theoretical exhibit would learn about the "class origins" of various customs and holidays and their role in "impeding socialist construction," but they would also come away with substantial knowledge about the Jewish religious calendar and life-cycle events associated with birth, marriage, and death. Similarly, Jewish folk medicine—the central topic of Pul'ner's published scholarship in 1929—would receive significant attention, ostensibly in order to demonstrate its "antiscientific basis" and its threat to public health. Finally, the status of Jewish women and changes in family life—topics on which Shternberg placed great emphasis in his lectures—were also prominently featured in Pul'ner's outline, albeit from the perspective of Soviet modernization. Regardless of whether Pul'ner wrote his article out of political conviction or necessity, his theorized museum exhibit virtually guaranteed that traditional Jewish culture would remain in the public eye. When viewed side by side, then, Pul'ner's manifesto of 1931, despite its repudiation of "ethnographer-populists," resembles something of an ideologically distorted homage to Shternberg's own program for Jewish ethnographic research from 1923 to 1924.

THEORY VERSUS PRACTICE: THE JEWISH SECTION
OF THE STATE MUSEUM OF ETHNOGRAPHY
ON THE EVE OF WORLD WAR

In his 1931 article, Pul'ner categorically rejected the idea that Jews constituted an ethnographic whole. Yet the Jewish Section of the State Museum of Ethnography that he agreed to head in 1937 would be founded
on thoroughly opposing principles.[43] The major research divisions and
exhibit spaces of the SME, formally established in 1934, were organized
largely according to the ethnogeographic principle. In the mid-1930s, a
debate took place among museum personnel regarding the proper ethnographic representation of Jews as an extraterritorial nationality within
the Soviet Union. Just as Pul'ner had done in his 1931 article, administrators discussed whether Soviet Jews should be represented collectively in
their own museum division, or as constituent members of their respective republics. This conversation was prompted by a number of concerns,
including the establishment of the JAR, which raised the possibility that
Jews deserved their own ethnographic department on administrative-
territorial grounds. Indeed, one participant in the discussion ventured
that the JAR would likely be elevated to republic status in the near future,
which argued in favor of a single Jewish Section.[44]

Another rationale offered in favor of consolidating a single Jewish Section was that Jews throughout the Soviet Union were united historically
by the ties of religion, even if religious observance was itself "irrelevant"
at the present time. Language as a constitutive element of national identity
was also cited as an important factor: Yiddish, it was reasoned, was spoken
by the vast majority of the USSR's Jewish population.[45] That this criterion marginalized non-Ashkenazic Jewish populations did not seem to
concern participants in the discussion, suggesting that the ethnographic
representation of "European" Jews was of utmost importance at this time.

While the finer points of Bolshevik nationality theory were debated,
it was ultimately pragmatic financial and political considerations that determined the museum's decision to consolidate Jews under the umbrella
of one Jewish Section. Chief among these were the prospect of obtaining
funding from Soviet Jewish agricultural organizations (the creation of a
Jewish Section would "flatter" the nationalist sentiment of Jewish orga-

nizations, one administrator argued) and the expectation that the JAR would advance from the status of an autonomous region to a republic, thereby justifying the eventual transition of the proposed Jewish Section to a full-fledged Jewish Department.[46] Last, but certainly not least, was the museum administration's unease at the prospect of having to publicly reiterate the history of Jewish suffering under the tsarist autocracy in every single republican division of the museum that happened to feature a Jewish minority. In the end, the reluctance of museum personnel to have to thank Comrades Stalin and Molotov repeatedly in multiple exhibits for their benevolent policies toward Jews seems to have been a particularly salient factor.[47] After much internal debate, then, a Jewish Section (not yet a department) was officially established with the mandate to represent all Jewish populations within the Soviet Union.

Yet another probable factor in the consolidation of a single Jewish Section was the growing influence of Nazi anthropology and racialist claims about the inferiority of the peoples of the USSR.[48] As head of the new section, Pul'ner was initially charged with curating an exhibit showcasing the construction of the JAR "as the creation of the Great October Socialist Revolution and of Leninist-Stalinist nationalities policy." Midway through the planning process, however, Pul'ner was informed that the exhibit would need to address the achievements of socialist construction for Jews throughout the USSR, and not only in the JAR. Within a very short period of time, Pul'ner and his staff had to assemble an exhibit intended to impress upon Soviet viewers the accomplishments of Soviet nationality policy for all Jews.[49] In all likelihood, the ubiquitous demonization of the *Ostjude* in Nazi propaganda also influenced Pul'ner's conceptualization of the exhibit: in searching for appropriate artifacts, for example, he expressed a particular eagerness to obtain objects of Jewish material and folk culture that would serve to disprove antisemitic stereotypes that Jews lacked innate cultural creativity.[50]

The exhibit that opened to the public in March 1939, "The Jews in Tsarist Russia and the USSR," encompassed the period 1881–1939, and consisted of over fifty displays featuring photographs, maps, lithographs, statistical charts, and ethnographic dioramas. Consistent with the Soviet ideological formula for ethnographic exhibits, the Jewish Section's display was organized as a "darkness to light" narrative, with two segments devoted, respectively, to Jewish oppression at the hands of the autocracy, and Jewish liberation under the benevolent policies of the Soviet state.[51] While the second half of the exhibit, showcasing the advancement of Jews under Communism, was the exhibit's ideological center of gravity, special emphasis was placed in the first, prerevolutionary half on Jewish workers' "folk creativity" and "optimism" as expressed in crafts, ornamentation, and the *Purim-shpil*. As the exhibit's detailed guidebook stated in a passage entitled "Culture and Folk Creativity," "The rich treasures of Jewish folk art and culture expose at the very root the claims of fascist cannibals that the Jewish people lack any aptitude for great art and craftsmanship."[52] While the announcement of the Nazi-Soviet Nonaggression Pact roughly five months after the opening must have been a shock to Pul'ner and his staff, it did not lead to a substantive alteration of the central narrative, and the exhibit remained on display until June 1941.

While Pul'ner and his team managed to acquire a range of artifacts from various Jewish collections throughout the Soviet Union for the purpose of staging the exhibit, and drew extensively on the An-sky collections for the first section of the exhibit, he was deeply concerned about flaws and gaps in the exhibit narrative, many of which were pointed out to him in visitor comment books.[53] As he wrote in a memo outlining plans for 1940, "This valuable material, the criticism of the masses, the voice of the people, has not been given proper attention up to now; these visitor comments are inexhaustible sources for the rectification of inadequacies and errors, and for the Museum's planning of future work on expeditions and exhibits."[54] Both before and after the exhibit opened, Pul'ner complained repeatedly to the director of the SME that the inventory of the Jewish Section was "underdeveloped" compared to other divisions. Pul'ner's memoranda regarding the state of the Jewish Section, written between 1938 and 1941, raise intriguing questions about how he perceived his role as a very public custodian of Soviet Jewish ethnographic knowledge. He was clearly exasperated by the experience of having to curate a major exhibit while simultaneously searching for artifacts ("That almost all the necessary items had to be acquired and studied in the process of building the exposition is, of course, completely abnormal").[55] Notwithstanding the riches of the An-sky collection, which Pul'ner himself had catalogued as a graduate student, he referred to the existing inventory as "random" and expressed frustration that he had to construct the Jewish exposition "literally from scratch."[56]

In a memo from March 1940, he summed up the status of Soviet Jewish ethnography as thoroughly deficient, particularly from the perspective of material culture: "The ethnographic study of Jews in the USSR is a relatively new area. Before the revolution there were no cadres of Jewish ethnographers (indeed, there are barely any now). Before the revolution, and with some rare exceptions after the revolution, the ethnographic study of Jews was conducted in a dilettantish fashion by nonspecialists, in fits and starts, randomly and superficially, by lone amateurs and travelers. In this way, research was carried out one-sidedly, involving primarily the collection of religious artifacts and folklore."[57] The collections of the State Museum of Ethnography, in his view, included "almost nothing reflecting the material culture of Jewish life (housing, utensils, clothing, food, modes of transportation, handicrafts, folk art, etc.)." As a result of the withering away of the old way of life, he added, many ethnographically and historically valuable artifacts of Jewish culture had "perished" and were irretrievably lost to scholarship: "Their remnants are dying out and disappearing with unbelievable rapidity."[58]

The fleeting nature of time thus emerges as a central theme in Pul'ner's ruminations to the museum administration. Not only was serious Jewish ethnographic research started "late" relative to the study of other groups, but the very speed of Sovietization that Pul'ner was supposed to champion in his museum exhibits was undermining his scholarly mission as an ethnographer. Indeed, he stated explicitly that valuable ethnographic material had been lost forever precisely because of the relentless momentum of "the socialist reconstruction of the life and culture of the Jewish population of the USSR." At the same time, he insisted that even the process of socialist construction among Jews itself was poorly documented, adding, "All of this places a special responsibility upon the State Museum of Ethnography and its Jewish Section to accelerate [*forsirovat'*] the ethnographic study of the Jews of the USSR."[59]

Between 1939 and 1940 Pul'ner made some limited progress in collecting supplementary ethnographic artifacts within Soviet Ukraine, but he complained bitterly about unpredictable financing and logistical support from the SME, which hampered his ability to plan expeditions and hire

FIGURE 6.1

I. M. Pul'ner, head of the Jewish Section of the State Museum
of Ethnography (1941). From the collection of the Russian
Museum of Ethnography, St. Petersburg, Russia.

support staff.[60] The conclusion of the Nazi-Soviet Nonaggression Pact and the subsequent Soviet invasion of eastern Poland, however, opened up a whole new avenue of research. While the Soviet regime depicted the invasion of eastern Poland as an act of liberation intended to unify historically Ukrainian and Belorussian lands,[61] for Pul'ner the annexation seems to have represented an exceedingly brief second chance to study aspects of traditional Jewish life that in his view no longer existed after two decades of Soviet rule. Although Pul'ner had ready access to the "traditional" artifacts of Jewish culture acquired by An-sky, these were largely religious in nature, and Pul'ner seemed to want something else: traditional Jewish culture in the present. Indeed, the possibility that the Soviet occupation represented something even more tantalizing—the opportunity to observe a vibrant secular Jewish Polish culture—is something that Pul'ner could not have articulated officially without attracting negative attention.[62]

In a memo dated June 4, 1941, Pul'ner outlined ethnographic research plans for the coming months. Time was critical: the process of Sovietization in the annexed territories was underway and there was a small window of opportunity to step back in time, as it were, ethnographically.[63] "It is proposed that fieldwork for the present year should be carried out in the western regions of Ukraine and part of Belorussia," Pul'ner wrote. "This is not incidental given that these locales have preserved to the present day most ethnographic materials on Jews, which, outside these areas, have to a significant degree disappeared, or been preserved as relics." Pul'ner was especially interested in acquiring specimens of Jewish clothing and ornamentation, since "the collection of clothes in the Section's inventory is paltry and the creation of such a collection constitutes an urgent and relevant undertaking. A delay in the collection of clothing, given its rapid disappearance and its replacement with European clothing, is akin to death for ethnography." Pul'ner saw a similar opportunity to collect information on Jewish housing, about which he added, "Practically speaking, nothing has been done up until the present time. And this question is the most relevant task of Jewish ethnography."[64] Pul'ner's interest in housing encompassed the study and collection of domestic utensils, artistic handicrafts, and folk architecture. "Th[is] latter question," he wrote, "is particularly important in connection with my refutation in 1939 of antisemitic and clerical tenets about the absence of civic architecture and art among Jews."[65] Pul'ner's memo also included a proposal to survey one or two "collectives" undergoing Sovietization. He identified L'vov, Tarnopol', Stanislavov, and Rovno and their respective vicinities as areas targeted for research (according to Pul'ner, the route had been recommended by a "senior researcher of the Jews of Western Ukraine," one Comrade Gol'dshtein, based in L'vov).[66]

In addition to fieldwork in the annexed territories, Pul'ner had already formulated an ambitious research agenda within the Soviet Union proper. Long-term projected plans included maintaining and updating the exhibit "The Jews in Tsarist Russia and the USSR"; the creation of a systematic bibliography of materials on Jewish ethnography in Yiddish, Hebrew, Russian, and other languages; the registration, inventory, and photographing of Jewish artifacts in the museum's holdings, which had been postponed in the rush to construct the 1939 exhibit; and the publication of an album of "The Jews in Tsarist Russia and the USSR" which would be used in conducting mass political-educational work among the Jewish populations of the western regions of Ukraine and Belorussia in order to "demonstrate the achievements in the socialist reconstruction of the life and culture of the Jews of the USSR."[67] Pul'ner also intended to publish popular brochures based on four specific themes explored in the exhibit: "The Prerevolutionary Shtetl," "Popular Theater: The *Purimshpil*," "Klezmer: Jewish Folk Musicians," and "The Jewish Woman in Tsarist Russia and the USSR."[68] He was particularly interested in creating a new exhibit devoted to the latter topic, which would both "show the achievements in the sphere of socialist reconstruction in the life of Jewish women in the USSR" and stimulate ongoing ethnographic research. This proposed exhibit, he argued, had a special political significance for the "socialist alteration of the life of Jewish women in the western regions of Ukraine and Belorussia," which is why he intended to develop it as a traveling exhibit.[69] In connection with plans for a special exhibit devoted to the ethnography of Jewish women, Pul'ner also hoped to draw on his graduate-level dissertation research to produce a special study on the subject "Marriage Among Jews in Tsarist Russia."[70] Throughout, Pul'ner stressed the need to study and act on the "scores" of visitor comments, "to which the museum, as an institution of mass political enlightenment and a servant of the people, is obligated to closely heed."[71]

Pul'ner estimated that his first expedition in annexed Poland would last for two and a half months. The anticipated departure date was to have been sometime between June 20 and June 25, 1941. On June 22, a little over two weeks after Pul'ner wrote this plan, the Nazis invaded the Soviet Union. The collections of the former Jewish Section would not be on view to the public again until the post-Soviet period.

SALVAGE ETHNOGRAPHY: BETWEEN MARXISM AND JUDAISM?

When he died at the age of forty-two during the Siege of Leningrad, Pul'ner left behind a host of unfinished projects, including his manuscript on the Jewish life cycle. On the eve of war, his vision for the Jewish Section of the SME was one of expansion rather than contraction: "The Jews in Tsarist Russia and the USSR" was still on view to the public, and he had plans to build the collection and add new displays. Despite his ongoing frustrations with the museum administration, his ambitious agenda implies confidence that basic institutional support would be forthcoming.[72]

Given Pul'ner's quest to study the Jewish life cycle and his liberal borrowing from the 1912 questionnaire in his unpublished notes, it is reasonable to ask whether or not he saw himself as a thwarted successor to An-sky. While his militant 1931 article in *Soviet Ethnography* suggests a politically savvy careerist, it is equally possible that he viewed himself as a cultural caretaker, salvaging and protecting what he could of Jewish ethnography while upholding a politically correct facade. When he fiercely insisted in memoranda to museum personnel that the "voice of the people"[73] (i.e., the visitor comments) must be heeded, it is possible that in these strikingly candid criticisms—perhaps a faint echo of An-sky's celebrated "Oral Torah"—Pul'ner had found a way to challenge the official narrative he had himself crafted.

Ultimately, however, the desire to ascertain whether or not Pul'ner was tragically torn "between two worlds," those of Judaism and Marxism, may say more about post–Cold War scholarly agendas than about the man himself.[74] After all, Pul'ner was seventeen years old at the time of the Russian Revolutions, and his educational and professional trajectory unfolded in an extraordinarily volatile and confusing political climate. If not a "true believer," he may very well have accepted the notion that Jewish assimilation into the Soviet "family of nations" was inevitable and desirable, and that the task of the ethnographer was to carefully preserve the "survivals" of Jewish civilization for purely scientific study. As someone involved in both bourgeois and Marxist-Leninist scholarly endeavors through the end of the 1920s, he eludes easy categorization both intellectually and ideologically.

Still, though many questions about Pul'ner remain unanswered, it is clear from archival records that he was acutely conscious of An-sky's legacy. Separated from An-sky by a generation, as well as by radically different institutional and ideological conditions, he shared his predecessor's fear that the window of opportunity for "salvage" was rapidly closing. The breadth and intensity of Pul'ner's various projects, which included ethnographic fieldwork, museum curatorship, bibliographic research, and administrative planning, seem consistent with someone trying to accomplish a serious cultural project within a finite amount of time. Unlike An-sky, however, Pul'ner was deeply implicated in the Stalinist system. In his articulation of Soviet-occupied Poland as Jewishly pristine terrain awaiting ethnographic excavation, his status as both agent and object of Soviet imperialism expresses itself most poignantly: a cynical act of aggression on a grand geopolitical scale inspires a scholar to plan a hitherto forbidden border-crossing in order to partake of the spoils of war, one Jew metaphorically "stealing" from another to replenish cultural treasures. In planning this act of salvage, moreover, Pul'ner was aware that he would simultaneously have to use the propagandistic tools of ethnography to promote Sovietization in the annexed territories.

In his last publication, "Questions of Jewish Ethnography," Pul'ner's mentor Lev Shternberg had cryptically remarked, "If [An-sky] has not found a successor, it is only because those who would like to continue his work do not know how."[75] In suggesting that Jewish ethnography had effectively ended with An-sky, was Shternberg alluding to a lack of qualifications among the current generation of scholars, or to the sheer political impossibility of carrying on such a legacy under Soviet conditions? The nature of the Jewish "ethnographic impulse" had changed radically since the time of An-sky's famed expedition into the Pale of Settlement. Even in the four years between Shternberg's lectures to a rapt graduate-student audience at the Leningrad Institute of Jewish History and Literature and the posthumous publication of his last article, much had changed. Ideology, always a constant companion of ethnography, now had behind it the power of the one-party state and a universalizing, transformational ideology. Roughly a decade later, when Pul'ner was appointed director of the Jewish Section of the SME, the ideological stakes were even greater. The politicization of ethnography in an era of fascism made Pul'ner's task all the more contradictory: faced with the challenge of using ethnography and folklore to refute Nazi claims of Jewish cultural inferiority, he also had to operate within a system dedicated to cultural homogenization. With the full implications of the Nazi threat still obscure, Pul'ner's plans for traveling ethnographic exhibits—though couched in predictable Marxist-Leninist rhetoric—may have represented a creative attempt at a compromise, a way to temporarily escape the center for the periphery in order to "go to the people" with less institutionalized mediation and supervision.

NOTES

I would like to thank the Russian Ethnographic Museum and the St. Petersburg branch of the Russian Academy of Sciences for access to the archival records on which this chapter is based, as well as the International Research and Exchanges Board (IREX) and the Memorial Foundation for Jewish Culture for providing the financial support that made this research possible. I am grateful to the anonymous reviewers, as well as to Mikhail Krutikov and Alexander Ivanov, for helpful comments and suggestions. Finally, I thank participants in the 2014–2015 Frankel Institute for Advanced Judaic Studies at the University of Michigan for a fruitful discussion of this chapter in its final stages.

1. See Ben-Cion Pinchuk, *Shtetl Jews under Soviet Rule: Eastern Poland on the Eve of the Holocaust* (Oxford: Basil Blackwell, 1990); and Jan T. Gross, *Revolution from Abroad: The Soviet Conquest of Poland's Western Ukraine and Western Belorussia,* exp. ed. (Princeton, NJ: Princeton University Press, 2002).

2. I. M. Pul'ner, "Plan komandirovki 1941 g. v zapadnye oblasti Ukrainy po izucheniiu i sboru materialov po etnografii evreev," June 4, 1941, Archives of the Russian Ethnographic Museum (REM), St. Petersburg, f. 2, op. 5, d. 49, l. 1. This document will be discussed in more detail below.

3. See Robert Weinberg, "Purge and Politics in the Periphery: Birobidzhan in 1937," *Slavic Review* 52, no. 1 (Spring 1993): 13–27.

4. On the A. E. Ratner gymnasium, see Hirsz Abramowicz, *Profiles of a Lost World: Memoirs of East European Jewish Life before World War II,* ed. Dina Abramowicz and Jeffrey Shandler, trans. Eva Zeitlin Dobkin (Detroit: Wayne State University Press, 1999), 158–159.

5. For more on this phenomenon, see Gabriele Freitag, *Nächstes Jahr in Moskau!: Die Zuwanderung von Juden in die sowjetische Metropole 1917–1932* (Göttingen: Vandenhoeck &

Ruprecht, 2004); and Yuri Slezkine, *The Jewish Century* (Princeton, NJ: Princeton University Press, 2004).

6. See Terry Martin, *The Affirmative Action Empire: Nations and Nationalism in the Soviet Union, 1923–1939* (Ithaca, NY: Cornell University Press, 2001).

7. On Soviet class categories, see Sheila Fitzpatrick, "Ascribing Class: The Construction of Social Identity in Soviet Russia," *Journal of Modern History* 65, no. 4 (December 1993): 745–770.

8. See Aaron Vinkovetskii, "Dos lebn un di arbet fun an etnograf," *Sovetish heymland* 12 (1975): 162.

9. In his CV, on file in the personnel archives of the former Saltykov-Shchedrin State Public Library in Leningrad (dated 1931, with additional material dated November 1935), Pul'ner indicates that he voluntarily withdrew from this Jewish "nationalistic" sports organization. His personnel file is accessible at the Russian National Library in St. Petersburg (Arkh. RNB), f. 10/1, l. 8. For a less detailed published version, see Ts. I. Grin and L. A. Shilov, eds., *Sotrudniki Rossiiskoi natsional'noi biblioteki: Deiateli nauki i kul'tura; Biograficheskii slovar'*, vol. 2, *Rossisskaia publichnaia biblioteka—Gosudarstvennaia publichnaia biblioteka v Leningrade 1918–1930* (St. Petersburg: Izd-vo Rossiiskoi Natsional'noi Biblioteki, 1999), 525–527. I thank Viktor Kel'ner for bringing the personnel file to my attention.

10. I. Pul'ner and D. Bentsionov, *Baveglekhe un sportive masn-shpiln in shtetl* (Moscow: Farlag Shul un Bukh, 1925). Featuring sports activities with names such as "Reds and Whites," "Wolf and Sheep," and "Attack," this publication sought to inculcate socialist collectivism, physical fitness, and a martial spirit among young and—based on the illustrations—predominantly male Jews.

11. I. M. Pul'ner, personnel materials for the State Museum of Ethnography, March 15, 1938–August 26, 1941, REM, f. 1/f. 2, op. 3, d. 188, l. 10b. Pul'ner's earlier Zionist affiliations require further research.

12. For information about Shternberg, see Sergei Kan's contribution to this volume, as well as his biography, *Lev Shternberg: Anthropologist, Russian Socialist, Jewish Activist* (Lincoln: University of Nebraska Press, 2009). On Bogoraz, see Sergei Kan, "My Old Friend in a Dead-End of Empiricism and Skepticism: Bogoraz, Boas and the Politics of Soviet Anthropology of the Late 1920s–Early 1930s," in *Histories of Anthropology Annual*, ed. Regna Darnell and Frederic W. Gleach, vol. 2 (Lincoln: University of Nebraska Press, 2006).

13. For a discussion of Shternberg's role in the shaping the curriculum, see Kan, *Lev Shternberg*, chap. 7.

14. E. Airapet'iants, P. Orlenko, and E. Shchapova, "Sviditel'stvo," July 19, 1936, REM, f. 1/f. 2, op. 3, d. 188.

15. See Francine Hirsch, *Empire of Nations: Ethnographic Knowledge and the Making of the Soviet Union* (Ithaca, NY: Cornell University Press, 2005); as well as Yuri Slezkine, *Arctic Mirrors: Russia and the Small Peoples of the North* (Ithaca, NY: Cornell University Press, 1994). Soviet populations were also categorized as either "western" or "eastern," terms that denoted perceptions of developmental distinction more than geographic distribution. See Martin, *The Affirmative Action Empire*, 23.

16. On museum exhibits, see Hirsch, *Empire of Nations*, chap. 5.

17. On the history of the *lishentsy*, or "disenfranchised" elements of Soviet society, see Golfo Alexopoulos, *Stalin's Outcasts: Aliens, Citizens, and the Soviet State, 1926–1936*

(Ithaca, NY: Cornell University Press, 2003). Pul'ner undoubtedly chose his words very carefully when describing his family's "social origins" on personnel forms, as any negative associations with the category *lishentsy* would have limited his educational and professional opportunities. I thank Alexander Ivanov for highlighting this point.

18. "Instruktsiia dlia obsledovaniia evreiskogo naseleneiia v etnograficheskom i ekonomicheskom i sotsial'nom otnosheniakh. Iz zapisei studentov na lektsiiakh, chitannykh v Leningradskom Institute Evreiskoi istorii i literatury professorom L. Ia. Shteinbergom [*sic*] v 1923/24 uchebn. godu," Russian State Archive of Sociopolitical History (RGASPI), Moscow, f. 272, op. 1, d. 532, ll. 1–9.

19. Lev Shternberg, "Problema evreiskoi etnografii," *Evreiskaia starina* 12 (1928): 11–16. Significantly, this article was published in one of the last issues of *Evreiskaia starina*, the journal of the Jewish Historical-Ethnographic Society, just before the JHES's closure.

20. For Pul'ner's reference to the original purpose of the expeditions as the study of Western Jews, see "Otzyvy E. Kagarova, V. Struve, V. Bank, I. Meshchaninova, A. Genko o deiatel'nosti i nauchnykh trudakh I. M. Pul'nera; zhizneopisanie; spisok nauchnykh trudov; perechen' ekspeditsii," July 5, 1935–November 14, 1935, REM, f. 9, op. 2, d. 35, l. 3.

21. I. M. Pul'ner, personnel records for the State Public Library in Leningrad, May 5, 1935, Arkh. RNB, f. 10/1.

22. See I. M. Pul'ner, "Iz zhizni goroda Gomela," in *Evreiskoe mestechko revoliutsii: Ocherki*, ed. V. G. Tan-Bogoraz (Moscow-Leningrad: Gosudarstvennoe Izdatel'stvo, 1926), 157–196. Given that the student contributions were not exclusively concerned with the shtetl as defined in contemporary Bolshevik discourse, the title of the published volume was not entirely precise. One study, for example, addressed an agricultural colony, and Pul'ner himself observed that Gomel had long ago transitioned from a shtetl to a major provincial center. It is possible that Bogoraz chose the title *The Jewish Shtetl in Revolution* to parallel the theme of socioeconomic transformation in the peasant village emphasized in his other edited volumes of student research. For more details about the expeditions and the resulting publication, see Deborah Yalen, "Documenting the 'New Red Kasrilevke': Shtetl Ethnography as Revolutionary Narrative," *East European Jewish Affairs* 37, no. 3 (2007): 353–375. On shifting ideological perceptions of the shtetl, see Deborah Yalen, "Tak nazyvaemoe 'evreiskoe' mestechko: Shtetl, bol'shevistskaia ideologiia i sovetskaia etnografiia v mezhvoennyi period," *Novoe literaturnoe obozrenie* 102 (June 2010): 145–157.

23. Pul'ner to Shternberg, July 27, 1927, St. Petersburg Branch of the Archive of the Russian Academy of Sciences (PFA RAN), f. 282, op. 2, d. 243, l. 10b.

24. An-sky's untimely death in 1920 prevented him from retrieving these articles, and they were eventually nationalized by the Bolshevik regime. The collection was later transferred to the State Museum of Ethnography in 1934. For an overview of communications between the JHES and the State Russian Museum regarding these artifacts, see Evgeniia Pevzner, "The Story of One Collection," *Pinkas: Annual of the Culture and History of East European Jewry* 2 (2008): 120–171. On the circumstances of An-sky's flight from Soviet Russia in 1918, see Gabriella Safran, *Wandering Soul: The Dybbuk's Creator, S. An-sky* (Cambridge, MA: Belknap Press of Harvard University Press, 2010).

25. On the original questionnaire, see Nathaniel Deutsch, *The Jewish Dark Continent: Life and Death in the Russian Pale of Settlement* (Cambridge, MA: Harvard University Press, 2011). For an example of Pul'ner's field notes drawing on the An-sky questionnaire, see I. Pul'ner, "Materialy ekspeditsii v Belorussiiu," July–August 1930, REM, f. 2, op. 5,

d. 12. For Pul'ner's dissertation, see "Dissertatsiia I. M. Pul'nera, 'Svadebnye obriady u evreev,'" n.d., REM, f. 9, op. 2, l. 9.

26. See V. V. Struve and D. A. Solovei, "V komitet po delam vysshei shkoly," July 7, 1939, REM, f. 1/f. 2, op. 3, d. 188, l. 10. On Pul'ner's dissertation, see Evgeniia Khazdan, "Evreiskaia svad'ba v dissertatsii I. M. Pul'nera," in *Krug zhizni v slavianskoi i evreiskoi kul'turnoi traditsii: Sbornik statei; Akademicheskaia seriia, vypusk 49,* ed. O. V. Belova (Moscow: Sefer, 2014), 207–222.

27. J. Pulner, "Zur volkskunde der georgischen Juden," *Mitteilungen zur Jüdischen Volkskunde* 31–32 (1929): 60–65.

28. Iosyp Pul'ner, "Obriady ï povir'ia, spolucheni z vahitnoiu, porodileiu ï narozhden-tsem u zhydiv (materiialy do porivnial'noho vyvchenyia narodnoï medytsyny ï fol'kloru u zhydiv)," *Etnohrafichnyï visnyk* 8 (1929): 100–114. For Pul'ner's reference to material col-lected in 1927 in Zaverezh'e (BSSR), see 103n2.

29. This exhibition, which was organized under the guidance of Vladimir Bogoraz, would become the basis for the State Museum of the History of Religion.

30. See, for example, the bibliographic material compiled by Pul'ner in his article "Itogi i zadachi izucheniia kavkazkikh (gruzinskikh i gorskikh) evreev," *Sovetskaia etnografiia,* no. 4–5 (1936): 105–121.

31. Pul'ner, personnel records for the State Public Library in Leningrad.

32. Also known as the "Revolution from Above," the "Great Break" refers to Stalin's radical shift from the New Economic Policy to a program of accelerated industrialization and mass agricultural collectivization. This process was accompanied by a "cultural revo-lution" which purged institutions of old "bourgeois specialists" and replaced them with politically loyal personnel.

33. The term *narodnosti* had been used by imperial ethnographers to denote "people" (as in *Volk*), but it took on additional nuances within the context of Soviet nationality policy. For a discussion of the evolving relationship between the classificatory terms *narodnosti* and *natsional'nosti,* see Hirsch, *Empire of Nations.*

34. See, for instance, various meeting minutes recorded by Pul'ner in 1931, PFA-RAN, f. 135, op. 1, d. 244.

35. On the reorganization of the museum system, see Hirsch, *Empire of Nations,* chap. 5.

36. While Pul'ner's 1929 contribution to the *Ethnographic Herald* of the Ukrainian Academy of Sciences did stress mutual cultural influences between Jewish and Slavic populations—a theme he would emphasize in far more dogmatic terms in his 1931 ar-ticle—there was little overt political rhetoric in the earlier article.

37. I. M. Pul'ner, "Voprosy organizatsii evreiskikh etnograficheskikh muzeev i evrei-skikh otdelov pri obshchikh etnograficheskikh muzeiakh," *Sovetskaia etnografiia,* no. 3–4 (1931): 156–163. It bears noting that around the same time, Meir Wiener, the head of the Section of Ethnography and Folklore at the Kiev Institute of Jewish Proletarian Culture, was formulating his own theories regarding the task of Soviet folkloric studies. Though beyond the scope of this chapter, a comparison of Wiener's and Pul'ner's activities in Kiev and Leningrad, respectively, merits further exploration. On Wiener, see Mikhail Krutikov, *From Kabbalah to Class Struggle: Expressionism, Marxism, and Yiddish Litera-ture in the Life and Work of Meir Wiener* (Stanford, CA: Stanford University Press, 2011).

38. Although Bogoraz harbored little interest in traditional Judaism and was trying at this time to refashion himself as a Marxist ethnographer, he had previously been vulner-

able to charges of Jewish nationalism in the Soviet Yiddish press. His introduction to the 1926 collection *The Jewish Shtetl in Revolution,* for example, was so preoccupied with pogrom statistics that it was dismissed by critics as "Zionist whining." See Yalen, "Documenting the 'New Red Kasrilevke,'" 367.

39. See Lev Shternberg, "Problema evreiskoi natsional'noi psikhologii (doklad v Evreiskom Istoriko-Etnograficheskom Obshchestve)," *Evreiskaia starina* 11 (1924): 5–44; and Kan, *Lev Shternberg,* 314–320.

40. See Hirsch, *Empire of Nations,* chap. 5.

41. The specific case of Jews had in fact been raised in previous discussions among museum personnel in the late 1920s. See Hirsch, *Empire of Nations,* 195.

42. Pul'ner, "Voprosy organizatsiia," 157. Although Pul'ner was grounding his argument in the ideological framework of Bolshevik nationality policy, it is important to remember that as a former affiliate of the J H E S, he would have already been exposed to discussions about Jewish plurality within the former Russian Empire from a very different political perspective. For more on the J H E S's approach to non-Ashkenazic Jewish populations within the Russian Empire, see Jeffrey Veidlinger, *Jewish Public Culture in the Late Russian Empire* (Bloomington: Indiana University Press, 2009), 274–282.

43. The State Museum of Ethnography in Leningrad was established in 1934 after its separation from the State Russian Museum. In 1948, it received collections from the Moscow Museum of the Peoples of the USSR, and was renamed the State Museum of Ethnography of the Peoples of the USSR.

44. D. Pozdneev, "Vozniknovenie evreiskoi sektsii v sostave G M E (po pamiati)," November 26, 1936, R E M, f. 2, op. 5, d. 22, l. 30b; and D. Pozdneev, "Postanovka evreiskogo otdela v G E M," January 1, 1937, R E M, f. 2, op. 5, d. 22, l. 11. The author is presumably the Orientalist Dmitrii Matveevich Pozdneev.

45. Pozdneev, "Postanovka evreiskogo otdela v G E M," l. 8.

46. As it turned out, the Society for the Settlement of Jewish Toilers on the Land (O Z E T) was liquidated in May 1938, and many of its archival materials were acquired by Pul'ner for the Jewish Section of the S M E. On the history of O Z E T, see Arkadi Zeltser, "Society for the Settlement of Jewish Toilers on the Land," trans. Yisrael Cohen, in *The Y I V O Encyclopedia of Jews in Eastern Europe,* accessed May 31, 2015, http://www.yivoencyclopedia.org/article.aspx/Society_for_the_Settlement_of_Jewish_Toilers_on_the_Land.

47. Pozdneev, "Postanovka evreiskogo otdela v G E M," l. 12.

48. For an overview of Soviet ethnography in the era of rising fascism, see Hirsch, *Empire of Nations,* chap. 6.

49. I. Pul'ner and M. Shakhnovich, "Iz opyta stroitel'stva ekspozitsii," 1940, R E M, f. 2, op. 5, d. 48, l. 20–21.

50. Pul'ner reflects on this in memoranda written after 1939. See, for example, Pul'ner, "Plan komandirovki 1941 g.," l. 2.

51. For a discussion of how this exhibit exemplified the "musealization" of the Jewish Soviet experience, see Alexander Ivanov, "'Evrei v tsarskoi Rossii i v S S S R'—Vystavka dostizhenii evreiskogo khoziastvennogo i kul'turnogo stroitel'stva v strane sovetov," *Novoe literaturnoe obozrenie* 102 (June 2010): 158–182. For the English translation, see Alexander Ivanov, "The Exhibition 'Jews in Tsarist Russia and in the USSR' and the Closure of the Jewish Modernisation Project in the Soviet Union, 1937–1941," *East European Jewish Affairs* 43, no. 1 (2013): 43–61.

52. Gosudarstvennyi Muzei Etnografii, *Evrei v tsarskoi Rossii i v sssr: Kratkii puto-voditel po vystavke* (Leningrad: Izdanie Gosudarstvennogo Muzeia Etnografii, 1939), 16.

53. See, for example, "Kniga otzyvov i pozhelanii po ekspozitsii 'Evrei v tsarskoi Ros-sii i v sssr'" for March 14, 1939–March 12, 1940, rem, f. 9, op. 3, d. 6; and for March 29, 1940–June 12, 1941, rem, f. 9, op. 3, d. 7. For a discussion of selected visitor comments, see Ivanov, "'Evrei v tsarskoi Rossii i v sssr,'" 172–176; and Deborah Yalen, "Red Kasrilevke: Ethnographies of Economic Transformation in the Soviet Shtetl, 1917–1939" (PhD diss., University of California, Berkeley, 2007), chap. 5. On the ideological function of visi-tor comment books in general at the State Museum of Ethnography, see Hirsch, *Empire of Nations*, 211–215.

54. I. M. Pul'ner, "Plan raboty evreiskoi sektsii gme na 1940 g.," January 21, 1940, rem, f. 2, op. 5, d. 47, l. 3.

55. Pul'ner and Shakhnovich, "Iz opyta stroitel'stva ekspozitsii," l. 20.

56. I. M. Pul'ner, "Plan komandirovki 1941 g.," l. 1.

57. I. M. Pul'ner, "Otchet I. M. Pul'nera o komandirovke k ukrainskim evreiam v g.g. Berdichev, Bershadi, Odessa, Kiev Ukrainskoi ssr c 27 iiulia–10 sentiabria 1939," March 25, 1940, rem, f. 9, op. 1, d. 25, l. 1.

58. Ibid.

59. Ibid., l. 2.

60. Ibid.

61. For background, see Gross, *Revolution from Abroad*.

62. I am grateful to David Fishman for illuminating this point, which merits further exploration.

63. Ben-Cion Pinchuk speaks of a rapid process of Sovietization among the Jews in the annexed territories. See Pinchuk, *Shtetl Jews under Soviet Rule*. On the Soviet side, how-ever, Alfred Abraham Greenbaum remarks on how the annexation seems to have sparked a "general Jewish cultural revival" among Soviet Jewish scholars working in Minsk. Greenbaum, for instance, cites an article dated April 12, 1941, in the American newspaper *Morgn frayhayt*, reporting on Minsk scholars' plans to research Jewish folklore in western Belorussia. See Alfred Abraham Greenbaum, *Jewish Scholarship and Scholarly Institutions in Soviet Russia, 1918–1953* (Jerusalem: Hebrew University of Jerusalem, Centre for Re-search and Documentation of East European Jewry, 1978), 62, 71.

64. Pul'ner, "Plan komandirovki 1941 g.," l. 1.

65. Ibid., l. 2. This "refutation" was implicit in the exhibit and its guidebook, but it is not clear if Pul'ner published a more explicit statement elsewhere.

66. This is most likely a reference to collector Maksimilian (Mordekhai) Gol'dshtein. For biographical information, see "Gol'dshtein, Maksimilian," *Elektronnaia evreiskaia en-tsiklopediia*, accessed May 24, 2015, http://www.eleven.co.il/article/11252. I thank Mikhail Krutikov for sharing this information.

67. Pul'ner, "Plan raboty evreiskoi sektsii gme na 1940 g.," ll. 1–6. Archival records indicate that the sme was also developing a new exhibit devoted to "the Peoples of West-ern Ukraine and Western Belorussia." Although this exhibit would primarily focus on Ukrainians and Belorussians, Jews are described alongside these two populations as vic-tims oppressed by the Polish nobility. See "Plan ekspozitsii 'Narody zapadnoi Ukrainy i zapadnoi Belorussii' i spisok kollektsionov predmetov," 1939–1940, rem, f. 2, op. 1, d. 730, ll. 11–12.

68. Pul'ner, "Plan raboty evreiskoi sektsii gme na 1940 g.," l. 6.

69. Ibid., ll. 1–2. Notably, Pul'ner intended to use the Yiddish classics of Mendele Moykher-Sforim, Y. L. Peretz, and Sholem Aleichem as sources for this exhibit, suggesting either that he accepted these works as reliable "ethnographic" records of Jewish life, or that their broad acceptance in the Soviet literary canon as politically palatable works of Jewish literature made their inclusion in the source base inevitable. For a discussion of how Yiddish literary representations of the shtetl came to be taken as historical truth, see Dan Miron, *The Image of the Shtetl and Other Studies of Modern Jewish Literary Imagination* (Syracuse, NY: Syracuse University Press, 2001).

70. Pul'ner, "Plan raboty evreiskoi sektsii GME na 1940 g.," l. 3.

71. Pul'ner, "Plan komandirovki 1941 g.," l. 1.

72. See I. M. Pul'ner and E. A. Mil'shtein, "Proizvodstvenno-tematicheskii plan na 1941-i god," January 15, 1941, REM, f. 2, op. 1, d. 833.

73. Pul'ner, "Plan raboty evreiskoi sektsii GME na 1940 g.," l. 3.

74. For a helpful discussion of how scholars conceptualize the relationship of Communist and Jewish identities in the interwar Soviet context, see Krutikov, *From Kabbalah to Class Struggle*.

75. Shternberg, "Problema evreiskoi etnografii," 16.

"Sacred Collection Work"

THE RELATIONSHIP BETWEEN
YIVO AND ITS ZAMLERS

SARAH ELLEN ZARROW

The folklorist Rubinshteyn set out for the fish market to gather
material. He came from a shtetl, as far out as Bialystok, to collect
folklore in the Jerusalem of Lithuania. . . . It was not so easy
for him; but what wouldn't one do for the love of folklore?

—AVROM KARPINOVICH, "Der folklorist"

Avrom Karpinovich, the Vilna-born Yiddish writer whose favorite subject was the city, wrote "Der folklorist" about a fictional
zamler, an avocational collector, for YIVO (Yidisher Visnshaftlekher Institut), the Yiddish Scientific Institute that had been founded in Berlin in
1925 and moved to Vilna two years later. Rubinshteyn, Karpinovich goes
on to tell the reader, "had gotten it into his head that all Vilna speech must
be saved, because if it were lost, God forbid [*kholile*], it would be a great
loss for culture. Due to his love of folklore, he even remained a bachelor.
How many matches they proposed, and good matches, but he refused. At
YIVO, they wanted to set him up with a graduate student, Zelde, an old
maid, a specialist in the history of Jewish food dating back to the twelfth
century."[1] Rubinshteyn refuses this match as well. In the fish market, he
meets and takes up with Khane-Merke, who piques his interest with her
colorful curses. But the relationship sours, as Rubinshteyn does not see

146

Khane-Merke as a whole person, but rather as an ethnographic informant. After she waits for Rubinshteyn to show up for half a day, an acquaintance remarks to Rubinshteyn, "Do you think that Khane-Merke is a sack full of curses and aphorisms, which you can bag together and drag off to write books? Khane-Merke also has a heart!"[2] Khane-Merke leaves Rubinshteyn, and he cannot find the words to explain his feelings for her. He buys a backpack, and hobbles away from Vilna to gather folklore in another city.

Karpinovich's Rubinshteyn is, of course, a send-up, but his characterization speaks to a logical extreme of the zamler type. Rubinshteyn loves "the people," but cannot love a person. To him, everyone is an object for study, and the passion with which he undertakes his *zamlung*, his collection activity, speaks to an intense drive to work on behalf of YIVO. YIVO has trained him well, and he has taken YIVO's aims to a ridiculous extreme. Rubinshteyn was very likely a zamler for YIVO's Ethnographic Commission, originally a part of the institute's Philological Section.[3] Indeed, YIVO was organized into various disciplinary sections: the Philological Section, the Economic-Statistical Section, and the Historical Section all relied heavily on zamlers, who carried out much of their work. These zamlers were long seen as a, if not the, quintessence of Jewish collection activity, particularly in interwar Poland.

In reality, zamlers did not behave like Rubinshteyn, traveling far and wide to serve the organization. Karpinovich's parody is, perhaps unwittingly, as much about YIVO's aims and goals as the individual zamler's. In this chapter, I explore the role of the zamler as both the leadership of YIVO and the zamlers themselves saw it. The relationship between members of the Ethnographic Commission—including folklorists Shloyme Bastomski, N. Khayes (who was also the secretary), N. Weinig, and Nekhame Epshteyn, philologist Max Weinreich, and lexicographer Zalman Reyzen—on the one hand, and the zamler force on the other, was unstable and fraught. It was a product of radically different notions of the place of Jews in interwar Poland, as well as a product of YIVO's own attempt to establish itself as a locus of Jewish identity within Poland as a whole. The Ethnographic Commission's membership and its zamlers frequently "talked past" each other in their correspondence, indicating radically differing aims. In addition to professionalizing a lay zamler corps, YIVO attempted as well to transform the fundamental relationship of urban-dwelling Jews to Jewish tradition. Appealing to the idea of a disappearing heritage, YIVO attempted to forge a relationship between Jewish urban intellectuals and shtetl Jews, albeit one with a critical and scholarly distance. The zamler stood for a new type of Jew, one who drew from heritage while remaining firmly in the modern world.

The Ethnographic Commission was, in a way, an institution in its own right. It had its own executive committee and subsections for, among other areas, music, folklore, history, art, and literature. It also maintained a museum, a library, and archives. Appeals for research went out in *Yedies fun YIVO* (News from YIVO), the institute's newsletter. While other sections of YIVO used zamlers to collect material, none relied on them as heavily as did the Ethnographic Commission.[4]

By the late 1920s, the Ethnographic Commission reported that it had collected over forty thousand individual items, including proverbs, anecdotes, customs, legends, and the like. The Ethnographic Commission clearly took pride in this vast collection, reporting that "the ethnographic holdings of the institute are, due to their scope and variety, among the richest collections of its type. The Ethnographic Commission has a few hundred zamlers and correspondents in Poland and in other countries of Jewish settlements."[5] In addition to the hundreds of zamlers it inspired, the commission included in its circles over five hundred respondents to numerous questionnaires, and counted eighty thousand items in its collection. A planned ethnographic museum had already collected "a substantial number of examples."[6] The museum had prepared, in addition, three monograph volumes, one of which had already been sent to press, on the history of Jewish literature.[7] Not all projects involved the collection of folklore, customs, and sayings, or what is typically considered "ethnography." Literature comprised another important domain for the Ethnographic Commission. The commission curated exhibits devoted to the Yiddish writers Sholem Aleichem and Y. L. Peretz, two writers who had offered a romantic picture of the "folk" that the Ethnographic Commission was eager to display to its zamlers.[8] Literature could prop up zamlung, and vice versa, according to YIVO. The resulting image of the Jewish folk would thus be a rich one, described and delineated in multiple ways.

Zamlung had an expansive meaning for YIVO's Ethnographic Commission. It was important for its scope—for the sheer numbers of items brought in to YIVO—as well as for the raw data it provided for museum exhibits and scholarly works. It was also significant for having brought a large number of people into YIVO's fold, increasing its visibility and spreading knowledge of YIVO's activities.

Who exactly was a zamler? Was he (and correspondence with zamlers in the YIVO archives indicates that zamlung was a predominately male avocation) merely a vehicle to produce real-life examples to reinforce the image of the shtetl Jew as portrayed in literature and art? Or were zamlers expected to challenge these tropes? Were the type and content of material to be collected dictated by explicit or tacit expectations on the part of the Ethnographic Commission? And what, precisely, was the relationship between YIVO and its zamlers, and what does that relationship tell us more broadly about YIVO, particularly its dual function as a social science organization—one that defined and depicted the contemporary Jew—and as a network of practitioners?

The idea of using zamlers for the Ethnographic Commission's work seems to have multiple origins. One of the inspirations for the commission was the S. An-sky Jewish Historical-Ethnographic Society (renamed for An-sky only after his death), founded in Vilna in 1919 as the successor to the Society of Friends of Jewish Antiquity, which was in turn founded in 1913 by Lev Frenkel. In 1939, the society's materials were merged with YIVO's, but it seems that there was substantial overlap in their working relationship before then.

An-sky had died in 1920, and his expeditions provided much of the basis both for the Ethnographic Commission's questionnaires and for the concept of the zamler. An-sky had organized his interviews around a series of questionnaires that traced the life cycle of a Jew, beginning with pregnancy and progressing through birth, childhood, marriage, and finally death. An-sky's questions were designed to explore the rituals and customs that enveloped the totality of the individual Eastern European Jew's life experience.[9] Of course, An-sky believed—and he was not necessarily incorrect—that these customs were fading, and in danger of dying out. This foreboding is reflected in the wording of the questions, which were often prefaced with phrases such as, "In the past, how did people . . . ?" The Ethnographic Commission was concerned both with capturing the "remnant" and with analyzing the processes of modernization, urbanization, and secularization that had created it.[10]

YIVO's questionnaires borrowed much of An-sky's language wholesale, but completely changed the way in which the questions were presented. YIVO's questionnaires came out one at a time, with ten to twenty questions apiece, and were organized thematically, rather than around the totality of a Jewish life. There are questions on holidays, on Jewish-gentile relationships, and on children. This was no accident. While both An-sky and YIVO saw traditional town-based Jewish life as something that was fading away, An-sky still understood his research to be about the totality of a Jew's life, from cradle to grave, something that the ethnographer (or, indeed, a lay zamler) might observe in its whole form. The focus was on what would be understood as traditional, though there were also questions on the modern gymnasium and the impact of enlightenment movements.

YIVO, on the other hand, structured its questionnaires with a specific idea of a zamler in mind, a person whose own experience lay somewhat outside the realm of what he observed. This imagined zamler would certainly be familiar with major holidays and common rituals, but he might not be familiar with some of the (by then) more obscure traditions of Jewish family life, particularly customs that had come to be regarded as more superstitious. The zamler would also likely practice some of the rituals in his own home, and would make reference to common customs and beliefs in his everyday speech. He would not, however, be so immersed in traditional life as to be privy to its nuances, nor would he be expected to spend extended periods of time conducting immersive ethnographic fieldwork. The zamler would have a limited temporal interaction with the informant; he would be more likely to sit down for a brief interview than move in for a month. The questions he would pose, therefore, were shorter and more pointed. Thus, YIVO's questionnaires, though many borrow An-sky's language, take on more bite-sized aspects of Jewish life with little pretense of reconstructing the entire Jewish life cycle.

It seems that originally, YIVO had intended to send out the *anketes,* the questionnaires, via YIVO *bleter,* YIVO's general academic journal. Recipients were originally expected to answer the questions themselves and return their completed questionnaires back to Vilna. In this case, respondents would have engaged in what Nathaniel Deutsch has called "auto-ethnography," improving the ethnographer's self-awareness.[11] By requiring them to reflect upon their own customs as informants rather than as zamlers, YIVO seems to have intended to stimulate among the Jewish youth a deeper knowledge of their own condition. This would serve not only to salvage declining traditions, but also to enable zamlers to construct a bulwark against potential future crises and losses. Thus, the act of zamlung would be generative, not merely preservationist. But this is not how the YIVO-informant relationship operated in practice.

Zamlers instead, perhaps mimicking An-sky, went out to people in their towns or in neighboring towns, and posed the questions to them. They also collected additional data that YIVO did not originally request —stories, sayings, and songs. YIVO's relationship with its zamlers took many forms. YIVO needed its zamlers to serve as intermediaries in a process of collection that would, in the end, produce an image of the Polish Jew.

Correspondence with zamlers indicates, however, that YIVO was also deeply engaged in a process of fashioning the zamler.[12] YIVO's lengthy replies to zamler queries and submissions indicate a great interest in the work of the zamler corps; even very casually written correspondence received replies. In many cases, YIVO wanted to request further work from the zamlers. A December 25, 1929, letter to one zamler, for instance, thanked him for his story "Minyen," which the letter praised as "one of the most beautiful stories in the Hasidic canon."[13] The letter continued by encouraging the zamler to collect more from the same informants.

YIVO often thanked zamlers for their submissions while gently reminding them to follow the professional standards it had outlined, such as recording the names of informants or writing on one side of the paper only. These regulations came directly from YIVO's pamphlet issued to would-be zamlers, *What Exactly Is Jewish Ethnography? A Handbook for Zamlers* (or, as YIVO's own slightly awkward English translation of the title read, *A Vade Mecum for Collectioners*), issued in 1929.[14] "Jewish ethnography" was not defined precisely as a discipline or field that was somehow separate from general ethnography, though the majority of examples and sources used in this handbook were about Jews. Indeed, though there were numerous other ethnographic projects functioning within Poland at the time, not to mention in the Soviet Union and in Germany, this booklet painted a picture of a Jewishly oriented practice, one whose proper object of study was Jews.

As the introduction to the handbook stated, "Up until this point, the activities of the Ethnographic Commission of YIVO have known that there is practically no ready-made zamler; he must be built. A large part of the correspondence that the Ethnographic Commission has overseen has been conducted with the aim of schooling its helpers." The handbook emerged from that correspondence.[15] The commission wrote that the handbook would clarify matters for "older helpers" and would also bring in a lot of new zamlers.[16]

The main concern of the handbook was ostensibly to ease the process of collecting data from the "*folksmentsh.*" An introduction noted that the farmer would look askance at the geologist or the botanist who clipped flowers and collected them in his sack, and likewise would be unenthusiastic about relating a story or singing a song. The hapless zamler would "stand there and not know how to answer the question: 'What's this silliness all about?'"[17] In other words, YIVO's Ethnographic Commission felt the need to equip the zamlers with the scholarly tools to explain their mission and to build trust among their potential informants. For the most part, however, the handbook provided less of a practical guide to ethnographic best practices than a scholarly introduction, complete with short bibliographies (generally of Yiddish- and Russian-language materials), to the craft of ethnography—it included, for instance, sections on groups in anthropological thought, material culture, superstitions, and folk songs. It also included a terminology glossary, to clarify some of the words used in the ethnographic craft. Finally, the handbook provided six succinct guidelines of ethnography, complete with explanations and clarifications:

- carry a pen and pad of paper
- ask reminder questions when an informant gets stuck

- everyone can lend a hand to the endeavor
- the work is hard and exhausting
- zamlers should seek out new subjects, not just in the city, but in nearby areas
- zamlers should publicize their work in local dramatic clubs, choirs, folk dance evenings, etc.

Eight additional rules were appended to the guidelines, including to copy everything down exactly, to use only one side of the paper, to write as much as possible in the local dialect, and not to correct the storyteller or singer.

The general advice to, and rules for, zamlers indicated an enormous investment in the zamler on YIVO's part. The assumption that zamlers would be interested in an overview of Jewish ethnography, or that such an overview would equip would-be zamlers with a sense of duty and mission, is belied by the work that zamlers did and by the actual relationships that the zamlers formed with YIVO.

Many zamlers expressed a general interest in the materials they collected, even if they didn't adopt a scholarly approach to them. Zamlers wrote notes accompanying their submissions that expressed their personal feelings about these materials, particularly subjective feelings about tales—how interesting or beautiful they were. Responding to one such letter, YIVO replied with a request to the zamler to remember to submit the names of the informants along with the stories. YIVO was also interested in the chain of transmission, and not just with the stories themselves, as befits an organization that saw itself as a modern scientific one. The zamlers, on the other hand, derived the most pleasure from hearing the stories themselves; the informant was not of primary importance to them. The act of listening superseded the scholarly work.[18] The experience of collecting, of hearing new and interesting stories, is a common theme in zamler correspondence to YIVO. YIVO, for its part, was far more interested in shaping the zamler's professional comportment than in fostering such positive experiences.

When zamlers wrote to YIVO for advice, their correspondence was often written in an apologetic tone, indicating a sensitivity to the need to conduct their research according to scientific standards. Herman Frume, for example, wrote to say that he had been collecting materials by himself, and that there were probably some mistakes in their organization. He asked if YIVO could send him some advice.[19] Others simply shared their excitement about collecting. Zalmen Knel, in a note sent with various questionnaires, expressed his hope that YIVO would be happy with the results, as he himself was happy when the stories were told to him. He also requested more questionnaires.[20]

Social prerogatives also served as motivating factors for zamlers. YIVO encouraged them to form clubs, and many zamlers organized themselves into *zamlerkrayzn* (collectors' circles). By 1927, there were twenty-four such krayzn, and by 1929, 139 Polish cities boasted zamlerkrayzn, as did 44 foreign cities.[21] It seems indeed that many zamlers preferred using their zamlung work to establish social ties rather than working alone (again, unlike our fictional Rubinshteyn). The zamlers' letters to YIVO may also be read as friendly overtures, intent on establishing a rapport and a larger social network. Zamlers sought not only to develop skills and pursue their hobby, but also to make friends and expand their social circles. The Ethnographic Commission's leadership, however, did little to foster networking and camaraderie.

The secretary of one such local circle, located in Warsaw, wrote to YIVO asking for a copy of *Der pinkes: Yorbukh fun der geshikhte fun der yidisher literatur un shprakh, far folklor, kritik un bibliografye* (The chronicle: Yearbook for the history of Yiddish literature and language, for folklore, criticism, and bibliography), edited by Shmuel Niger, the predecessor to YIVO's *Filologishe shriftn* (Philological writings), for their scholarly library; such requests for the book were frequent. M. Grome, the secretary of the Warsaw group, added in his letter that their krayz had been operational for three years, and had thirty members. Grome noted that the group had been collecting ethnographic and bibliographic materials and sending them to YIVO in Vilna, and had also been publicizing YIVO's work at evening activities held in larger auditoriums. Some members had been involved in Noah Prylucki's research seminar.[22] Grome and his krayz clearly saw the zamler relationship with YIVO as one of give and take, where the group would help YIVO with both its work and its publicity, and YIVO would provide financial resources. YIVO does not seem to have viewed the relationship in this way.[23]

The requests for information and new questionnaires indicate that not every individual zamler, and indeed perhaps very few zamlers, were very connected with YIVO. YIVO regularly published the questionnaires in YIVO *bleter*, and YIVO's records of its own correspondence indicate sending regulations for zamlers out after the handbook was published, which was as late as 1929. We might surmise, then, that zamlers learned of the Ethnographic Commission from friends or by word of mouth, rather than through regular contact with YIVO.

There are also examples of zamlers who were eager to enter into cooperation with YIVO. It is important to remember at this juncture that "zamler" was not an official title, and that zamlers were more or less self-appointed; this seems to have caused some tensions with the Ethnographic Commission at times. One such enthusiastic zamler, B. Tishler from Stanisławów (Stanislavov; today's Ivano-Frankivsk), entered into an extended correspondence with YIVO. Tishler sent his first letter to YIVO in 1929, explaining at the beginning that "due to various economic reasons, I haven't taken part in the important activities of the above-named institute. I believe that there won't be further unfortunate disturbances, and if free time permits, I will dedicate myself to cooperation in the development of folklore."[24] Tishler had not followed YIVO's questionnaires but had taken on his own project—"I have tried to collect all folk expressions that characterize man, and compare them to various other societies around the world," he wrote. According to Tishler, expressions were the least-explored branch of folklore, and though he was certain that he had left out some possible comparisons, he nevertheless came off as extremely self-assured, hoping to secure YIVO's agreement that he had, indeed, collected important examples. He also requested copies of books and periodicals from YIVO, as well as a short overview of YIVO's recent history and some guidelines for zamlers. Tishler signed his letter, "Your Donor."

The Ethnographic Commission's reply informed Tishler that the purpose of the commission was not just to collect, but also to work with and publicize important research materials. "But you yourself understand," the letter went on, "that between the zamler's inscriptions and publication is a large process of classification, ordering, examining, and comparing the materials from one Jewish area to another, comparing our folklore to that of other people, and determining reciprocal influences." The commission agreed to send a volume to Tishler, but urged that if he truly loved his work, he should "see well whether *your* collection should be quickly published or not." The commission further informed him that it could evaluate his materials for potential publication, and that it would welcome regular packages of collected materials from him.[25]

Tishler replied two weeks later. "I noted," he wrote, "how you answered in a sharp tone about what I wanted to know. Would you think a bit about giving me something about Jewish folklore?" He did not want, he went on to say, to know about his few contributions, but rather to learn about folklore itself, and he believed it was the responsibility of YIVO to assist him. Now he wanted to know specifically whether there were mistakes in his work, and if so, if YIVO could correct them.[26] Unfortunately, this is where the correspondence chain stops, but it is clear that Tishler desired a more cooperative relationship with YIVO, and had a strong sense of his own potential importance within the organization. Whereas Tishler sought guidance and training, YIVO mistook Tishler's exuberance for a desire to see his work in print. It seems that their relationship soured because of this misunderstanding.

It is important at this juncture to mention the use YIVO had for the materials the zamlers collected. Y. L. Cahan, chief folklorist for YIVO operating out of New York, was responsible for analyzing and compiling the contributions. A collected volume, *Yidisher folklor* (Jewish folklore), appeared in 1938. While YIVO was to act as curator, in actuality it acted for quite some time as more of a repository, as the work of sorting and categorizing the materials collected by zamlers did not begin for some time after the establishment of the Ethnographic Commission. Thus, the zamlers' work would not be elevated except in YIVO's own correspondence to the zamlers and in periodic lists of zamlers that YIVO published. The zamlers were in many instances eager to see the fruits of their labor, and a misunderstanding developed about the pace of work and the accreditation that would be afforded to zamlers in book-length publications; they were not YIVO's collaborators but rather more like suppliers of raw material.

Some zamlers were devotees, acolytes of YIVO, who ended up making pilgrimages to YIVO in Vilna and becoming deeply wrapped up with the organization. One twenty-four-year-old zamler wrote about his experience for YIVO's 1934 autobiography competition.[27] As a young man born in the province of Volhynia, R. had applied, and been rejected from, the Lwów art academy. His autobiographical contribution exhibited clear artistic tendencies: it was arranged in chapters with novelesque titles such as "National Feeling Grew in Me," and began with an extended poem. R. explained that he had read the Warsaw-based Yiddish literary journal *Literarishe bleter* (Literary papers), had sent in his own poems to the journal, and had organized a Yiddish literary group in his town. He also sent poems to YIVO, and in June 1926 received a letter from YIVO co-founder and Yiddish linguist Max Weinreich, which he quotes in part in his autobiography. Weinreich's encouragement, and his suggestion that R. work with YIVO, seems to have moved R. greatly. According to him, he drew two of his friends to the "sacred collection work in service of YIVO" (*heyliker zamler arbet letoyves dem YIVO*). This work thus replaced, for R., his earlier artistic work and gave him a sense of purpose (though he later abandoned this work when he became a Zionist). He also referred to the work of the zamler as a *"sheyne kulturele arbet"*—beautiful cultural work.[28]

Two of the friends he brought in to his newfound obsession were not originally aficionados of Yiddish, he wrote. As students in Tarbut schools (Hebrew-language schools with a Zionist orientation), they had learned that Hebrew was the true Jewish language, whereas Yiddish was only a jargon.[29] But R. convinced them of the merits of Yiddish, and noted that "until this very day they remain true to everything Yiddish. . . . We remain three loyal Yiddish-watchmen."[30] But R.'s self-appointed language guardianship, like his zamlung, did not last long. Ultimately it was a passing fad. His story indicates the fervor with which some took up the work of zamlung, but also the ways in which this fervor could be merely one aspect of youthful dramatics and mercurial temperament.

Shloyme Zanvil Pipe was a particularly committed zamler who eventually took on zamlung as a profession. Pipe enrolled in YIVO's *aspirantur* program, an unofficial graduate studies program, with a project proposal to research the folklorization of Yiddish song, particularly Dovid Edelstadt's labor anthem "Der arbeter" (The worker). In 1928, he wrote to YIVO, submitting a few stories that he collected from women. He asked YIVO whether the stories were widespread, and indeed, all of Pipe's correspondence indicates a great interest in taking part in YIVO's mission. Pipe later participated in a seminar led by Y. L. Cahan in Vilna, and became an *aspirant* from 1935 to 1939, during which time he researched folk songs for YIVO's first volume of folklore and made various scholarly contributions to folklore research, especially Yiddish folk songs and their variants and sources. The vast majority of zamlers, however, seemed more drawn to the experience of collecting as a social activity than to the social scientific aspects of scholarly ethnography.

Pipe was an aberration, though we know more about him than about perhaps any other zamler. Indeed, few of them expressed, at least in their correspondence with YIVO, the remotest scholarly interest in the content of what they had collected, at least not in a systematic way—at most, they were pleased with the stories they had heard. Most zamlers expressed satisfaction with having collected a certain amount of material, or excitement at the prospect of simply being a zamler.

The Ethnographic Commission also hosted a variety of open meetings and programs for schools. Announcements regarding the May 30, 1929, meeting, for example, indicated that leading writers, journalists' organizations, historical-ethnographic societies, and a Jewish teachers' union took part. In the late 1920s or early 1930s, YIVO began to organize "enlightenment programs" (*oyfkler aktsies*) in schools. Through "conversations and lectures on folklore themes," YIVO informed Vilna's teachers and schoolchildren about folklore and, presumably, about its work.[31]

YIVO's collection activities were not limited to the Ethnographic Commission. The theater museum and archive acquired donations from individuals, institutions, and zamlerkrayzn. A report in *Literarishe bleter* notes that the museum found a "warm reverberation" in all circles of artists and theater activists.[32] The uniqueness of the museum had much to do with its appeal. An anonymous correspondent wrote in *Literarishe bleter* that "the museum is the only public Yiddish theater museum in the whole world, and every person associated with the Yiddish theater and artists had, therefore, an obligation to help enrich and endow the museum with all available materials in the realm of Jewish theater."[33]

YIVO attempted to extend the reach of its zamler network as well. YIVO was not the only Jewish ethnographic and collecting organization to operate in interwar Poland; there were different models of what such organizations might look like. Whereas in the 1920s, these organizations—museums, clubs, etc.—had divergent aims, by the mid to late 1930s, they had begun to see themselves as participants in the same mission. But YIVO presented itself as the Jewish collecting agent par excellence; it actively tried to expand its geographical reach and convince other organizations that they were involved in the same project. In 1934, for example, Tsemakh Szabad and Zalmen Reyzen, leaders at YIVO, sent a telegram congratulating the founders and patrons of the newly opened Jewish Museum in Lwów. "Let us hope," they wrote, "that the establishment of a museum to protect the traces of the Jewish past will also be dedicated to the further development of Jewish creativity."[34] This was not completely congruent with the Lwów museum's aim, which was to "illustrate the artistic achievements of the Jewish people in their historical development . . . and to inculcate understanding, love, and respect among the populace for the cultural monuments of the Jewish people."[35] The Lwów museum was much more focused on Jews as a shining example of a minority people contributing to high culture. The museum did not use zamlers, though it did employ a few photographers to travel around eastern Galicia and photograph synagogues and other Jewish sites. But because the museum focused its attention on high culture rather than folk culture, attempts to include folk traditions within the museum were trumped by other ideals. But Shabad and Reyzen wanted to encourage the Lwów museum's leaders to embrace YIVO's project of documenting Jewish folk life.

YIVO certainly did intend to intervene in the scholarly discourse about the nature of Jews and Jewish life, but this was not its only, or even its primary, aim. The public display of the Jew, whether in a museum or a publication, never became YIVO's main focus. Analysis of the questionnaires was infrequent. Rather, YIVO's greater mission, in later practice if not in its original goals, was to fashion the experience of the zamler. The remote training of zamlers, the promotion of groups of zamlers, and the creation of programs designed to spur youth into research and self-discovery all point to the mission of transforming Jews into zamlers. The zamler would be the intermediary between the folk—the bearers of folklore, tradition, and the vanishing past—and the modern scholarly institute—the collector, documenter, and social scientific organization.

What would the popularization of this idea mean for YIVO? Other than the perpetuation of YIVO as an institution, which should not be discounted, and its ongoing interaction with wide swaths of the Jewish people in Poland, the promotion of the zamler-Jew would have two main implications for YIVO. First, the zamler would be naturally positioned in relation to the people he studied; he would have access to them while not being exactly *of* them. The handbook for zamlers implied this aim, noting that the general public could lend a hand to the ethnographic endeavor. The handbook was designed to appeal particularly to intellectuals who closely interacted with what YIVO regarded as the common folk: school-teachers, cultural activists, and club leaders.[36] The zamler corps, in actuality, had its own aims, and with few exceptions it focused on pleasure, not on scholarship.

As "the people" disappeared, losing their customs to urbanization, emigration, and modernization (as YIVO's questionnaires, and, as demonstrated above, An-sky's as well, assumed a priori), the zamler might be an advocate on their behalf, absorb some of their ways through osmosis, or become a memory-bearer.[37] He would in some way become responsible for the perpetuation of local color, of the distinctiveness of the Jews of Poland's small towns. But the zamler would not become traditional. He would instead act as a purveyor of heritage. Barbara Kirshenblatt-Gimblett has written that the transformation of a locally rooted custom into a piece of heritage intended for display "'preserves' custom without preserving the 'custom-bound' self. Indeed, heritage becomes a resource in the process of fashioning the self."[38]

YIVO's fashioning of the zamler, however, was not an attempt to merge the zamler with his collected material, that is, to encourage the zamler to take on the persona of the people from whom he collected. The second implication of the Jew-as-zamler was the creation of a new type of Jew. The zamler was fashioned as modern—YIVO made no efforts, for example, to appeal to Hasidim or the traditionally religious, and prior to the autobiography competition, did not encourage introspection or autoethnography. The zamler would be modern, but rooted. Informed by an idea of the past, and by a "direct experience" with the past in the guise of the informant, the zamler would nonetheless remain thoroughly modern. He used modern scientific collection methods, making sure to accurately transcribe dialect and speech quirks, and to present his work in a uniform manner. He was also a traveler, even if he was only traveling within his own town.

YIVO's focus on fashioning the person of the zamler rather than merely producing an image of the Jew was both inward- and outward-looking. YIVO's appeals to the community—to individuals, to libraries and schools, to teachers' groups and scouting organizations—far from being merely about fundraising or gathering volunteers, was designed to instill this modern image within Jewish society, and to create more modern Jews. The idea that Jews would have a unique set of traditions, folklore, and songs, and that these artifacts were worthy of collection and documentation, was a unique one within Poland, different from other Jewish collection projects. Although YIVO, and the program of zamlung, has been held up as a statelike actor for Jews in interwar Poland, or as the paradigmatic example of collection practice, it was in fact sui generis.[39] The Ethnographic Commission's interactions with its zamler corps thus also serve as a lens into the unstable character of Jewish life in interwar Poland.[40]

Rubinshteyn, the fictional zamler in the fish market, would in reality likely not have been so divorced from regular everyday life, or so dedicated to his work as to forsake the other aspects of his life. Real-life zamlers approached zamlung as a crucial and participatory act. Being a zamler was not only work, but a sacred calling, holy work. Most zamlers had other jobs and communities. They usually came to collection work as part of a zamlerkrayz, as a social activity, rather than as solitary scientists. The notion of Jew-as-zamler propagated by YIVO's Ethnographic Commission ultimately failed to gain widespread adherents from the actual zamlers themselves.

Karpinovich's portrayal of the "scientific" zamler, however—seeking out the people in their place, devoted entirely to cold calculation—does show us the extent to which YIVO's portrayal of the Jew-as-zamler took hold in the popular imagination, if not the lived experience of the zamlers. For while YIVO's initial investment in the fashioning of the zamler was considerable, in the end, the interests and desires of the zamlers were often at odds with YIVO's designed program.

NOTES

A version of this chapter was first presented at the YIVO Institute for Jewish Research on November 13, 2013.

1. A[vrom]. Karpinovich, "Der folklorist," in *Baim wilner durkhoyf* (Tel Aviv: Y. L. Peretz Publishing House, 1967), 69.

2. Karpinovich, "Der folklorist," 78.

3. In 1930, the Ethnographic Commission changed its name to the Folklore Committee, but I will continue to refer to it as the Ethnographic Commission to avoid confusion.

4. See Cecile Esther Kuznitz, *YIVO and the Making of Modern Jewish Culture: Scholarship for the Yiddish Nation* (New York: Cambridge University Press, 2014), esp. 72–80.

5. Administration meeting minutes, n.d., YIVO Institute for Jewish Research, New York, RG 1.1, f. 7.

6. Administration meeting minutes, n.d., YIVO, RG 1.1, f. 9.

7. Ibid.

8. On S. An-sky, see Eugene M. Avrutin, et al., eds., *Photographing the Jewish Nation: Pictures from S. An-sky's Ethnographic Expeditions* (Waltham, MA: Brandeis University Press, 2009); Nathaniel Deutsch, *The Jewish Dark Continent: Life and Death in the Russian Pale of Settlement* (Cambridge, MA: Harvard University Press, 2011); Gabriella Safran, *Wandering Soul: The Dybbuk's Creator, S. An-sky* (Cambridge, MA: Belknap Press of Harvard University Press, 2010); and Gabriella Safran and Steven J. Zipperstein, eds., *The Worlds of S. An-sky: A Russian Jewish Intellectual at the Turn of the Century* (Stanford, CA: Stanford University Press, 2006), as well as Nathaniel Deutsch's contribution to this volume. For an in-depth discussion of Peretz's folklore contributions, as well as an analysis of the Ethnographic Commission's work, see Itzik Nakhmen Gottesman, *Defining the Yiddish Nation: The Jewish Folklorists of Poland* (Detroit: Wayne State University Press, 2003).

9. For more on An-sky's expeditions, see Deutsch, *The Jewish Dark Continent;* and Safran, *Wandering Soul.*

10. See Deutsch's contribution to this volume, especially the section on An-sky's sense of the ideological potential of autoethnography.

11. Deutsch, *The Jewish Dark Continent,* 28.

12. As mentioned above, zamlers seem to have been almost exclusively male. Women, perhaps most notably the Warsaw-based Regina Lilientalowa, participated in folklore collection and writing in other capacities, but rarely as zamlers.

13. Ethnographic Commission to A. Shertl, December 25, 1929, YIVO, RG 1.2, f. 4.

14. *Vos iz azoyns yidishe etnografye (hantbikhl far zamler)* (Vilna: YIVO, 1929). On the authorship of this pamphlet, see Gottesman, *Defining the Yiddish Nation,* 206n125.

15. *Vos iz azoyns,* n.p. (introduction).

16. Ibid.

17. Ibid., 5.

18. I thank Gabriella Safran for her observation on this disconnect between YIVO and its informants.

19. Herman Frume to Ethnographic Commission, YIVO, RG 1.2, f. 2.

20. Zalmen Knel to Ethnographic Commission, YIVO, RG 1.2, f. 2.

21. Cecile Esther Kuznitz, "The Origins of Yiddish Scholarship and the YIVO Institute for Jewish Research" (PhD diss., Stanford University, 2000), 175.

22. M. Grome to Ethnographic Commission, YIVO, RG 1.2, f. 2. On Prilutski and the *forsh-seminar,* see Gottesman, *Defining the Yiddish Nation.* Also see Keith Ian Weiser, *Jewish People, Yiddish Nation: Noah Prylucki and the Folkists in Poland* (Toronto: University of Toronto Press, 2011).

23. The idea that one worked as a zamler not just for the love of it, but also as a type of remunerated work, should not be surprising, given the harsh economic climate in which zamlers worked.

24. B. Tishler to Ethnographic Commission, October 23, 1929, YIVO, RG 1.2, f. 4.

25. Ethnographic Commission to B. Tishler, July 1930 [?], YIVO, RG 1.2, f. 4.

26. B. Tishler to Ethnographic Commission, July 24, 1929, YIVO, RG 1.2, f. 4.

27. "Ikh vil nisht shtarbn: Mayn skeletishe oytobiografiye farn konkurs fun YIVO" [I do not want to die: My skeletal autobiography for YIVO's competition], 1934, YIVO, RG 4, #3547. The entrant's name has been obscured to preserve anonymity.

28. Ibid.

29. Ibid.

30. Ibid.

31. Ethnographic Commission to Gimnazie Gezelshaft far Pedagogn, YIVO, RG 1.2, f. 5.

32. *Literarishe bleter,* no. 31, reprinted as "Teater-muzey" in *Yedies fun yidishn visnshaftlikhn institut* 25, August 8, 1928, YIVO, RG 1.1, f. 466, unpaginated.

33. Fani Shapiro, "Der teater-muzey in nomen fun ester-rokhl kaminski baym YIVO," *Literarishe bleter* 8, no. 303 (February 21, 1930): 152.

34. Tsemakh Szabad and Zalmen Reyzen to the Jewish Museum of Lwów, May 14, 1934, Central State Historical Archives of Ukraine in Lviv (TsDIAL of Ukraine), f. 701, op. 3, d. 1667, l. 3.

35. "Statut Muzeum gminy wyzn. żyd. we Lwowie," n.d., TsDIAL of Ukraine, f. 701, op. 3, d. 1369, l. 10.

36. *Vos iz azoyns,* 30.

37. See Deutsch's contribution to this volume.

38. Barbara Kirshenblatt-Gimblett, "From Ethnology to Heritage: The Role of the Museum" (keynote address, International Society for Ethnology and Folklore, Marseilles, April 28, 2004), 2.

39. See Gottesman, *Defining the Yiddish Nation;* and Kuznitz, "The Origins of Yiddish Scholarship."

40. See, for example, Ezra Mendelsohn, "Interwar Poland: Good for the Jews or Bad for the Jews?," in *The Jews of Poland between Two World Wars,* ed. Yisrael Gutman et al. (Waltham, MA: Brandeis University Press, 1989), 130–146; Szymon Rudnicki, "Anti-Jewish Legislation in Interwar Poland," in *Antisemitism and Its Opponents in Modern Poland,* ed. Robert Blobaum (Ithaca, NY: Cornell University Press, 2005), 149–170; and Jerzy Tomaszewski, "The Civil Rights of Jews in Poland, 1918–1939," *Polin: Studies in Polish Jewry* 8 (2004): 115–127.

8

The Last Zamlers

AVROM SUTZKEVER AND SHMERKE
KACZERGINSKI IN VILNA, 1944–1945

DAVID E. FISHMAN

On July 13, 1944, the day that Vilna, the "Jerusalem of Lithuania," was liberated from German occupation by the Soviet army, one of the city's most illustrious sons, the Yiddish poet and partisan Avrom Sutzkever, found himself in a writers' sanitarium in Voskresensk, outside Moscow. When he read the news, splashed across the front page of *Pravda*, his reaction was immediate: "I can't stay here. . . . I must go to my home city and see our destruction." He left for Moscow and went straight to Justas Paleckis, the titular president in exile of Soviet Lithuania. Paleckis had, five months earlier, convinced the Soviet authorities to extract Sutzkever from a partisan base in the Narocz Forest and bring him to Moscow by military airplane. This time Sutzkever pleaded with Paleckis to provide him with transportation in the opposite direction—from Moscow to Vilna—immediately.[1]

The Lithuanian president in exile and the Jewish poet traveled to Vilna (in Lithuanian, Vilnius) together, and reached the city on the night of July 18, just five days after the city's liberation. In a note that Sutzkever wrote at the time, he reflected,

> If not for the hidden cultural treasures, I don't know if I would have had enough strength to return to my home city. I knew that I wouldn't find any of my loved ones. I knew that everyone had been executed by the murder-

ers. I knew that my eyes would be blinded with pain as soon as I saw the Wilia [the river that ran through the city]. But the Hebrew letters planted in Vilna's soil sparkled at me from a thousand kilometers away. And I remembered Zelig Kalmanovitch's words: "New Jews will be born [after the war in Vilna], but there won't be any new *seforim* [holy books]."[2]

As inmates of the Vilna ghetto, Sutzkever and Kalmanovitch had been slave laborers for the Einsatzstab Reichsleiter Rosenberg, the Nazi German agency responsible for looting cultural treasures that belonged to Jews and other enemies of the Reich. The work brigade included Sutkever, Kalmanovitch, and eighteen other Jewish intellectuals, and was assigned the task of "sorting" and "processing" Vilna's Jewish libraries, archival collections, and museums. They were ordered to set aside the valuable items for shipment to Germany, first and foremost to the Institut zür Erforschung der Judenfrage (Institute for the Study of the Jewish Question) in Frankfurt, and to send the remaining, worthless materials to paper mills, where they would be mixed into a pulp and recycled as paper. The Rosenberg Detail set a quota: no more than 30 percent of the processed material was to be considered valuable; 70 percent was to be destroyed. Ghetto inmates gave the Jewish forced laborers a nickname: the "Paper Brigade." They were assigned the task of participating in the physical destruction of their own culture.

The members of the Paper Brigade decided to sabotage the Germans' plans. They secreted away thousands of books, documents, manuscripts, and works of art, smuggled them into the ghetto, and placed them in underground bunkers, secret compartments, and other hiding places—an operation that extended over one and a half years. These hidden treasures were the Hebrew letters planted in the soil that sparkled at Sutzkever and drew him back to Vilna. His coworker Zelig Kalmanovitch, one of the prewar directors of the Yiddish Scientific Institute (YIVO), died of typhus in a German labor camp in Estonia. Survivors of the camp who disposed of his body reported that they discovered a tiny Bible hidden in his clothing.[3]

Now, upon his return to Vilna, Sutzkever joined the efforts to retrieve and dig up the Jewish cultural treasures, which had been initiated by Shmerke Kaczerginski, his close friend and fellow poet from the literary group Yung Vilne. Kaczerginski had been joined by Abba Kovner, the last commander of the Fareynikte Partizaner Organizatsye (FPO) partisan organization in the Vilna ghetto. On July 26, 1944, thirteen days after Vilna's liberation, the three of them—Sutzkever, Kaczerginski, and Kovner—established a Jewish Museum under the auspices of the Arts Administration of the People's Commissariat of Education of the Lithuanian SSR. The museum, initially located in Sutzkever and Kaczerginski's apartment on Vilna's main thoroughfare (now named Gedimino Street), was the first Jewish institution in the newly liberated city; a synagogue began to function a month later, in late August, and a Jewish orphanage and boarding school opened in September.

The three heads of the museum enlisted volunteers among Jews who surfaced in the city—partisan fighters from the forests, former ghetto inmates who had survived in hiding, and Jewish Red Army soldiers. The group's initial survey of the Paper Brigade's hiding places yielded mixed results: The YIVO building had been burnt to a crisp by bombing, and the materials hidden in its attic were now soot and ashes. Stray pieces of paper could be retrieved amidst the rubble. The *malina* (hiding place) inside the ghetto library at 6 Strashun Street had been discovered by the Germans shortly before their retreat; they removed all the materials and burnt them in a bonfire in the courtyard. On the other hand, the hiding places at 1 Strashun Street and 8 Strashun Street were intact, as was a bunker at 6 Shavl Street.[4]

The initial work focused on the bunker on Shavl Street. Kaczerginski described the activity there in his diary, in an entry dated August 5: "On a daily basis, sacks and baskets of treasures are transferred from the bunker—letters, manuscripts, and books by famous Jewish personalities. . . . The Polish inhabitants of the courtyard are constantly calling in policemen and other officials; they think we are digging for gold. They can't understand why we need these dirty pieces of paper that are stuffed amidst the feathers of pillowcases and blankets. None of them realize that we have found letters by Peretz, Sholem Aleichem, Bialik, and Avraham Mapu, the handwritten diary of Theodore Herzl, manuscripts by Dr. Solomon Ettinger and Mendele Moykher-sforim." But in addition to the Shavl Street bunker and other hiding places, Poles and Lithuanians began to bring materials that Jews had given them for safekeeping. The same diary entry noted, "We are bringing in Torah scrolls that are lying scattered across the city."[5]

Some members of the retrieval team dug with shovels, while others used their hands. The partisans in the group worked with machine guns hanging over their shoulders. The group used mainly makeshift wooden handcarts to transport materials to the museum (that is, to Sutzkever and Kaczerginski's apartment).

Sutzkever reported the following incident: As he and his comrades dug up artwork buried in the Shavl Street bunker, they hit upon a sculpture of King David by the nineteenth-century Russian-Jewish artist Mark Antokolsky. Next to it, an arm extended from underneath the surface, and Sutzkever grabbed it, thinking it was another sculpture. He shuddered when he realized that the arm was made of human flesh, not of clay. The engineer who had built the bunker, Gershon Abramovitch, explained to Sutzkever that a group of Jews had hidden there for several weeks after the ghetto's liquidation. When one of them died, the group buried him alongside Antokolsky's King David.[6]

Sutzkever and Kaczerginski's apartment on Gedimino Street was filling up quickly with material. A correspondent who visited in August described the scene: Sutzkever's room was full of packages of leather-bound volumes, whose bindings had been blackened by dampness and aging; there were piles of Torah scrolls lined against the wall; the floor was covered with mounds of papers and manuscripts; on the desk table there stood a cast clay statue, scratched, with one of its arms broken off. There was hardly space for Sutzkever to sleep. The room was eerie at night. It was like sleeping in a cemetery, amidst tombstones and open graves.[7]

Pages from Jewish books surfaced unexpectedly, and in disturbing places. In one of the city's open-air markets, the Polish saleswomen wrapped herring in pages from the Vilna Shas (the famed edition of the Talmud issued by the Romm Press). When an outraged Jewish partisan yelled at them for their callous behavior, they replied that they didn't know the pages were from the Zydowska (Jewish) Talmud. The partisan informed Kaczerginski of the situation, and the latter went straight to the marketplace and began waving his fist at the saleswomen. He threatened to beat them up and denounce them to the Soviet police as looters of Jewish property if they didn't hand over all the pages of Jewish books immediately. Upon seeing that Kaczerginski was serious, the market women acquiesced.[8]

The minutes of the meetings held by the "initiative group" of the Vilna Jewish Museum (Sutzkever, Kaczerginski, and Kovner) indicate that they conceived of the institution as a continuation of the Paper Brigade, but that they also expanded its mission. Their objective was not only to collect and preserve prewar Jewish cultural artifacts, but also to collect documents from the war years on Jewish life and death in the ghetto, and on the atrocities perpetrated by the Germans. These documents included the records of the Judenrat/ghetto administration, diaries and chronicles, poems and scholarly studies, posters and letters, German orders and memoranda.

In an August 2 meeting with some sixty Jewish partisans, the museum leadership appealed to their audience for help. Sutzkever spoke emotionally: "This is a gathering of the last remaining Jews, the survivors. . . . In order to justify our lives, we must be creative while sitting on top of the ruins. A group of Vilners has undertaken the first task: to bring together the remaining cultural treasures, to gather the remnants. Before we begin to ask others to help, let every one of us search among our belongings and in our immediate environment for the remains of our exterminated [farshnitn] life."

Kovner followed, and addressed the partisans as comrades in arms, many of whom had been under his command in the ghetto and the forests. He gave them new orders that explicitly tied the armed resistance of the FPO to the spiritual resistance of the Paper Brigade: "In the bunker at 6 Shavl Street, thirty crates of valuable YIVO materials were hidden. And that is also the place where the FPO hid its machine guns. This symbolizes the great importance of our work. We must rescue whatever remains; we must document our struggle, and transmute it into a political force. The destruction of our cultural treasures is perhaps a greater tragedy than the tragedy of our blood."[9]

For Sutzkever, Kaczerginski, and Kovner, retrieving the remaining Jewish cultural treasures was an obvious, self-evident need, a precondition for the resumption of Jewish life, wherever or however it would take place. But other museum activists were mainly or even exclusively interested in documenting the war years, not in preserving the prewar treasures. They were intent on using the ghetto documentation for political, judicial, and educational purposes.

Alongside the retrieval of documentation, the museum began almost immediately to record the testimony of survivors. Sutzkever and Kaczerginski's apartment was a beehive of activity, with staff members sitting at the table interviewing former inmates of the Vilna ghetto and other ghettos. In keeping with YIVO's prewar interest in collecting material on everyday life, the museum recorded first-person essays on various aspects of life under the Nazi occupation, not only on leaders and major events. There were essays called "Song and Music in the Ghetto," "I Worked for the Gestapo," "How I Created an Underground Printing Press," "The Official German Bordello on Subocz Street," "A Polish Hospital Murders a Jewish Patient," and "The Ghetto's Burial Department."[10]

But the museum encountered indifference and outright hostility from Lithuanian Soviet officials. There was no budget for salaries, transport, or supplies. The Ministry of Culture eventually allocated a building for the museum: the burnt-out edifice of the ghetto library and its adjacent structures, in the territory of the abandoned ghetto. The building's interior was in ruins, with mountains of rubble. The roof had large gaps through which one could see the sky, and there was no furniture and no glass in the windows. By late August, Sutzkever, Kaczerginski, and Kovner were frustrated and angry at the authorities, and the relations did not improve over the ensuing months.

In early September, an enormous mountain of materials was found, not in a hiding place, but in the courtyard of the Vilnius Municipal Trash Administration (Soyuzutil). The Germans had disposed of scores of tons of Jewish materials as trash for shipment to paper mills. But because of the hostilities with the advancing Soviet army, several tons of paper were not sent onward to the mills. A Jewish partisan discovered the trove and brought in a sample package of materials to show to his colleagues. When they opened it, the first item they found on top was a manuscript by the early nineteenth-century Hebrew Enlightenment author Joseph Perl. Underneath it were newspapers, pedagogical materials, and small sculptures —all from different parts of the YIVO archives. The work of transporting and sorting the mountains found at the Trash Administration occupied the museum's staff for more than half a year.[11]

As word spread concerning the excavation and retrieval activities in Vilna, the response among the Moscow Jewish intellectuals was one of excited enthusiasm and gratitude. The Yiddish novelist Dovid Bergel-son wrote to Sutzkever, "There was recently an article in 'Eynikayt' [the Moscow Yiddish newspaper] about the great work you are performing in Vilna. It is truly great work. I don't know whether anyone is doing anything more important now for our culture than you are." Shakhna Ep-shtein, executive secretary of the Jewish Anti-Fascist Committee, wrote to Sutzkever in a similar tone: "We are following your activity with the greatest interest. Your achievements are truly historic. May your hands be strengthened!"[12]

Sutzkever returned to Moscow on September 10, 1944 to focus on his literary activity. Kovner left the USSR illegally in November, and eventu-ally settled in Palestine. This left the museum in Kaczerginski's hands. The man underwent a remarkable transformation. Before the war, he had been an ardent Communist sympathizer who had served time in Polish prisons for illegal political activity. Now, he dedicated himself to rescuing Torah scrolls, pages of the Talmud, rabbinic books and manuscripts, even wooden synagogue *shtenders*. People observed that he was the only Jewish Communist in Vilna who had cast off his previous ideological blinders, and who was, in the aftermath of the destruction, a new person. Kaczer-ginski took on the role that had been played by Khaykl Lunski, the head of the Strashun Library, Vilna's Jewish communal library. The murdered Lunski, a rabbinic scholar and Zionist, was replaced by Kaczerginski, a Communist sympathizer and atheist.[13]

In addition to directing the museum's operations, Kaczerginski under-took a personal research project: to collect the texts and melodies of the songs that were sung in the ghettos of Vilna, Kovno, and Shavl. He tapped his own memory and interviewed friends, comrades in arms, and survi-vors. By October 1944, he compiled a draft book manuscript with forty-nine songs. In his original introductory essay to the manuscript, Kacz-erginski explained that the martyrs and victims should be remembered in their own words—the words of the songs they wrote and sang, that expressed their fears and hopes, determination and despair. He consid-ered the songs to be the martyrs' last will and testament to future genera-tions. Kaczerginski signed a contract with the Moscow publishing house Der Emes in 1945 to publish part of his collection under the title *Songs of the Vilna Ghetto,* but the Moscow edition never appeared. Kaczerginski published the book two years later, in Paris, after having left the USSR.[14]

Writing in Paris, Kaczerginski recalled his motivation for undertaking the "songs of the ghettos" project. He had belonged to a group of folklore zamlers in the Vilna ghetto, led by Moshe Lerer, a longtime folklore zamler for YIVO who became a staff member of the institute. People considered Kaczerginski, Lerer, and the other folklorists maniacs for recording all the "nonsense" that people said and sang in the ghetto. With death hanging over the inhabitants like a sword, who cared what expressions people used, and how they used them? How old they were and where they were born? But the circle of folklorists grew, and it even secured some funding from the ghetto administration for its work.

After Vilna's liberation, Kaczerginski realized that not only was his home city destroyed, but virtually no one from the zamler group had survived, and nothing from their folklore collection had been retrieved. While digging up and sorting through documents, he discovered a memo by Lerer to the members of the zamler group, giving a list of genres and themes to collect, as well as methodological guidelines. "That document was for me the last will and testament of my dear colleagues," he wrote. "The document didn't let me rest until I resumed the work that had been interrupted."[15]

By the spring of 1945, Kaczerginski had lost all faith in the Soviet system and in the prospects for building Jewish culture in Soviet Lithuania. The last zamlers became smugglers of Jewish cultural treasures. Sutzkever and Kaczerginski lifted thousands of documents, manuscripts, and books from the museum's premises, and packed suitcases full of materials, which they took with them across the border to Poland. They also enlisted the help of friends who emigrated to Poland, and of activists in the Bricha who were skilled in the ways of illicit border-crossing and smuggling. From Poland and later from Paris, Sutzkever and Kaczerginski sent most of the materials to YIVO in New York, but held on to a significant proportion, which they eventually donated to the National Library of Israel, Yad Vashem, and other institutions. Of the materials that remained behind in Soviet Vilnius, some were destroyed at the time of the Jewish Museum's liquidation in 1949. The surviving materials are now held in the Lithuanian National Library, the Lithuanian Republican Archive, and the Vilna Gaon Jewish State Museum.[16]

Sutzkever and Kaczerginski's postwar retrieval endeavor was the final chapter in the YIVO tradition of *zamlen*. But never had zamlen been conducted under such tragic and heartbreaking conditions: the historic Jewish quarter of Vilna consisted of row after row of demolished buildings, 90 percent of the city's Jews had perished, and the survivors were struggling to find food and clothes and to establish a meaning and direction to their lives. Under such circumstances, the original goal of zamlen was now untenable: the pieces of folklore, literature, and history would *not* serve as the basis for creating a new modern Jewish culture in Eastern Europe, as Simon Dubnow and S. An-sky had imagined. The items were now the "remains of our exterminated life," in Sutzkever's words; "the last will and testament of the martyrs," in Kaczerginski's words. The objective was to commemorate. The fact that they called the institution they founded a museum, rather than a library or an institute, conveyed the sense of a static, finite culture that could be displayed in glass cases, not of a vibrant culture that would grow and develop. After all, this was a museum that did not mount any exhibits, and whose collection consisted mainly of books, with relatively little art. The word "museum" carried a commemorative, even funereal overtone.

In the final analysis, Sutzkever and Kaczerginski were driven by an elemental sense that a self-respecting people could not abandon its cultural legacy, any more than it could leave behind surviving children in Christian hands. For the fragments of Jewish history and culture to flourish and return to life, they, like the children, would have to leave Soviet Vilnius.

NOTES

1. Avrom Sutzkever, "Ilya Ehrenbnurg," in *Baym leyenen penimer* (Jerusalem: Yiddish Department, Hebrew University of Jerusalem, 1993), 142–143.

2. Notes by Avrom Sutzkever, n.d., National Library of Israel, Jerusalem, Min Hahurban Collection, no. 4 1703, file 219.

3. Sutzkever described his work for the Rosenberg Detail in his book *Vilner geto: 1941–1944* (Paris: Farband fun di Vilner in Frankraykh, 1946), esp. 108–113; Kalmanovitch did so in his posthumously published ghetto diary, *Yoman be-geto Vilnah u-khetavim min ha-'izavon she-nimtse'u ba-harisot* (Tel Aviv: Moreshet Bet-Edut al shem Mordekhai Anilevits, 1977), 65–140 passim; and in "Togbukh fun Vilner Geto (fragment)," *YIVO bleter*, n.s., 3 (1997): 43–113.

4. Sutzkever, *Vilner geto*, 229. On the early work of the museum, see Kaczerginski's diary notes in Shmerke Kaczerginski, *Tsvishn hamer un serp* (Buenos Aires: Der Emes, 1950).

5. Kaczerginski, *Tsvishn hamer un serp*, 35.

6. Sutzkever, "Vos mir hobn geratevet in Vilne," *Eynikayt* (Moscow), October 12, 1944; Sutzkever, *Vilner geto*, 230.

7. A. Matatkov, "Geratevete kultur-oytsres (a briv fun vilne)," *Eynikayt*, August 17, 1944; Chaim Grade, "Fun unter der erd," *Forverts*, July 8, 1979. The central hero of Grade's serialized novel is a fictionalized version of Kaczerginski. Since Grade and Kaczerginski were close friends who lived together in Łódź and Paris during the years 1946 and 1947, we may safely assume that this depiction is based on Kaczerginski's own account.

8. Leyzer Engelshtern, *Mit di vegn fun der sheyres ha-pleyte* (Givatayim: Igud Yotse Vilna veha-Sevivah, 1976), 101–102; the story about Kaczerginski is also told in Grade, "Fun unter der erd," *Forvets*, March 15, 1979.

9. "Protokol fun baratung fun partizaner aktivistn bam muzey fun yidisher kultur un kunst," in the notebook "Protokoln fun zitsungen fun der initsiativ grupe," YIVO Archives, New York, Sutzkever-Kaczerginski Collection, RG 223, file 757, 9–11, unpaginated.

10. National Library of Israel, Min Hahurban Collection: "A yid fun Gestapo dertseylt," file 223, pp. 27–32; Y. Kovalski, "Umlegale tsaytungen," file 223, pp. 33–47; Vera Gavronski-Libo, "Muzik un gezang in geto," file 223, pp. 47–50; "A yid afn operatsye tish," file 223, pp. 64–66 (also in YIVO, Sutzkever-Kaczerginski Collection, RG 223, file 712); Akiva Gershater, "A daytshisher melukhishe bardak," file 223, pp. 75–77; Grinshtein, "Der beys oylem opteyl in geto," file 234.

11. Kaczerginski, *Tsvishn hamer un serp*, 49–50.

12. Bergelson to Sutzkever, n.d., National Library of Israel, Sutzkever Archive, Dovid Bergelson file; Epshtein to Sutzkever, September 7, 1944, Sutzkever Archive, Shakhna Epshtein file.

13. This portrait is based on Grade, "Fun unter der erd," *Forverts*, March 25, 1979.

14. The draft manuscript of the collection is held in the Central State Archive of Lithuania, Vilnius, fond 1390, "The Jewish Museum," op. 1, file 50. The contract with Der Emes is reproduced in Kaczerginski, *Tsvishn hamer un serp*, 68. Kaczerginski's *Dos gezang fun Vilner geto* was published in Paris in 1947, and was followed by the fuller work *Lider fun di getos un lagern*, published in New York in 1948.

15. Shmerke Kaczerginski, ed., *Lider fun di getos un lagern* (New Tork: Tsiko, 1948), xix–xx.

16. I deal with this subsequent history in a forthcoming book.

Part II

Findings from the Field

Ethnography and Folklore among Polish Jews in Israel

IMMIGRATION AND INTEGRATION

HAYA BAR-ITZHAK

An examination of how the definition of "folklore" has changed from the eighteenth century to the present can explain why research was focused on particular groups and why certain questions were asked about them. Romanticism and the rise of nationalism in Europe, which stimulated the study of folklore, saw that study as mainly involving what Herder called the "ancient national spirit." Accordingly, the group that was deemed most appropriate for study was the peasantry, considered to be a relatively stable group that had not yet been "spoiled" by civilization.[1] This led to the prevalent assumption that the songs and stories they preserved reflected the ancient national spirit and permitted its reconstruction.

From the mid-nineteenth century, folklore studies in England was influenced by the British anthropology of Edward Tylor, who saw evolution as a reflection of human history. Folklore studies was viewed as a historical discipline that compared and identified archaic survivals of beliefs and customs.[2] It was still assumed that these survivals were to be found chiefly in relatively stable populations, and no one imagined that other groups might be appropriate objects of study.

The changing definition of folklore, starting with William R. Bascom, who saw folklore as a verbal art, and continuing with Dan Ben-Amos and

Robert A. Georges, both of whom see folklore chiefly as a communicative process using the artistic medium, helped move the study of folklore beyond that of a salvage operation and opened new horizons for modern research.[3] It is no longer assumed that folklore exists in a situation of social stability. Hence new groups—including immigrants—became the object of study, and new questions were asked.

Robert Georges demonstrates how the British anthropological tradition of studying survivals continued to influence the study of North American immigrant and ethnic folklore decades after this tradition ceased to be the dominant school.[4] Folklorists continued to see themselves as engaged in a campaign to rescue folklore. Immigrant traditions were viewed as survivals that had to be documented at once, before they vanished as a result of contact with the new culture. However, as Georges shows, with the passage of time new research orientations emerged and scholars began to focus on the process of transition and how the immigration experience itself modified the folklore that the immigrants brought with them from their countries of origin. In these studies change is viewed as a natural part of folklore, not as an unfortunate but inevitable development whose final outcome must necessarily be the absolute elimination of the cultural differences between ethnic groups and the dominant culture.[5]

THE STUDY OF IMMIGRANT FOLKLORE IN ISRAEL

In the study of immigrant and ethnic folklore in Israel, the emphasis seems to have been placed chiefly on folklore as a project of salvage. Expressions like "saving the immigrants' traditions," "rescuing what can still be saved," and "studying the folklore that is still alive" are very common. Although scholars have studied the changes in traditional folklore brought about by immigration, they have paid less attention to the creation of original folklore as a direct result of contact with the new place and new culture.[6]

With the influx of mass immigration in the early years of Israeli statehood, David Ben-Gurion's government elaborated a national absorption policy. In Ben-Gurion's formulation, the purpose of statehood was to facilitate the cultural absorption of immigrants. This formulation sought to expedite the process of "blending" the returning exiles through a set

of values and symbols that placed emphasis on what the different population groups had in common and that hallowed the principles of national
unity and state sovereignty. This "statist" approach combined universal
values rooted in socialist Zionism with a rigid concept of national unity,
which was interpreted as uniformity, and rejected the traditional customs
and folk cultures of the different Jewish ethnic groups as divisive manifestations left over from the diaspora.[7]

Some policymakers regarded the new immigrants' acquisition of values developed in the pre-state period as inevitable, and even applied the
term "assimilation" in concluding that there was no room for the preservation of "cultural enclaves" in Israeli society.[8] Some, like Spiegel, even
asserted that the assimilation of Mizrahim (Middle Eastern and Oriental
Jews) into Ashkenazic Israeli culture was essential, owing to the absence
of equality between the cultures, "inasmuch as they have little of value
to offer to modern culture. Therefore they must abandon their demand
to preserve their culture and their folklore, for they thereby foster the
persistence of alienation and divisiveness among sections of the people."[9]
However, the traditional background of the Sephardim and Mizrahim
made it difficult for the concepts and symbols of socialist Zionism to appeal to them. Thus, during the period of mass immigrant absorption in
the 1950s, many veteran Ashkenazic Israelis rejected the cultural values
that more recent immigrants from North Africa and the Middle East
brought with them.

FOLKLORE OF IMMIGRATION AND
INTEGRATION OF POLISH JEWS

I conducted my ethnographic project with immigrants from Poland who
arrived in the late 1950s in Upper Nazareth (then Qiryat Nazereth). Historians refer to this wave of immigration as the "Gomułka Aliyah," after
Władysław Gomułka, the Polish Communist leader of the period. This
wave brought 42,289 Polish Jews to Israel between 1956 and 1960. Because
the peak year was 1957 it is also known as the "1957 Aliyah." The large exodus from Poland followed the change of government there in 1956, when
the new regime unleashed a new torrent of antisemitism and opened the
gates for Jewish emigration. Comparing this wave of emigration with the

"first wave" of Polish emigration that immediately followed World War II
and the Kielce pogrom, Hersh Smolar noted,

> Then [in 1945–1946], many Jews who had not yet had a chance to settle
> down fled in panic. Many were still sitting on their suitcases. Things were
> different with the "second wave." Families came then who had already
> integrated, who had apartments, furniture, jobs, a livelihood. The children
> were in school, the teenagers were working or in high school. In this situa-
> tion the decision to throw everything away and leave was far from easy. . . .
> Unlike the "first wave," after the Kielce pogrom, when masses of ordinary
> folk fled in confusion, the "second wave" was marked by the departure
> of many who had no contact with a Jewish environment, assimilated per-
> sons who frequently made a public show of their Polishness.[10]

Whereas sociologists and anthropologists had studied the waves of immigration from Asia and North Africa in the 1950s, few had conducted any
research on the contemporaneous immigration of Polish Jews. When I
asked sociologists why there had never been a study of these immigrants,
they answered that this was not a problematic group and had consequently not drawn scholarly attention. I believed that collecting and analyzing the folklore created by these immigrants could provide an explanation, even if only a partial one, of the "nonproblematic" nature of this
group, since the immigrants themselves, as we shall see, were exposed to
many difficult problems of integration.

In Upper Nazareth I found a town that was established in part to absorb
this wave of immigration and in which Polish Jewry arrived as a group.
The town was founded in 1957 on a ridge in the lower Galilee, adjacent
to old Nazareth, but as a separate municipality with the name Qiryat
Natzeret. The reasons for establishing the town were related to demog-
raphy and security, that is, setting up a Jewish town near an Arab urban
center, with the idea that it could eventually become the capital of Galilee and northern Israel—an idea realized in 1974 when it received full
municipal status.[11] As a first step, eleven families of veteran Israelis were
recruited to provide the administrative infrastructure for the new community (administrators, teachers, and the like). These families first met
at the site in January 1957, the same month that the initial fifteen families
arrived from Poland. Throughout the year more Polish immigrants arrived, along with the families of additional veteran Israelis.[12] In addition

to those from Poland, immigrants from Hungary and especially Romania were sent to Qiryat Natzeret. In 1960, the first wave of immigrants from North Africa (Algeria, Tunisia, and Morocco) arrived. The immigrants were employed in industry, construction, and other services. There were also some first stirrings of private enterprise, chiefly retail stores, although most purchases were made in the markets of Arab Lower Nazareth.

In my fieldwork since the 1980s, I have conducted interviews with forty-nine adults and their families, all of whom arrived in Upper Nazareth in the first years of its establishment.[13] When I started my fieldwork, I expected to find chiefly family stories, the kind of absorption stories that are handed down in families and that deal with the experience of immigration and the challenges of absorption. However, I found much more new folklore that went beyond the family circle—aphorisms, phrases, and stories with similar themes that expressed a formal identity shared by the entire group. I found that new folklore was created at the interface of the traumatic encounter between the immigrants and their new reality.[14]

"OUR NAME OF THE PLACE"

Eastern European Jewish folklore was always polyglot and preserved this multilingualism through the experience of immigration, but with a significant change. Whereas in Poland the language that served as the distinctive identifying and unifying code was Yiddish, supplemented by a few words of Hebrew, in Israel the situation was inverted. This is particularly conspicuous in the epithet the immigrants applied to their new home, Qiryat Natzeret, drawing on the tradition of homiletical derivations of names they had brought with them from the diaspora. In their legends of origin about the earliest Jewish settlements in Poland, Polish Jews derived the name Poland from the Hebrew *Po-lin*, meaning "lodge here," because it was the place where their ancestors had found rest after years of persecution and wandering. That is, the Polish word was Judaized and a new etymology was invented based on a play on Hebrew words. We also find this kind of wordplay, or name *midrash*, in Polish Jewish folklore about various cities.[15]

In Israel the immigrants called their new home Qiryat Natzores—"a town on troubles." As one of my informants put it, "We didn't call it Qiryat

Nazereth, our name was Qiryat Natzores." The Hebrew word *Natzeret* was given the Ashkenazic pronunciation *Natzores* and was then further distorted to give it a meaning in Polish and Yiddish. In Polish, *na* means "on," while in Yiddish, *tsorres* means "troubles." The immigrants' reference to their new home as a "town on troubles" expressed the problems they encountered in their attempts to integrate.

PHYSICAL CONDITIONS AND TRANSITION

The first large category of folklore dealt with the initial encounter with the physical conditions of the new country. For immigrants from Europe, the Israeli climate was hard to bear. This immediately led to homiletical derivations of words and names. Thus *ḥamsin*, the name for the dry hot desert wind that the immigrants learned from the old-timers, was given a Polish etymology based on phonetic similarity: *ḥamsin* became *chamski syn*, Polish for "son of a hoodlum," and so they called this cruel weather.

The immigrants remember that there were few buildings, and those that existed were built from stone, an architecture unfamiliar to them. There was little greenery, and the ground was rocky. The wild landscape and unfamiliar animals were the source of great anxiety. Snakes, scorpions, lizards, and chameleons were seen as primeval creatures, known to them previously only from books. This was the background for the "monster" story that circulated among the Polish immigrants. The formal structure of the monster story runs as such:[16]

1. The hero (the narrator or someone he knows) steps over an object without noticing it.
2. The "object" wakes up and turns out to be a snake, scorpion, or lizard that traps the hero.
3. The trapped hero looks for a way to defend himself and lights on some object quite inappropriate for this (usually some object provided to immigrants by the Jewish Agency, such as an aluminum bucket, a broom, a stool, or a kerosene lamp).
4. The hero uses this implement to fight off the "monster" and wins the battle (he kills the animal or chases it away).
   In a number of stories, there is another narrative function:
5. A veteran Israeli who happens to pass by informs the hero that the animal in question was quite innocuous.

The following is an example of the monster story that I recorded from Yosef Goldman. The recording has since been deposited in the Israel Folktale Archives (IFA):

> When we arrived, the place was utterly desolate. I sent my wife and daughter to my sister in Haifa and stayed here alone. Every afternoon I used to go out and try to plant a garden. One day I come back and cross the threshold. I saw there was a stick on the threshold, but I didn't pay any attention to it and stepped over it. No sooner had I entered the room than I see that the stick is following me—it wasn't a stick but a snake, which began to dance in front, while blocking my path back to the door.
>
> What could I do? There was no place to run to, and in Poland I had never had anything to do with snakes. I look around and next to me I see the bucket we had received from the Jewish Agency. In those days, when we came from Poland, I was healthy—I must have weighed around a hundred kilos. I grab the bucket, put it over the snake's head, and sit on it, and, what do you expect, my weight severed its head. I was petrified! I took the snake by the tail and ran to my upstairs neighbors, who were old-timers from Afula. They heard the story and began to roar with laughter because the snake wasn't poisonous.[17]

What these stories expose, first of all, are the anxieties of the narrating society. But they also provide a way to vent these anxieties by the mere act of expressing them. The story is a metaphor for the condition of the immigrants, who feel that they have come to a primordial wasteland. From this perspective, the story expresses a binary opposition between nature and culture, to use the concepts of Claude Lévi-Strauss.[18] The hero resembles a person who has gone from a civilized habitat to a place where nature lies bare and exposed, overrun by primeval monsters. Settling in an unfamiliar place, asserts Mircea Eliade, resembles an act of creation. Strange districts are associated with chaos, with pre-creation. Settlement is tantamount to converting chaos into cosmos by means of a ritual that actualizes it.[19] The transition story is both an expression of and part of the ritualistic act. The transition itself, represented in the stories by the crossing of the threshold, leaves the hero trapped and with no way out, his back to the wall, with monsters dancing in front of him and barring his way. This is how the immigrants conceive of their own situation. They know there is no way to return to the former situation, which, although it did not lack difficulties, was known and familiar. They know the only way out is to deal with the Israeli "monster" and to overcome it, if possible.

The hero of the story has no means appropriate for dealing with the new situation. He does not know the nature of the monster, and the various objects provided by the Jewish Agency are not really meant for self-defense. This, of course, constitutes implicit criticism of the absorption methods themselves. Nevertheless, the hero is a doer. Instead of throwing in the towel, he takes up the unsuitable tools, because they are the only ones at hand. But in addition to them, he also applies the wealth he retains from his past—experience of life, the ability to improvise, a capacity to withstand perilous situations and survive. Indeed, despite the inappropriate implements, his readiness to act and his powers of invention lead him to victory.

Interwoven throughout the story is a vein of humor that the narrator directs at the hero, who is sometimes himself or his alter ego. The fact that an experienced adult lets himself be trapped creates the self-directed irony so typical of Eastern European Jewish humor. The hero's duel with a threatening monster, armed only with an aluminum bucket or a kerosene lamp, is a genuinely comic scene.[20] The humorous climax of some of the stories turns the entire plot into a tempest in a teapot and reflects the narrator's attitude toward himself and his peers and displays his ability to see the amusing side of his own anxieties.

Nevertheless, even though the monster turns out to have been a totally harmless creature, the narrating society does not view the incident as much ado about nothing. The incident is important precisely because it highlights the trap in which the immigrant finds himself and forces him to take a stand and act. This reveals the optimism of the immigrants from Poland, who, having experienced the horrors of the Holocaust, know that one must persevere, no matter what. The story also makes it clear that even though Israeli society has not provided the immigrants with the appurtenances that would facilitate their integration, they can make do by calling upon other resources derived from their earlier experiences—determination, perseverance, power of invention, and the ability to get by in situations of pressure and distress. From this perspective, the story confirms the positive self-evaluation of the narrating society alongside its characteristic self-directed irony.

FOOD

The food in Israel, too, was quite new. Many immigrants told of bad stom-achaches during their first days in the country. The new foods became the subject of many stories, such as one I call "The Camouflaged Plums." The formal structure is as follows:

1. The hero (the narrator or someone he/she knows) is invited to a meal at the home of someone who has been in the country longer (a relative, a veteran immigrant on a kibbutz, etc.).
2. The host puts a dish of tiny plums on the table.
3. The hero is astonished by their small size and compares them in his/her mind with the plums he/she remembers from Poland.
4. The hero tastes the plums (the narrator first describes the hero's anticipa-tion of the taste of the dearly loved fruit) and spits them out.
5. The host laughs at the hero and makes fun of him/her: "They're olives!" he announces.

The epilogue to these stories may be, "To this day I can't eat them," but it may also be, "And today I've learned to eat and enjoy them." I recorded one example of this story from Moniek Zand:

> The old-timers never stopped trying to recruit me to join the Mapai Party. They organized outings to kibbutzim and persuaded me to come along. Around noon we came to the dining room, where I saw lots of tiny plums in a bowl on the table. I didn't understand why they were serving dessert before the main course and why the tour organizers were eating them even before the meal. For me, in Poland, plums were dessert. But the plums in Poland were colossal, maybe the size of apples, and so sweet. What can I tell you, throughout the meal I thought about the plums and could already taste their sweetness in my mouth. When the meal was over I took a tiny plum and popped it into my mouth. The taste was so bitter that I spat it out. I couldn't restrain myself. They just laughed and laughed. "What, you didn't know they were olives?"[21]

This story circulates broadly among Polish Jews in Israel, far beyond Up-per Nazareth. Here, too, we encounter the typical humor of self-irony, a result of the description of an adult who behaves like an infant—putting things into his mouth without knowing what they are and then spitting them out. The story also expresses the longings for one's native country, or at least cravings for familiar things and tastes from home. The description of the hero anticipating the flavor of the plums is comic, because the adult hero is portrayed as a gluttonous child. The story also expresses the immigrant hero's lack of self-confidence, reflected by his joy when he finally believes, erroneously as it turns out, that he has encountered something familiar.

The story presents two fundamental oppositions between the plums of Poland and the supposed plums of Israel. First is their size—large in Poland, small in Israel. This can be interpreted as a metaphor for the situation of the immigrant, whose stature has become dwarfed not only in the perceptions of the veteran society (which laughs at his reaction) but also in his own eyes. The second contrast is that of sweet versus bitter. The hero's mouth waters at the thought that he is about to taste the sweet fruit of his native country; instead he fills his mouth with the acrid bitterness of the Israeli fruit. This can be understood as a symbolic expression of disappointment when faced with the difficulties of absorption, which leave an unexpected bitter taste in the immigrant's mouth. What is more, he is not familiar with Israel and its fruits, of which the olive is one of the most important and sacred, one of the biblical Seven Species.

Explicit laughter erupts twice in this story. The first time is within the narrative, where the object of the laughter is the disappointed hero who spits out the bitter fruit, and those amused are the old-timers, who know quite well what an olive is. But there is also laughter in the narrative situation. Here the narrator and his audience chuckle at the hero, their alter ego, because in the wake of such an incident they too know what an olive is. The incident in which they are portrayed as risible heroes is perceived as having been worthwhile after all, because it taught them something, brought them closer to the new reality, and helped them internalize it.

THE SPHERES OF THE SOCIAL ENCOUNTER: THE *VEYTIQ*

Folklore reflects tensions in contact between immigrants and old-timers, who, as already noted, occupied all the key positions in Upper Nazareth, leaving the immigrants extremely dependent on them. In 1950s Israel, one's seniority in the country was still a criterion for determining social status and the allocation of resources.[22] Sometimes political pressures

were exerted on immigrants by the bureaucrats of the agencies they depended on for their daily bread. At first the immigrants found hardly any
arena where they could enjoy a full and equal social partnership with the
old-timers. It is true that the veteran society, which saw itself as the integrating society, drilled into the immigrants the notions of full equality,
solidarity, and partnership in the creative enterprise—but on the condition that the host society's existing groupings and parties were deemed
suitable to all the immigrants' desires, needs, and aspirations. The under-
lying conception of immigrant absorption in those years, which advocated assimilation into existing social orientations and values to the greatest extent possible, and as a corollary rejected the diaspora experience,
produced great tension.[23] The immigrants felt that even that which was
precisely dearest to them, their own language—Yiddish even more than
Polish—was denigrated and rejected. So the immigrants called on this
language to respond to the veterans, tit for tat. The epithet the immigrants
affixed to the old-timers was based, once again, on a verbal echo with a
Yiddish word and a borrowed signification. The Hebrew word *vatiq*, "veteran" or "old-timer," became *veytiq*, which in Yiddish means "pain." This
epithet became a unifying code word for the group, demarcated its difference from the host group that perceived itself as an elite, and, through
the connotation attached to the word, challenged this perception. In fact,
the *veytiq* figures in many stories and expresses the relations between immigrants and old-timers.

ENCOUNTER WITH OTHER JEWISH ETHNIC GROUPS

As noted above, immigrants came to Upper Nazareth from Hungary and
Romania as well, and later, in 1960, from North Africa. There is evidence
of a great deal of mutual segregation at first, expressed in folklore through
epithets and stereotypes. The term *igen-migen*, for instance, culled from
the Hungarian word *igen* (yes) was used to refer to immigrants from Hungary. This epithet was associated with the jocular Yiddish rhyme "We
called them *igen-migen, khap di fligen* [catch the flies]." Romanian emi-
grants were called *Romaneshte* or *Romeiner-ganev* (Romanian thief), while
Moroccan Jews were called *shvartze* (black). The Poles looked down on
this last group, as reflected in the following story.

1. The hero or heroine goes to the home of new immigrants from Morocco.
2. The hero or heroine is invited to stay for dinner.
3. The hero or heroine asks to use the facilities, only to discover that the toilet bowl is being used as a crock for curing pickles!

I recorded one example of this story from Ya'acov Goldberg:

> Moroccans moved into the other end of the tenement house. What can I tell you—the first time I saw them, after they arrived, I thought the prophet Elijah had come to the block. They wore white dresses with a three-cornered hat and triangular white shoes. With the beard they looked just as I had always imagined Elijah the prophet.
>
> There was one man whom I used to greet cordially every morning and he returned the greeting. One evening, when I was coming home, he was standing outside. He took me by the hand and gestured that he wanted me to come inside with him. I didn't want to, but it wasn't nice to refuse. We went inside and he called his wife, who began to run back and forth and put food on the table, all sorts of delicacies. He pushed everything into my mouth. The food was spicy, but I had no choice, I had to eat it. Finally my stomach began to hurt and I had to go to the bathroom. I went in there and what did I see? The toilet was stuffed full of cucumbers! That's how it was back then. They didn't know what a toilet was for.[24]

This story, which I recently heard directed at Jews from Ethiopia (in a slightly different form), is always told in a context that turns it into an apologetic tale, namely, as a reason the narrator preferred to keep his distance from this group at the time of their first encounter. The ethnic group targeted in this story is one that, according to the tale, does not draw one of the most basic distinctions in the civilized world—that between food and excrement. The story recounts the "primitive" nature of the members of that community when they arrived in Israel and is presented to justify the attitudes of the narrator and his or her community at that time.

ENCOUNTER WITH ARABS

The encounter with Arab society, too, was a shock. The immigrants who were brought to Qiryat Natzeret had to pass through the streets of Lower Nazareth in order to reach their new home. The encounter produced many stories of astonishment at the sight of men in dresses and headscarves. But the relations that developed between the two groups were for the most part positive. The immigrants appreciated the business sense of the Arabs of Nazareth, sold them goods they had brought from Poland, traveled with Arabs in Arab buses, and were delighted to discover not only that some of the Arabs spoke Polish, having come into contact with General Władysław Anders's army during its stay in the country during World War II, but also that the Arabs were quick to learn Yiddish and did not condemn it, as the veteran Israelis did.

At the same time, there was an uneasiness about intimate relations, which stemmed precisely from the mutual attraction of east and west. The following narrative, which was also in broad circulation, embodies this anxiety.

1. The heroine is a woman known to be intimate with Arab men (the narrator does not refer to a specific woman but takes pains to indicate that everybody knew her).
2. The heroine is warned against continuing this unacceptable conduct.
3. The heroine pays no attention to the warnings and continues to behave this way.
4. The heroine's head is shaved in the middle of the night.
5. The mortified heroine cannot leave her house.

The narrative function of the head shavers is filled by various figures in different stories. Usually we are told that "nobody knows who they were," a mechanism that aligns the story with sacred legends by alluding to the intervention of celestial powers, even though most of the Polish immigrants were not religious. Sometimes they are "some of our young men," and sometimes "they were young fellows from the *shvartzes*" (in the Israeli context, this meant immigrants from North Africa), "who are hotheaded and hate Arabs."

This is a story about setting boundaries. After their arrival in Israel, the immigrants were confronted with a situation in which values and norms were blurred; many of the values they had brought with them from their country of origin were rejected by the dominant culture. This disjuncture, as we have noted, produced alienation and even hostility. Arab society, despite its differences and remoteness, did not threaten the immigrants. On the contrary, it treated them with the respect and esteem that was so conspicuously absent in the attitude of the Jewish host society. The cordial relations and close proximity between Jews and Arabs stoked anxiety over the potential for intimate relations to develop between the two communities, an intimacy forbidden by Jewish religious law and considered taboo by most of the immigrants and the larger society. The story attempts to set these limits clearly, casting a woman who transgresses those boundaries as the victim. Her punishment of having her hair cut off alludes to the many connotations of hair in Jewish tradition, while at the same time borrowing a penalty that was commonly meted out in Europe during World War II to women who were too friendly with the enemy.

To conclude, my main motivation in starting this project was to help remedy the absence of sociological research on this immigration wave of Polish Jews to Israel, in contrast to the numerous studies of immigration from Asia and North Africa during the same period. I wanted to see if ethnographic work collecting folklore among this group could help explain why sociologists were viewing Polish-Jewish immigrants as "nonproblematic." My findings show that immigrants from Poland *did* have many problems. The shock of the encounter with Israeli society and culture was no less strong, and in some areas perhaps even stronger, than that experienced by other groups of immigrants. Nevertheless, an analysis of their folklore reveals three central traits that reflect the Polish immigrants' cultural outlook. First, the heroes of the stories are optimistic. Even when the situation seems desperate, they do not throw up their hands in despair, but rather fight on bravely, even though the only weapons available are quite inappropriate for the task at hand. Secondly, the heroes display high self-esteem, even though it is not shared by the host society. This is reflected in their attitude toward the old-timers as well as toward immigrants of other ethnic groups. And third, the heroes—and the narrators—display humor, a willingness to see the amusing and absurd side of a situation and to laugh at themselves even in painful settings. Even the most traumatic situations are ultimately seen as having been worthwhile, despite the ridicule the hero endured. The hero of the story comes out the winner, because he or she learns from what happened, becomes more familiar with the new situation, and internalizes it.

A study of the folklore of Polish immigrants to Israel demonstrates the importance of immigrant folklore. Folklore emerged as a means of coping with every challenge immigrants faced: the physical surroundings, the food, status, their encounters with other groups of immigrants, and their relations with Arab society. Their folklore is not only an expression of the chaos they experienced, but also a means of turning this chaos into cosmos, using cultural implements from the past and adapting them to the new reality. In this way folklore serves as a means to digest change, to cope with it, and to construct a bridge while using resources drawn from both cultures, the old and the new.

NOTES

1. For an exhaustive treatment of the subject see William A. Wilson, "Herder, Folklore and Romantic Nationalism," in *Folk Groups and Folklore Genres: An Introduction*, ed. Elliott Oring (Logan: Utah State University Press, 1989), 21–37.

2. Edward B. Tylor, *Primitive Culture* (London: John Murray, 1871).

3. William R. Bascom, "Folklore and Anthropology," *Journal of America Folklore* 66 (1953): 283–290; Dan Ben-Amos, "Gishot ḥadashot le-ḥeker ha-folklor," *Ha-sifrut* 20 (1975): 1–8; Robert A. Georges, "Folklore," in *Sound Archives: A Guide to Their Establishment and Development*, ed. David Lance (Milton Keynes: International Association of Sound Archives, 1983).

4. Robert A. Georges, "Gishot meḥkar be-folklor 'etni," *Jerusalem Studies in Jewish Folklore* 4 (1983): 7–26.

5. As studies of this kind, Georges lists Robert Bogdan Klymasz, *Ukrainian Folklore in Canada: An Immigrant Complex in Transition* (New York: Arno, 1980); and Beatrice S. Weinreich, "The Americanization of Passover," in *Studies in Biblical and Jewish Folklore*, ed. Raphael Patai, Francis Lee Utley, and Dov Noy (Bloomington: Indiana University Press, 1960), 329–366.

6. Galit Hasan-Rokem,"Tahalikhey shinui shel ha-sipur ha-'amami," *Jerusalem Studies in Jewish Folklore* 3 (1982): 129–137; Haya Bar-Itzhak and Aliza Shenhar, *Jewish Moroccan Folk Narratives from Israel* (Detroit: Wayne State University Press, 1993); Haya Bar-Itzhak, "Interrelationship between Jews and Gentiles in Folk Narratives Told by Polish Jews," *Jewish Folklore and Ethnology Review* 13, no. 1 (1991): 8–10; Esther Schely-Newman, "Self and Community in Historical Narratives: Tunisian Immigrants in an Israeli Moshav" (PhD diss., University of Chicago, 1991).

7. Charles Liebman and Eliezer Don-Yehiya, *Civil Religion in Israel: Traditional Judaism and Political Culture in the Jewish State* (Berkeley: University of California Press, 1983).

8. K. Frankenstein, "The Psychological Approach to the Problem of Ethnic Differences," *Magamot* 3(a) (1951): 158–170.

9. G. Spiegel, "Hishtalvut 'edot be-kfafot meshi," *Keshet* 5, no. 17 (1963): 147–148.

10. Quoted in Yisrael Gutman, *Ha-Yehudim be-Polin aḥare milḥemet ha-'olam ha-sheniya* (Jerusalem: Zalman Shazar Center, 1985), 111.

11. Baruch Kipnis, "Hitpat̲h̲ut yeshuvim Yehudim ba-Galil 1948–1980," in *Artsot ha-Galil*, ed. Avshalom Shmueli, Arnon Sofer, and Nurit Kliot (Haifa: Society for Applied Social Research, University of Haifa, 1983), 723–724; Dan Rabinowitz, *Overlooking Nazareth: The Ethnography of Exclusion in Galilee* (Cambridge: Cambridge University Press, 1996), 6–7.

12. Despite this fact, an information sheet put out by the Upper Nazareth municipality in 1984 states that "the first settlers came to Nazareth hills at the beginning of 1957. Most of them were veteran Israelis—managers, military personnel, and others who wanted to participate in the establishment of a new and developing community." This reflects the Israeli official policy at that time toward the status of new immigrants.

13. For the first findings of this ethnographic project see Haya Bar-Itzhak, "Les Juifs polonais face an 'monstre' israélien: Récits d'aliya en Israël des Juifs *polonaise*," *Cahiers de littérature orale* 44 (1998): 191–206; and Haya Bar-Itzhak, *Israeli Folk Narratives: Settlement, Immigration, Ethnicity* (Detroit: Wayne State University Press, 2005).

14. Notably, other folklorists who focus on the immigrant experience have made similar observations. For instance, in her study of Eastern European immigrants to Canada, Barbara Kirshenblatt-Gimblett associated cultural shock with the creation of folklore. Kirshenblatt-Gimblett, "Culture Shock and Narrative Creativity," in *Folklore in the Modern World*, ed. Richard M. Dorson (The Hague: Mouton, 1978), 109–121.

15. Haya Bar-Itzhak, *Jewish Poland: Legends of Origin* (Detroit: Wayne State University Press, 2001), 27–44.

16. The attempt to establish a formal text of the folktale is best known from the work of Vladimir Propp, *Morphology of the Folktale* (Austin: University of Texas Press, 1968). His method differentiates between content and form and establishes a division into two categories, one variable and the other fixed. On the plane of each individual narrative there are the characters and their actions, and these may change from one story to another. The analytic level is the fixed formal level. On this level he suggests the narrative roles and their functions, which are abstract, general, and unchanging.

17. Yosef Goldman, interview with the author, Israel Folktale Archives (IFA) 22849.

18. Claude Lévi-Strauss, *Structural Anthropology* (New York: Basic Books, 1963), 206–231.

19. Mircea Eliade, *The Myth of the Eternal Return; or, Cosmos and History* (Princeton, NJ: Princeton University Press, 1991), 9–10.

20. Dov Noy, "Ha-kayemet bedih̲at 'am Yehudit?," *Mahanayim* 67 (1962): 49–56; Elliott Oring, *Jokes and Their Relations* (Lexington: University Press of Kentucky, 1992).

21. Moniek Zand, interview with the author, IFA 22850.

22. Shmuel N. Eisenstadt, *Israeli Society* (London: Weidenfeld and Nicolson, 1967), 166–182.

23. Liebman and Don-Yehiya, *Civil Religion in Israel* (see note 7).

24. Ya'acov Goldberg, interview with the author, IFA 22851.

10

The Use of Hebrew and Yiddish in the Rituals of Contemporary Jewry of Bukovina and Bessarabia

ALEXANDRA POLYAN

In a seminal 1959 article, Charles Ferguson coined the term "diglossia" to describe situations in which a single "speech community" uses two or more varieties of the same language under different conditions. Usually a standardized version of the language is designated as a high variant and local dialects are designated as low.[1] Although Ferguson focused on cases in which the registers are variants of the same language, subsequent scholars have since applied this model to communities in which two unrelated languages coexist, such as Arabic and Turkish in the Ottoman Empire, Latin and German in medieval Europe, or Yiddish and Hebrew in pre–World War II Eastern Europe.[2]

With the rise of nationalism in the nineteenth century, former vernaculars were transformed into standardized national languages, often rendering speakers of regional variants outsiders. The process of language standardization influenced speakers' metalinguistic reflection and—in some sense—their *Weltanschauung*.[3] As Susan Gal writes, "Multilingual speakers of regional languages are often stigmatized—and denigrate themselves—for being 'traditional' or insufficiently modern, and for the practice of code switching between languages."[4]

How can Hebrew and Yiddish be described within the framework of Ferguson's diglossia? It is widely recognized that "language and religion have been the two most important markers of ethnonational identity: sometimes linked, sometimes at odds."[5] In this case, Jewish ethnonational identity can be said to have two main markers: Judaism and Hebrew.[6] However, in the Eastern European Ashkenazic context Yiddish played an important role as well; Hebrew and Yiddish coexisted and were used in a diglossic manner. Contrary to popular perceptions, Hebrew was not a dead language prior to its nineteenth-century "reinvention," nor was its use restricted to a miniscule elite, as was the case for Latin in medieval Christendom.[7] By contrast, a large percentage of the Eastern European male Jewish community utilized Hebrew for communication, either with other people or with God.[8] Literary works, philosophical treatises, polemical works, and letters were written in Hebrew, and it was employed as a vehicle of oral communication, albeit only under special circumstances. Hebrew also successfully united different people coming from disparate communities, who spoke mutually incomprehensible vernacular languages.

Joshua Fishman characterizes the distribution of functions between Hebrew and Yiddish as "compound bilingualism"—a situation that occurs when choice of language depends on communication, topic, or addressee.[9] Sometimes, the difference between the two languages has been described as one between the sacred and the profane. Max Weinreich argued that it was the difference between oral and written communication: Hebrew was used for transmission of existing written texts or creating new ones, while Yiddish served as a mode of oral communication.[10] Other scholars, notably Dovid Katz, have complicated this division by pointing to both the often-overlooked history of early modern Yiddish literary productivity and Hebrew orality.[11]

This chapter analyzes Jewish diglossia and perceptions of language usage in early twenty-first-century Bukovina and Bessarabia. It is based on interviews recorded by the Center for Biblical and Jewish Studies of the Russian State University for the Humanities and the Center for Teaching Jewish Studies in Universities "Sefer" (Moscow). The interviews were recorded between 2005 and 2012 during expeditions that Maria Kaspina led to Bukovina and Bessarabia.

There are several reasons for choosing this region. During World War II Bukovina and Bessarabia were under Romanian as opposed to German occupation, as a result of which its percentage of Holocaust survivors was much higher than it was elsewhere in the Soviet war zone. The second reason is that in Bukovina and Bessarabia traditional Jewish culture, ritual, and language are preserved better than in adjacent Podolian regions, due to the fact that Bessarabia and Bukovina had been part of Romania rather than the Soviet Union during the interwar period. As a result, the Jewish community was not subject to Soviet antireligious campaigns, and Jewish religious practice and education were permitted to continue without interruption. Therefore our informants, born in the 1930s and earlier, still remembered the traditional shtetl and local Yiddish dialects.

The linguistic situation has been undergoing some changes recently. The generation of monolingual Yiddish speakers and bilingual Yiddish-Hebrew speakers has largely disappeared from the region, and the present generation, comprising mainly bilingual or trilingual speakers, is surrounded by people who speak either Russian, Ukrainian, or Moldavian.[12] Further, throughout the twentieth century Yiddish, like other European languages, underwent a process of standardization; it now possesses an interdialectal standard of pronunciation as well as lexical and grammatical standards. Thus, a kind of inner diglossia has appeared in Yiddish. The place of the high language has been taken by the *klal-shprakh* (standardized language), whereas local dialects are considered low languages.

For instance, Yefim Yakovlevich Vaynshteyn, whom I recorded with Nataliya Golant in 2012 in Beltz, told us, "Literary Yiddish is the language spoken by the Jews of the Birobidzhan region. It was a pure literary language. Newspapers were published in it, prose was written, Jewish poems.... This was genuine Yiddish!" When we asked him to expand on the difference between this Yiddish and his Yiddish, he replied, "Many words are pronounced differently: we say *gekimen*—and they say *gekumen*. It is a simple example. *Fardrisn—fardrosn*. There is a difference.... We have an ensemble which sings pure Birobidzhan Yiddish. This is literary Jewish Yiddish. And all the rest—Ukrainian, Moldavian, Uzbek, Tajik Yiddish—this is all ... folklore!"[13]

Vaynshteyn explained that writers, editors, and other literati had come to an agreement in Birobidzhan on how Yiddish was to be written and pronounced. Vaynshteyn, who grew up in the Soviet Union, perceived the Jewish Autonomous Region of Birobidzhan to be the global center of Yiddish and its leadership to be the leading authority on the language. He suggested the existence of an ideal place where the correct language variety is spoken. Ironically, his idea of a genuine language is that of a standard language: it is not a folk variety, but a literary language that possesses a press and a literature. We can see how, even in naive speculations on the topic, standardization of a language leads to popular perceptions of language purism—"an ensemble which sings pure Birobidzhan Yiddish," in Vaynshteyn's words. Indeed, our informants frequently described the *klal-shprakh* as "regular," "correct," "literate," or "pure." But as Joshua Fishman has noted, "Where standard variety does exist it does not necessarily displace the non-standard varieties from the linguistic repertoire of the speech community for functions that are distinct from but complementary to those of the standard variety."[14] *Klal-shprakh* is a variety suitable for formal usage in the press and literature, whereas local dialects are preserved in the realm of everyday speech. The informant's own dialect is perceived as a softer and more beautiful idiom.

The concept of *literarishe shprakh* (literary language) is related to *klal-shprakh*. When informants speak of *literarishe shprakh,* though, they can mean two different things: the interdialectal pronunciation standard, which is phonetically close to the northern dialect, or the written language of the Yiddish literary classics, epitomized first and foremost by Sholem Aleichem, who, ironically, used one of the southern dialects. For instance, Lazar' Mikhaylovich Gurfinkel of Czernowitz told us in 2007, "Ikh red nisht literaturish, nisht vi Sholom-Aleykhem ot geshribm, a bisl ondersh, a bisl ondersh" (I do not speak the literary language, not the language Sholem Aleichem wrote, in a slightly different way, in a slightly different way). Similarly, Khayim Davidovich Kotlyar of Czernowitz explained in 2009, "Mainly it [*klal-shprakh*] has the same words, but the accent is different. They speak Sholem Aleichem's Yiddish, and I speak Moldavian."

As daily usage of Yiddish has declined in Eastern Europe, a language shift has taken place, in which Yiddish has become a cherished piece of heritage rather than a vernacular language.[15] Like other vernaculars, which had not been valued and were taken for granted, Yiddish has become an object of reflection and even a matter of national pride. Our informants perceived Yiddish as a language with a vast literary tradition. They speculated about its beauty and about the culture it represents. Sometimes they even associated Yiddish with antiquity. When asked in 2012 which language was older, Yiddish or Hebrew, Yevgeniya L'vovna Bass of Beltz told me, "Idish. Val idish is e-he-he-he-he! Nor ivrit . . . dakht zikh mir us, az nysht. Rabunem obm gelernt ivrit, ober idish iz, dakht zikh, elter." (Yiddish is. Because Yiddish is e-he-he-he-he [from time immemorial]! And Hebrew . . . I believe, it is not. The rabbis learned Hebrew, but Yiddish seems to be older.) This trend culminates in the sacralization of Yiddish. Esther Raytses, a Habad emissary's wife in Ukraine, told me in 2011 that she spoke to her children only in Yiddish, even though she did not know it well and had to replace many words with English ones. The explanation she gave was as follows: "Der Alter Rebe hot gezogt, az yidish iz di heylike shprakh" (The Alter Rebe said that Yiddish is the sacred language).[16] Even when our informants belonged to the younger generation with limited command of the language, or even no knowledge of it whatsoever, they still tended to respect Yiddish because of its historical association with the rich culture of the older generation, and they tended to praise it for its emotional richness.[17]

The revival of Hebrew as a spoken language has also influenced the status of Yiddish in Eastern Europe and introduced a new diglossia into the speech community, this time between modern vernacular Hebrew and *loshn-koydesh* (the Holy Tongue), a term that refers to biblical and rabbinical Hebrew.[18] Sometimes our informants perceived the difference between the two variants of Hebrew in terms of old and new. In our 2010 interview Abram Yakovlevich Krupnik of Novoselitsa referred to the shift from the Ashkenazic pronunciation's emphasis on the penultimate syllable to the Sephardic emphasis on the last syllable. The Ashkenazic pronunciation mirrors the pronunciation of Yiddish, whereas the Sephardic is preferred in modern Israeli Hebrew: "I would like to say that now people read Hebrew some other way, not like I do. That is, if I ask you—me, a resident of Novoselitsa, how the things are in Israel, I would say, "Ma *nish*ma bizrail?" [How are things in Israel?]. And nowadays people do not put it this way, they would not say "Ma *nish*ma," but rather "Ma nish*ma* be-Izrail." And as for me, I use the old way." Daniil Grigoryevich Grinberg of Beltz also noted the shift in pronunciation of the Hebrew letter *tav* from the Ashkenazic to Sephardic custom, which he regarded as a simplification of the language: "The words were pronounced some other way before. One used to read 's' instead of 't.' Now we read *itgadal*, and the old version is *isgadal*. And today we read like one reads contemporary Hebrew, simply."

The skill of being able to read "old" Hebrew, that is, the Holy Scriptures and the prayer book, in the Ashkenazic pronunciation was a matter of pride for our informants, even among those who otherwise disparaged traditional religious education. The prestige of Yiddish and the affiliated Ashkenazic pronunciation is much higher than that of contemporary Hebrew, for the latter is considered a language devoid of culture.

In contemporary times, aspects of the traditional Ashkenazic culture, particularly *loshn-koydesh* and Yiddish, are employed primarily in ritual. In the situation of genuine diglossia, translation from the high variety to the low one or vice versa is problematic, although it does exist.[19] In the frame of ritual, however, the linguistic hierarchy is much more flexible. There are several texts, such as notes left on the graves of *tsadikim* and spells which exist both in *loshn-koydesh* and in Yiddish, that can be uttered or written in both languages.[20] Another example of contemporary diglossia comes from the realm of everyday life, in which synonymic texts of small genres like clichés are not translated when uttered. For instance, when mentioning someone who is deceased, it remains customary to recite in *loshn-koydesh* the phrase *ulev a-shulem* (may he rest in peace) or the Yiddish phrase *zol zikh min* (may he solicit on our behalf). Similarly, both the *loshn-koydesh* phrase *leshune toyve* (to a good new year) and the Yiddish phrase *a git in mozldik yur* (a good and happy new year) are common holiday greetings.

Yiddish texts are commonly used in contemporary Bukovina and Bessarabia in funerary rites and when making appeals to the dead, particularly when visiting the graves of *tsadikim* and deceased relatives. Visitors address the dead with a highly changeable text, but with a stable opening: *loyf in beyt* (run and beseech). The deceased is expected to beseech God on behalf of the living, for the dead are regarded as being in closer proximity to the Lord. When asked for a specific example, Grigoriy Vladimirovich (Rivn ben Zeyev) Gitman of Czernowitz volunteered, "Nu, akh bet dekh, zol zayn, zolsti beytn Got far mikh, far di kinder, in me zol . . . mir zoln zan gezint, zoln ubm parnuse—in azoy vayter" (I beseech you that . . . that you ask God on behalf of me, my children, that He give us health and

earnings—and so on). When we asked Polina (Pesya) Samuilovna Rippel
of Czernowitz in 2011 if it would be proper to say *loyf in beyt*, she replied affirmatively and added, "If you address one deceased person then *loyf beyt
ar indz*, but if I address many of them, I mention all of them and put it in
plural: 'ir zolt loyfn beytn far indz . . . far mir, tsi far veymen . . . farn kind,
far veymen, ikh veys'" (May you run and beseech God for us . . . for me or
for whom . . . for the child, for whom). Yiddish is the main language used
for communicating with the dead—either when visiting their graves or
when dreaming about them. The text begins with the standardized phrase
loyf in beyt, but the rest of the recitation is customarily changed and ad-
justed to the circumstances.

Postnatal rites also often employ Yiddish. The most common such rituals are those geared toward protecting the infant from the evil eye, particularly the "spell of three women."[21] A variant we recorded from Abram Yakovlevich Krupnik in 2009 went, "Dray vaber zenen gezesn of eyn shteyn.
Eyne'ut gezugt, Ployni ot an oyg; di ondere'ut gezugt, neyn; in di drite ut
gezugt, fin vonen es iz gekimen, ain zol es geyn" (Three women sat at one
stone. One of them said, the So-and-So has an evil eye; the other one said,
he doesn't; and the third one said, from whence it came, there it must go).[22]
Recital of this text also requires ritual action. Klara Moiseyevna Katz of
Czernowitz explained to us in 2007,

> My mom would take a glass of water . . . one had to keep silent at that
> time. No one was allowed to be in the room—you and your baby only.
> And no one could talk to you, you could not answer anything! Take a
> glass of water, cold water. Take a piece of bread, divide it into nine pieces,
> and throw this bread into the glass. If it goes up—a man had put the evil
> eye; if it goes down—that's a woman. Then take this bread out of the
> glass piece by piece, throw [it] and say, "Fin vi s'iz gekimen—ahin zol es
> geyn" [From whence it came—there it must go]. After you've thrown one
> piece—fin vi s'iz gekimen. . . . Ofn pripetchik zitsn dray vaber. Eyne zugt,
> yo, eyne zugt, neyn, eyne zugt, fin vi s'iz gekimen—ahin zol es geyn.
> [From whence it came. . . . Three women sat at an oven. One of them said
> yes, the other one said no, and the other one said, from whence it came—
> there it must go.] And throw it into all the corners of the room until no
> piece is left.

Maria Kaspina recorded an interesting gloss from Sarah Gorodetskaya,
who was born in Brichany. Gorodetskaya explained that the Yiddish word

anore (a contraction of the Hebrew phrase "the evil eye") is derived from the contemporary Israeli Hebrew word *nora* (awful).

Finally, Yiddish texts related to holiday rites were well preserved among our Bessarabian and Bukovinian informants. Among the more common rites recalled was the *fir kashes* (four questions) asked by children during the Passover seder. Usually our informants remembered only one or two of the four questions. In 2005 Roza Ovshiyevna Shterenberg of Czernowitz recalled,

> Tote, ikh vil dikh freygn di fir kashes. Di ershte kashe vil ikh dikh freygn. Farvus ole tug fin a gonts yur viln mir esn khumec, viln mir esn motse, ober di dozike teg fin yontef esn mir nor motse? Hob ikh dikh gefregt eyn kashe. Di tsveyte kashe vil ikh dikh freygn. Farvus ole tug fin a gonts yur viln mir esn ungeleygt, viln mir esn nisht ungeleygt, ober di dozike nakht fin Peysakh esn mir nor ungeleygt?

> (Dad, I would like to ask you the four questions. I am going to ask you the first question. Why do we eat chometz as well as matzo the whole year, but during these days of the holiday we eat matzo only? I asked you the first question. I am going to ask you the second question. Why do we eat reclining or not reclining the whole year, but this very night of Passover we eat only reclining?)

We have also recorded parody versions of this text. For instance, Anna Iosifovna Ivankovitser of Czernowitz remembered in 2006, "Tate, zug mir nor, tate. Far vus a top ... a top ot a lokh—di vaser rint aroys. A galosh ot a lokh—di vaser rint arayn.... A top ot an oyer—eyngt. Di ost tsvey oyer—di eyngst nit!" (Dad, tell me, Daddy. Why if a pan ... a pan has a hole—water runs out. If a galosh has a hole—water runs into it.... A pan has a handle [literally, eye]—and hangs. You have two—and you don't hang!)

The realm of Hebrew is wider because it includes everyday individual prayer as well as the ceremonial recitation of the Torah and prayers in the synagogue. Beyond the synagogue, it is also used in funerary and holiday rites. Two particularly well-preserved funerary sacral texts are the *El male rakhamim,* commonly referred to as the *Mule,* and the Kaddish. Mikhail (Moyshe) Khaimovich Royf of Czernowtiz, whom we interviewed in 2011, recited the Hebrew *Mule* for us, explaining how both the deceased's name and the name of the one giving charity in memory of the deceased are inserted into the prayer:

Eyl mule rakhmim shoykhen bemroymim, amtse menekhoyne tas kanfe ashkhine be-males kedoyshim utoyrim kzoyer rakia mazhirim nishmas —and here you mention the late person's name—sheulokh loylmo-, "he who passed away" this means—bavir—who gives tsduke [charity], do you know what tsduke is? Tsduke bavir—here I mention the late person's name . . . and the name of the person who gives tsduke . . . nudav tsduko ba-nishmuso, b'an Eyden te' menikhuso, lokheyn bal a-rakhmim yastireyhi . . . bitsroyr akhayim es nishmuso . . . nakhluso, veyunikh beshloymo beshlum veneymar umeyn.

Other Hebrew texts our informants remembered came from *piyutim* and prayers sung before and during Yom Kippur. These texts are characterized by specific phonetic features employed when the sacred texts are recited outside of the ritual context. Unlike the phonetics of what Max Weinreich termed "Whole Hebrew,"[23] in these instances the stress is shifted so that the historically ultrashort vowels are reduced (*naxluso* instead of *naxalusoy* and ba*vir* instead of *baavir*), vowels in syllables following the stressed ones are reduced (*nishmuso* instead of *nishmusoy* and *tsdukə* instead of *tsduku*), guttural consonants are omitted (*yey* instead of *yehey* and *kzoyer* instead of *kezoyhar*), and entire unstressed syllables are omitted (*menekhoyne* instead of *menikhu nekhoynu*).[24]

In addition to these rituals, our informants also mentioned the complex wedding ritual, but could not recall its specifics, which included not only prayers and blessings in Hebrew but also a number of Yiddish songs, greetings, and farewell sayings. Several informants also still remembered the ritual of *krishme leyenen*. The word *krishme* is derived from *kries-Shma* (reading the Shema prayer), and refers to the ritual of inviting *kheyder* pupils to visit a newborn baby and its mother several days after birth—before circumcision in the case of a boy—in order to protect the baby. In both cases, only snippets of the ritual recitation of Yiddish and Hebrew texts had been preserved among the Bessarabian and Bukovinian Jews we visited.

Our research has shown that while the use of Yiddish as a daily language of communication has declined, its value has been preserved in ritual. The very fact of its use in ritual has also contributed to a rise in its status. As a result, Yiddish, which was once regarded in opposition to Hebrew, has been drawn closer to Hebrew: both are used primarily in ritualistic settings, and many rituals can be performed with utterances in either or both languages. The main difference between the ways that Hebrew and Yiddish function today is that Hebrew ritual recitations are derived from written texts and are generally stable, whereas Yiddish ritual recitations are transmitted orally and can easily be changed.

Speech communities can be defined by the symbolic values they assign to a language, regardless of how many languages are spoken within it.[25] Popular fluency in the language is not even relevant: there are speech communities that regard their language as a symbol of national identity even if few of their members have mastered it.[26] A new speech community is being formed today in Bessarabia and Bukovina around Yiddish. Yiddish is being extruded from oral communication but continues to be perceived as a literary language possessing a vast cultural tradition, and almost as a sacred language. At the same time, Yiddish is also being used in ritual, conflating its role with the position traditionally held by *loshn-koydesh*. A new diglossia has been created in parts of Eastern Europe.

NOTES

1. Charles A. Ferguson, "Diglossia," *Word* 15 (1959): 325–340.

2. See, for example, Joshua A. Fishman, "Bilingualism with and without Diglossia; Diglossia with and without Bilingualism," *Journal of Social Issues* 23, no. 2 (1967): 29–38.

3. James Milroy, "The Ideology of the Standard Language," in *The Routledge Companion to Sociolinguistics*, ed. Carmen Llamas, Louise Mullany, and Peter Stockwell (London: Routledge, 2007), 133–134.

4. Susan Gal, "Multilingualism," in Llamas, Mullany, and Stockwell, *The Routledge Companion to Sociolinguistics*, 153.

5. John Edwards, *Language and Identity* (Cambridge: Cambridge University Press, 2009), 100.

6. See, for example, Max Weinreich, "*Yiddishkayt* and Yiddish: On the Impact of Religion on Language in Ashkenazic Jewry," in *Readings in the Sociology of Language*, ed. Joshua A. Fishman (The Hague: Mouton, 1970).

7. Chaim Rozen, "Tahalikhe lashon," *Leshonenu la-'am* 25 (1951): 3–32; Jack Fellman, *The Revival of a Classical Tongue: Eliezer Ben Yehuda and the Modern Hebrew Language* (The Hague: Mouton, 1973); Chaim Rabin, "Language Revival and Language Death," in *The Fergusonian Impact: In Honor of Charles A. Ferguson on the Occasion of His 65th Birthday*, ed. Joshua A. Fishman et al. (Berlin: Mouton de Gruyter, 1986), 2:543–554; Shelomo Haramati, *Ivrit ḥaya bi-merutsat ha-dorot* (Givatayim: Masada, 1992); Shelomo Morag, *Iyunim ba-'ivrit, ba-aramit u-vi-leshonot ha-yehudim* (Jerusalem: Magnes Press of Hebrew University of Jerusalem, 2003); Rachel Elior, "'Ivrit mi-kol ha-'avarim," in *Leshon rabim: Ha-'ivrit ki-sefat tarbut*, ed. Yotam Benziman (Jerusalem, Van Leer, 2013).

8. Weinreich, "*Yiddishkayt* and Yiddish," 414; Joshua A. Fishman, "The Sociology of Language: An Interdisciplinary Social Science Approach to Language in Society," in *Advances in the Sociology of Language*, ed. Joshua A. Fishman (The Hague: Mouton, 1971), 1:290.

9. Fishman, "The Sociology of Language," 304–305.

10. Weinreich, "*Yiddishkayt* and Yiddish," 410–414. See also Chava Turnianski, "Evreiskie iazyki v traditsionnom ashkenazskom mire," in *Tysiacha let kul'tury ashkenazov*, ed. Jean Baumgarten et al. (Moscow: Lechaim, 2006), 379.

11. Dovid Katz, *Words on Fire: The Unfinished Story of Yiddish* (New York: Basic Books, 2007), 45–77.

12. See Valeriy Dymshits, "Idish v byvshikh stetlakh Podolii (po materialam polevykh issledovaniy 2004–2009 gg.)," in *Idish: Yazyk i kul'tura v Sovetskom Soyuze*, ed. M. Kupovetskiy, L. Katsis, and M. Kaspina (Moscow: RGGU, 2009), 347–350.

13. Our interviews, conducted originally in Russian, are quoted in English translation only. In cases in which they were conducted in Yiddish, I will quote them in Yiddish and then provide an English translation.

14. Fishman, "The Sociology of Language," 229.

15. For related developments in the American context, see Jeffrey Shandler, *Adventures in Yiddishland: Postvernacular Language and Culture* (Berkeley: University of California Press, 2008). See also Joshua A. Fishman, *Language and Nationalism: Two Integrative Essays* (Rowley, MA: Newbury, 1972), 52–53. On metalinguistic reflection, see, for example, Larisa Fialkova and Maria N. Yelenevskaya, *Ex-Soviets in Israel: From Personal Narratives to a Group Portrait* (Detroit: Wayne State University Press, 2007), 239–266; and John A. Lucy, "Reflexive Language and the Human Disciplines," in *Reflexive Language: Reported Speech and Metapragmatics*, ed. John A. Lucy (Cambridge: Cambridge University Press, 1993), 9–32.

16. The Alter Rebe (Shneur-Zalmen of Liady, 1745–1813) was the founder of the Chabad-Lubavitch Hasidic movement. Dovid Katz states that the Alter Rebe had never proclaimed Yiddish to be a sacred language, but his descendants had. (Katz, conversation with the author, November 25, 2012.)

17. Larisa L. Fialkova and Maria N. Yelenevskaya also note that "many immigrants admit that they failed to transfer their knowledge of Yiddish to the children, but this has not decreased the symbolic value of the language." See Fialkova and Yelenevskaya, *Ex-Soviets in Israel*, 251. One of our informants, who speculated on love and tenderness, which could be expressed in Yiddish only, told us about her grandmother who addressed her with a very cute and tender phrase. The phrase turned out to be "Farmakh dem pisk!" ("Shut up!").

18. See Uzzi Ornan, "Hebrew Is Not a Jewish Language," in *Readings in the Sociology of Jewish Languages*, ed. Joshua A. Fishman (Leiden: Brill, 1985), 22–26.

19. See, for example, B. A. Uspenskiy, "Iazykovaya situatsiya i iazykovoye soznanie v Moskovskoi Rusi: Vospriiatie russkogo i tserkovnoslavianskogo iazyka," in *Vizantiia i Rus'*, ed. G. K. Vagner (Moscow: Nauka, 1989), 206–226.

20. See, for example, Maria Kaspina, "'Dray vaber zitzn af a shteyn . . . ': Predstavlenie o durnom glaze v traditsionnoi kul'ture evreev Ukrainy," in Kupovetskiy, Katsis, and Kaspina, *Idish*, 336–340.

21. See Yelena Okolovich, "Zametki po evreiskoi narodnoi demonologii (po materialam fol'klora na idishe)," in *Mezhdu dvumia mirami: Predstavleniia o demonicheskom i*

potustoronnem v slavianskoi i evreiskoi kul'turnoi traditsii, ed. O. V. Belova (Moscow: Sefer, 2002), 136–162.

22. For other variants of this text, including its long version found in printed sources, see Kaspina, "'Dray vaber zitzn af a shteyn. . . .'"

23. Max Weinreich, *Geshikhte fun der yidisher shprakh* (New York: YIVO, 1973), 1:251–253.

24. See Dovid Katz, "The Phonology of Ashkenazic," in *Hebrew in Ashkenaz: A Language in Exile,* ed. Lewis Glinert (New York: Oxford University Press, 1993), 47–61.

25. Joshua A. Fishman, "The Sociology of Language," 232–234. See also John Gumperz, "The Speech Community," in *International Encyclopedia of the Social Sciences,* ed. David L. Sills (New York: Macmillan, 1968), 381–386.

26. Jerzy Smolicz, "A Language as a Core Value of Culture," in *Elements of Bilingual Theory,* ed. H. Beardsmore (Brussels: Vrije Universteit Brussel, 1981), 104–124.

11

Food and Faith in the Soviet Shtetl

JEFFREY VEIDLINGER

M inutes after Dov-Ber Kerler and I first met Khayke Gvinter on the streets of Bershad in 2002 while interviewing Yiddish speakers for our oral history and linguistic project, she was offering us gefilte fish. When we explained that we had to be on our way, she sent her husband, Yuzik, across the yard into her home, to bring us some of her homemade fish, wrapped in paper. "For the road," she insisted. She made her gefilte fish just like her mother did, and could even pull up carrots from the very same garden. The passing on of food traditions, always an important aspect of identity construction, is particularly important among the Jews of small-town Ukraine, where culinary traditions are almost all that remain of a culture that once flourished in the region. Recipes and food often remind them of loved ones who were murdered in their youth or otherwise perished before their time.

In the interwar Soviet Union, the Jewish Sections of the Communist Party, with the support and encouragement of the state and party apparatuses, embarked upon a campaign to destroy traditional Jewish religious practice, the mainstay of Jewish culture. Throughout the 1920s, numerous *kheyders* and synagogues were closed by official fiat throughout the Soviet Union. In addition to the closing of synagogues, the Jewish Sections initiated a massive antireligious campaign designed to discredit religion

and to mock rabbinical authorities. Books of anticlerical jokes were published in Yiddish and schoolchildren were taught songs mocking Judaic
religious practice. The Jewish Sections established mock courts to put the
Jewish religion "on trial," and published "Red Haggadahs," retelling the
Passover story as deliverance from capitalist oppression. According to
official Soviet publications, the results were initially successful: reports
in newspapers and ethnographic reports boasted of the early successes
of the Jewish Sections, telling how the youth of the shtetls were cooper-
ating in liquidating synagogues and exposing Jewish superstitions. Yet
other sources, including internal Jewish Section reports from the late
1920s, complain of a resurgence in synagogue attendance and a rejection
among many Jews of Soviet atheist propaganda, particularly in the shtetls
of Ukraine and Belorussia. In other words, Jews were presented as both
enthusiastic early adapters of Soviet atheism and as obstinate believers in
archaic religious customs.[1]

This chapter suggests that many Jews in small-town Ukraine persisted
in their religious practices and faith, but under state pressure relocated
much of their ritual from the public synagogue to the domestic home. In
addition to venerating the synagogue—the most visible symbol of Judaism in the shtetl—as the most salient expression of Jewish life, many experienced their religious lives in the form of what anthropologist Barbara
Myerhoff termed "domestic religion," the informal inculcation of religious identity through home ritual, which she contrasted with the formal
channels of dogmatic education, "the Great Tradition."[2] Since Myerhoff's
1979 observation, scholarly attention to the role of religion in identity
has shifted from public demonstrations of proscribed ceremony—in the
church, the mosque, or the synagogue—to embrace expressions of faith
and spirituality within the constant and routinized domestic observances
of the home. Among scholars of the Soviet Union, in particular, interest
in domestic or "popular" religion has helped us understand the impact
of formal attacks on institutional religion.[3] In the case of Jewish practice,
domestic religion includes the Sabbath observance, the display of religious artifacts, and most importantly foodways.

Recent scholarship on the implementation of antireligious campaigns
in Vitebsk province and Minsk have provided an increasingly complex
and detailed picture of religious life in the provinces. These studies have

utilized extensive archival evidence to demonstrate the persistence of religious practice through the 1920s and into the 1930s. Arkadii Zeltser, for
instance, has shown that the central Soviet government did not regard the
oppression of Judaism as a priority, and measured the benefits of Jewish
religious suppression against the political expediency of guarding against
accusations of antisemitism. At the same time, the state concentrated its
earliest antireligious campaigns on the confiscation of church and monas-
tic property; since Jewish communal property was not as extensive, many
Jewish religious buildings were left intact. Although central authorities
declined to allocate significant resources to the suppression of Judaism,
local Jewish Sections often acted virulently in their antireligious campaigns. Similarly, Elissa Bemporad, in her study of Minsk, demonstrates
the persistence of key religious rituals such as *shkhite* (kosher slaughter)
and circumcision through the 1930s.[4]

These studies have shown how the Yiddish press often exaggerated the
successes of governmental policies, reveling in informing readers of how
their co-religionists had voted to close synagogues and establish Saturday as a workday in select villages and towns with the hopes of pressuring
others to do the same. Many of the more enthusiastic reports tended to
exaggerate the successes of antireligious campaigns by reporting only the
immediate public reception of these campaigns, while leaving long-term
effects aside. Thus, a trial of the Jewish religion may have been attended
by a large crowd that followed the narrative attentively, even laughing
at appropriate times, but then returned home to prepare a Sabbath meal
and light Sabbath candles. As Anna Shternshis has demonstrated, the
extent of Soviet Jewish religious beliefs and practices cannot be measured by archival and published sources alone. While these sources can
be effective in demonstrating the institutional history of religious organizations, they reveal little on the matter of personal faith.[5] They aid
scholars in ascertaining the public facts, but tell us little about the role
religion played in the home and even less about the role personal faith
played in the hearts and minds of ordinary individuals. In the interwar
Soviet shtetl, Jewish traditions were practiced first and foremost in the
home, away from prying public eyes but surrounded by loving family,
and most commonly at the kitchen table, where food became a symbol of
faith.

This chapter draws upon oral history, in particular the Archives of Historical and Ethnographic Yiddish Memories (AHEYM) at Indiana University, led by Dov-Ber Kerler and myself. The project conducted videotaped oral history and linguistic interviews with 380 individuals in some one hundred towns, villages, and cities in Eastern Europe, mostly in Ukraine. We interviewed informants in their homes, places of work, and around towns, and entirely in Yiddish, even if at times in a stilted Russified Yiddish. We sought informants born before 1930, as we were primarily concerned with memories of Jewish life and Yiddish language in the region before World War II. We also sought informants who were still living in the town or district in which they spent the interwar years. This allowed us to take tours of the town with our informants as guides who could show us the sites of former synagogues, Jewish homes, Jewish stores, baths, and other communal sites, all of which serve as *lieux de mémoire* (sites of memory).[6] The interviews were recorded on digital videotape and have been deposited in the Archives of Traditional Music at Indiana University.

A few caveats are in order. First, we do not claim to have interviewed a typical sample of the population: by interviewing only those who spoke Yiddish, we have already excluded those segments of the population that were most assimilated in the 1920s and 1930s. Whereas in 1926, 76 percent of Jews listed Yiddish as their mother tongue, by 1939, the number of Jews claiming Yiddish as their mother tongue had declined to 40 percent. Since most of our informants were only reaching adolescence by the outbreak of World War II, they can be counted among the minority at the time whose mother tongue was still Yiddish. Further, by focusing on small towns in the traditional centers of Jewish life in Ukraine, the historical regions of Podolia and Volhynia, we examined one of the regions where the persistence of traditional Jewish practice continued longest. Finally, by conducting all our interviews in situ, we excluded the large number—even the majority—of Ukrainian Jews who had left Ukraine for Israel, North America, or elsewhere in Europe. Jews who migrated internally, from small villages to larger cities like Kiev, were also excluded on these grounds. There are numerous reasons why the individuals we interviewed chose to stay in the villages and towns of Ukraine, but the vast emigrations since the collapse of the Soviet Union undoubtedly tainted the sample of those who remained.

Elizaveta Bershadskaia was born in 1927 in Chernyatka near Bershad, where her father worked as a barber and her mother as a seamstress. In 1938 she moved to Bershad, her mother's hometown. She reported that although there was no synagogue in Chernyatka, which was a town of only about fifteen Jewish families, there was a *minyen* (prayer quorum) that met in a private house, where the worshippers read from a *seyfer toyre* (Torah scroll). Although there was no *shoykhet* (kosher butcher) in Chernyatka, she explained, kosher meat was easily obtained from nearby Bershad. She also remembered matzo being brought in from Bershad. Although she insisted that her father went to synagogue regularly and taught her to pray when she moved to Bershad, she could not recall any prayers or songs, even when prompted. She told of celebrating Passover seders in her home, but could not remember the four questions traditionally recited at the meal. She recalled spinning a little toy during the festival of Hanukkah, but could not recall the name of it (*es dreyt*, it spins, she kept saying, but could not come up with the word *dreydl*), nor could she recall a single Hanukkah song, even when prompted.

Most of Bershadskaia's memories are typical of those we encountered in the region. In particular, we often found individuals who warmly and enthusiastically recalled being reared in strictly observant communities, but who were unable themselves to remember any prayers and had only the vaguest notions of Jewish festivals, holidays, and religious rituals. Many women reared in religious households, in particular, had clear memories of individual holidays and the foods associated with them, but were entirely unable to expound upon the meaning of the holiday or to recite a single prayer. Bershadskaia, for instance, recalled clearly that on Fridays her mother would bake challah and they would eat cholent over Sabbath; on Passover they would eat latkes made from matzo meal; and on Hanukkah they ate potato latkes.

Gisia Leiderman, who was born in Bershad in 1924, told us that she came from a religious family: her father went to synagogue on every holiday, put on tefillin every day, and observed the Sabbath by refraining from lighting fires. Yet her only association with many holidays was the food: she remembered eating gefilte fish on Sabbath and making matzos on

Passover. Evgeniia Kozak, who was born in Bershad in 1926, also recalled the meals her mother baked for Sabbath (cholent, challah, soup, gehakte fish), Passover (latkes from matzo meal, gefilte fish, kugel), Purim (humentashn), and Shavuot (cheese blintzes). She also remembered putting up a succah on Succoth and receiving gelt on Hanukkah. Yet she, like the others mentioned, could not recall a single song from the Passover seder or any Jewish prayer, including the benediction over the candles, traditionally sung by women, nor could she explain the significance of any of the holidays she mentioned. Yet she described her family's weekly Sabbath preparation in detail. At the mention of chopped fish, her thoughts became nostalgic: "It's been a long time since I've eaten chopped fish," she mused.

Often the memory of food evokes visceral emotions that beautify the moment: "Since it was Sabbath everything we cooked was good," recalled Beyle Vaisman of Berdichev. The Sabbath time was sacred, rendering even the profane good. For those who formally welcomed the Sabbath with prayer on Friday evenings, lighting Sabbath candles and eating traditional challah bread was an important part of the custom.

Asya Barshteyn, who grew up in Sharhorod, also ascribed special meaning to the Sabbath meal, describing the challah "as though God had baked it": "At home, on Sabbath. We had an oven. You could bake bread, you could bake challah. During the week, you would eat bread, but on Sabbath it was challah, as though God had baked it. Like you were supposed to. Cooked and baked with all types of cookies and baked goods that my mother cooked. Everything like you were supposed to do. And on Sabbath we would light candles. I light candles. Every Sabbath I light candles." Barshteyn's insistence that she did everything "like you were supposed to do" (*azoy vi me hot gedarft*) was echoed by many of those we interviewed, who insisted that they followed religious strictures "just as they were supposed to," or occasionally described how they performed a custom even though "you are supposed to do it differently."[7] These phrases indicate a strong sense that the performance of religious ritual was a requirement that they had agreed to fulfill in accordance with established guidelines and custom. In their narrative, religious obligations trumped the expected behavior of a Soviet citizen, for whom religious performance was not an obligation, but rather an infringement. In 1930s

Soviet Ukraine, one was certainly not "supposed to" light Sabbath candles and bake challah bread.[8]

Another popular Sabbath meal was gefilte fish, which could either be
served Friday evening during the welcoming of the Sabbath or dished
cold on Saturday afternoon. Sofia Palatnikova was born in 1927 in Teplyk,
but lived from 1930 until the war on a collective farm named after Com-
missar of Enlightenment Anatoli Lunacharskii, not far from Simferopol
in the Crimea. She told of large Passover seders with lots of children, and
recalled the construction of succah booths all over the collective farm.
She told of observing Rosh Hashanah, fasting on Yom Kippur, eating humentashn on Purim, and receiving gelt on Hanukkah while living there.
She also remembered the Sabbath gefilte fish, which she explained she
continued to cook from the recipe her mother taught her and which she
described for us in detail:

> I take off the skin. That's right, and I take out the bones. And then I put
> the fillet through a meat grinder. My mother did it with a chopping knife.
> She used to say that when you use the grinder it doesn't taste as good.
> But I use the meat grinder. Then I add raw grated onion, then fried on-
> ion—just fried a little. Pepper. Salt to taste. Eggs. . . . And if there's matzo
> meal—I have matzo meal almost all year round. I take matzo—it's good
> for fish. I also sometimes use little biscuits, non-sweet ones, "croquettes."
> I had taken off the skin, so the place where I had cut it, that's where I
> stuff it. Then I set it out on a plate, with the head, the tails, and then the
> middle part, you get a whole fish. And after that I stuff it, I put it in a
> pan and fry it a little. And to the bottom of the pan I add carrots and raw
> onions and fried onions and a bay leaf and pepper and salt and let it cook
> over a low flame for two hours. And it comes out just right. . . . My mother
> made it like that. They say my fish is good. I give some to the non-Jews. . . .
> They don't know how to make fish.

In this description, Palatnikova subtly turned what seemed to be a straight-
forward recipe for gefilte fish into a value-laden identity marker. She concluded her recipe by vouching for its authenticity—"My mother made it
like that"—establishing the recipe as esoteric knowledge, available only to
her exclusive group—"They [non-Jews] don't know how to make fish." The
use of matzo in the recipe further marked it as Jewish. On the other hand,
she also asserted the universal appeal of the dish by insisting that the
non-Jews, although they were incapable of making it, still acknowledged

its supremacy. In some respects, the gefilte fish recipe Palatnikova shared is reminiscent of Kabbalistic knowledge—it is esoteric and can only be created by the initiated, but it has a potency recognizable to all. A good gefilte fish transcends ethnic boundaries.

In addition to the role that special dishes and food preparation play in the periodic holidays of Judaism, food practices, particularly observance of the laws of *kashrut,* have traditionally served as a major boundary marker for Jews. Whereas kosher meat remained readily available in the 1920s, its acquisition became increasingly difficult throughout the Soviet Union during the 1930s. It was almost impossible to obtain kosher beef; the state confiscated cows, and the slaughter of cows was heavily regulated. Chickens, however, were more easily obtained, and legal kosher butchers continued to exist in certain locales: in 1935 there were twenty-one kosher butchers in the city of Kiev alone. The state targeted kosher butchers during the Great Terror of 1937, but in small towns some continued to practice clandestinely through the war.[9]

While most of the people we spoke to had also overcome Jewish taboos against mixing milk and meat and eating pork products, many continued to associate their Jewish identity with specific food customs. In her recollections of Sharhorod, Asya Barstheyn told us, "They sold only kosher meat—no lard at all. All the Jews bought only kosher meat. My mother only went to the kosher butcher shop to get meat." Sofia Palatnikova's father, who owned a butcher shop in Teplyk until 1930, also remembered that if the meat was not kosher, nobody would buy it. The Jews ate only kosher meat, and the non-Jews, she explained, did not eat meat at all. When we asked why, she ventured, "Why? I should know? They didn't have anything to buy it with. My father explained that there were a lot of fast days. . . . For a month and a half they don't eat meat." Presumably Palatnikova was referring to Lent, but she also distinguished pork from meat, alluding to a perception that Jews ate beef and chicken, whereas Christians ate only pork. The Jewish dietary restrictions, even when they were not followed, were so highly ingrained that they influenced the semantic meaning of meat.

Of all the Jewish festivals and holidays, Passover is the one most Soviet Jews remember observing. Many imagine Passover as the defining Jewish holiday, and it is the food of Passover—the matzo—that most represents the holiday itself. Other scholars have written about the Soviet emphasis on the celebration of Passover. Memoirs from the period and reports from foreign visitors also often note the importance Soviet Jews ascribed to obtaining matzo for the holiday.[10] Rabbis in the Soviet Union even made numerous appeals to foreign Jews in the 1920s requesting that matzo be sent from abroad, and in 1929 the government responded to popular pressure by briefly permitting the importation of matzo. Passover was the most observed Jewish holiday in the interwar Soviet Union, as well as the most persecuted. One reason for its observance may be that in contrast to Rosh Hashanah and Yom Kippur, it is observed in the home rather than the synagogue. In an environment where synagogue attendance was difficult, people were more likely to celebrate a holiday based in the home. The Jewish Sections recognized the popularity of Passover celebrations and so concentrated much of their propaganda on combating its observance through the use of Red Haggadahs and trials of Passover.

Tatiana Marinina of Teplyk, who spent much of the 1930s living on the Lunacharskii collective farm in the Crimea with her sister, Sofia Palatnikova, recalled how Passover brought the whole collective farm together: "All the children and grandchildren would come to the seder. They used to come. . . . My father had friends and they would come. My mother would cook up a wonderful chicken soup with matzo meal. She would make Passover pancakes from potatoes and beetroots. We used to pickle, I'm not sure you know this, but Jews also pickle borscht." Once again the holiday is associated primarily with food and the matzo serves as an identity marker, separating the Jews from their neighbors. But in Marinina's memory, it was also the custom of pickling borscht—that most Ukrainian of dishes—that defined what it meant to be a Jew during Passover.

Several people we interviewed noted the custom of throwing a hot stone into a pot in order to render certain utensils kosher for use during Passover. Evgeniia Krasner of Shpykiv told us, "In the oven we would heat stones to make them glow and we would throw these stones and prepare all of the pots and pans—earthenware pots—and we would put the stones in and pour water over them, and steam would rise up over everything." Marinina told us that her mother "would take down the dishes from the attic, and throw a stone in the oven. There wouldn't be a crumb of bread in the whole house." When we spoke with her, she explained that she had revived these practices for herself, but regretted that she had not been able to pass them down to her own children: "I do the same now. We also have matzo here. I buy matzos—you're supposed to do it differently—but I buy them all year round. And I make latkes and fresh matzo. I make a Passover pancake from sour beetroots and potatoes. In my book, Passover is Passover! No bread comes in my house! I am alone. When I had children, I couldn't do it. Now that I'm alone, though, why shouldn't I do it when it is such a pleasure?" There is a wistfulness in her implication that during that period of her life when she was bringing up children to pass these traditions on to, she was unable to fulfill them. Only now, when she is alone in a new democratic Ukraine, is she able to perform them. But her children have grown up without learning the customs, and will never have these rituals embedded in the fabric of their lives.

Her insistence that she buys matzo year round is also indicative of the degree to which matzo has become associated with Judaism. Even though the ritual eating of matzo is only required for eight days of the year—and it is precisely the extraordinary nature of the diet that renders the ritual significant, as symbolized by the question, "Why is this night different from all other nights?"—the display of matzo and occasional eating of it is a year-round activity for many Jews in Ukraine today. Ukrainian Jews use matzo not only as an essential ingredient in their gefilte fish, but also as a means of expressing their identity publicly. Although we conducted our interviews during either the summer or the winter season, months away from the Passover festival, countless homes we visited proudly displayed a box of matzo on the mantelpiece. The boxes distributed annually by the Federation of Jewish Communities in Ukraine are even designed as keepsakes: they are colorfully illustrated and include a list of useful phone numbers for Jewish organizations throughout Ukraine. The federation suggests that the matzo has a shelf life of one year. Matzo boxes are clearly intended not just to hold the matzo for consumption during Passover, but also to be displayed year round and kept as visible identity markers. No longer used exclusively for ritual purposes in accordance with the periodic calendar of festivals, matzo continues to have a deep symbolic value as a public expression of ethnic identity.[11]

The Passover holiday is a domestic affair and is intricately bound up with memories of family and loved ones. For Beyle Vaisman, memories of the Passover seder provided a concrete and specific memory she could attach to the family she lost during the war:

> I remember Passover, with the four questions.... And the plates. We were daughters, three daughters. There were no brothers, so there was nobody to ask the four questions, but I remember we would open the door ... for Elijah the prophet. We had separate dishes. Everything would be koshered.... We had a very religious family and that's why I remember the laws. A very religious family. My father would keep Passover and we would have a seder. And we kept kosher. There was a *shoykhet*. He would slaughter a cow that people took to him. And there was a *shoykhet* for poultry.... We led a very religious life, a religious family. And in addition to this, my father was very learned. We had a big family with cousins, aunts, uncles. All of them would celebrate Passover with us, and Sabbath back then. It was so interesting. My father was so learned. He would tell such interesting stories. We children never wanted to go because we just wanted to hear these Jewish stories. They were so interesting. And Hitler took and murdered these people.

The last sentence of her description—"And Hitler took and murdered these people"—seems at first to be out of place in her memory of Passover. But the phrase reveals that the memory is not really about Passover—it is about her loved ones and her loss. The holiday's significance does not lie in the commemoration of the biblical Exodus from Egypt. Rather it is given meaning because the seder meal is tied to so much else that has disappeared, most importantly loved ones and familial heritage. Passover, like the Sabbath, is remembered today primarily because it evokes memories of family, food, and domestic harmony. Passover's central rituals—eating matzo, cleaning the house of bread products, and the seder meal—are focused on the home rather than the synagogue, just as the Sabbath meal and rest are domestic rituals. Both holidays can be observed in private, inconspicuously, and with few resources. Although both also have a synagogue component, it is the home rituals that define the holiday. Passover was and remains a cherished holiday neither because of its universal message of liberation nor because of its centrality as one of the three pilgrimage festivals in the Jewish religious tradition, but rather because the unique tastes and smells associated with its specific dietary restrictions evoke a nostalgic longing for childhood. This nostalgia was perhaps best expressed by Pesia Kolodenker and Yente Tolkovitz of Tulchyn. After discussing the

Passover meals, Pesia remarked, "Everything we ate, everything we baked back then was very tasty," to which Yente added, "Now it's not good."

The testimonies that our project has recorded paint a picture of a shtetl population in Ukraine whose life was still steeped in the culture of Jewish religion in the interwar period. Synagogues remained a regular part of life, but it was the Jewish holidays celebrated in the home that were most cherished. Even the men who were able to sing holiday songs and recite prayer fragments they remembered from their *kheyder* days displayed little knowledge of the meaning of the prayers and the significance of the holidays. While this could be attributed to a lack of religious observance, it is also a function of Eastern European *kheyder* education, which focused on the performance of ritual, paying little attention to the significance of holidays and the stories associated with them.

So much of the old world that the elder generation of Ukrainian Jews knew was rendered unrecognizable by Sovietization. Parents were deprived of the pleasures of passing many of their most cherished traditions on to their children. Schools and clubs taught their children to reject their elders' prayers, religious rituals, and customs. Traditional modes of healing and curing the evil eye were mercilessly mocked as harmful superstitions. Even their workways could not be passed on, as the state spurned traditional artisanal skills in favor of factory work, and interpreted business acumen as hostile "antigovernment" activity. Yet Soviet ideologues not only tolerated ethnic food customs, but even encouraged them as part of the ethnic kaleidoscope that constituted the Soviet Union. National minorities were encouraged to retain visible markers of ethnic difference, such as dress and food, provided that they were emptied of any national sentiment. The Soviet government often showcased the colorful peasant dresses and exotic spices of its national minorities as a means of asserting the ethnic diversity of the Soviet Union. Foodways, along with language, was the most tangible tradition that could safely be passed from generation to generation, and represented the last link with the older generation. A gefilte fish recipe could become a cherished family heirloom.

This was even more the case for communities devastated by war. Small-town Jewish communities could hardly erect a monument in the center of town, honoring the murdered Jews, nor could they publicly commemorate the war with an annual "Jewish parade" or other memorial. Instead, private remembrance was the predominant means of evoking the past, and the kitchen represented a sphere as close to private as could be. The eating of a gefilte fish made in accordance with a traditional recipe was a literal imbibing of the past and a means of merging oneself with one's ancestors, sharing a meal with them across time.[12] Food is also a major stimulant to memory. Taste and smell can work synesthetically, evoking seemingly unrelated memories. In immigrant communities, food often becomes a metonym for a wider cultural context, for the lost world of the old country.[13] This diasporic evocation was exacerbated in the Soviet Union, where foodways provided one of the few means of expressing ethnic identity and memory. For small-town Soviet Jews, food provided a means of memorializing and commemorating a past that could not be publicly expressed.

NOTES

This chapter is drawn from material I previously published in Jeffrey Veidlinger, *In the Shadow of the Shtetl: Small-Town Jewish Life in Soviet Ukraine* (Bloomington: Indiana University Press, 2013).

1. See the analysis by Mordechai Altshuler, *Soviet Jewry on the Eve of the Holocaust: A Social and Demographic Profile* (Jerusalem: Hebrew University of Jerusalem, 1998), 98–102; and Mordechai Altshuler, *Religion and Jewish Identity in the Soviet Union, 1941–1964* (Waltham, MA: Brandeis University Press, 2012).

2. See Barbara G. Myerhoff, *Number Our Days: A Triumph of Continuity and Culture among Jewish Old People in an Urban Ghetto* (New York: Dutton, 1979); and Robert Redfield, *Peasant Society and Culture: An Anthropological Approach to Civilization* (Chicago: University of Chicago Press, 1956), 67–104. Anthropologists and scholars of religion have demonstrated that these two phenomena often coexisted, but the distinction is still a useful one. This relationship is similar to what Russian scholars have termed "daily religion." See particularly A. S. Lavrov, *Koldovstvo i religiia v Rossii, 1700–1740* (Moscow: Drevlekhranilishche, 2000).

3. See, for instance, Moshe Lewin, "Popular Religion in Twentieth-Century Russia," in *The Making of the Soviet System: Essays in the Social History of Interwar Russia* (London: Methuen, 1985), 57–71; and Glennys Young, *Power and the Sacred in Revolutionary Russia: Religious Activists in the Village* (University Park: Pennsylvania State University Press, 1997).

4. Arkadii Zel'tser, *Evrei sovetskoi provintsii: Vitebsk i mestechki, 1917–1941* (Moscow: Rosspen, 2006); Elissa Bemporad, *Becoming Soviet Jews: The Bolshevik Experiment in Minsk* (Bloomington: Indiana University Press, 2013).

5. Anna Shternshis, *Soviet and Kosher: Jewish Popular Culture in the Soviet Union, 1923–1939* (Bloomington: Indiana University Press, 2006).

6. Pierre Nora, "Between Memory and History: Les Lieux de Mémoire," in "Memory and Counter-Memory," ed. Natalie Zemon Davis and Randolph Starn, special issue, *Representations* 26 (Spring 1989): 7–24.

7. These words were also used by Barbara Myerhoff's informant in Venice, California, who insisted, "That's just how things are supposed to be." See Myerhoff, *Number Our Days*, 234.

8. For the norms of religious behavior in Soviet cities of the 1930s, see Natalia Lebina, *Povsednevnaia zhizn' sovetskogo goroda: Normy i anomalii, 1920–1930* (St. Petersburg: Neva, 1999), 119–158.

9. A. A. Gershuni, *Yehudim ve-yahadut bi-Verit ha-mo'atsot: Yahadut Rusyah mi tekufat Stalin ve-'ad ha-zeman* (Jerusalem: Feldheim, 1970), 86–87.

10. For analyses of Passover in the Soviet Union, see Yaacov Ro'i, "Ha-pesaḥ mul ha-mishtar ha-sovyeti," *Bar ilan* 24/25 (1989): 173–195; and Anna Shternshis, "Passover in the Soviet Union, 1917–1941," *East European Jewish Affairs* 31, no. 1 (2001): 61–76.

11. Alice Nakhimovsky has observed a similar phenomenon among urban assimilated Jews in the Soviet Union, who divorce food from its association with the ritual calendar and instead utilize it as a general signifier of intimacy and a symbol of Jewish life. See Alice Nakhimovsky, "You Are What They Ate: Russian Jews Reclaim Their Foodways," *Shofar* 25, no. 1 (2006): 63–77.

12. For a discussion of the role food can play in traversing the private and public spheres, particularly in regard to memorialization, see Jon D. Holtzman, "Food and Memory," *Annual Review of Anthropology* 35 (October 2006): 361–378.

13. For some anthropological and historical studies of food and memory, see David E. Sutton, *Remembrance of Repasts: An Anthropology of Food and Memory* (Oxford: Berg, 2001); Joelle Bahloul, *The Architecture of Memory: A Jewish-Muslim Household in Colonial Algeria, 1937–1962* (Cambridge: Cambridge University Press, 1996); and Hasia R. Diner, *Hungering for America: Italian, Irish, and Jewish Foodways in the Age of Migration* (Cambridge, MA: Harvard University Press, 2003).

12

Undzer Rebenyu

RELIGION, MEMORY, AND IDENTITY
IN POSTWAR MOLDOVA

SEBASTIAN Z. SCHULMAN

When applied to the study of the past, the ethnographic approach allows for keen insight into overlooked events, ignored historical actors, and marginalized social groups whose presence has been diminished or lost in the traditional historical record. For more recent historical events, these anthropology-influenced methodologies are often engaged to produce what has come to be known as "microhistory," or those studies that provide a tight focus on the local in order to shed light on broader matters and contexts. As Carlo Ginzburg writes on the genre, "A close-up look permits us to grasp what eludes a comprehensive viewing, and vice versa."[1] The biography of Khayim-Zanvl Abramovitsh (ca. 1892–1995) is one such case where small-scale activities and individual actions can reveal much about wider issues.[2] Known as the Ribnitser Rebbe, Abramovitsh was a central figure in northern Bessarabian religious life and folklore, a Jewish mystic and healer celebrated by Jews and non-Jews from the region, but little known outside the circles he personally touched. Despite the limited scope of his activities, however, the implications of his works and the stories told about him have potentially profound consequences for our understanding of Soviet Jewish history, post-Soviet Jewish identity, and contemporary Hasidic culture.

Mention the name Khayim-Zanvl Abramovitsh, or even simply Khayim-Zanvl, to a Jew who lived in any one of a certain group of northern Moldovan towns from the 1940s to the 1970s, and you are likely to be bombarded with detailed stories. From wonder tales and reports of miracles to discussions of Jewish continuity and tradition, these accounts speak to the widespread influence of the rabbi, leader, and teacher known today as the Ribnitser Rebbe. Active in the region before, during, and after World War II, Abramovitsh is said to have touched the lives of countless Jews in the Soviet Union's western borderlands, fulfilling religious functions and providing spiritual inspiration to communities in times of crisis. Based in the industrial Moldovan city of Rybnitsa from 1941 until his emigration to Israel and then to the United States in the early 1970s,[3] Abramovitsh was brazen in his observance of Jewish religious practice under Communism, often facilitating the performance of rituals for his fellow Jews in the area and indeed sometimes throughout the USSR. Among certain groups of post-Soviet Jews today, Abramovitsh is in fact still remembered as a heroic, respected, and endearing figure. Since his death in 1995, he has also achieved an almost mythic status in Hasidic circles, revered as a true *tsadik,* or holy man, whose miraculous acts, collected and embellished in hagiographic works, have brought the Jewish people one step closer to redemption.

Integrating rarely accessed archival materials with ethnographic interviews that I and others conducted with Jews living today in Moldova and elsewhere, in this study I seek to differentiate fact from fiction and discern the reality of Abramovitsh's activities and their impact among Jews in the postwar Soviet Union. As a healer, ritual slaughterer, and prayer leader, the Ribnitser Rebbe enabled the persistence of prewar religious and folkloric traditions in this region. At the same time, for those Jews who came of age in the postwar period in these peripheral communities, Abramovitsh inspired the articulation of a kind of Soviet Jewish identity that remains largely unstudied in the dominant historiography, which has focused mostly on the country's more assimilated urban Jews. From this perspective, the Ribnitser Rebbe's biography can be considered a critical lens through which to reexamine much of the postwar Soviet Jewish experience. The following thus attempts to outline the effect of Abramovitsh's efforts on his community across generations and offer a few hypotheses as to how he was so successful in these endeavors.

In addition to uncovering some of the historical facts regarding the Rebbe's life and activities, these oral testimonies will also be examined for what they reveal about how this region's Jews perceive themselves, their Soviet past, and their place in the contemporary Jewish world. As post-Soviet Jewry now constitutes a global diaspora, tales told about Abramovitsh occupy a central part of how some informants reimagine and resituate their local traditions in a worldwide context. The narrative that emerges is indeed often a pointed critique of Western Jews and their perceived patronizing, paternalistic attitude toward their formerly Soviet brethren. Instead, in pointing to an enduring religious tradition, these Moldovan Jews suggest the moral rightness of the local over the global and seek to shift their story from one of liminal interest to one of central importance.

According to governmental sources, Jewish religious life in the town of Rybnitsa had officially come to an end in 1927, when its last synagogue was closed as part of a wider campaign against religious activities in what was then the Moldavian Autonomous Soviet Socialist Republic (MASSR).[4] Although informal religious activities, such as *minyonim*, or small prayer groups, and private holiday celebrations, continued relatively unmolested into the 1930s, many Jews who grew up in the town during this period emphasize the thoroughly Soviet character of their city. Despite the fact that a plurality of the town's residents in this period identified as Jewish,[5] many informants describe Jewish life in interwar Rybnitsa as being governed more by the developing norms of life in the new socialist state than by the precepts of Jewish tradition. Citing the ideological goal of "friendship of the peoples," for instance, several informants made special note of the fact that social networks and romantic relationships often crossed ethnic boundaries between Ukrainians, Jews, and Moldovans as "constructing the Communist future" became the new commonplace.[6] And even though a Soviet Yiddish school operated in the town for several years, the consensus among those interviewed was that in Rybnitsa, at least at this time, Russian not only was becoming the "language of interethnic communication," but was also the preferred form of expression in the Jewish home.

During World War II, Rybnitsa fell under Romanian occupation and was the site of a ghetto and transfer station where approximately three thousand Jews were held captive and thousands more murdered. Significantly, imprisoned in the ghetto were not only Jews from the MASSR and Soviet Ukraine, but also Jews from the Romanian region of Bessarabia as well. Abramovitsh himself, then a resident of the Bessarabian shtetl of Rezina, was among the thousands of Jews forced from their homes into the Rybnitsa Ghetto. After the ghetto's liberation in 1944, this mix of Jews who had lived in the Soviet Union before 1940 and *zapadniki,* or so-called Western Jews, from territories only later annexed to the USSR, was to define the Jewish community of Rybnitsa for the rest of the Soviet period, especially as the town's burgeoning postwar industries in metallurgy and food production attracted migrants from across the country. It was in this diverse community that Abramovitsh was to earn his reputation as the Rebbe of Rybnitsa.

In the mid-1940s, when the Soviet government adopted, ostensibly for war-related strategic reasons, a more favorable view of Jewish religious life, Abramovitsh played a leading role in officially registering the Rybnitsa Jewish community, serving as the group's unanimously elected "minister" and liaison with the authorities.[7] When this official recognition was rescinded sometime in the early 1950s, Abramovitsh continued his leadership role, sometimes in direct conflict with the government, but more often in a less provocative and more clandestine manner.

During an interview I conducted in 2011, Leye Freydkina (née Boiarskaia, b. 1946) described her father Srul's upbringing in the aforementioned shtetl of Rezina, just across the Dniestr River from Rybnitsa, as "pious and poor." Born in 1927, Srul, according to his daughter, had a traditional Jewish religious education and despite his youth enjoyed spending time in the company of his learned neighbor, one Khayim-Zanvl Abramovitsh, who was then one of the town's rabbis. Srul was, as his daughter retells the story, an inquisitive youth who both literally and figuratively "spoke the same language" as Abramovitsh, sharing intellectual interests and often engaging in long conversation. As Freydkina relates, this was the beginning a lifelong friendship between the two, a strong relationship that survived the profound dislocations of war and genocide, as well as decades under Communism in the Soviet Union.

Although Freydkina's stories of her father's precocious youthful be-havior—before she herself was born—cannot necessarily be taken at face value, her own memories of her father's association with Abramovitsh in the postwar years are more reliable. In this regard, Freydkina describes how Abramovitsh's efforts in organizing daily prayer groups, providing proper slaughter for kosher meat, acquiring religious literature and cer-emonial items, performing ceremonies, and fulfilling many other duties enabled her father and others in his circle to maintain many ritual and cultural aspects of their prewar lives. It was not the simple fact that these opportunities existed in the town, Freydkina emphasizes, but that they were integrated into her father's and others' daily routines. Abramovitsh's twice-daily *minyonim* for instance, were organized in such a way that they took place in a different private home each day. As in other cities, Frey-dkina clarifies, this scheme was intended to throw off frequently visiting out-of-town KGB operatives, preventing them from discovering the extent of the Rebbe's activities. Within Rybnitsa, however, Abramovitsh's deeds were considered somewhat of an open secret, and the local authorities could not be so easily fooled. Instead, Freydkina reports, the *minyen* mem-bers told their employers that they went from home to home each day in order to commemorate a *yurtsayt*, or the anniversary of a loved one's passing, in a different family, an excuse that took advantage of a supposed legal loophole, often invoked especially in the early postwar years, that al-lowed for leniency for missed days of work where funereal practices were concerned. Whether employers believed these justifications or actually let their employees miss work so frequently is not yet verifiable.[8]

The open secret of Abramovitsh's extensive efforts was not lost on those Jews who, unlike Srul, did not grow up in a religious environment. Jews who grew up in Rybnitsa or in other parts of the Soviet Union before the war and had lost a connection to tradition were also affected by Abramo-vitsh's actions. Often, this resurgent interest in Judaism or Jewishness was thought to be a reaction to the traumas of life during and after the war, a need for spiritual and communal sustenance after tremendous loss and hardship. In his memoir of the Rybnitsa Ghetto, for example, Isroel Fingurt describes in amazement how Soviet Jews returned to the faith of their ancestors under Abramovitsh's stewardship during the war: "This was the miracle of the return of the formerly godless back into the fold.

In the camp, dozens of people, who for some 10 to 15 years hadn't gone to synagogue, hadn't opened a prayerbook or a Bible [*khumash*], started to regularly go to Rabbi Khayim-Zanvl's tiny crooked room to participate in prayer and hear words of Torah."[9]

The testimony of Zlata Kotliar, a current Jewish resident of Rybnitsa, born in 1927, is indicative of this prewar generation of Soviet Jews who reconnected to *yidishkayt* thanks in part to the presence of the Rebbe in their town. While Kotliar had attended her town's Soviet Yiddish school for three years, she had little other formal exposure to Jewish culture in her youth. Spurred by the loss of family during the war and a desire to identify Jewishly, Kotliar credits "that kind soul" Abramovitsh with the fact that after the war she was able to speak Yiddish without shame and mark Jewish holidays with others.[10]

In addition to these Jews born before the war, many Rybnitsa Jews born after the war also expressed a strong connection to Abramovitsh. Leonid Tul'chinskii (b. 1952), for example, told numerous stories about "Reb Khayim-Zanvl" during an interview I conducted with him in Moldova in 2011. Tul'chinskii's connection with the Ribnitser Rebbe began just eight days after he was born, when Abramovitsh performed and officiated over his circumcision. Much like Leye Freydkina's father, Tul'chinskii's grandparents were regularly involved in Abramovitsh's meetings and celebrations, and they sought to involve their grandson as much as possible in these happenings. After he reached the age of thirteen, and was thereby considered an adult by Jewish law, Tul'chinskii was a frequent presence in *minyonim* whenever it did not conflict with his schooling. Tul'chinskii's experience of Judaism was a major part of his life, he declares, but nevertheless it took on an informal quality. Having had no opportunity for formal religious learning, for Tul'chinskii, practicing his faith was in many ways more about being part of a community of his coethnics than about fulfilling any spiritual needs. As he said, "I didn't really understand the services. I opened the book and when they would stand, I would stand. When they would sit, I would sit. And afterward, Reb Khayim-Zanvl would give me a bottle of beer. But it was important to be together. We knew that."

For Tul'chinskii, practicing Jewishness was not exclusively about community solidarity, however. Being Jewish had a moral component as well.

"How can I tell you? I know what it means," he said simply. "I know what it means to be a Jew, to be a good person." Tul'chinskii explained how he absorbed these less tangible lessons by focusing on the outpouring of Jewish mutual assistance after a flood ruined much of the town's lower half in 1967. Unprepared for this natural catastrophe, thousands of Rybnitsa's residents lost their homes in this flood, including Abramovitsh and many other Jews who had lived in the town's traditionally Jewish neighborhood. In the wake of disaster, Tul'chinskii reported, Abramovitsh began an informal campaign to help victims of the flood, organizing a way to receive and distribute material donations and find temporary shelter for those affected. While he initially refused any aid, Abramovitsh stayed for over six months with Tul'chinskii's grandparents while, he recalled with astonishment, local Jews pooled their resources to purchase the Rebbe a new home in the upper part of the town. Only a teenager at the time, Tul'chinskii had been deeply moved to learn that being Jewish did not only have social and ceremonial aspects, but an ethical imperative as well.

Until recently, most scholarship on the history of Soviet Jewry has downplayed the role of religion in the lives of the USSR's Jewish citizens.[11] Even those monographs written on the basis of the rich archival materials made available by the Soviet Union's collapse have tended to focus on the creation of a new secular Jewish culture that emerged after the Bolshevik Revolution rather than on the persistence and transformation of earlier ways of life.[12] As the present study has shown, however, for many Jews in the postwar Soviet Union, religion remained one of the most salient ways in which one articulated, practiced, and perceived of one's Jewishness. In this regard, Judaism resembles many faiths that, despite state antireligious campaigns, proved vital and enduring throughout the Soviet period.[13]

Of course, not every Jew in Rybnitsa was shaped by Khayim-Zanvl or his presence in the town. Nor was the Rebbe the only such figure in Soviet Moldovan Jewish life. At least in the early postwar years, there were other Jewish religious leaders with similar goals active throughout the republic. Rabbi Iosif Epel'baum (1893–1962), for instance, served as a rabbi in Chişinău (Kishinev), then the capital of the MSSR, in the city's only postwar synagogue, acting throughout the late 1940s as a community activist, spiritual guide, and advocate for local Yiddish culture and the establishment of Jewish schools. In 1949, he was removed from his post by the local branch of the Council on the Affairs of Religious Cults (CARC) for "nationalist activity."[14] Perhaps under greater pressure from the authorities than Abramovitsh because of his more visible presence in the republican capital, Epel'baum remained occasionally active in Jewish life in the city, but never again attempted to play as influential a role as he did in the early postwar years.

In more peripheral locales as well, smaller Jewish communities in these same postwar years sought to rebuild and revive Jewish life in their towns and villages. Returning from the front or from evacuation in central Asia, these reassembled and often devastated communities petitioned authorities, sometimes on the local level and sometimes in letters addressed directly and simply to "Kremlin, Moscow," for the right to formally establish their communities, reclaim synagogues, or open new spaces for prayer. While these requests were almost always refused, their number and wide geographic spread from across the MSSR and on both sides of the former Romanian-Soviet border indicate an intense, if unfulfilled, desire for Jewish religious expression throughout the republic in the early postwar period. Written in formulaic language, these letters do not reveal the emotional content of their writers' appeals, but do demonstrate the ways in which many Romanian-born Jews, at least, hastily learned to "speak Bolshevik," employing the particulars of Soviet bureaucratic speech and argumentation to make demands of their new government. Yet, with few exceptions, even these painstakingly crafted epistles were met only with rejection.[15]

Looking over this correspondence and the numerous letters of refusal, it appears that no figure was as doggedly persistent or as ultimately successful, both in his struggles with the authorities and in his spiritual work in his community, than Khayim-Zanvl Abramovitsh. While the efforts of so many others had been curtailed, this Rebbe was able to provide almost three decades of consistent guidance and leadership to his community and at times to others in regions outside the MSSR, such as Podolia and Transcarpathia. What, then, explains Abramovitsh's outsized success? Can it be attributed solely to his alleged power to perform miracles? Correspondence between the Rybnitsa district government and the republican-level branch of the CARC indicates that Abramovitsh may have been a point of contention and intrigue between competing government agencies. The district government, perhaps feeling under greater threat because of Abramovitsh's ability to capture hearts and power, or perhaps motivated by simple antisemitism, often painted the Rebbe as a rabble-rouser, denying his applications and issuing repeated reprimands for his transgressions. The CARC branch in the republican capital, by contrast, seems to have taken a laissez-faire approach to Abramovitsh and his go-ings-on, preferring to turn a blind eye to his supposed offenses in order to avoid conflict and/or to distract the locals from larger issues.[16]

Oral history testimonies potentially add a third layer to this supposed bureaucratic competition. Several informants reported on rumors they heard of KGB agents, both Jewish and non-Jewish, who regularly visited the Rebbe, sometimes with their families in tow, not to punish Abramo-vitsh but rather to receive the renowned mystic's blessings for themselves and their children.[17] No KGB surveillance file for Abramovitsh has yet been uncovered that would determine the veracity of these retellings. Nevertheless, even if such documents do exist, they are unlikely to cor-roborate the occurrence of such fantastical encounters. Yet these stories do point to the possibility that Abramovitsh had close and maybe even personal relationships with Soviet officials. Perhaps he achieved his goals not by making miracles happen, but as so many other Soviet citizens did—by taking advantage of the USSR's famously corrupt government insti-tutions. Adopting Soviet modes and methods to accomplish decidedly un-Soviet tasks, Abramovitsh, a Romanian-born Jew, with his dealings indicates just how quickly some *zapadniki* (Westerners) could adjust to Soviet reality. At once undeniably Jewish and at the same time wholly So-viet, Abramovitsh and his community represent a distinct group of Soviet Jews who combined tradition and innovation, ancient ritual and modern discourse, to meet the challenges of living Jewishly in a state that offered few sanctioned opportunities for positive, substantive Jewish expression, especially in the religious sphere.

In a certain sense, the narratives told about the Ribnitser Rebbe re-semble tales recorded by Bessarabian Jews regarding other earlier *tsadi-kim*, such as the Ruzhiner Rebbe (Yisra'el Friedman, 1796–1850) and his son and grandson, the two Rebbes of Ştefăneşti (Menachem Nokhem, 1823–1869, and Avrom Mattisiyahu, 1847–1933). While there are almost no Hasidic dynasties native to Bessarabia, there is a rich tradition of Jews (and even some non-Jews) from this area visiting renowned Jewish mystics just beyond the region's borders, the Prut and Dniestr Rivers, for blessings, advice, or healing.[18] As Maria Kaspina has written in her study on the legends of the second Shtefeneshter Rebbe, in this peripheral region far away from the centers of power, Jewish holy men and mystics often filled the gaps when the state, science, medicine, or other trappings of "modernity" were deemed suspicious, unhelpful, or simply inefficient.[19] In a similar fashion, Abramovitsh in many of the stories cited above is shown fulfilling spiritual, social, and humanitarian needs for which the Soviet state seemingly failed to provide.

Yet as Annette Wieviorka writes in her work on Holocaust interviews, "Testimonies . . . express the discourse or discourses valued by society at the moment the witnesses tell their stories as much as they render an individual [past] experience."[20] Oral history interviews tell the listener not only about the historical episode that the narrator describes, but also about the world in which the informant currently lives. Long seen as impediments to the use of oral texts for the study of history, the intervening effects of memories, experiences, and current circumstances on an informant's testimony, if properly interrogated, can in fact be quite revealing.

The narratives about the Ribnitser Rebbe, for instance, uncover a great deal about present-day attitudes among Moldovan Jews toward religion and Jewish identity. For many Jews in Rybnitsa, although Abramovitsh has not been physically present for several decades, he is still seen as central to their understanding of themselves as Jews. Pictures of the Rebbe are a frequent sight in many homes, hung almost in the fashion of Russian Orthodox icons, signaling the continued spiritual presence of Abramovitsh in their lives. Indeed, Abramovitsh is today seen by many Jews in the region as a figure representative of a disappearing "authentic" form of unstructured, oral, and home-based Judaism that was practiced in Soviet times when more public and formal manifestations of Jewish faith were discouraged.[21] This sort of "unregulated religiosity" is considered by these informants to be a more genuine form of Jewishness than the more hegemonic Western models of supposedly "proper" Jewish living taught by foreign humanitarian organizations present in their communities, such as the Jewish Agency for Israel (Sochnut), Chabad-Lubavitch, and the American Jewish Joint Distribution Committee (JDC, or "the Joint"). While each of these organizations provides crucial humanitarian support for these impoverished communities, in their cultural assistance they have also privileged modes of being Jewish related to, but sometimes directly at odds with, local practices and ways of thinking. These tensions have been aggravated by the fact that younger members of these communities, who may have been raised after the mass emigration of large numbers of actively Jewish neighbors and with fewer Jewish traditions, have been quick to adopt, at least in part, these new models of being Jewish. Perceiving material and social advantages to be reaped by associating with outside aid organizations, younger generations often view these foreign approaches to Jewish culture and spirituality as potentially more lucrative, and therefore more desirable, than local forms. This dynamic creates further internal fissures within the community, and not just with their foreign sponsors.

These dislocations between local and foreign understandings of Jewishness have been documented by other scholars of the region. A recent article by ethnographer Ekaterina Lazareva, for instance, details a conflict between a Jewish woman in Balti, Moldova, and the local Chabad emissary (*shaliach*) over practices, such as intermarriage, that have become normative in the Moldovan community, but that remain outside the norms of traditional Judaism.[22] Another particularly clear illustration of this disconnect between local and foreign models of Judaism comes from my own fieldwork, from an interview conducted with a Jewish woman in Balti as part of an expedition led by the Moscow-based Sefer Judaica Institute. In this instance, the informant insisted that the summertime celebration of Shavuot that had recently been marked in the local JDC-sponsored community center represented a wholly distinct and unrelated holiday from the "Shvies" (as the holiday is called in the local Yiddish dialect) of her childhood.[23]

What distinguishes those narratives in which the Ribnitser Rebbe appears, however, is their discourse about morality. Often Abramovitsh is evoked as a kind of moral foil for corrupt community officials, inattentive foreign aid workers, and unethical religious functionaries. As Iosif Belous, a current resident of Chişinău, states,

> You want to know who was a good person, a leader in our community? That was Reb Khayim-Zanvl. He would have never done the things

FIGURE 12.1

A portrait of Khayim-Zanvl Abramovitsh (ca. 1892–1995), the
Ribnitser Rebbe, hangs on the wall of the common room in the Jewish
community center in Rybnitsa, PMR, Moldova. Photograph by the
author with permission from the Jewish community of Rybnitsa.

[the local Chabad rabbi] does today, kick my grandchildren out of synagogue because their mother is Russian. And he cared about more than
just money like those businessmen in the community do. The Americans
think we weren't Jews before perestroika, before the Joint came. No. We
were Jews. You could hear Yiddish in the streets, we had holidays, we
prayed, we helped each other when times were bad. We already had
community. We lived a Jewish life here.[24]

In the latter part of this statement we hear how descriptions of the kind
of religiosity that the Ribnitser Rebbe enabled and the "Jewish society"
of which it formed a part are sometimes employed to refute the claims
of Western Jewish organizations that before their arrival, Soviet Jewish
life was one of unmitigated hardship, assimilation, and repression. In-

stead, by telling the stories of their resident spiritual hero, these informants construct a kind of "oppositional memory," an alternative historical narrative that attempts to reassert the place of a local and supposedly morally better way of being Jewish. Rather than being simply the recipients of Western aid, these informants seem to say, the Jews of this region are the carriers of a proud tradition.

In Rybnitsa, these conflicting understandings of Jewishness continue to exist side by side, and are even embedded into the physical space of the town's JDC-sponsored Jewish community center. In the building's common room, where most indoor communal activities occur, a large photographic portrait of the Rebbe hangs by the door, greeting visitors as one of the first visible objects in the room. Some older community members report that they "talk" to Abramovitsh through this picture upon entering the room, sharing a few words with their old friend.[25] The rest of the wall space in the room, however, is taken up by small placards explaining the meaning of Jewish holidays, a half-erased whiteboard with announcements for "Shabat" (*sic*), and, facing the Rebbe on the opposite three walls, Zionist posters ardently advertising the better (Jewish) life to be had in Israel (see figure 12.1).

For those in the community who have immigrated to Israel and elsewhere, a similar sort of dissonance is expressed between the different forms of Jewishness in their old and new homes. Here too, the memory of the Ribnitser Rebbe is again evoked as a form of opposition, inspiration, and individuation. For Mir'iam Shub (b. 1923), for example, a Moldovan Jewish immigrant to Israel and survivor of the Rybnitsa Ghetto, Abramovitsh represents the only religious leader she has ever respected. An avowed atheist, she believes that all rabbis and priests are out only to make money (*parnuse*) from their congregants. Khayim-Zanvl, on the other hand, is an exception, a true believer who cared profoundly for "his Jews." In fact, according to Shub, Abramovitsh left Israel, where he lived for a short time in the early 1970s, for the United States, solely to continue his stewardship of "our Jews," whose language, culture, and way of life were disappearing from the Jewish state.[26] In creating a dichotomy between "our Jews" and the Jews of Israel, Shub uses the figure of the Rebbe to underline her dissatisfaction with life in her adopted home and reaffirm her own perception of Judaism as morally correct.

FIGURE 12.2

Detail from previous illustration: Khayim-Zanvl Abramovitsh,
the Ribnitser Rebbe. Photograph by the author with
permission from the Jewish community of Rybnitsa.

It is worth noting that in her testimony, Shub identifies Abramovitsh not as a mystic or a miracle worker, but as a fellow migrant who, while she holds him in particularly high esteem, suffered through the same trials and tribulations as she did. Indeed, even for those informants who express a belief in Abramovitsh's supernatural abilities, the Rebbe is always seen as an equal member of their group, or as a sort of "first among equals" who through magic, piety, or moral uprightness cared for his community in extraordinary ways. Abramovitsh may have led an ascetic and devout lifestyle that set him apart, these narrators seem to say, but he was a ghetto inmate, a Jew deprived of religious freedoms, a flood victim, an immigrant, and so forth, "just like us." This image of a tsadik as "one of us" is in many ways a striking departure from the traditional image of the tsadik as a spiritual superman that has come to typify the Hasidic Rebbe. It is made more remarkable by the fact that Abramovitsh spent his childhood at the court of the second Shtefeneshter Rebbe, who lived in wealth and grandeur, imitating the "regal way" of his grandfather, the Ruzhiner. In the contemporary Hasidic world, Abramovitsh has become a true saintly figure; for many Moldovan Jews, wherever they may currently reside, he remains "Reb Khayim-Zanvl," an advocate to this day for their fast-disappearing way of life, and a spiritual leader who can nevertheless still be called an "old friend."

In retrospect, there is a temptation to characterize the Ribnitser Rebbe and his community during the Soviet period as heroic religious resisters against a totalitarian atheist regime. These pious Jews do bear some resemblance to other groups, such as Soviet Jehovah's Witnesses, who engaged in clandestine and sometimes illegal activities in order to practice a faith out of step with state ideological goals. Yet the actions that Jews in these communities took to maintain their practices and beliefs are far from the more aggressive stances that Witnesses and other groups took against the state in their antimilitarism, proselytism, and overall disengagement from and rejection of secular society.[27] For these Jews who sought to blend their Jewishness, even in a religious sense, with their Sovietness, another model is necessary to replace the binary model of dissent versus conformity.

Perhaps one paradigm can be found within Abramovitsh's grassroots style of leadership and lack of ostentation. While his style was undoubtedly a product of ideological and theological choices made by the Rebbe himself, it also seems to reflect a particular postwar Soviet Jewish sensibility about ethnic identification and the socialist state. In her study of Moldovan Jewish economic practices in the postwar USSR, anthropologist Anna Kushkova argues that activity by Jews in the so-called "second economy" and outside of prescribed Soviet norms more broadly served to strengthen ethnic belonging and a sense of collective Jewish identity.[28] Along these same lines, the Ribnitser Rebbe can perhaps be seen as a kind of underground spiritual entrepreneur who opened a religious "black market" where Jews could operate outside the state's restrictions and form an ethnic and ethical community of their own. His memory continues to be evoked in a similar manner, as those who remember him tell his stories and assert once more the authority of their fading, yet still living, tradition.

NOTES

1. Carlo Ginzburg, "Microhistory: Two or Three Things That I Know about It," trans. John Tedeschi and Anne C. Tedeschi, *Critical Inquiry* 20, no. 1 (1993): 26.

2. Much of Abramovitsh's biography in the decades before World War II remains clouded by the mists of legend. Documents from the Soviet Council on the Affairs of Religious Cults (CARC) give the year of his birth as 1892 (Arhiva Nationala din Republica Moldova [ANRM], Chişinău, f. 3305, op. 1, d. 20), while *Sefer halikhot ḥaim: Rabenu hakadosh me-Ribnits* (n.p.: Grunter, 1999), a popular Hasidic hagiography of the Ribnitser Rebbe, states that he was born sometime between 1890 and 1902. Unless otherwise noted, all translations in this chapter are my own.

3. Today, the city of Rybnitsa is located in northern Transnistria (the Pridnestrovskaia Moldavskaia Respublika [PMR], or Pridnestrovie, in Russian), a separatist state within the Republic of Moldova.

4. For more on the Soviet antireligious campaigns in the MASSR, see Charles King, *The Moldovans: Romania, Russia, and the Politics of Change* (Stanford, CA: Hoover Institution Press, 2000), chap. 4.

5. I. Pilat, *Iz istorii evreistva Moldovy* (Chişinău: Ob-vo Evreiskoi Kul'tury, 1990). According to the 1926 Soviet census, Rybnitsa was 38 percent Jewish, 33.8 percent Ukrainian, 16 percent Moldovan, and 12.2 percent Other.

6. E.g., Shoah Foundation Visual History Archive (VHA), University of Southern California, Los Angeles, Maia Fel'dman 27615, Efim Sandler 36535; Archives of Historical and Ethnographic Yiddish Memories (AHEYM), Indiana University, Bloomington, MDV 197 Zlata Kotliar; Zlata Kotliar, interview with the author, Rybnitsa, PMR, Moldova, August 2011.

7. Materials on the denial of registration to the Jewish religious community of the city of Rybnitsa, 1949–1956, CARC Moldavian SSR, ANRM, f. 3305, op. 1, d. 20.

8. Mordechai Altshuler also mentions similar exploitation of this seeming leniency toward funereal prayers and religious study in private homes in other parts of the Soviet Union. See Mordechai Altshuler, *Religion and Jewish Identity in the Soviet Union, 1941–1964* (Waltham, MA: Brandeis University Press, 2012), 155.

9. Isroel Fingurt, *Obrechennye* (Chișinău: Menora, 1994), 47.

10. A H E Y M, M D V 197 Zlata Kotliar; Kotliar, interview.

11. Recent exceptions to this trend in the historiography include Altshuler, *Religion and Jewish Identity in the Soviet Union;* Elissa Bemporad, *Becoming Soviet Jews: The Bolshevik Experiment in Minsk* (Bloomington: Indiana University Press, 2013); and Jeffrey Veidlinger, *In the Shadow of the Shtetl: Small-Town Jewish Life in Soviet Ukraine* (Bloomington: Indiana University Press, 2013). Other exceptions in the field of anthropology include Sascha Goluboff, *Jewish Russians: Upheavals in a Moscow Synagogue* (Philadelphia: University of Pennsylvania Press, 2003); and V. A. Dymshits et al., *Shtetl XXI vek: Polevye issledovaniia* (St. Petersburg: Izdatel'stvo Evropeiskogo Universiteta v Sankt-Peterburge, 2008). One should also note the work of Judith Deutsch Kornblatt on Jewish converts to Russian Orthodoxy, which argues that religion, albeit in Christian form, was one way some Jews, paradoxically, engaged with Jewish tradition, culture, and identity; see Judith Deutsch Kornblatt, *Doubly Chosen: Jewish Identity, the Soviet Intelligentsia, and the Russian Orthodox Church* (Madison: University of Wisconsin Press, 2004). On so-called "Judaizing Christians" in the Soviet Union, see Aleksandr L'vov, *Sokha i piatiknizhie: Russkie iudeistvuiushchie kak tekstual'noe soobshchestvo* (St. Petersburg: Izdatel'stvo Evropeiskogo Universiteta v Sankt-Peterburge, 2011).

12. See, for example, David Shneer, *Yiddish and the Creation of Soviet Jewish Culture* (Cambridge: Cambridge University Press, 2004); Jeffrey Veidlinger, *The Moscow State Yiddish Theater: Jewish Culture on the Soviet Stage* (Bloomington: Indiana University Press, 2000); Anna Shternshis, *Soviet and Kosher: Jewish Popular Culture in the Soviet Union, 1923–1939* (Bloomington: Indiana University Press, 2006); and Ber Boris Kotlerman, *In Search of Milk and Honey: The Yiddish Theater of Soviet Jewish Statehood* (Bloomington, IN: Slavica, 2009).

13. As a faith that held a privileged status in relation to the state throughout the Soviet period, there is a rich historiography on Russian Orthodoxy in the USSR and its sometimes conflictual, sometimes conciliatory relationship to the state, particularly in the revolutionary and interwar periods. Works especially relevant to the present study include Robert Greene, *Bodies like Bright Stars: Saints and Relics in Orthodox Russia* (DeKalb: Northern Illinois University Press, 2010); Edward Roslof, *Renovationism, Russian Orthodoxy, and Revolution, 1905–1946* (Bloomington: Indiana University Press, 2002); and Glennys Young, *Power and the Sacred in Revolutionary Russia: Religious Activists in the Village* (University Park: Pennsylvania State University Press, 1997). Pertinent works on other faiths include Emily Baran, *Dissent on the Margins: How Soviet Jehovah's Witnesses Defied Communism and Lived to Preach about It* (New York: Oxford University Press, 2014); Douglas Rogers, *The Old Faith and the Russian Land: A Historical Ethnography of Ethics in the Urals* (Ithaca, NY: Cornell University Press, 2009); and Yaacov Ro'i, *Islam in the Soviet Union: World War II to Perestroika* (New York: Columbia University Press, 2000).

14. Altshuler, *Religion and Jewish Identity in the Soviet Union,* 127–128; Materials on the registration of the Jewish religious community in the city of Kishinev, 1948–1950, C A R C Moldavian S S R, A N R M, f. 3305, op. 2, d. 22.

15. Materials on the denial of registration to the Jewish religious communities of Soroca, Balti, Edineti, Capresti, and Otaci, n.d., CARC Moldavian SSR, ANRM, f. 3305, op. 1, d. 13, 16, 26, 31, 35.

16. Materials on the denial of registration to the Jewish religious community of the city of Rybnitsa, 1949–1956, CARC Moldavian SSR, ANRM, f. 3305, op. 1, d. 20. For more on such interbureaucratic competitions in other parts of the Soviet Union, see Yaacov Ro'i, "The Reconstruction of Jewish Communities in the USSR, 1944–1947," in *The Jews Are Coming Back: The Return of the Jews to Their Countries of Origin after WWII*, ed. David Bankier (Jerusalem: Yad Vashem in association with Berghahn Books, 2005), 186–206.

17. Leye Freydkina, interview with the author, Rybnitsa, PMR, Moldova, June 2011; Leonid Tul'chinskii, interview with the author, Rybnitsa, PMR, Moldova, June 2011; AHEYM, MDV 195–196 Abram Shargorodskii; Shoah VHA, Abram Shargorodskii 37039.

18. The one Hasidic dynasty native to Bessarabia was the small court established in the town of Bendery in 1814 by Aryeh Leib Wertheim (ca. 1772–1854). See Gad Sagiv, "Savran-Bendery Hasidic Dynasty," trans. Jeffrey Green, *The YIVO Encyclopedia of Jews in Eastern Europe* (2010): http://www.yivoencyclopedia.org/article.aspx/Savran-Bendery_Hasidic _Dynasty.

19. Maria Kaspina, "Pochitanie Shtefaneshtskogo rebe: Proshloe i nastoiashchee," in *"Staroe" i "novoe" v slaviaskoi i evreiskoi kul'turnoi traditsii*, ed. O. Belova (Moscow: Sefer Judaica Institute, 2012), 120–135.

20. Annette Wieviorka, *The Era of the Witness*, trans. Jared Stark (Ithaca, NY: Cornell University Press, 2006), xii.

21. The study of Judaism as a "lived religion" in the postwar Soviet Union, especially as it was practiced outside of larger urban centers, has only begun recently. See, in particular, Veidlinger, *In the Shadow of the Shtetl*; and Dymshits et al., *Shtetl XXI vek*.

22. Ekaterina Lazareva, "Pratika obrashcheniia k ravvinu i rasskazy o chudesakh: Traditsiia i novshestva," in Belova, *"Staroe" i "novoe,"* 136–142.

23. The often fraught encounter between local Jewish communities and some of these global Jewish organizations is of course not unique to Moldova or to the former Soviet Union. For recent descriptions of two such meetings outside Eastern Europe, see Alanna Cooper, *Bukharan Jews and the Dynamics of Global Judaism* (Bloomington: Indiana University Press, 2012), chap. 9; and Marcy Brink-Danan, *Jewish Life in Twenty-First-Century Turkey: The Other Side of Tolerance* (Bloomington: Indiana University Press, 2012), 126–127n7. A similar dynamic between Ukrainians and American evangelical churches has been described in Catherine Wanner, *Communities of the Converted: Ukrainians and Global Evangelism* (Ithaca, NY: Cornell University Press, 2007).

24. Shoah VHA, Iosif Belous 37961.

25. Kotliar, interview.

26. Shoah VHA, Mir'iam Shub 40094.

27. Baran, *Dissent on the Margins*.

28. Anna Kushkova, "An Essay on the Jewish Ethnic Economy: The Case of Belz, Moldova," *East European Jewish Affairs* 43, no. 1 (2013): 77–100.

Part III

Reflections on the Ethnographic Impulse

13

Ex-Soviet Jews

COLLECTIVE AUTOETHNOGRAPHY

LARISA FIALKOVA AND
MARIA YELENEVSKAYA

The method of autoethnography is comparatively new. Even its spelling has not stabilized yet: in some sources it appears as one word while in others it is hyphenated. One of the key figures theorizing its application, Carolyn Ellis, attributes the coining of the term to David Hayano. However, Hayano refutes his authorship and writes that he first heard it in 1966 in Sir Raymond Firth's structuralism seminar.[1] Techniques of autoethnography became widespread in qualitative research only in the 1980s–1990s and are closely related to interest in narratives. Autoethnography is a method of studying one's own people in which the researcher is a full insider by virtue of being "native," possessing an intimate familiarity with or achieving full membership in the group being studied.[2] "The forms of autoethnography differ," write Carolyn Ellis, Tony E. Adams, and Arthur P. Bochner, "in how much emphasis is placed on the study of others, the researcher's self and interaction with others, traditional analysis, and the interview context, as well as on power relationships."[3] Autoethnography emerged when many researchers in the field came to realize that the mainstream methods no longer met the requirements of the changing situation in the field. First, a growing number of students belonging to minority groups and non-Western cultures received training as ethnographers and in their own investigations began to question the authority of their Western peers in understanding their own cultures. Second, funding for field research abroad shrank and scholars had to look instead for research topics in their own backyards.[4]

It is also worth mentioning that autoethnography comes to the foreground in periods of crisis and rapid changes in the surrounding social structure and in the personal lives of all the citizens, including researchers. The disintegration of the Soviet Union, the emergence of new states, and mass emigration were among the factors that stimulated post-Soviet autoethnographic research. In this period of sociopolitical change, ethnographers equipped with theoretical knowledge and skills in fieldwork techniques and used to reflecting on external events became interested in their own lived experiences as objects of study.[5] On the one hand, autoethnography guards researchers against a paternalistic position and helps them to avoid statements and conclusions made from a privileged position: "I know better than an aboriginal who he is."[6] On the other hand, this method makes an autoethnographer vulnerable; researchers are sometimes criticized for a failure to distance themselves from their subject of study and for self-advocacy. It also breaks the unwritten contract of the discipline: the subject and the object of the study shouldn't coincide. As Victor Shklovskii poignantly remarked, "They say that in order to be an ichthyologist one doesn't have to be a fish."[7]

Scholars engaged in qualitative research distinguish between evocative and analytical autoethnography. The evocative paradigm, also referred to as emotional or heartful, is motivated by the desire to connect social science to literature, academic interests to personal ones, emotions to cognition, and theoretical abstractions of social life to everyday living.[8] This approach is very popular but is sometimes criticized for being merely experiential and for encouraging self-indulgence.[9] To a large extent, it rejects other more traditional approaches to ethnography, is skeptical about the possibility of understanding the "other," and shuns generalizations. By contrast, the analytic paradigm is an attempt to bridge the gap between traditional ethnography, which focuses on the other, and the study of the self. Leon Anderson singled out its five key features: complete member researcher status, analytic reflexivity, narrative visibility of the researcher's self, dialogue with informants beyond the self, and commitment to theoretical analysis.[10] In our own work we adhere to the analytic paradigm, and in the rest of this chapter will show how these key features are manifested in the autoethnography of ex-Soviet Jews.

Some researchers interpret the term autoethnography literally and focus exclusively on themselves. We can even see the confusion of genres: personal diaries or memoirs are presented as ethnographic studies.[11] We agree with Sara Delamont's justified critique of this approach.[12] Although it may seem to be a contradiction in terms, autoethnography can be done collaboratively and can be community-based.[13] In this framework, a dialogue is conducted not only between informants' narratives but also between the stories of the researchers participating in the project. Like other forms of autoethnography, the collaborative version is primarily inductive; that is, it studies the self in order to understand more deeply the whole of the researchers' group. On the other hand, it can begin with research into the culture of the group as a way of interpreting one's own values, feelings, and behavior.

Not every study of one's own group belongs to autoethnography or is perceived as such by the author. First, autoethnography presupposes conscious reflections about the self as an individual and as a member of a specific group, constant movement from the individual to the collective, and critical assessment of behaviors and attitudes observed. We realize that our selection of material for analysis is a result of our theoretical approach, and some researchers whose work we analyze below may contest our interpretation of their studies as autoethnography. This is likely to happen when membership in the group under study is not revealed either consciously or semiconsciously. In some cases, though, a researcher may intentionally disguise himself or herself as an anonymous subject. It is important to emphasize that the degree of researchers' visibility depends on various factors, including a desire to be "objective," fear of self-disclosure, and career considerations.

Autoethnography of Soviet Jews began when the Soviet Union collapsed. Soviet ethnographers excelled in investigations into the everyday life and traditions of the ethnicities populating the extreme North, Siberia, and the Far East, but Jewish studies were not part of the ethnographic agenda. Foreign researchers who were interested in pursuing such studies met with obstacles created by the authorities and fear on the part of potential informants. As a result, most of the information available in the West about the lives of Soviet Jews came from dissidents who made up a tiny section of Soviet society and were not representative of the whole group. Their reports were primarily self-reflections motivated by the struggle against Soviet power and could not substitute for real fieldwork. Among the most vivid examples of such materials are a collection of essays edited by immigrants of the 1970s about Jewish identities in the Soviet Union and dissidents' attempts to reinvigorate Jewish life,[14] and Natan Sharansky's memoirs about his imprisonment.[15]

We believe that the terminology of Ronald Jackson's cultural contracts theory is useful to explicate the situation of post-Soviet Jews and changes in their identities. This theory seeks to analyze identity negotiation in the process of changing one's worldview. It is concerned with identity outcomes in contacts with members of other cultural groups and distinguishes three types of contracts: "ready to sign" (assimilation), "quasi-completed" (adaptation), and "co-created" (mutual valuation).[16]

The ready-to-sign cultural contract between the Soviet state and its Jewish citizens came to an end in the late 1980s to early 1990s. Jews got an opportunity to review and evaluate their assimilated past when Jewishness was a liability reducing their social upward mobility and was widely perceived as a "disability of the fifth group."[17] During perestroika, when glasnost' began, Soviet history came to be reappraised and the borders of the country opened for travelers in both directions. Jewishness all of a sudden became an asset as it gave access to new resources. In the period of economic deprivations Jews received help from charity organizations in the form of humanitarian aid, be it food parcels, clothes, or free canteens. The Jewish Agency and Joint Distribution Committee (JDC) launched free Hebrew-language courses, summer camps, and Sunday schools for Jewish children and helped create community centers. Moreover, Jewishness offered a ticket to ethnically privileged migration. But it turned out that the new resources presupposed new ready-to-sign contracts designed to promote new types of assimilation, this time with the traditional view of Jewishness. Donors invested in bringing Soviet Jews back to the fold expected the latter would be eager to learn about the forgotten tradition and embrace it. But while few rejected new resources, many were not ready to pay the price by changing their behavior, and more importantly by accepting a different definition of who a Jew is.

The problem of resistance arose among the Jews of the former Soviet Union (FSU), but also in the transplanted communities in Israel, Germany, and the United States. Although the consequences of noncompliance with the new ready-to-sign contracts differed in these countries, in all of them ex-Soviet Jews were confronted with the dilemmas of halachic versus nonhalachic descendants of mixed marriages, nationality versus ethnicity, and blood relations versus religious affiliation. These dilemmas raised questions that may sound paradoxical or oxymoronic: Can a Jew recite Kaddish in a Russian Orthodox Church?[18] Are Russian Orthodox Jews apostates or Jews of Christian faith?[19] Is there an exit from the deadlock of the halachic definition of Jewishness?[20] How can one combine affinities with Israel and the former Soviet Union, which came to be called "historical" and "prehistorical" fatherlands?[21] What is the ex-Soviet Jews' native language: Russian, in which they formulated their first sentences; Yiddish, which they occasionally heard from their parents and grandparents; or Hebrew, although some did not even suspect it existed before mass emigration began?[22] Whose diaspora are ex-Soviet Jews in Israel: a returning diaspora or part of an incipient Soviet diaspora?[23] These questions were particularly acute for immigrants, because they had to establish themselves as individuals and as communities vis-à-vis the host societies.

Mass migration of ex-Soviet Jews triggered a plethora of research projects about this group, and already in the mid-1990s there were immigrant researchers among the authors. Among those who began to study their own communities were not only ethnographers, but also political scientists, sociologists, psychologists, educators, linguists, folklorists, and scholars of literature. Few of them had been concerned with Jewish history or culture prior to immigration. In 2008 we conducted a study in which we analyzed the careers of immigrant researchers engaged in immigration studies. We found that in some cases émigré scholars changed the direction of their research due to necessity. One of our Israeli respondents said that she had to expand into immigration studies because her main field hardly interested anybody in her new academic environment. Some other respondents pointed out that they had taken up immigration studies on the advice of colleagues. It was suggested to them that they choose a niche where they would have a clear priority over others. Although the term autoethnography was not used, this advice clearly pointed to the advantage of having privileged access to the group under study, stemming from complete member status in it. Similar advice was given to one of us (Larisa) on the eve of her emigration by the literary scholar Vladislav Krivonos. Sensing Larisa's anxiety about her professional future he said that if he faced emigration, he would use it as an opportunity to become a mediator between the culture of the old country and the culture of the receiving society. Immigration studies proved to be a good application of this advice.

Responses to our short questionnaire also showed that researchers' investigations of their own groups were guided by the desire to sort out their own experiences. This was clear in the answers of older adults, as well as in those of young researchers who did their professional studies after immigration.

- I think it was the desire to make sense of and digest one of the most important events in my life.
- Only part of my research is on immigrants, so I am not an expert in immigration studies, but, of course, it's trying to understand your own experience and also to address injustices that were inflicted on immigrants that guided me.
- Immigration problems are my problems. My parents have become factory workers. Their Hebrew is nonexistent, and their Soviet degrees are worth nothing. Their social status plummeted and Soviet-like obsessive fear has become overwhelming in the new country. All of this *is my life and the life of my parents in Israel.* Why not write about things close to you, things that hurt? It is easy for me to write about immigrants, it is easy to avoid writing something ridiculous. It is easy to spot interesting details. . . . My command of Russian and my immigrant origin are my "relative advantages," and it's a shame not to utilize them.[24]

Retrospectively, it is clear to us that among the first triggers of our own research in the field of immigration studies was not only a desire to understand the self, but also a need to put our own experiences in a more general context, together with the wish to analyze the dynamics of the wider group's social life. Both of us were novices in the field: Larisa had specialized in Russian literature and Maria in text linguistics and foreign language pedagogy.[25] Yet we both started recording our reflections about our new environment. In the first months after moving to Israel each of us, like many other immigrants, rendered our impressions, observations, and emotional responses to the new country in letters: Maria in regular letters, Larisa in tape recordings. Unfortunately, none of these have been preserved. But in that first period we were not yet ready for autoethnography.

We were able to start analyzing new experiences only after some time had passed and we could distance ourselves from the trauma of resettling. Without a time lag, observations charged with excessive emotions would have been purely evocative. Trying to overcome nostalgia, fear of uncertainty, and cognitive and emotional confusion, we looked for solutions to numerous dilemmas in scholarly literature on immigration in general and ex-Soviet Jews in Israel in particular. Reading about "homecoming," Zionist aspirations, or the total absence of any elements of Jewish identity in the "sausage aliya," as the immigration wave of the 1990s was often called in the media, we could hardly recognize ourselves or our in-group. This was an additional trigger for choosing the topic: a desire to contest what we saw as a distorted picture of Russian-speaking immigrants to Israel, and to present our own vision of the group, its collective identity, and its values.

As Garry Freeman aptly observed, "The history of social sciences is marked by attempts of scholars belonging to oppressed or marginal groups to draw attention to their plight. Women's studies are dominated by women, minority studies by minorities, etc. Migrant scholars bring with them special insight and commitment and deserve credit for much of the field's growth."[26] This is definitely the case with immigration studies in Israel in the last two decades. At the same time, we fully agree with Anderson that research should not be confused with political activism and that "the autoethnographer must not allow herself or himself to be drawn into participating heavily in activities in the field at the expense of writing the field notes."[27]

And here the difficult question of ethnographic ethics arises: in whose interest are studies done? Researchers conducting in-depth interviews with fellow immigrants are inevitably confronted with the expectations of the informants that their opinions and attitudes are fully shared by virtue of common background. Moreover, they expect that published research will promote the status of the group and individuals participating in the study and are sometimes disappointed when they read critical analyses of the interviews in the published research. This comes out strongest where such sensitive issues as interethnic relations and political orientation are concerned. For example, after our book on personal narratives of ex-Soviets was published, Russian-speaking readers, including some of our colleagues and reviewers, were ready to accept that the symbolism of the threat of the opposition of East and West and the special features of the Soviet personality that came up in our analyses indeed influenced the discourse and behavioral patterns of the FSU immigrants. On the other hand they refused to interpret these as mythology but insisted that "they are based on reality."[28] Although their general evaluation of our work was positive, they thought that in our treatment of interethnic tensions we had betrayed group interests.[29]

As mentioned earlier, immigrant scholars conducting qualitative research are not always aware that when investigating their own group they apply methods of autoethnography. As a result, one of the key features of analytic autoethnography—researcher visibility—is not always internalized and sometimes is even concealed. This can be observed in the research of those who were trained in the Soviet academic tradition as well as in the work of young researchers educated after immigration. In the majority of publications we are familiar with, the authors' interest in their own group is not mentioned at all. The visibility, then, is manifested in the insider knowledge about the group and its antecedents, comparisons between cultural traditions of the home country and those of the host society, the language in which fieldwork is conducted, and the familiarity with the scholarly literature of the country of origin.[30] An important factor revealing hesitation in becoming visible is adherence to the typical style of Soviet academic tradition, which aspired to reveal the "objective truth" and avoid the subjectivity associated with pseudoscience. One of the manifestations of this trend was a discursive style abounding in impersonal structures and the use of the safe "we" instead of the responsible "I."[31]

In some studies researchers are semivisible. They speak openly about belonging to the group and explain that their choice of topic stems from a desire to relate to and analyze personal experience. At the same time, their own narratives are not quoted, or they are concealed as informants' stories. For example, in their investigation into Russian-speaking Israelis' attitudes toward religion, Larissa Remennick and Anna Prashizky specify that the "questionnaire in Russian was developed by the authors, drawing on their previous research and personal experience as immigrants in Israel."[32] Similarly, Narspy Zilberg indicates that besides ethnographic interviews, her work on cultural codes of secular Russian Jews of Jerusalem was based on her personal observations: "Living in Jerusalem among immigrants, I became a natural witness to the most important events and sociocultural phenomena of the everyday life of diverse immigrant groups making up the Russian-speaking community."[33] Two other co-researchers, Claudia Zbenovich and Julia Lerner, note that their interest in the subject of interpersonal educational communication in a cross-cultural setting is explained not only by their scholarly work in the field of immigration, but also by their own experience of being Russian-speaking parents in Israel wishing to bring up bilingual and bicultural children.[34]

The passage from invisibility to visibility is not always easy. Thus, in our first joint publications we did not interview each other but recorded some of our own narratives which were part of our stable storytelling repertoire. Yet we hid them under assumed names in order to retain equal status with other narrators we quoted. Moreover, analysis of these stories was done not by the narrator herself but by her co-author. When we interviewed some of our kin we applied the same strategy. This enabled the narrators to include details that would have been possibly omitted as superfluous in a conversation with a family member. Later we came to the conclusion that our methods should be more transparent to the reader, and in a book devoted to personal narratives we included a section in which we reflected on folk groups and researchers' roles when they investigate their in-group.

Visibility does not always come voluntarily, but can be enforced by publishers. And again we turn to our own experience. An anonymous reviewer of our book on personal narratives insisted that in the section on folk groups our biographical details and political standing should be stated in the text. We must admit that this demand was in sharp contrast with academic conventions we were used to, and at first we perceived it as coercion. It reminded us of the ideological pressure in Soviet academia, which made references to Marx, Engels, and Lenin obligatory in PhD dissertations in the social sciences and humanities irrespective of the topic of the reported research. Moreover, we were convinced that our analyses clearly revealed our ideology on the key issues of Israeli discourse: inter-ethnic relations, tension between religious and secular sectors, tolerance of multiculturalism, and above all attitudes toward the Arab-Israeli conflict. We did add a required paragraph but tried to be as concise as possible.[35] Today we see this requirement in a different light and our writing of this chapter testifies to our greater adaptation to Western academic conventions.

Some immigrant scholars achieve full visibility. They not only cite their own immigrant experience as the basis of their choice of topic, but also explicitly refer to it in analyses and include their narratives under their own names, thus combining the roles of the analyst and the analyzed. A good example of immigrant researchers' full visibility is a study by the family therapist Alla Sumbaeva. She works for the organization Advancement of Adolescents, which is affiliated with the Israeli Ministry of Education. In explaining the problems of immigrant adolescents she recounts her personal difficulties and her growing alienation from her parents. Distressed by the difficulties of adaptation they failed to see how much their daughter needed emotional shelter and instead relied on her, trying to take advantage of her proficiency in Hebrew:

> I recall an episode from my own life. I came to Israel with my parents at the age of sixteen. For a long time after arrival a simple request by my parents to translate this or that word made me furious. I believe I experienced negative emotions because every time it happened my parents made me feel how confused and helpless they had become if they had to turn to me for help. But myself, I was badly in need of their support and help. I remember that in irritation, probably caused by my own helplessness, I would tell them to consult a dictionary.[36]

Another young immigrant scholar, Adi Kuntsman, whose autoethnographic work exemplifies full narrative visibility, writes about queer migration, which was previously completely ignored in studies of Russian Jews.[37] The focus of her research is sexuality and its role in immigrants' integration. She interviewed fourteen young lesbians and quoted in her article five autobiographical stories, beginning with her own. Her study shows that her and her subjects' integration into the Israeli lesbian community went hand in hand with a rejection of Russianness, which these young immigrants associated with the homophobia of the totalitarian society. Comparing her own story to those of her interviewees she reflects on changes that she and some of her subjects underwent in the course of research. Having established themselves in the queer community of middle-class educated Ashkenazic Jews they reconsidered their cultural belonging, created Russian enclaves in the Israeli queer community, and established connections with queer communities in their country of origin.

Changes that the self and members of the in-group undergo in the course of integration processes concern many immigrant scholars. An interesting example of critical reflection on the influence of academic studies and research in the sociology of immigrants' identities can be found in the work of Julia Lerner.[38] She writes that in the courses she teaches, she uses herself as an example, thus trying to disrupt stereotypes of Russian-speaking immigrants that have evolved in Israeli society. Exposed to various social theories in the course of their studies, she and her fellow students learned not to take anything for granted and started to question ideologies, social hierarchies, and power relations. She attributes her gradual shift to left-wing political views to the internalization of knowledge she acquired at the university and to research activities she was engaged in.

Indeed, many Israeli academics have left-wing leanings and are often criticized for this by the media and despised by the lay public. This trend is particularly pronounced in the Russian-speaking community, where left-wingers are labeled with the pejoratives *levaki* (lefties) and *golubi* (pigeons). Left-wingers are treated as "useful idiots" or as traitors to the Jewish state. As far as left-wing Russian-speaking scholars are concerned, their political orientation is seen as an indication of a lack of independent thinking or as a career strategy. Each of us has a history of clashes with some of our Russian-speaking friends and relatives who are convinced that every Russian speaker in Israel is a right-winger and anti-Arab. This is often viewed as the legitimation of the group's position in the host society. We would like to quote from memory two recent episodes, both of which took place during table talk at parties. During a visit to Upper Nazareth, Maria defended the right of Arab Israelis to buy apartments in this town.

One of the guests looked at her with amazement and said, "Come on, are you a left-winger?"

"Yes, I am," Maria replied.

"Well, then there is nothing for us to talk about."

Larisa, for her part, was visiting her relatives in Netania. The conversation dwelt upon neutral issues, but then one of the guests got bored and asked, "Why don't we ever talk politics?"

"In order not to quarrel," Larisa said.

"What? Are you a left-winger?"

"Yes."

"It cannot be true. You are Russian and Russians cannot be lefties!"

"In her university everybody is a lefty," said another guest.

Like Lerner, we believe that it is our knowledge of Israeli society, which we have acquired in the process of teaching heterogeneous student audiences, through collaboration with colleagues, and through research activities, that has influenced our political views.

Reflections about the self and fellow immigrants include analyses of family relations, in particular bringing up the young, the second-generation immigrants.[39] Everyday observations of one's own children and those of friends, decisions about the choice of kindergartens and schools, and communication with the staff of educational institutions opened up new topics, most of them related to emerging bilingualism, the maintenance or abandonment of customs, and the habits of the old country. These studies reveal tensions between Jewishness, Israeliness, and Russianness in individuals and the community as a whole, and shed light on various types of hybridity. Some made conscious decisions, others acted intuitively. However, it turned out that the intention to preserve the culture was not sufficient for success. As shown by Shulamit Kopeliovich, who studied language maintenance and attrition among children in religious Russian-speaking families, only self-discipline and consistency bring about success in raising children as balanced bilinguals.[40] Since the author herself belongs to this subsection of society, this study can also be considered auto-ethnography. It is not only interesting from the linguistic point of view; it also reveals that preservation of linguocultural Russianness is essential for intergenerational continuity, not only in secular Russian-speaking Jewish and mixed families but also in religious Orthodox families.

Not surprisingly, many of the studies devoted to ex-Soviet Jews are interdisciplinary. Despite inevitable acculturation processes, more than twenty-five years after the beginning of the fourth wave of Russian emigration, symbolic boundaries between F S U immigrants and host societies have not disappeared.[41] Russian speech is still heard in public spaces, and various services, ranging from clinics run by Russian-speaking doctors through afternoon schools to tourist agencies, are offered to immigrants by their coethnics. While the circulation of conventional immigrant news media is in decline, numerous internet portals and specialized sites have sprung up and are visited by Russian-speaking users residing in different corners of the world. The repertoire of leisure activities offered to immigrants in their mother tongue in Israel, Germany, the United States, and other countries can satisfy any age and taste and includes shows and concerts, literary contests, bard festivals, national and international performances of the student cabaret K V N (the Club of the Merry and Resourceful), and so on. Many of these activities remain outside the purview of immigration scholars belonging to the host societies. They require not only sophisticated language knowledge, but also a common cultural and experiential background. Moreover, we have to admit that like other minority communities, Russian-speaking immigrants are not always willing to cooperate with outsiders.

Cultural phenomena of immigrants' lives have been observed and documented in numerous studies devoted to émigrés of the fourth wave. Most of these investigations dwell on the hybridization of identity. Thus, Zinaida Ilatova and Shmuel Shamai postulate that ethnocultural self-identification of immigrants to Israel should be regarded in the framework of a bi-dimensional rather than monodimensional model. The monodimensional model presupposes that as immigrants acquire and accept the culture of the host society, their original culture retreats. By contrast, the bi-dimensional approach demonstrates that the combination of the two cultures in immigrants' identities can vary without creating cognitive dissonance.[42] The bi-dimensional model of acculturation, and as a result the hybridization of identity, was confirmed in a study of immigrant youth in Israel by Marina Niznik, who showed that cultural integration of young people is not linear—they are bicultural or globalized rather than assimilated into the dominant Hebrew culture.

Her findings are "in line with the segmented assimilation theory and also exemplify a 'limited' or 'selective' acculturation scenario."[43] Although the author's personal involvement is invisible in this work, clearly her interest in the Russian-Israeli youth culture stems from her profession as a teacher of high-school- and university-level Russian language and literature in school and university, and from her role as a mother.

Thanks to autoethnography, researchers have developed new approaches to understanding their own communities. The problems they discuss include Russian-Jewish attitudes toward children's upbringing, fractured memories of the Jewish tradition suppressed by the state, the preservation of Russian cultural traditions in immigrant Jewish Orthodox families, and dialectics of Russian-Israeli belonging in the immigrant queer community, to name but a few. Autoethnography reveals how customs and cultural symbols are blended in ways that seem to outsiders to be mutually exclusive, but which in effect reflect the hybridization of identities. Relying on constant participant observation, autoethnography enables differentiation between declared values and real everyday practices. There are many signs that cultural hybridization has been inherited by one-and-a-half- and second-generation immigrants, who have already started passing on their cultural habits to their own children.

What began as isolated everyday attempts by ex-Soviet Jews to explain their culture, habits, and values to members of their new host society— colleagues, neighbors, or incidental acquaintances—developed into formal formats of communication. Media publications, works of fiction, and academic texts are different manifestations of negotiations of the group's place in a new society. We believe this should lead to "signing" a co-created contract based on mutual valuation.

NOTES

This chapter is a joint project and both authors contributed to it equally. We alternate priority of authorship in our joint publications. We would like to express our gratitude to Jeffrey Veidlinger, Dov-Ber Kerler, Julia Lerner, and anonymous reviewers for their comments and valuable suggestions on the previous drafts of this chapter.

1. Carolyn Ellis, *The Ethnographic I: A Methodological Novel about Autoethnography* (Walnut Creek, CA: Altamira, 2004), 38; David Hayano, "Auto-Ethnography: Paradigms, Problems, and Prospects," *Human Organization* 38, no. 1 (1979): 99.

2. Carolyn Ellis and Arthur P. Bochner, "Autoethnography, Personal Narrative, Reflexivity," in *Handbook of Qualitative Research,* ed. Norman K. Denzin and Yvonna S. Lincoln (Thousand Oaks, CA: Sage, 2000), 739.

3. Carolyn Ellis, Tony E. Adams, and Arthur P. Bochner, "Autoethnography: An Overview," *Forum: Qualitative Social Research* 12, no. 1, art. 10 (January 2011), http://www.qualitative-research.net/index.php/fqs/article/view/1589/3095.

4. Hayano, "Auto-Ethnography," 99.

5. Anna Gotlieb, "Avtoetnografia (Razgovor s samoi soboi v dvukh registrakh)," *Sotsiologia 4M* 19 (2004): 6.

6. Natalia Kozlova, *Sovetskie liudi: Stseny iz istorii* (Moscow: Evropa, 2005), 16–17.

7. Victor Shklovskii, "Tetiva: O neskhodstve skhodnogo," in *Izbrannoe,* vol. 2 (Moscow: Khudozestvennaia Literatura, 1983), http://philologos.narod.ru/shklovsky/tetiva.htm.

8. Carolyn Ellis, "Evocative Autoethnography: Writing Emotionally about Our Lives," in *Representation and the Text: Re-Framing the Narrative Voice,* ed. William G. Tierney and Yvonna S. Lincoln (Albany: State University of New York Press, 1997), 117.

9. Paul Atkinson, "Rescuing Autoethnography," *Journal of Contemporary Ethnography* 35, no. 4 (2006): 400–404; Paul Atkinson, Amanda Coffey, and Sara Delamont, *Key Themes in Qualitative Research: Continuities and Change* (Walnut Creek, CA: Altamira, 2003), 49–70; and Sara Delamont, "Arguments against Auto-Ethnography," *Qualitative Researcher* 4 (2007): 2–4.

10. Leon Anderson, "Analytic Autoethnography," *Journal of Contemporary Ethnography* 35, no. 4 (2006): 378.

11. During the SIEF Congress 2013, one of us attended a panel discussion where a presenter was criticized by one of the participants for including interview material in her paper instead of focusing exclusively on her own experiences and feelings. Sadly, no participant in the discussion except Maria Yelenevskaya defended the interview-based studies.

12. Delamont, "Arguments against Auto-Ethnography."

13. See Heewon Chang, Faith Wambura Ngunjiri, and Kathy-Ann C. Hernandez, *Collaborative Autoethnography* (Walnut Creek, CA: Left Coast Press, 2012); and Satoshi Toyosaki et al., "Community Autoethnography: Compiling the Personal and Resituating Whiteness," *Cultural Studies, Critical Methodologies* 9, no. 1 (2009): 56–83.

14. A. Voronel and V. Yakhot, eds., *I Am a Jew: Essays on Jewish Identity in the Soviet Union* (Moscow: Academic Committee on Soviet Jewry and Anti-Defamation League of B'nai B'rith, 1973).

15. Natan Sharansky, *Fear No Evil: The Classic Memoir of One Man's Triumph over a Police State* (New York: Random House, 1988).

16. Ronald L. Jackson II, "Cultural Contracts Theory: Toward an Understanding of Identity Negotiation," *Communication Quarterly* 50, no. 3–4 (2000): 362.

17. This jocular phrase alludes to the documents issued by Soviet authorities to rank citizens. In internal passports ethnicity appeared as the fifth entry. Physically and mentally challenged people carried papers that specified what "group of disability" was assigned to them, depending on the graveness of their disease. Since Jewishness hindered

socioeconomic mobility, the neutral "fifth entry" in the passport was often referred to as the fifth group of disability.

18. Anna Shternshis, "Kaddish in a Church: Perceptions of Orthodox Christianity among Moscow Elderly Jews in the Early Twenty-First Century," *Russian Review* 66 (2007): 273–294.

19. Mikhail Krutikov, "The Jewish Future in Russia: Trends and Opportunities," *East European Jewish Affairs* 32, no. 1 (2002): 9; and Elena Nosenko-Stein, "Chuzhie sredi chuzhikh: Sushchetsvuet li pravoslavnaia evreiskaia identichnost'?," *Etnograficheskoe obozrenie* 3 (2009): 20–35.

20. Viktor Moin, Liudmila Krivosh, and Moshe Kenigshtein, "Smeshannye russkoiazychnye semi v Izraile: Problemy i osobennosti adaptatsii," in *"Russkoe" litso Izrailia: Cherty sotsial'nogo portreta,* ed. Moshe Kenigshtein (Moscow: Mosty Kul'tury; Jerusalem: Gesharim, 2007), 194–217; and A. Sinel'nikov, "Evreistvo tol'ko po materi—put' v tupik: Gde vykhod?," *Diaspory* 3 (2004): 100–124.

21. Larisa Fialkova and Maria Yelenevskaya, *Ex-Soviets in Israel: From Personal Narratives to a Group Portrait* (Detroit: Wayne State University Press, 2007), 37–87.

22. Gennadii Estraikh, "From Yiddish to Russian: A Story of Linguistic and Cultural Appropriation," in *Studia Hebraica,* ed. Felicia Waldman, vol. 8 (Bucharest: University of Bucharest, 2008), 62–71; Fialkova and Yelenevskaya, *Ex-Soviets in Israel,* 254; and Anna Verschik, "Jewish Russian and the Field of Ethnolect Study," *Language in Society* 36, no. 2 (2007): 213–232.

23. Larissa Remennick, "Transnational Community in the Making: Russian-Jewish Immigrants of the 1990s in Israel," *Journal of Ethnic and Migration Studies* 28, no. 3 (2002): 515–530; Larisa Fialkova and Maria Yelenevskaya, "Incipient Soviet Diaspora: Encounters in Cyberspace," *Narodna Umjetnost: Croatian Journal of Ethnology and Folklore Research* 42, no. 1 (2005): 83–99; and Sabina Lissitsa, "'Russian' Israelis: The Emergence of a Transnational Diaspora," in *Every Seventh Israeli: Patterns of Social and Cultural Integration of the Russian-Speaking Immigrants,* ed. Alek Epstein and Vladimir (Ze'ev) Khanin (Tel Aviv: Bar Ilan University, 2007), 231–256.

24. Maria Yelenevskaya and Larisa Fialkova, "The Case of Ex-Soviet Scientists," in *Transnationalism: Diasporas and the Advent of New (Dis)order,* ed. Eliezer Ben-Rafael and Yitzhak Sternberg (Leiden: Brill, 2009), 627.

25. See the ethnography of our research collaboration in Larisa Fialkova and Maria Yelenevskaya, *In Search of the Self: Reconciling the Past and the Present in Immigrants' Experience* (Tartu: ELM Scholarly Press, 2013), 9–13.

26. Garry P. Freeman, "Political Science and Comparative Immigration Politics," in *International Migration Research: Constructions, Omissions and the Promises of Interdisciplinarity,* ed. Michael Bommes and Ewa Morawska (Aldershot, UK: Ashgate, 2005), 115.

27. Anderson, "Analytic Autoethnography," 389.

28. Fialkova and Yelenevskaya, *Ex-Soviets in Israel,* 153–156.

29. See Fran Markowitz's autoethnographic account of similar moral dilemmas. Fran Markowitz, "Introduction: Edgy Ethnography in a Little Big Place," in *Ethnographic Encounters in Israel: Poetics and Ethics of Fieldwork,* ed. Fran Markowitz (Bloomington: Indiana University Press, 2013), 1–20.

30. See, e.g., Nelly Elias and Natalia Khvorostianova, "Russian Cultural Institutions in Beer-Sheba: Building a Community," *Sociological Papers: Immigrant Scholars Write about Identity and Integration* 12 (2007): 47–65; Julia Lerner, "'Russians' in Israel as a Post-

Soviet Subject: Implementing the Socialization Repertoire," *Israel Affairs* 17, no. 1 (2011): 21–37; and Liza Rozovsky and Almog Oz, "Generation 1.5 Russians in Israel: From Vodka to Latte; Maturation and Integration Process as Reflected in the Recreational Patterns," *Sociological Papers: The Emerging Second Generation of Immigrant Israelis* 16 (2011): 39–57. Rozovsky is a young immigrant scholar.

31. When Larisa's book manuscript, written in Israel, was sent to the publisher in Ukraine, the editor insisted on replacing "I" with "we" because "the use of this pronoun ["I"] is incompatible with the conventions of academic writing." Larisa Fialkova, *Koly hory skhodiat'sia: Narysy ukrains'ko-izrail's'kykh fol'klornykh vzaemyn* (Kiev: Instytut Mystetstvoznavstva, Fol'klorystyky ta Etnolohii im. M. T. Ryl's'kogo, 2007).

32. Larissa Remennick and Anna Prashizky, "From State Socialism to State Judaism: 'Russian' Immigrants in Israel and Their Attitudes towards Religion," *Sociological Papers* 15 (2010): 11.

33. Narspy Zilberg, "Simvoly, kul'turnye kody i sekuliarnye traditsii russkikh evreev v Ierusalime," in *Izrail' glazami "russkikh": Kul'tura i identichnost'; Posviaschaietsia pamiati Barukha Kimmerlinga,* ed. Elena Nosenko (Moscow: Natalis, 2008), 279.

34. Claudia Zbenovich and Julia Lerner, "*Vospitanie eto rabota:* Intercultural Encounters in Educational Communication within Russian-Speaking Families in Israel," *Russian Journal of Communication* 5, no. 2 (2013): 119.

35. Fialkova and Yelenevskaya, *Ex-Soviets in Israel,* 27–31.

36. Alla Sumbaeva, "Trudnye podrostki-immigranty: Gumanisticheskaia model' gruppy podderzhki," in Kenigshtein, *"Russkoe" litso Izrailia,* 384.

37. Adi Kuntsman, "Double Homecoming: Sexuality, Ethnicity, and Place in Immigration Stories of Russian Lesbians in Israel," *Women's Studies International Forum* 26, no. 4 (2003): 299–311.

38. Julia Lerner, "Da'at be-hagira: Studentim yotse rusia ba universita ha-israelit" (Working Papers of Shaine Center of Research in Social Sciences, Jerusalem, 1999), 123–156.

39. See Zbenovich and Lerner, *Vospitanie eto rabota.*

40. Shulamit Kopeliovich, *Reversing Language Shift in the Immigrant Family: A Case Study of a Russian-Speaking Community in Israel* (Herstellung: Dudweiler Verlag, 2009).

41. The first wave of emigration from Russia began in the wake of the Bolshevik Revolution of 1917. The second occurred in the 1940s, during World War II and the first postwar years. The third wave was in the 1970s, and the fourth wave began during perestroika in the late 1980s and intensified as a result of the disintegration of the USSR. These waves are called "Russian" in terms of the language and cultural affiliation of the émigrés. The third and fourth waves were largely made up of Soviet Jews. See David R. Andrews, *Sociocultural Perspectives on Language Change in Diaspora* (Amsterdam: John Benjamins, 1999), 2–4; and Elena Andreevna Zemskaia, *Iazyk russkogo zarubezhia: Obschie protsessy i rechevye portrety* (Moscow: Iazyki Slavianskoi Kul'tury; Vienna: Weiner Slawistischer Almanach, Sonderband 53, 2001), 35.

42. Zinaida Ilatova and Shmuel Shamai, "Dvukhmernaia model' etno-kul'turnoi identifikatsii russkoiazychnykh emigrantov v Izraile," in Kenigshtein, *"Russkoe" litso Izrailia,* 123–125. Ilatova is an immigrant scholar.

43. Marina Niznik, "Cultural Practices and Preferences of 'Russian' Youth in Israel," *Israel Affairs* 17, no. 1 (2011): 104.

14

Family Pictures at an Exhibition

HISTORY, AUTOBIOGRAPHY, AND THE
MUSEUM EXHIBIT ON JEWISH ŁÓDŹ
"IN MRS. GOLDBERG'S KITCHEN"

HALINA GOLDBERG

In my parents' home any time was a story time. Sure, sometimes tales were told during leisurely strolls through old Łódź; other times over dessert at the old-fashioned café at the Grand Hotel. But most often they unfolded at my parents' dining table—the hearth of family and social life—during the carefully choreographed meals that organized my parents' retired lives around food. Some stories were narrated during breakfast, while we took delight in lox and matias *herring (good herring is better than the best lox, Dad would say), accompanied by the obligatory single shot of medicinal cognac that was purported to cure several of Dad's old-age ailments. (If the conversation was particularly enjoyable, an additional shot of cognac was permissible.) But the most abundant storytelling came between the midday and evening meals— sometime around 4 or 5 PM when my parents would take their late-afternoon snack:* a gleyzele tey un a shtikl kukhn. *It was during that hour, while the skies slowly darkened, that they talked to me about their lives, which were divided by* di milkhume *(the war) into the idyllic time before it (far der milkhume) and the real time after (nakh der milkhume). The most fascinating of their stories took place during the in-between time (beys der milkhume), which comprised the surreal experience of their wartime Soviet exile. The words* beys der milkhume *also screamed out the silent horror of the slaughter of our families: silent because our relatives who stayed behind in the Łódź Ghetto did*

256

not survive to tell their stories.[1] *My parents could only echo that silence and tell me of the Immense Absence they experienced. They continued to carefully study any archival photographs from the Łódź Ghetto and the camps that they got their hands on, in hopes of recognizing one of the haggard faces in them as that of a loved one, searching for the smallest clue that would lead them to our families' untold stories.*

These pictures of "my" people—nameless and anguished, a handful of pre-war family photographs that survived di milkhume*—and my parents' stories were a part of my life as far back as I can remember. As a child I listened to them eagerly, assembling in my mind images of the grandparents, aunts, uncles, and cousins I never knew. Years later, when I started my regular visits back to Łódź from my new home in New York, I attended to these recollections with the awareness of a historian. Looking back, I cannot tell whether it was the childhood fascination with my parents' stories that awakened the historian in me, or the innate historian in me that caused me to be drawn to hear these tales over and over (after all, my older brother did not have the same penchant for listening). Within every human being there is a book; those cursed with "living in interesting times" often carry within them several poignant books. I grew up surrounded by such remarkable human books, Jewish and gentile alike, and every time one of those people departed this life, I didn't just grieve for the person, but also felt an intense regret over the irretrievably lost stories, as if with the loss of each person the last copy of an invaluable book was care-lessly committed to fire. By the mid-1990s, aware of the relentless march of time, I started to record the books within my parents.*

I taped the recollections of my parents, Maria (Mania) and Zenon (Zanvl) Goldberg, without a specific plan in mind—I simply felt compelled to hold on to their stories. The project for which these recorded conversations provided framework and soundtrack developed naturally and unexpectedly years later, after both my parents were already gone and I was closing the Łódź apartment they called home for sixty-five years. Many of their belongings, furniture in particular, dated back to the early twentieth century—of course they did not come from my parents' childhood homes ravaged by the Germans, but were acquired by them, secondhand, after the war. Nonetheless they were period appropriate for

the wooden weavers' houses that were moved from various locations in
Łódź to form the Open-Air Museum of Łódź Wooden Architecture at the
Central Museum of Textiles.[2] I offered to donate them to the museum,
suggesting in passing to the museum's director, Norbert Zawisza, that
since there were weavers on both sides of my family, it would be great
if he could use the donated objects to remember *Jewish* weavers. A couple
of months later I got an enthusiastic e-mail from an Anna Dąbrowicz, who
had been appointed by Zawisza to curate an exhibit about Jewish weavers
of Łódź. She was uniquely suited to curate this exhibit—not just because
of her professional qualifications, but also because she has resided for
much of her adult life in what used to be the very heart of Łódź's Jewish
quarter, and has been experiencing the absence of Lodzer Jewry every
time she steps out of her apartment. Once she learned about the handful
of prewar materials I inherited and the recordings of my parents' recollections, she decided that it was best that museum visitors learn the story
of prewar Jewish Łódź directly from my parents. Commandeered by the
ingenious and energetic Ania, as she is known to her friends, I did not even
realize that I was becoming her collaborator in designing and creating "In
Mrs. Goldberg's Kitchen": it was an unanticipated journey full of wonder
into my family's past.

In the ten months that it took to create the exhibit, I found myself jug-
gling three roles: museum exhibit designer, scholar, and autobiographer.
The most familiar of these roles was that of a scholar: as a musicologist,
I have been studying history through music and the history of music my
entire adult life. I am comfortable with the careful scrutiny of information and the nuanced conclusions that it typically produces. Moreover,
I am trained and train my students to be critical, maintain objectivity,
and not seek refuge from multifaceted evidence in simple narratives. But
as a museum exhibit designer, having taken up a métier at which I was a
complete novice, I had to embrace the simply stated goals of the exhibit, to
communicate within a limited amount of time an abridged version of history that would be comprehensible to a broad range of audiences. While
the scholar in me felt imprisoned in a straitjacket (and we did go to great
lengths to make sure that even if we did not tell the full story, we were at
least careful to work with reliable information), the creative "me" spread
her wings—I was granted an unexpected opportunity to explore sound as

historic material in ways that were completely new to me. As for my third role, I guess it is possible to argue that the function of an autobiographer is familiar to all of us, but that is not entirely correct: it is not simply having a story but telling it—the deliberate examination of recollections and the search into one's (or one's family's) past—that produces self-discovery and reflection, and makes an autobiographer.

Autobiography and history have a long-standing and uneasy relationship. In his study of what he calls the "two ways of narrating and preserving the past," Jeremy Popkin explores these tensions within the context of autobiographies written specifically by historians.[3] Nineteenth-century efforts to construct history as an objective, critical academic discipline, as *Wissenschaft,* resulted in the exclusion of first-person narratives from historical scholarship.[4] Their subjectivity and their affinity with literary fiction genres undermined their reliability as historical sources. Aware of the tensions between these two lenses on history, Popkin nonetheless shows that first-person narratives written by historians can help in developing more nuanced interpretations of historical events.

I hope to extend Popkin's point, to suggest that something can be learned from investigating the convergence of the *three* ways of narrating and preserving the past that I experienced while preparing "In Mrs. Goldberg's Kitchen": autobiography, history, and museology. In the following discussion of the making of "In Mrs. Goldberg's Kitchen," I explore my reflections on the three roles I adopted and their cautious coexistence. To highlight the dissimilarity of these personas, I switch my narrative voice back and forth between that of an objective report from a scholar and museum exhibit designer and that of a child subjectively recalling her parents and the world of their youth that was destroyed long before she was born.

JEWS IN ŁÓDŹ

Łódź, located in central Poland, is the country's third largest city. On the eve of World War II Łódź was a multiethnic and multidenominational urban center, home to a vibrant Jewish community, the second largest in Poland. During the course of the nineteenth century, the population of Łódź exploded, growing from 767 souls, 259 Jews among them, in 1820, to 665,000 in 1938, of whom over 200,000 claimed Jewish faith. The city's rapid growth came about as a result of an 1820 decree from the Polish Kingdom government that included Łódź among new industrial settlements, thus laying the foundation for its development as a center of the textile industry. Attracted by the city's growing economy, people flocked from far and near in hopes of employment and opportunities. As they moved to Łódź, the Jews, who at the start of the nineteenth century held traditional jobs as consignment traders, laborers, and stallkeepers, often acquired skills that were better suited to the economic opportunities offered by this city: many became weavers; some built small and large textile businesses of their own. Set aside in 1822 as the Jewish quarter of the city, the small area around the Old Town market, or as the Jews called it, *di alte shtut,* quickly became overpopulated. After 1862, when restrictions on Jews residing elsewhere in Łódź were lifted, the Jewish intelligentsia and the well-off middle and upper classes began to settle in the city's center, but the less affluent and the poor continued to crowd around the Old Town market and in the northern district of Bałuty—the area turned later, during World War II, into Łódź Ghetto by the Nazis.

THE EXHIBIT

The exhibit focuses on the working-class Jews of Bałuty during the period between the two world wars: it seeks to portray the hustle and bustle of everyday life, but also to present the astounding changes that took place at the threshold of modernity. The younger generation, which benefited from reforms undertaken during the brief flowering of independent Poland, was quickly adapting to new trends and mores. Interwar Bałuty was a world at the crossroads of tradition and modernity; *yidishkayt* and acculturation; Judaism, Marxism, and Zionism.

Conceived as a microhistory lesson, the multimedia exhibit tells the story of the Lodzer Jewish community through the eyes of a single family: surrounded by old furniture and objects, the visitors listen to my parents' personal experiences and observations. The exhibit exists in two dimensions: symbolic and archival. The symbolic dimension endeavors to capture the cozy atmosphere of my parents' home, in which they—as virtual hosts—spin tales about the Bałuty of their youth. The majority of furnishings that help create this intimate environment came from the

FIGURE 14.1

A view into the main exhibit room. "In Mrs. Goldberg's Kitchen,"
House No. 6, Open-Air Museum of Łódź Wooden Architecture,
Central Museum of Textiles, Łódź. Photograph by Klaudia Zarębska.

Łódź apartment in which they resided during the years 1945–2010. Although these objects had a connection with my family only after the war,
they are of prewar Łódź provenance. Therefore they serve as a bridge connecting the present, my parents' postwar space, and prewar Łódź in a general sense. The archival dimension consists of documents, photographs,
and sound and video recordings, all drawing on the work of scholars and
collectors. In this dimension, sound serves as the bridge connecting the
present, my parents' postwar space, and prewar Łódź. The soundtrack,

available in Polish and English versions, makes use of recorded interviews with my parents, made during the years 1998–2002; archival recordings of popular music from the 1920s and '30s; and historical commentary.

Thus the exhibit employs audio and visual narrations (stories told by my parents are reflected in pictures and documents). Our family tree—presented as a beautifully detailed papercutting that draws on traditional Jewish symbolism—and the attendant map serve to highlight the variety of occupations performed by my ancestors, and demonstrate how nineteenth-century technological and economic trends resulted in migrations to industrial centers and the adoption of new vocations by Jews in the new urban environment.[5] Electronic media further enhance the virtual experience of the past (for instance the "magic mirror," a new technology offered only in one other museum in the world, which uses a special film projection screen that also acts as a reflecting surface to bring mirror images of the visitors into the filmed representation of the past).

More than a decade passed between the period when I taped my parents' recollections and the first time I heard the recordings. During that stretch of time their health and ability to recall the past declined; our interactions became less about sharing our time together and more about me caring for them. The easygoing dinner-table conversations that we all enjoyed so much became less and less common. And then they left this world—first Dad and a few years later Mom—and I stowed the recordings away: they were precious as documents of my family's history, but the prospect of hearing my parents' voices "from the other side" was too emotionally charged. I couldn't get up the nerve to revisit our dinner-table gatherings.

The first time I heard my parents' recorded voices was soon after I agreed to work on the exhibit. There was none of the uneasiness I anticipated! We were together again, sitting around the dining room table—talking, laughing, quarreling. The phone would ring and interrupt our conversation; the chime of the doorbell would bring in an unannounced but welcome guest whose voice would mingle with ours. In the recordings, as in their day-to-day conversations, the voices of my mom and dad moved fluidly between Polish and Yiddish. This linguistic in-betweenness, the grain of their voices, and their tales provided me with a sense of comfort—of safety that a child feels in her parent's arms—that

I never thought I'd be able to experience again. During the ten months that I worked on the exhibit I was with my parents every day.

    Their tales took me back to their prewar lives, wartime journeys, and even recollections of especially interesting moments in postwar Stalinist Poland. Some of the stories told repeatedly over the years, especially by Mother, seemed entirely improbable. She claimed, for instance, that my grandmother Nechuma, whose maiden name was Jochimek, was actually born Abbe, and that she was related to Samuel Abbe, the owner of the textile factory in the Radogoszcz district of Łódź, which the Nazis turned into the infamous political prison.[6] "He visited us often," Mother would say, "because he was in love with your grandma." Pressing the issue further (for instance, by asking why Grandma married a poor wagoner rather than a well-to-do manufacturer of wool textiles) would only produce more preposterous claims: "He wanted to marry her, but he couldn't because she was his aunt." The explanations got even more complicated when I tried to figure out why Grandma did not carry the Abbe name. I suspected that, if indeed she was an Abbe, the lack of clarity was intended to cover up some extramarital doings of my ancestors.

    My parents' storytelling depended on the sense of togetherness they built in their sixty-seven years as a couple. Over the course of their lives, their stories became intertwined into a narrative so conjoined that even for the individual memories of their childhoods, before they knew each other, each depended on the validation of the other ("Zanvl, what year did I start school?"). Then there were the attendant spats ("We were in Białystok!" "No, Mania, you jumble up everything—we were in Lwów!"): Father was the keeper of exactitude; Mother contributed narrative verve and color. The day my dad died, Mom, who outlived him by six years, stopped telling stories.

THE MAKING OF THE EXHIBIT (I)

My parents' recorded conversations about life in interwar Łódź served as the conceptual starting point for designing the archival dimension of the exhibit. In addition to my audio recordings, we used excerpts from hours of interviews with my parents conducted and taped by Patrick Le Besco, whose primary interest was the Lodzer dialect of Yiddish, and a few selections from a video interview with my father made for the Visual History Archive of the Shoah Foundation at the University of Southern

California. Out of the rich fabric of my parents' stories, we pulled out topical threads that, in our view, best captured selected aspects of everyday life. We identified ten such topics: (1) living conditions, (2) work at home (women), (3) work outside the home (men and, increasingly, women), (4) children at school, (5) children at play, (6) religious holidays, (7) secular leisure time, (8) courtship, (9) military service, and (10) political and cultural life. At the heart of the soundtrack for each of these themes we placed an excerpt or two in which my parents' voices recall their experiences. Similarly, around each such snippet of oral history, we built the exhibit's visual layer that tells the story through photographs and documents.

In defining the ten thematic areas for the exhibit and selecting specific audio and visual materials to present these themes to the visitors, we followed a set of objectives that were articulated during the early stages of our project. The most direct purpose of the exhibit was to knit the history of Jewish weavers back into the existing narrative of the history of the textile industry in Łódź, from which they are largely absent. In this prevailing narrative Jews—if they make an appearance at all—are presented as factory owners (the most famous of them being the absurdly wealthy Izrael Poznański);[7] nothing is said of their Jewish employees or Jewish weavers toiling in the countless small workshops. A related goal, therefore, was to counteract the stereotypes of Jews that are perpetuated in historical narratives and everyday culture, instead drawing attention to the Jewish working class. A broader aim was to draw awareness to Łódź's multicultural, multiethnic, and multidenominational past. Before World War II Łódź was a real melting pot, featuring not only a large Jewish community but also a sizable population of Polonized Germans, some of whom attended the city's Lutheran churches, and a smaller Russian Orthodox community. These linguistic/religious/cultural groups coexisted side by side and interacted in mostly constructive ways. Close associations and friendships were not uncommon. After the war, not only did the city become a monoculture, but the historic traces of these groups and their interactions became invisible to the average person.

Thus we set out to correct some of these misconceptions and fill in gaps of historical knowledge that characterize the typical visitor. We aimed to create an exhibit that would reach a broad range of audiences

(Polish and foreign; gentile and Jewish) across various educational backgrounds and age groups. But from the onset, the primary addressees of "In Mrs. Goldberg's Kitchen" were the young people of Łódź (and Poland, as the museum routinely hosts school tours from other cities). The youth of today's Poland are by and large growing up without direct contact with Jews. Even with the reemergence of interest in All Things Jewish after the fall of Communism,[8] Polish cultural memory strongly favors the easily identifiable, distinctly "other" Hasidic Jew. For example, musical Jewishness is routinely located in the "exotic" klezmer and cantorial sounds at the expense of popular and art music composed by and for Jews, which cannot be easily labeled as Jewish. As for the visual imagination of Jewishness, the peculiar persistence of stereotyped Jewish mannequins and figurines has already been noted by Ruth Ellen Gruber and by the cultural anthropologist Joanna Tokarska-Bakir, who focuses on the most pervasive and troubling of these wooden simulacra of Jewishness: the grotesque and half-demonic "Jew with a coin," believed to bring money into the household it guards.[9] As fascinating an ethnographic and commercial phenomenon as it may be, it is troubling that the most prevalent Polish image of Jewishness, one that is imprinted on the minds of people who know no other Jews, is that of the traditionally attired Orthodox Jew who has the power to control one's financial fortunes.[10] Moreover, young people, especially in Łódź, are routinely exposed to blatantly antisemitic vocabulary and imagery adopted by soccer fans to denounce and put down the rival team.[11] Motivated by concerns about these persisting biases toward Jews, we sought to broaden the thinking of young Poles beyond the stereotypes of "Jewish moneylender," "Jewish industrialist," or "Hasidic Jew" by exposing them to the lives of young, modern Polish Jews typical of the working class in a large industrial city in pre–World War II Poland—a group so well represented in Bałuty before the war but today mostly forgotten.

It was our intention from the start to abstain from directly discussing the Holocaust. After decades of silence under the Communist government, the horrifying fate of Bałuty's population has finally been publicly memorialized—during the post-Communist years monuments have been built and commemorations of the dreadful events observed. Nowadays, in the public spaces of Łódź the memory of the Lodzer Jewish community is intrinsically connected to the moment of its horrific death. In contrast, this exhibit focuses on the remembrance of the lives of Bałuty Jews. By recalling Bałuty as a vibrant, living Jewish quarter, however, the exhibit puts into sharp relief the current absence of Lodzer Jewry. We also reasoned that since viewing the past through the lens of a specific family personalizes history, the young people visiting "Mrs. Goldberg's Kitchen" would have the opportunity to develop a sense of personal connection to individual human beings.[12] They would be encouraged to see *themselves* in history. This, we felt, would be a good foundation on which to undertake sometime later the more difficult conversations about the Nazi destruction of Polish Jewry or the complexity of Polish-Jewish relations.

Having articulated our objectives for the exhibit and determined its thematic areas, we proceeded to research the historical context for my parents' observations. This exploration of primary sources and scholarly literature informed our selection of specific excerpts from the interviews, helped us choose the appropriate music for each topic, and served as the basis of the narration in which the fragments of music and interviews are embedded.[13] Whereas our research broadened our knowledge and made us keenly aware of the complex and nuanced circumstances we were studying, our task was to narrow down, select, and simplify. This process of expanding and refining my understanding of the history of Jews in Łódź while at the same time condensing it and making it comprehensible to lay audiences gave rise to continuous negotiations between my inner scholar and my outer exhibit designer. We made every effort to remain honest about the broader historical picture, but we were also acutely aware that most of the time only a carefully selected slice of history was presented.

A good example of a choice that had to be made is provided by the audio materials concerning my mother's friend Ola. Ola, Mom's childhood best friend, was an ethnic German who lived with her parents and two sisters in Bałuty, a couple of buildings down from Mom's childhood home. We selected for the soundtrack an excerpt in which Mom and Dad, in their characteristic manner, interweave their recollections of relations between Jews and Germans with specific references to Mom's relationship with Ola: "The Germans usually communicated with the Poles in Polish . . . and in Yiddish too. My wife had a girlfriend, who lived in the next building. . . . Her building was number eight and mine was twelve. . . . They could not live without each other. . . . Ola spoke Yiddish. . . . She sung Yiddish songs!"

But the story, as is often the case, was far more complicated—and infinitely more interesting. In a larger excerpt of the conversation Mom talks about all three sisters: Ola, Ela, and Dora. Ela had a Polish fiancé (*a husn*); Dora, on the other hand, already as a young girl, well before the war, joined the Hitlerjugend (the significance of which was not apparent to my mom at the time). My mom encountered them after the war, during their brief return to Łódź, before they permanently relocated to Germany. Dora was keeping a very low profile in fear of someone remembering her Hitlerjugend years (*zi hot moyro ahaym tsi gayn*; she was afraid to go home). Mom helped her secure safe lodgings; Ela "got rid" of her Polish boyfriend and was dating a German; Ola—already married to a German officer— also came back, but when she and Mom met they were unable to recapture the affection and closeness they had shared before the war. The full story reveals that relationships between ethnic groups during the prewar period, even when friendly, had the potential for problems—an account corroborated by documents and scholarship on this topic. The postwar epilogue describes personal relations that shifted under the heavy weight of historical events, but also captures the sense of this multiethnic city during a transitional phase, when people were still returning to the place they used to call home, while trying to understand their position in the new and frighteningly unfamiliar reality.[14] Perhaps the most fascinating aspect of the story is my family's willingness to help Dora in spite of now fully understanding the damage inflicted by the ideology she had already embraced before the war, even if she herself was not directly involved in murderous acts (a subject they appear not to have broached during their brief reacquaintance).

The choices we made in this and other cases were dictated by specific needs. We had no more than three minutes to present each of the ten subject areas—that included the narrative as well as excerpts of interviews and music. Thus, for each subject, interview fragments had to add up to one minute or less. Preparing the soundtrack was certainly an exercise in conciseness! Limited by the need for narrative clarity and by time constraints, we selected for presentation the angle that was likely to be the least familiar to our audiences. Typical historical narratives portray the relationships between ethnic groups in Łódź as tense, and their coexistence, especially in the milieu of the Jewish quarter of the city, as one of apartness; we opted to show the opposite—to call attention to the presence of gentiles in Bałuty and their interactions with Jews. The mingling of my parents' voices in this passage—a sonic effect that evokes the spontaneity of a real conversation and strengthens the impression of their living presence in the room—was an added bonus.

Such decisions were replicated hundreds of times. For the musical underscoring of the narrative, we were able to access the contents of hundreds of 78 rpm records from private and institutional collections.[15] Again time limits were stringent, since for the presentation of each subject, the sum of musical fragments typically could not exceed one minute. Tapping into the rich and beautiful musical soundscape of this period, we searched for the most direct means of evoking the atmosphere of Jewish Łódź at the threshold of modernity. The choice of music was vital to communicating our message clearly and convincingly.

We summoned the musical ambience of interwar Bałuty through the sounds of tangos and foxtrots, Yiddish and Polish cabaret, and Yiddish theater in the tradition of Goldfaden, sidestepping the klezmer sound that today is so often imposed on this world. In this manner, the auditory sphere of the exhibit depicted a world that was being transformed not only through new social, economic, and political circumstances, but also by the latest entertainment technologies: the gramophone, the radio, and the newest craze—talking movies. While not many among the impoverished residents of Bałuty could afford to buy a radio or a gramophone, young people heard popular songs while socializing in dance halls and in movie theaters, of which even Bałuty had several. Music delivered through these media came from the Americas and conveyed new values, changing the younger generation's attitude toward age-old Jewish traditions. In American entertainment, jazz and Mae West, an actress renowned for her overt sexuality and risqué wit, embodied these new morals. In fact, the tale of a musician making a choice between jazz and liturgical synagogue music was retold in various contexts as an allegory for this generational transformation.[16]

The foxtrot "Sex Appeal" serves as a good example of underscoring for the exhibit's soundtrack that was intended to capture this transformation. The song comes from the 1937 Polish film comedy *Piętro wyżej* (One floor up), where it is performed by a man (played by the unrivaled Eugeniusz Bodo) impersonating none other than Mae West. For this film, Poles of Jewish descent contributed the screenplay (Emanuel Szlechter and Ludwik Starski), direction (Leon Trystan), and music (Henryk Wars). This song, like our other selections for the soundtrack, emphasizes the importance of Jews in Polish popular culture, music especially, as composers, lyricists, conductors, instrumentalists, and singers. Moreover, by selecting the Yiddish version of the song, performed by Menasze Oppenheim, we wished to draw attention to the fact that Jews also constituted a large segment of the audience for this music. Numerous popular songs of that era focused on Jewish characters and spoke to the Jewish experience. Like "Sex Appeal," several even existed in Yiddish variants; others were recorded in Hebrew versions for the enjoyment of Polish Jews who relocated to Palestine. For the generation of Bałuty Jews born during the period between the world wars, these beautifully crafted and expressively performed popular songs mingled with the sounds of Hebrew prayers, traditional tunes, and songs of Yiddish theater to create a distinctive soundscape of their youth.

The continuing popularity of "Sex Appeal"—the song has returned in at least one new rendition in every generation since World War II—assures its familiarity to the exhibit's audiences and helps them maintain ownership of the song while learning about its unfamiliar early contexts. Several other songs selected for the soundtrack have had similarly bountiful performance histories and would be known to even younger museum guests. The unspoken aspect of history associated with the music accompanying the exhibit is the fate of its creators. In the case of "Sex Appeal," the singer and composer (Menasze Oppenheim and Henryk Wars) survived the war and emigrated to the United States; the lyricists, Emanuel Szlechter for the Polish text and S. Korn-Tayer (Igor S. Korntayer) for the Yiddish, perished during the Holocaust. By including their songs in the exhibit we endeavored to honor them, to bring the public's attention to their works, and to use their songs as a pathway to a conversation about their creators' lives and deaths.

The documents that spoke of history were stored in an old wardrobe that dominated my parents' room. The huge four-door armoire not only held Mom's and Dad's clothes, but also safeguarded their most precious mementos. Mother kept hers in a lavish red cardboard box marked in Russian "Zolotaia zvezda" (Gold star) and decorated with a five-pointed star surrounded by a laurel-and-oak wreath. The box, which originally contained a perfume set, must have been given to Mom as an extravagant gift in the early fifties. Paradoxical in its convergence of the prerevolutionary Russian art of perfumery with a staunchly ideological allusion to the Gold Star Medal, the highest state honor granted to Heroes of the Soviet Union, mostly for bravery in World War II, the red box recalled a rare instance of Stalin-era indulgence in luxury. Dad's keepsakes were kept in a wooden box, carved with a landscape of one of Poland's favorite vacation spots. The wardrobe was also the place where they kept the album with their most valued photographs.

For me the wardrobe was a place of secrets. On the infrequent occasions when my parents left me home alone, I would dive into its vast interiors that smelled of lemons, naphthalene, and marsh tea. I would carefully handle their keepsakes, and slowly page through the photograph album, stopping at the few pages with sepia-toned prewar pictures of the relatives who perished in the Holocaust. Only my maternal grandma Nechuma's photograph was framed and left on display in the room; other pictures remained in the album. In those rare moments I could leisurely gaze into the faces of my other grandma, my aunts, and my cousins, trying to get to know them.

Another wooden box, on top of the wardrobe, held valuable documents. I knew better than to snoop around there. Over the years, my parents let me see much of its contents. Among them were the military ID card that accompanied Dad through the opening battles of World War II, a certificate releasing my parents from the Soviet labor camp, and a handful of letters written by our relatives and sent to my parents from the Łódź Ghetto. One time—I was maybe six or seven—my dad hid a book on top of the wardrobe. Of course I had to see it! It didn't take long for me to understand why he tried to keep it away from my curious eyes: the ghastly images documenting the Nazi killing machine kept me awake for many months—not just because they were so graphic, but also because I knew that among the emaciated naked bodies piled up for disposal might have been those of the relatives whose faces I knew so well from the photographs—my grandmothers, aunts, and cousins. The wardrobe was the classroom for my earliest, often shocking, history lessons.

THE MAKING OF THE EXHIBIT (II)

The photographs and documents from my parents' wardrobe became the kernel of the visual narration of the exhibit. Prewar pictures of family members were framed and hung on the walls of "Mrs. Goldberg's kitchen," referencing the microhistory of the *balabuste*'s family.

FIGURE 14.2

"Family Tree." Papercutting by Anna Dąbrowicz.
"In Mrs. Goldberg's Kitchen," House No. 6, Open-Air Museum of
Łódź Wooden Architecture, Central Museum of Textiles, Łódź.
Photograph by Anna Dąbrowicz.

Among the documents in the wardrobe, we found some that provided enough clues to get us started on genealogical research. The very existence of Łódź was predicated on the Industrial Revolution, and as such the city was witness to epochal social shifts: massive migrations, and changes in mores, education, and occupations. By contrast, the sleepy shtetls, which we often imagine as the paradigmatic idyllic locus of old-world Eastern European Jewish life, experienced a much slower pace of change. By showing my family's history we intended to convey some elements of these momentous social and economic shifts. We were able to track down direct ancestors on both sides of the family, all the way back to the late eighteenth century, and show how the traditional Jewish occupations gradually gave way to new professions. At the same time we were able to present the attendant geographic relocations from smaller villages and towns to the big industrial city (to take, for instance, the two lineages of weavers in my family: the Goldbergs came from Piaseczno, now a suburb of Warsaw, and from the neighboring Ger/Góra Kalwaria; and the Abbes from Zduńska Wola, also in central-western Poland). Yes, the Abbes! As we followed the trail of the documents, we discovered that my mother was a reliable informant after all. Grandma Nechuma was indeed the youngest progeny of Dawid Wolf Abbe,[17] who died before he had a chance to register her as his child. The Samuel Abbe who "couldn't marry her because she was his aunt" was, in fact, the son of Grandma Nechuma's half-brother Lajb, thirty-eight years older than she was. *Sorry for making fun of your stories, Mom!* With her pedigree clarified, Grandma Nechuma, from her framed photograph next to that of Grandma Fajga of the Goldbergs, could overlook the kitchen in full dignity.

While the framed photographs of my relatives provided a personal connection to the past, the broader visual description of prewar life in Bałuty was presented in the photo wallpaper, a stratum that emerges in several spots of the "kitchen" from beneath a few layers of historically appropriate wallpapers and visually describes the topics addressed in the corresponding audio narration. The bulk of the pictures in the photo wallpaper came from the State Archives in Łódź: we selected 127 photographs from some 800 that were relevant to our exhibit. Photographs and pertinent articles from the Polish- and Yiddish-language press (*Nasz przegląd, Republika,*

Haynt, Der Lodzer shpigl, Ilustrirṭer Poylisher Manchester, among others) were also woven into the wallpaper layer.

The process of aligning visual and audio narrations can be demonstrated by examining the thematic area dedicated to Jews in the military. Here, a document—my father's military ID card—served as the starting point. Dad served in a combat engineering unit during the years 1935–1937. In August 1939, on the eve of World War II, he was mobilized, sent to defend the eastern borders of the country, and captured as a prisoner of war by the Soviets. This ID was issued at the end of his active service in 1937 to be used in the case of mobilization, and traveled with him through the opening battles of World War II and beyond. To set this document in a broader context we selected several archival photographs relevant to military service in interwar Poland. We also included excerpts from newspapers printed the day after Poland was attacked by Germany. Of particular importance were the appeals from the Association of Rabbis in Poland (Orthodox), the Gathering of Rabbis with Higher Education (Reform), and the Association of Jewish Veterans of Wars for Poland's Independence, calling on Jews to give their "property and lives" to defend their "beloved Homeland."[18] In this corner we placed framed family photographs of Dad as a soldier: a portrait picture of a handsome twenty-year-old in his spanking new uniform; photographs of Dad among a group of soldiers rowing in a boat and resting on a river bank; and Dad on leave, strolling through Łódź in his winter uniform.

It was important to tell this story: providing the visitors with information about Jewish participation in the Polish armed forces would help them to better assess questions concerning Jewish loyalty in the face of confrontation with the enemy and the ability of Jews to perform as soldiers.[19] Unfortunately, these stereotypes, established as early as the nineteenth century and exploited by the Nazis, persist in modern discourse in Poland and require a corrective. We wanted to draw attention to the history of Jewish participation in the Polish military campaigns that framed the interwar period. During World War I, Jews fought for the country's independence in the Polish Legions, led by Commandant Józef Piłsudski. They also participated in the Polish-Soviet War of 1920. In interwar Poland, Jews, like other citizens of Poland, were drafted into military service.

A large number of Polish Jews took part in the opening battles of World War II and many died in combat. Of those who were taken prisoner by the Germans, scores did not survive. Tens of thousands of Jews serving in the Polish military were taken into custody by the Russians; countless Jews died in camps or were executed (for instance, in Katyń, the Soviets murdered more than two hundred Polish officers of Jewish descent).

In narrating this story, it was essential to cite numbers—hearing specific figures has a strong impact on people. Only by making the point that my father's participation was the norm, rather than an exception, could we get across our message. But, as can be imagined, the estimates concerning Polish armed forces during the opening battles of World War II are notoriously unreliable: assessments of the overall number of soldiers mobilized in 1939 into the Polish armed forces range from as low as six hundred thousand to around one million; the numbers for Jewish soldiers among them range from one hundred thousand to the highly improbable two hundred thousand.[20] These vast discrepancies bear witness to the diplomatic and military chaos that characterized the weeks leading up to the war and its opening battles. Poland had a clear and ambitious mobilization plan, but early mobilization was thwarted by Poland's allies, who worried that it would provoke Hitler into starting the war. By the time the late mobilization call was issued, the destruction of roads and railroads disrupted travel and made it impossible for soldiers to reach their designated units. Thus the mobilization process was delayed, ongoing, and ultimately not completed. Historians wisely stay away from committing to specific estimates, but our ability to convey the message to the exhibit's audiences depended on including concrete numbers in our narrative. The scholar in me still cringes when I reflect on having to settle on and cite problematic numbers without explanation, without equivocation, and without a footnote.

THE MAKING OF THE EXHIBIT (III)

If my parents' recorded conversations and the documents and photographs from the wardrobe served as the conceptual starting point for designing the archival dimension of the exhibit, objects from their home provided the framework and inspiration for its symbolic component. Our goal here was to create a personal, intimate space in which the visitors could experience a different time and the immediacy of their hosts' presence. A lot of the furniture and household items that came from my parents' apartment were of early twentieth-century provenance. The kitchen furnishings, for instance, were in the apartment in 1945, when my parents moved in. Before that, they served a German family, probably stationed in Łódź during the war, who most likely inherited these articles from the prewar inhabitants of the apartment. As a child I disliked these pieces for being outdated and worn, but over the years I came to recognize that in their simplicity, everydayness, and patina they embodied what the Japanese call *sabi*, a beauty that comes from having grown old well. These objects' symbolic power was located in their having been marked by time and history, and in their connection with the specific family hosting the exhibit. We wanted the visitors to feel invited to sit at the table and thumb through the facsimiles of prewar materials, which we left there for their perusal.

They did. Our efforts to create the feeling of visiting a welcoming, familiar private home were recognized by countless visitors, who recorded their impressions in the guestbook. As one reviewer wrote in an online journal, "In Mrs. Goldberg's kitchen we are not subjected to the museum stuffiness that typically paralyzes the visitor. We enter a cozy, intimate space, emanating an atmosphere of authentic, everyday life. When we sit at Mrs. Goldberg's table, we only lack a cup of coffee and some cookies."[21]

This atmosphere of familiarity and hospitality had one unexpected and touching outcome. Even as we were designing the exhibit, people around us—friends, employees of the museum, collaborators—started to associate "Mrs. Goldberg's Kitchen" with the kitchens of their parents and grandparents, and the tales of prewar life they heard in them. Not a week went by without someone making an unsolicited contribution of a small treasure or family memento. Some of the toys used in the exhibit, for example, came from the childhood home of museum director Zawisza and the prewar German Lodzer family of our graphic artist, Paweł Myszkowski; Anna Dąbrowicz's mom sent us a 1937 atlas she used as a girl in school. My dear friend Barbara Grabowska gave us the only memento that she had from her Jewish grandmother: a beautiful old Singer sewing machine. There were other Jewish objects that for some seventy years waited for an appropriate home. A set of chairs, which before the war belonged to a Jewish family, came from Anna Dąbrowicz's Bałuty apartment, located

FIGURE 14.3

Objects in the main exhibit room, including donated family treasures.
"In Mrs. Goldberg's Kitchen," House No. 6, Open-Air Museum of
Łódź Wooden Architecture, Central Museum of Textiles, Łódź.
Photograph by Jarosław Trościankowski.

in a building that during the war housed several ghetto bureaus, including the room in which *The Chronicle of the Łódź Ghetto* was compiled. Another tenant of the same building, Władysław Zaremba, gave us Jewish books he found in the building's attic. Agnieszka Szygendowska, who worked on the restoration of the furnishings for "Mrs. Goldberg's Kitchen," donated three beautiful hand-embroidered Sabbath tablecloths. Somehow they came into the possession of her distant aunt (perhaps she found them in her postwar apartment among the objects left there by its prewar Jewish tenants). After the aunt's death they were passed on to Szygendowska, who held on to them in hopes of one day giving them a proper home.[22] In the process of absorbing these objects, a transformation took place: "Mrs. Goldberg's Kitchen" became a space that symbolically encompassed the histories of many families associated with Łódź, a witness to the city's multicultural and multidenominational past, resonating the waves of migrations that swept through it, and the tragic fates of many of the objects' owners.[23]

In narrating my remarkable experience of creating the Łódź exhibit I have deliberately drawn attention to some of the tensions that arise when the three modes of narrating and presenting the past coexist in close proximity. Working within the context of a museum exhibit necessitated brevity and directness of message, which were often not compatible with scholarly modes of analysis and presentation. The decision-making process was further impacted by the element of subjectivity: after all, when narrating history through the experiences of our loved ones, we cannot easily resist being swayed into choosing emotionally charged materials and viewpoints. But I also hope to have opened additional space for discussing the potential contributions of subjectively constructed material to our historical knowledge. Not only, as Jeremy Popkin argues, do autobiographical narratives allow more nuanced perspectives on historical events, but within the context of museum exhibits, they help visitors engage with history in a more direct, personal manner.

Perhaps most importantly, it was our deeply personal perspectives that helped Ania and me answer the difficult question, how does one tell the story of the Jewish inhabitants of Bałuty? Yes, we realized that to withhold the account of their death would be historically irresponsible, and would dishonor their suffering. But we also felt that the city already had memorials to the death of Lodzer Jews and that telling the story of their lives was just as important. Without it, they would remain in our memory as the Nazis have left them—humiliated, dehumanized victims; piles of shrunken, depersonified corpses to be tallied up as numbers. By remembering their lives in prewar Bałuty we felt we restored to them at least a sliver of the dignity that was so violently and completely taken away from them. In the face of all the death and destruction, I, for one, want to carry in my mind the image of my aunt Hela with her little daughter Zisele that was captured by a photographer's lens in the last moment of pre-Holocaust normalcy— a dainty girl catching a piggyback ride on her smiling mother's shoulders in the carefree brightness of late-summer Polish fields.

FIGURE 14.4

Prewar photograph of Hela and Zisele Świerc.
From the private collection of Halina Goldberg.

NOTES

1. Our closest relative to have lived through the horrors of the Łódź Ghetto and Auschwitz was my mother's cousin Reginka/Riwka (Piwnik) Andersson. She is turning 102 in Sweden as I write these words, but after the war she said very little about the terror she experienced (mostly in confidence to my mother, to whom she was very close), and she is no longer able to share her recollections.

2. Housed in Ludwig Geyer's White Factory (built in 1835), the Central Museum of Textiles has been in existence since 1960 and is one of the world's most prestigious such museums. The museum has 16,000 square meters (172,000 square feet) of exhibition and storage area. Over the years it has organized over one thousand exhibitions. Since 1972 it has been host to the International Triennial of Tapestry, the world's oldest and largest international exhibition competition promoting contemporary fiber art, which typically attracts some 140 artists representing fifty to fifty-five countries. This and other exhibitions at the museum are visited by some fifty thousand people every year. The latest addition to the museum is the Open-Air Museum of Łódź Wooden Architecture, consisting of several wooden architectural objects that date to the mid and late nineteenth century, moved to the museum from various locations in Łódź. Since Jewish and gentile weavers often lived in these types of dwellings, selecting one of them as the site of our exhibition was perfectly suitable.

3. Jeremy D. Popkin, *History, Historians, and Autobiography* (Chicago: University of Chicago Press, 2005), 4.

4. A reminder: *Musikwissenschaft* is the German term for my own home discipline of musicology.

5. The papercutting was created by Anna Dąbrowicz, who, in addition to a specialization in museology, has a degree in fine arts.

6. Erweitertes Polizeigefangnis, Radegast. In January of 1945, as the Red Army was entering the city, the Nazis set the prison on fire, killing 1,500 people, nearly the entire prisoner population. Today, the remains of the building house the Museum of Martyrdom (http://www.muzeumtradycji.pl/1-historia/?lang=en).

7. Izrael Poznański (1833–1900) served as a model for one of the protagonists of Israel Joshua Singer's 1937 novel *Di brider Ashkenazi* (The brothers Ashkenazi).

8. The earliest overview of this phenomenon was provided by Ruth Ellen Gruber, *Virtually Jewish: Reinventing Jewish Culture in Europe* (Berkeley: University of California Press, 2002). Since then, Gruber and other scholars of the "Jewish revival" have sought to further nuance discussion of the motivations and outcomes of Polish engagements with Jewish culture. See Gruber, "Beyond Virtual Jewishness: Monuments to Jewish Experience in Eastern Europe," Erica Lehrer, "Virtual, Virtuous, Vicarious, Vacuous? Towards a Vigilant Use of Labels," and Gruber's response to the latter, as well as other essays, in *Framing Jewish Culture: Boundaries and Representations,* ed. Simon J. Bronner (Oxford: Littman Library of Jewish Civilization, 2014). Lehrer's thoughtful observations are presented in more detail in *Jewish Poland Revisited: Heritage Tourism in Unquiet Places* (Bloomington: Indiana University Press, 2013).

9. Gruber, *Virtually Jewish*, 130; and Joanna Tokarska-Bakir, "Żyd z pieniążkiem podbija Polskę," *Gazeta wyborcza*, February 18, 2012, http://wyborcza.pl/1,75475,11172689,Zyd_z _pieniazkiem_podbija_Polske.html. There is a broader historical context to figurine representations of Jews in Poland. The 2013 exhibit "Souvenir, Talisman, Toy" at the Seweryn

Udziela Ethnographic Museum in Kraków, curated by Erica Lehrer, sought to nuance the multivalence of historical and social meaning that these images carried in order "to promote inter- and intra-ethnic dialogue and analyze its limits." I am grateful to Lehrer for reading a draft of this chapter and sharing with me the English-language draft of her article "'Most Disturbing Souvenirs': Curative Museology in a Cultural Conflict Zone," published in Polish as "Niepokojące pamiątki: Kurator i muzeum w strefie konfliktów kulturowych," trans. Ewa Klekot, *Zbiór wiadomości antropologii muzealnej* 1, no. 2 (2015): 175–200. Information about the exhibit can be found at http://www.luckyjews.com/.

10. These stereotyped images of Jews invariably shock American visitors to Poland, who see in them echoes of Aunt Jemima and other racist depictions of African Americans. The problematic nature of these images remains lost on most people in Poland.

11. A brief summary of this complex and troubling phenomenon can be found in Helene J. Sinnreich, "Reading the Writing on the Wall: A Textual Analysis of Łódź Graffiti," *Religion, State and Society* 32, no. 1 (March 2004): 53–58.

12. Of course, this viewpoint is not new to museology: in the last couple of decades, numerous museums have used the subjective approach to help visitors relate to history. Most notably, such an approach is the basis of the United States Holocaust Memorial Museum experience.

13. Among the most helpful studies were Bohdan Baranowski and Jan Fijałek, eds., *Łódź: dzieje miasta,* vol. 1, *do 1918 r.* (Warsaw: Państwowe Wydawnictwo Naukowe, 1988); and Adam Dylewski, ed., *Dzieje Żydów w Rzeczypospolitej: ludzie, kultura, tradycja* (Bielsko-Biała: Dragon, 2011).

14. On Jewish returns and relocations to postwar Łódź, see the historian Shimon Redlich's autobiographical *Life in Transit: Jews in Postwar Lodz, 1945–1950* (Brighton, MA: Academic Studies Press, 2010).

15. In its final form the soundtrack uses recordings from the private collections of Grzegorz Musiał, Peter Nahon, and Jerzy Płaczkiewicz, and from the Judaica Sound Archives at Florida Atlantic University Libraries in Boca Raton (http://www.fau.edu/jsa).

16. The most famous of these is of course *The Jazz Singer.* See Jeffrey Knapp, "'Sacred Songs Popular Prices': Secularization in *The Jazz Singer,*" *Critical Inquiry* 34, no. 2 (Winter 2008): 313–335; and Mark Slobin, "Some Intersections of Jews, Music, and Theater," in *From Hester Street to Hollywood: The Jewish-American Stage and Screen,* ed. Sarah Blacher Cohen (Bloomington: Indiana University Press, 1983), 29–43. There are other films in which tradition meets modernity through music, for instance Sidney Goldin's 1923 Yiddish-language *East and West* (with Molly Picon) and the 1928 *Lucky Boy* (with George Jessel).

17. Dawid Wolf Abbe, the patriarch of the large Abbe clan, was a fascinating character—the first Jew to have been admitted as a master into the Weavers Guild, he has been credited by historians with the discovery of a new method of yarn production. Izaak Kersz, *Szkice z dziejów gminy Żydowskiej oraz cmentarza w Łodzi* (Łódź: Oficyna Bibliofilów, 1996), 31.

18. Związek Rabinów Polski, Zrzeszenie Rabinów Polski o Wyższym Wykształceniu, and Związek Żydów Uczestników Walk o Niepodległość Polski, *Nasz przegląd,* September 2, 1939.

19. For the historic contextualization of these topoi, see Sander Gilman, *The Jew's Body* (New York: Routledge, 1991), 38–62.

20. The lowest number of mobilized Polish soldiers, six hundred thousand, is given in J. Bowyer Bell, *Besieged: Seven Cities under Siege* (New Brunswick, NJ: Transaction, 2006), 162. As for the percentage of Jewish soldiers in the September Campaign of 1939, the rather high 18 percent is proposed by Benjamin Meirtchak in *Żydzi-żołnierze Wojsk Polskich polegli na frontach II wojny światowej*, trans. Zbigniew Rosiński (Warsaw: Bellona, 2001). Meirtchak, a Jewish veteran of the September Campaign and the Battle of Lenino, gathered information needed to create lists containing thousands of names of Jewish officers in Polish military forces during World War II. Stefan Zwoliński offers a much more conservative 10 percent, having arrived at it by comparing the highest estimate of overall mobilization numbers to the lowest estimate of Jewish soldiers mobilized. See Zwoliński, "Żydzi w polskich regularnych formacjach wojskowych podczas II wojny światowej," in *Żydzi w obronie Rzeczypospolitej: materiały konferencji w Warszawie 17 i 18 października 1993 r.*, ed. Jerzy Tomaszewski (Warsaw: Cyklady, 1996), 145.

21. "W kuchni pani Goldbergowej nie wyczuwa się muzealnego zaduchu, który na ogół paraliżuje zwiedzającego. Wchodzimy do kameralnego, wręcz intymnego wnętrza, w którym panuje atmosfera codzienności i autentycznego życia. Gdy siedzimy przy stole u Goldbergowej, brakuje nam tylko filiżanki kawy i kawałka ciasta." Miłosz Słota, "Na kawie u Goldbergowej," accessed January 11, 2015, http://old.reymont.pl/muzea_archiwum.php?mode=time&time=2012-07. In addition to an overwhelmingly positive response in the press, the exhibit also received a Sybilla 2012 Award nomination in the category of Historical Exhibits from the Polish Ministry of Culture and National Heritage.

22. In 2013, Szygendowska's short story about these Sabbath tablecloths received first prize in the XI Sholem Asch Nationwide Literary Competition held in the great Yiddish writer's hometown of Kutno.

23. Inspired by the visitors' desire to contribute objects and stories to "Mrs. Goldberg's Kitchen," Anna Dąbrowicz developed a new project titled "Our Wardrobe," a virtual museum of objects and their associated stories. See http://szafa.muzeumwlokiennictwa.pl. This project also has a physical component—the visitors can enter a wardrobe located next to "Mrs. Goldberg's Kitchen" to record their own family stories and listen to those contributed by others.

15

Seamed Stockings and Ponytails

CONDUCTING ETHNOGRAPHIC FIELDWORK
IN A CONTEMPORARY HASIDIC COMMUNITY

ASYA VAISMAN SCHULMAN

B eginning with the expeditions of S. An-sky in 1912, the ethnography of Ashkenazic Jews has focused geographically on Jews living within the former Pale of Settlement or on immigrants from the area. In the twenty-first century, however, the largest population of Yiddish-speaking Jews consists of second- and third-generation residents of Hasidic communities worldwide, including New York, Jerusalem, London, Antwerp, Montreal, and Vienna. In Hasidic communities, Yiddish was retained (or sometimes reinstituted) as one of the markers of *yidish-kayt*, along with other traditional markers, such as dress, food, and folk customs. After the Holocaust and the reestablishment of Hasidic communities in other countries, these features of Jewish life in Eastern Europe were canonized and acquired a new importance due to the destruction of the Old Home (*alte haym*).

Contemporary studies of Hasidic communities, however, are conspicuously lacking in key fields of cultural inquiry: anthropology, sociology, linguistics, and ethnomusicology. This deficiency is due in part to the insularity of the communities and the perceived difficulty in gaining access to their members. As a result, many fascinating aspects of Hasidic life and manifestations of their rich culture have been largely unexplored by scholars. In this chapter, I will discuss my approach and methodology in conducting original fieldwork in Hasidic communities, my steps toward gaining access to the women of the communities, and my experience with gaining trust from community members. By learning to conform to community norms, such as observing Hasidic standards of dress, sparking the interest of potential interviewees in my project by speaking fluently in their native language, and making connections through acquaintances associated with the community, I was able to conduct extensive ethnographic research with Hasidic women in Brooklyn, Jerusalem, London, and Antwerp. In contrast to the experiences of other ethnographers, I demonstrated that it is not necessary to be Hasidic or to pretend to be interested in becoming Hasidic in order to study Hasidic culture.

In the fall of 2004, as a second-year graduate student in Yiddish language and literature, I enrolled in a class called Research Methods in Ethnomusicology. I have always been interested in Yiddish music; I grew up listening to and singing Yiddish folk songs, theater songs, and art songs from Eastern Europe and America and participating in Yiddish music and culture festivals. As a Yiddish student in an ethnomusicology class, I knew that I wanted to do my final project on some aspect of Yiddish music, but I did not have a specific topic in mind.

One of our first assignments that semester was to select a work on ethnomusicology from a list provided by the professor to read and present to the rest of the class. The title of Ellen Koskoff's book, *Music in Lubavitcher Life,* sparked my interest, and I began reading. Lubavitch Hasidim in America, unlike many other Hasidic groups, primarily use English as their vernacular, partially because of their greater involvement with the secular world and the large proportion of *ba'ale tshuve* (Jews who were not raised Orthodox but became so in later life).[1] Koskoff's work thus focused on English- and Hebrew-language songs and on *nigunim,* melodies sung to vocable syllables. As I read, I began to wonder about the musical life of other, non-Lubavitch Hasidim, ones who use Yiddish as their vernacular, particularly when I came to the chapter on women's music. Koskoff described the influence of *Kol be-Isha,* a Jewish religious law restricting women's voices, on the opportunities for women to participate in vocal music.

Because of Kol be-Isha, Hasidic women are usually unable to publicly perform or commercially record songs, as their voices are considered to be sensually attractive to men.[2] I wondered whether Yiddish-speaking Hasidic women sang in contexts similar to those of the Lubavitch women and how their repertoires differed. I was especially curious to learn whether there was any overlap between songs in the repertoire of contemporary Yiddish-speaking Hasidic women and the non-Hasidic Yiddish songs with which I was familiar. After finishing Koskoff's book, I decided that for my final project, I wanted to do some fieldwork with Hasidic women in Williamsburg, New York.

I thus began conducting the research for what would become my dissertation topic. Crucial to understanding my findings are the methodology I used in acquiring data and material, the process through which I gained access to the insular Hasidic communities that I studied, and my relationships with my informants. This chapter will describe how and where I met the women that I spoke to, my changing status as an outsider in their community, and the challenges that I encountered during my fieldwork. I will illustrate these experiences with ethnographic descriptions of several relevant episodes that occurred as part of my research.

GAINING ACCESS

New York

By November 7, 2004, I had used up all of my daytime cell phone minutes for the month. The vast majority of them were spent on phone calls to area-code 718 numbers in Williamsburg. A friend had given me the numbers of two women she had stayed with in that neighborhood on previous weekends, and I spent hours (and days) playing phone tag and being sent over the wires from one woman's aunt to her sister's mother-in-law to their mutual acquaintance: each woman claimed either that she did not have any time on the Sunday I was to do my fieldwork, or that she did not know any songs, unlike her aunt/sister's mother-in-law/acquaintance. Several people additionally gave me the phone numbers of their relatives in Monsey, New York, so that I could conduct phone interviews.

Despite all of my efforts, however, by the morning of Sunday the seventh I had only two appointments lined up: one with Taybl Glikman, a woman my friend had stayed with, and one with a play therapy teacher with whom I had managed to make an appointment only on Friday afternoon.[3] The first appointment was at 11 AM and the second was at 4 PM, so I spent my subway ride to Brooklyn planning creative ways to approach people on the street during the time I would have between the two meetings.

When I got off the subway, I was somewhat surprised to find the streets lined with people—mostly older men and small girls with their mothers—and I soon discovered that the marathon was passing through on that day. Groups of Hasidic girls held up cups of water to the occasional runners, and everyone cheered when someone ran past. I was encouraged by such friendliness toward the strangers and hoped to take advantage of the gathering to conduct some interviews. As practice, I asked one of the mothers for directions to Mrs. Glikman's house. Although I posed the question in Yiddish, she repeated it in English and gave me directions in English; as I walked away, she continued speaking to her children in Yiddish.

When I walked into Mrs. Glikman's apartment, she was playing solitaire on her computer. The apartment was small and rather cluttered; Mrs. Glikman was in her sixties. During our phone conversation two weeks earlier, she had told me that she knew a number of Yiddish songs but did not have a good voice. On the day we finally met, after a few preliminary questions (in English) about her family, job, and language background, I asked Mrs. Glikman about the songs. "I'm not into singing," she replied, insisting that she never sang and was not into songs at all.[4] Instead, she offered to play a tape of a boys' choir that she had borrowed, along with the tape player, from her neighbor for my benefit.

I had not planned on such a turn of events and was not sure how to proceed. When I reminded Mrs. Glikman of our phone conversation, she reluctantly conceded that she did know a few songs. When she began singing, it turned out that one of the songs was actually a lengthy ballad to which she knew all of the words. For the remainder of the twenty-minute interview, Mrs. Glikman repeated at intervals, "I can't say that I really know songs or [am] into songs," "From me you're not going to get too much songs," and "I'm not into singing at all, no." This was a recurring pattern during almost every interview I conducted that day: women would deny knowing or singing songs and would then proceed to sing (usually with the aid of their children) for about twenty minutes.

At the end of my interview with Mrs. Glikman, she asked me what I planned on doing until my next appointment. I told her that I was going to try to speak to some of the women watching the marathon. Mrs. Glikman immediately assured me that no one would speak to me, "unless . . . I know somebody and I would ask them to speak to you, they might speak to you. But if you just stop somebody . . . You want to try it? You'll see, nobody's going to talk to you." My confidence about approaching strangers in Williamsburg was significantly affected by Mrs. Glikman's pronouncement so early in the day that I was certain to get no results.

Mrs. Glikman explained that she had agreed to talk to me because she did not consider herself to be a full-scale member of her society. Having grown up with a learning disability at a time when such children were stigmatized and labeled stupid, Mrs. Glikman had a very difficult life. She got married, but her husband divorced her when her children were still babies. She took a job in a factory and struggled to make ends meet. To alleviate her loneliness, she bought a television and a radio some time before, a practice forbidden in her Hasidic community. Her father renounced her, and her lifestyle at this point did not conform to Hasidic standards. While she was still an observant Jew, she was seen as a marginal member of her community. Mrs. Glikman attributed her willingness to speak to me to this liminal status.

She explained, "I don't know if people are interested. . . . I mean, I don't care, because I'm not as [observant], I mean, I don't belong into the crowd, you understand? But most people . . . I mean, you want to try it? But most people wouldn't want . . . Just looking at you . . . I mean, you're a very nice girl. But most people are not going to speak to strangers. You understand? That's the Williamsburg mentality." With these comments, Mrs. Glikman was referring to the fact that despite my best efforts to dress according to ultra-Orthodox community standards for this weekend, it was clear to anyone in the community that I was an outsider.

Although Mrs. Glikman had previously denied both on the phone and in person that she knew anyone else whom I could interview, she now offered to take me to her neighbors' apartments. Fortunately, most of the neighbors on whose doors we knocked were home, and only two refused to speak to me. I was thus able to interview six additional women (not counting their small children). The first neighbor we approached was the one who had lent Mrs. Glikman the tape. She would not let us into her apartment, but after much persuasion from Mrs. Glikman, she did agree to come into Mrs. Glikman's apartment with her small daughter. Although she agreed from the beginning that she knew a few songs, she claimed that she never sang them. When asked more specific questions, however, she consented, "I sing to myself, to my children a little bit."

I ended up acquiring a rather large repertoire on that Sunday. The songs ranged from religious Sabbath songs to children's songs about body parts to elaborate songs from Hasidic musicals to some original compositions by the last woman I spoke to that day. I had only heard two of the songs before—"Khanike oy Khanike" (Chanukah oh Chanukah), a very common holiday song that has been translated into English and is sung by much of American Jewry, and "Volt ikh gehat koyekh" (If I had the strength), a Sabbath song that is known to be of Hasidic origin. I was surprised by my findings—I had expected to record several lullabies and simple folk songs, and to then write a short paper comparing the collected songs to the secular songs with which I was familiar. Instead I discovered a treasure trove of complex, original compositions created by women and girls in the community over the past fifty years, a cultural wealth completely inaccessible to the greater outside world and even to the male members of the Hasidic community. My exercise in ethnography quickly turned into an ever-expanding project as I uncovered more and more layers of meaning in the data I was collecting, and as the amassed repertoire grew with insightful songs that shed light on many aspects of the lives of Hasidic women.

I went on my second field trip several months later. This time I was in New York for a week in late August, and I had no appointments. I took the subway to Williamsburg and began a fieldwork method that I would continue using on and off for the next three years. My initial encounter with Mrs. Glikman, and her conviction that no one in the community would agree to speak to me, had led me to believe that I needed an intermediary to establish contact with potential informants. My interviews with the women to whom Mrs. Glikman introduced me, however, did not go as well as I had hoped, and on my second trip (and thereafter) I decided to try working on my own, not knowing whether I would be more or less successful than I had been with Mrs. Glikman's assistance.

On an average day, I would walk along the side streets between Marcy Avenue, Lee Avenue, and Bedford Avenue, the heart of the Hasidic neighborhood, and approach women who looked like they could stop for a moment to talk to me. After much trial and error, I learned strategies that worked best for identifying women who would be most likely to respond to me. I avoided women carrying heavy bags, women who looked like they were in a rush, and women who looked particularly unfriendly. I also targeted women who covered their hair with more than just a *sheytl* (wig), a sign that they were from a Hasidic group in which women were more likely to speak Yiddish as their primary language.

Many authors have described the challenges that fieldwork presents, particularly for a novice ethnographer. I found that Bruno Nettl's description of his foray into a village in the northern plains of the United States to study Native American music mirrored my own experiences and anxieties most directly.[5] Much like Nettl, I found it difficult initially to "get up the nerve" to speak to potential informants, not knowing how to begin a conversation, and missed opportunities by taking too long to think of the right thing to say.

Particularly toward the beginning of my research, I would let many women pass me by before mustering up the courage to actually stop one. Finally, I would decide on a suitable candidate, and ask her, in Yiddish, if she could spare a minute. Most women were sufficiently intrigued by the fact that I approached them in Yiddish to find out what I wanted. Early on in my research, the women were puzzled by the fact that I spoke Yiddish although my outward appearance did not mark me as one of them—I did not look like a Hasidic woman or girl, but I spoke the insider language. As I discovered more about the community and gained experience, I gradually learned to modify my dress and appearance to blend in more and more.

Once I had a woman's attention and confirmed that she spoke Yiddish, I would tell her that I was a student interested in learning about Yiddish songs that women in Williamsburg sang. I would then ask the woman if she knew any songs in Yiddish. If the answer was affirmative, I would ask if the woman might have some time to meet with me in the coming days. I would explain that I was in New York for a limited time, and that I would like to arrange for a meeting as soon as possible. Again, it took weeks of daily trips into the community before I found the sequence of opening lines that was most likely to gain me entrance into a woman's home.

The responses I received varied. Often the woman would claim to be extremely busy, primarily with taking care of her large family. Alternatively, she would suggest that she did not really sing, and that instead I should speak to her friend or relative. Very commonly, women suggested that I speak to younger girls, go to girls' schools, or listen to tapes. About one out of three women would actually agree to a later meeting. I would then get the woman's phone number and ask when a convenient time would be for me to call to schedule the appointment. Sometimes, the woman did not give me her number but asked for mine. I tried to avoid this situation, as in such cases the woman almost never followed up. After the exchange of contact information, the woman would either walk away or start asking me questions. She would want to know where I was from, where I studied, whether I was Jewish, how observant my parents were, why I wanted this information, and, all too frequently, whether I was single and interested in being set up with a potential marriage partner.

After several hours of walking around and collecting phone numbers, I would return home, type up my notes, and begin making phone calls. Typically it would be several days before I finally reached one of the women who had given me her number. When I called at the appointed time, a child or husband would usually answer the phone and inform me that Mrs. Shtern was busy, at a wedding, at her sister's house, visiting her mother, or in labor. When I would ask if I could call back at a later time, the person on the other end would say that by the time Mrs. Shtern got back, it would be too late to call; I could leave a message or call back the following day.[6]

When I did get through to one of the women, I would remind her of our meeting on the street and attempt to schedule an appointment. We would agree on a time—usually when the children were at school and the husband was away—and on a place—almost always the woman's apartment. I would get the woman's address and then ask if there was anyone else she thought I could contact who could help with my project. Occasionally, I would get another phone number this way, but most often, the woman would think that she was the only one in the community who would want to speak to me.

One afternoon, I approached a woman in her thirties who was waiting on the street for the school bus to bring her son home. She was wearing a house robe and her hair was covered with a turban. I asked her my usual set of questions, and unlike most of the women that week in August, she agreed to meet with me the following day in her apartment. When I arrived, the table was covered with homemade song booklets and sheets of notebook paper. After the interview portion of our meeting, the woman—Faygi—began singing some of the songs from the booklets. She explained that they were from Satmar camp, some from her own days as a camper and others borrowed from her teenage nieces.[7]

Throughout my encounter with Faygi, I experienced for the first time the hospitality that is characteristic of many people in the Hasidic community. *Hakhnoses orkhim*—welcoming guests—is a *mitzvah* (positive commandment) for Orthodox Jews. During my first trip to Williamsburg, many of the women I spoke to were not friendly to me, some even refusing to let me into their homes. At the time, I thought that they reacted to me in this way because I was an untrustworthy outsider. After the successful experience I had with Faygi (and with the many other women that followed), however, I decided that the distrust with which the first group of women received me probably stemmed in part from the fact that they were introduced to me through Mrs. Glikman—an intermediary seen by them as somewhat disreputable and unconventional.

When I met Faygi, on the other hand, I was alone and dressed in accordance with the conventions of modesty. Faygi was very friendly to me, offering me refreshments during the interview and engaging in conversation. At the end of the interview, she even invited me to spend *shabes* (the Sabbath) at her house later that week. I gladly accepted Faygi's invitation, since spending a weekend in a Hasidic home would give me the opportunity to engage in participant observation. I realized that the success of my research efforts depended more on the extent to which I strove to fit into the norms of the community than on being introduced to potential informants by another community member, particularly if that liaison herself was seen as eluding norms.

While of course only some of the women that I approached in Williamsburg (and later in Borough Park) ended up giving me interviews and singing songs for me, I believe that my method was ultimately successful. During a typical interview, I would ask the women about their background, Hasidic affiliation, and professions. The women usually gave one-word answers and sometimes asked why I needed certain pieces of information. Then I would ask about singing context: when, where, and with whom did women and girls sing, where did they learn the songs that they sang, and what was the provenance and authorship of these songs. Very often, women had trouble coming up with answers to questions, or they would suggest that they sang only in one context (usually school or camp), and that they learned songs only by one method (usually from tapes). I would then begin listing other possible answers, and almost always, the women would find that a lot more of the contexts and learning methods applied to them than they initially thought.

Finally, I would ask the women to sing as many songs as they could remember or had time for, and I would ask them to give me as much information about each song as they could. If lyric sheets of the songs were available, I would ask to borrow them to make photocopies. If a woman had sung everything she could think of and still had time to continue, I would prompt her with suggestions of other songs she might know. When the singing was complete, I would list the titles and sing the first lines of several non-Hasidic Yiddish songs and ask if the woman had ever heard of any of the songs, and if so, if she ever sang them. At the end of the meeting, I would thank the woman, and either arrange for another meeting (if we had run out of time but had more material to cover) or ask if she could suggest other friends or family members who might be able to help me.

The largest portion of my research took place from February 2007 until June 2008, when I lived in New York and took regular trips to Williamsburg and Borough Park to interview women and visit Hasidic girls' schools. While I met most of the participants in my research project during those months using the method described above, there were a few cases when I met women by other means. In one instance, a Jewish studies colleague put me in touch with his brother, who had become Hasidic. The brother, in turn, invited me to his home to meet with a Hasidic schoolteacher, Suri Gold, with whom I ended up having the longest and most informative interview of all my contacts. In a special case, a Hasidic woman whom I met in a linen store refused to let me interview her but convinced her younger friend, Dvoyre Horowitz, to meet with me. Dvoyre became an invaluable contact: not only did she share with me a wealth of songs and knowledge about singing contexts, but she also invited me to her home for the Passover holiday and introduced me to a very musical friend of hers.

When I first conceived of my project, I was expecting to do a study on song lyrics. The process of meeting individual Hasidic women, however, showed me that there was much to discover not only about these women's songs, but also about their lives and the significance of music in their culture. By interacting with a wide variety of Hasidic women, I gained an appreciation for what I learned both about their individual experiences and about their role in Hasidic society in general. The model of conducting individual-based ethnography that I developed to find informants who could teach me about songs and singing was perfected over time and was crucial for expanding my fieldwork from individuals to Hasidic institutions, including girls' schools.

GAINING TRUST

As I perfected my method of conducting research in Brooklyn, my status in the community—both as an outsider and, to some extent, as a partial insider—played an important and ever-changing role in the process. This section will present an overview of the existing self-reflective literature on the status of the female ethnographer in a Hasidic community, and will describe how my own experiences and approach differed from those of the other researchers. I will discuss the way I presented myself to my informants, the role my religious and geographic background played in shaping my status in the community, and the process I went through of adjusting to community standards.

Almost everyone who has done ethnographic research with Hasidim has commented on the significance of being Jewish for the extent to which they succeeded in gaining access to the community.[8] In my case as well, many of my informants asked me if I was Jewish, and, often, whether I was observant. Although the women never said so explicitly, my understanding was that if I had not been Jewish, they would not have been as willing to participate in my research project. I do feel, however, that my experience differed on many levels from that of many of my colleagues in the field.

In the chapter of her dissertation titled "Relevant Issues in Ethnomusicological Research," Ruth Rosenfelder discusses the limitations of an ethnographer, particularly one studying a closed community.[9] She cites a number of researchers who have done work with Hasidim to indicate that "ethnological research into all but the most accessible sects, as represented by Lubavitch, requires of the scholar either personal connection with the Hasidic community or, failing that, a sponsor from within the group." She refers, for instance, to a personal communication with Ellen Koskoff, who studied the music of Lubavitch Hasidim, in which "Koskoff observes that in order to gain access to the more closed sects such as Satmar, the researcher must be a member of the religious Jewish community."[10]

Janet Belcove-Shalin, who studied Hasidim in Borough Park, reflects in an essay on her status as an unobservant Jew in a Hasidic community.[11] She writes that initially, community members had a "negative perception of me as someone radically different from themselves . . . someone viewed with a combination of contempt and incredulity," and she felt that "if I could not find the way to overcome some of their negative perceptions of me, my fieldwork would never advance further than a preliminary research prospectus."[12] She finally discovered that "it was only after I encouraged (or chose not to actively discourage) their belief that one day I might become more observant that they began to take me seriously and to open their doors to me."[13]

Ayala Fader, who wrote her dissertation on the education of Bobov Hasidic girls in Borough Park, similarly found that "despite repeated explanations of my research project . . . Hasidic women I met and worked with often assumed I was on the way to becoming or already was a returnee to the faith."[14] This assumption was based partially on the fact that Fader dressed modestly, out of respect for community practices and to facilitate entrance into the community. While she initially denied this status, she found that when she "neither made claims nor denied the influence of being exposed to their community," she was best able to forge connections with her informants and become a participant observer.[15] Fader describes, however, one undesirable consequence of this approach: "Perhaps it was my effort to conform and offend no one that made my time in Boro Park feel constraining and stifling."[16]

Rhonda Berger-Sofer, who studied Hasidic women in the Meah She'arim neighborhood of Jerusalem, established contact with people in that neighborhood by first becoming acquainted with the Lubavitch Hasidim living there, whom she believed to be the most open of the Hasidic groups. After attending religious classes in the community for over a month, she approached the rabbis teaching the classes and asked them to help her in her project. Unlike Belcove-Shalin and Fader, she explained that she was not a *ba'alas tshuve,* but because she had "behaved 'properly' and showed a sincere interest in learning by faithful attendance at [the] lessons," the rabbis agreed to help her and found her a family with which to live.[17] In exchange, Berger-Sofer had to make some personal sacrifices: for the duration of her research, she had to adhere to the Hasidic lifestyle in full, which included not reading secular books and newspapers and not listening to the radio or watching television. In order to be able to live with a Hasidic family, she "conformed to their dress codes and the general concepts of *tznee'iss* [sic] [modest] behavior, which is a guideline for female interaction and behavior."[18]

While my experiences as an ethnographer in a closed community had much in common with those described above, my unique background and approach to presenting myself ultimately shaped my status among the women in the Hasidic community differently. Despite the fact that I am not Hasidic or ultra-Orthodox, I was able to do fieldwork with some of the most insular groups, such as Satmar, and the vast majority of my research was done with no sponsors from the groups that I studied. I do, however, consider myself to be an observant Jew, unlike most of the ethnographers mentioned above, and this fact affected both the attitude of the Hasidic women toward me and my own level of comfort among my informants.

Although my level of religious observance and lifestyle differs significantly from that of my informants, I was able to answer affirmatively when asked whether I was *shomer shabes* (observant of the Sabbath) and *shomer kashres* (observant of the laws regarding dietary restrictions). I did not go into detail about how exactly I observe these laws, and, satisfied by my answers, the women never pursued these questions further. The Hasidic women with whom I came into contact therefore did not identify me as someone interested in becoming religious. Because they did not attempt to convince me to change my religious beliefs or observance, I did not feel the tension between my own beliefs and ideologies and those I was expected to manifest to the same degree as some of the other ethnographers did.

When I went into the Hasidic community to speak to people or to observe performances, I also attempted to outwardly conform to Hasidic standards as much as possible. I thus chose articles of clothing and hairstyles most similar to what girls in the community wore. Because of my unmarried status, I chose to imitate the outward appearance of Hasidic girls, which differs markedly from that of married women. Despite the fact that I was significantly older than the girls in the community, I felt that I could not dress as a woman, since that would have required covering my hair and misleading community members as to my status, which would have caused problems upon further questioning. Yet while I attempted to resemble community members in appearance, I never claimed to be Hasidic or lied about my affiliation when asked. I tried to give honest answers that were as vague as possible about my relationship to Jewish law, and to quickly steer the conversation to other topics. I found that the more time I spent with the community and the better I learned to blend in, the fewer detailed questions were asked about my level of observance.

By living within a short commuting distance of the Hasidic neighborhoods that I studied, I was able to act in accordance with Hasidic norms while doing research, without having to completely modify my lifestyle as Berger-Sofer did when living among her informants. Although I was based in my own apartment in Manhattan, I spent time as a guest in a number of Hasidic households for periods ranging from a weekend to a week. While living consistently with a Hasidic family during fieldwork certainly has its merits, I feel that I was able to get a better sense of singing as it occurs in the family by visiting a number of different households.

My background as a Jew from the former Soviet Union (FSU) also worked to my advantage in my interactions with Hasidic women. Whereas most secular Jews are disparaged by Hasidim for consciously abandoning religion and are even often equated with non-Jews in the Hasidic worldview, Jews from the FSU, both secular and religious, are accorded a special status. They are perceived as having lost their connection to religion due to forces beyond their control, coerced to stray from Torah ways by the allegedly malevolent Russian government. At the same time that Russian Jews are seen as victims, they are also associated with an imagined righteousness that Jews from the old country somehow embody. These Jews are therefore viewed with much more tolerance than the largely secular American Jewish community, because they carry within themselves the possibility of redemption, namely, religious observance. Because I, as a Russian Jew, had become observant on my own, the Hasidic women treated me with more respect, and this fact facilitated my gaining access into their world.

Despite my observance and special immigrant status, certain aspects of my lifestyle were problematic for the women with whom I communicated. As several other ethnographers have described, higher secular education is scorned among the Hasidim, particularly for a woman. My informants, on the one hand, had trouble understanding why I was pursuing a higher degree, rather than getting married and raising a family. On the other hand, the fact that my degree was in Yiddish and Jewish studies somewhat mitigated the situation; as Belcove-Shalin observes, for example, Hasidim have a particularly negative opinion of anthropologists, whom they associate with the theory of evolution, which is seen as being in opposition to Hasidic beliefs. Studying Yiddish, in contrast, was perceived by some of the women as another indicator of my quest to reconnect to my Jewish roots.

Learning to assume the outward features of a Hasidic lifestyle for my trips into Brooklyn was a lengthy and gradual process. While I knew the general rules of *tsnies* (modesty), such as wearing long-sleeved shirts and below-the-knee skirts, avoiding singing in the presence of men, and minimizing direct contact with males in general, there were many nuances of the Hasidic interpretation of these rules with which I was unfamiliar. Through conversations with informants and close observation I learned, for instance, that in many communities it is unacceptable for girls with curly hair to be seen in public with their hair worn down and curly. In order not to stand out, I had to straighten my curls and often wore my hair in a ponytail; I also needed to keep my hair approximately shoulder-length. From a book about modesty that I bought in Brooklyn, I learned which colors were seen as too flashy and attention-grabbing, and I discovered that it is unacceptable for Hasidim to wear clothing made of denim, as the material is seen as being too casual.[19]

Another significant element of the way in which I presented myself was language. Although I spoke fluent Yiddish when I began my project, the dialect that I had learned was distinctly different from the Yiddish spoken among the Hasidim with whom I interacted. For the first several weeks of my fieldwork, consequently, women whom I approached in Yiddish would respond to me in English. As I learned over time, part of the problem was that I was speaking the "standard" form of Yiddish, which is close to Lithuanian (or Northern) Yiddish and sounds foreign and comical to Hasidim, whose Yiddish is somewhere between the Hungarian and Polish dialects.

I had studied Yiddish dialects in university, so I knew the general features of the Hungarian and Polish dialects, but applying the changes to my own speech was a difficult process. Hasidic Yiddish in America is furthermore characterized by a fairly high proportion of loan words from English. Even after I had more or less learned to speak in the Hungarian Yiddish dialect, my language still sounded peculiar to my collocutors, because I did not have a feeling for which Yiddish words ought to be replaced with English ones.

I was nonetheless able to establish a rapport with a number of women. In addition to interviews and school visits, I had the opportunity to engage in participant observation on several occasions, when women with whom I had formed relationships invited me to spend the Sabbath or a holiday with their families. By engaging in participant observation in a Hasidic home, I gained greater insight into the role of song in a woman's life. I was able to acquire this experience only because I learned to adapt to the Hasidic community enough to become a partial insider. I demonstrated my ability to gain the trust of my informants by not singing in the presence of men, dressing properly, underscoring my country of origin, and speaking Yiddish. Despite the limitations in my ability to speak Hasidic Yiddish, the overall experience was successful and beneficial to my project.

To conclude, the fieldwork that I conducted with Hasidic women was an evolving, ever-changing process based on learning and growing from each experience. In order to initially gain access to the community, I tried meeting informants both with and without a sponsor, and I found that working alone while attempting to conform to community norms resulted in more successful research than associating with a marginal member of the society.

Once I gained access to informants, I worked on earning their trust both by modifying external facets of myself such as clothing and language and by emphasizing what were my assets in the community: my observance and Russian heritage. Despite encountering a number of challenges, I was able to conduct more and more nuanced and targeted interviews and to engage in participant observation on weekends and holidays, immersing myself in the community. In contrast to the experiences of other ethnographers, I demonstrated that it is not necessary to be Hasidic or to pretend to be interested in becoming Hasidic in order to study Hasidic culture.

NOTES

1. Ellen Koskoff, *Music in Lubavitcher Life* (Urbana: University of Illinois Press, 2001).

2. The Kol be-Isha prohibition can be traced to the Babylonian Talmud, Berachot 24a, which states, "A woman's voice is *ervah* [an erotic stimulus], as it is written, 'For your voice is pleasing and your appearance attractive' (Song of Songs 2:14)." This line has been interpreted to mean that a woman's voice could lead a man to engage in impure thoughts and possibly actions, and thus it is prohibited to him; it is generally accepted that this prohibition applies only to a woman's singing voice, and not to her speaking voice.

3. All names of Hasidic women have been altered to protect their anonymity.

4. Taybl Glickman, interview with the author, November 2004.

5. Bruno Nettl, *The Study of Ethnomusicology: Thirty-One Issues and Concepts* (Urbana: University of Illinois Press, 2005), 133–135.

6. Rhonda Berger-Sofer describes the typical evening activities of a Hasidic woman in her dissertation on the Hasidic women of Meah She'arim, Jerusalem: "Since most families are large and live [in the same neighborhood], a family may go to . . . celebrations [such as weddings, engagement parties, or bar mitzvahs] several times during the week. Often celebrations may even conflict, and individuals can only attend a celebration for part of the time, running to the other celebration which they also may be obligated to attend." Rhonda Berger-Sofer, "Pious Women: A Study of the Women's Roles in a Hasidic and Pious Community, Meah She'arim" (PhD diss., Rutgers University, 1979), 79. I have found the situation to be similar in the communities in Brooklyn.

7. Faygi Eisner, interview with the author, August 2005.

8. Works include Berger-Sofer, "Pious Women," 32–39; Ruth Rosenfelder, "Hidden Voices: Women's Music in London's Lubavitch and Satmar Hasidic Communities" (PhD diss., City University, 2003), 106–123; Janet Belcove-Shalin, "Becoming More of an Eskimo: Fieldwork among the Hasidim of Boro Park," in *Between Two Worlds: Ethnographic Essays on American Jewry*, ed. Jack Kugelmass (Ithaca, NY: Cornell University Press, 1988), 77–102; Ellen Koskoff, *Music in Lubavitcher Life,* and quoted in Rosenfelder, "Hidden Voices," 109; Israel Rubin, *Satmar: Two Generations of an Urban Island* (New York: Peter

Lang, 1997), 12; and Harry Rabinowicz, *A World Apart: The Story of the Chasidim in Britain* (London: Vallentine Mitchell, 1997), cover.

9. Ruth Rosenfelder studied the women's music of Lubavitch and Satmar Hasidim in London.

10. Rosenfelder, "Hidden Voices," 109.

11. Belcove-Shalin, "Becoming More of an Eskimo," 77–102.

12. Ibid., 85, 88.

13. Ibid., 88.

14. Ayala Fader, "Gender, Morality, and Language: Socializing Practices in a Hasidic Community" (PhD diss., New York University, 2000), 25.

15. Ibid., 26.

16. Ibid., 28.

17. Berger-Sofer, "Pious Women," 33.

18. Ibid., 39.

19. Rabbi Pesach Eliyahu Falk, *Modesty: An Adornment for Life* (Nanuet, NY: Feldheim, 1998), 396–400.

Part IV

By Way of Conclusion

16

c/D

From Function to Frame

THE EVOLVING CONCEPTUALIZATION
OF JEWISH FOLKLORE STUDIES

SIMON J. BRONNER

The writings of S. An-sky may not have been the first words on Jewish folklore, but, as many of the chapters in this collection have shown, they were instrumental in raising the visibility of folklore in the contentious discourse that arose in the early nineteenth century regarding the stake Jews held in modernity. Signifying a move in Jewish consciousness from a social connection based on ancient sacred texts and theology to more contemporary cultural expressions, An-sky's vision of folklore was not just about salvaging traditions in the wake of modernization, but was also a symbol for the perpetuation of Jewish identity, and ultimately Jewish nationalism.[1] An-sky invoked the notion of "expedition" rhetorically, associating it with geographic exploration to suggest the comprehensive charting of traditions in Jewish locales as a way to gauge the viability of these roots as Jews modernized. The scouring of remote locales relatively untouched by industrial movements allowed for contemplation of the evolution of Jewish customs into the present and their comparability to other remote Jewish corners of the world. Yet there was a powerful etiological statement in the presentation of stories and songs hailing from the Pale of Jewish Settlement as a special historic place and social space, that is, a font of *yidishkayt* defined for the intrepid ethnographers as cultural Jewishness. Folklore from the Pale, particularly for a group without a country, emerged as the poetic soul for Jews elsewhere, and this was a quality to hail, rather than hide, for post-enlightenment Jews.

Exposing material such as superstition, ritual, and craft by the ethnographers venturing into the Pale bore the risk of confirming the stereotype of Jewish culture as primitive and stubbornly antiprogressive, but An-sky's team presented these traditions as the mother lode of authentic, and valuable, cultural ore out of which Jewish social consciousness was or could be forged. An-sky's great project looked to Eastern Europe as the cultural source area of traditions that appeared to have disappeared elsewhere with modernization. In addition, by inquiring into the role of oppression in the cultural progress of Jews, the expedition questioned how shtetl traditions could serve as the foundation of a new, and often problematic, Jewish identity then forming in industrial, democratizing societies.

Rather than view the traditions of the shtetl as backward or bizarre, An-sky took a cue from the romantic nationalistic ideology of the folkloristic Grimm Brothers, Wilhelm and Jacob, in celebrating peasant expression as vernacular artistry at the heart of sustaining national creativity and identity.[2] For Dov Noy, the American-educated, Polish-born doyen of Jewish folklore in Israel, An-sky "anticipated the basic precept of modern ethnography concerning 'ethnicity'—i.e., that a custom is Jewish even if its origin and language are not, provided that it is performed in a clearly Jewish context."[3] Fellow Israeli folklorist Haya Bar-Itzhak additionally credited An-sky with the neologism "ethnopoetics," which in describing a group's aesthetic systems on its own terms became central to modern folklore studies.[4] In the United States, Slavicist Gabriella Safran observed that "earlier than others, An-sky described folklore as the dynamic product of interactions among people and nations. He grasped that the stories people tell depend on who is listening, and he strove to vanish into the background as he heard them, to be indistinguishable from the people he was studying."[5]

Despite these claims to setting a theoretical course for the analysis of folklore as prime "dynamic" evidence of a subaltern ethnic group in the broader realm of culture, An-sky is noticeably absent from citations of folklore and ethnography outside the Jewish world. Much as An-sky suspected that his expedition was distinctive among the cultural forays of the time, An-sky, like his Jewish subject, was largely overlooked in academic social sciences. Historiographies of field-inspired theory have emphasized both the regionalist study of Christian north European peasant societies spurred by Swedish folklorist Artur Hazelius (1833–1901) and the evolutionist "English anthropological school" of George Laurence Gomme (1853–1916), Andrew Lang (1844–1912), and Edwin Sidney Hartland (1848–1927) more prominently than An-sky's contributions.[6] Some of the omission, or ignorance, of An-sky's expeditions might be attributable to the lack of reports in English, French, and German, but a more likely explanation is that the literary- and evolutionary-minded folklorists who dominated European cultural studies had difficulty with (and possibly prejudice against) the Jewish subject in their hierarchical framework for folklore as evidence of stages of social progress and cultural nationalism.[7]

Although Noy and Bar-Itzhak tried to publicize An-sky's contributions to their academic colleagues, they also realized that An-sky's largest notice was among Jewish intellectuals who had an insider discourse about Jewish destiny. Noy and Bar-Itzhak addressed their fellow Jews to make the case that An-sky's lasting contribution was not so much in his literary or political work, but in his representation of directly experienced folklore from the shtetl as the expressive lifeblood of a dispersed, assimilating people in need of a cultural transfusion. Even if his post-Holocaust audience did not accept some of An-sky's romantic notions of the shtetl, he provided a model of the Jewish cultural task ahead by identifying folklore in situ as a deep voice that could clearly benefit shallow moderns stripped of their heritage. Noy and Bar-Itzhak suggested that An-sky associated folklore with the everyday grassroots of culture, implying that it could be adapted and function in communities elsewhere.

Despite organizing, in Bar-Itzhak's words, "the first fieldwork in the study of Jewish folklore that applied the research tools of modern folkloristics," that is, ethnography and ethnopoetic/functional analysis, many scholars of Jewish culture and identity found An-sky problematic as a progenitor of folklore studies because of his apparent archaeological ob-

session with the relict minutiae of the past in isolation, and his neglect
of emerging practices and situated performances in modern everyday life,
including those that took place in urban and multicultural settings.[8] He
still approached folklore as a relic of a bygone age surviving in remote
locations. Later scholars, though, mined his materials to find new meanings in their expressive content and symbolism. The "modern" in Noy's
ethnography and Bar-Itzhak's folkloristics was at bottom process- rather
than product-oriented. Instead of romantically imagining the Jewish
nation through its people in their home locales, as An-sky hoped, later
scholars framed folklore in the processes of variable social interactions
in a mobile, transnational society. Folklore, as a topic and a vision, was
tied less to place and more to a portable, intangible heritage or even state,
and projection, of mind. It defined a malleable, adaptable Jewishness that
could be enacted on certain occasions rather than constituting an isolated,
totalistic "folklife."

The question I take up here in light of the effort more than a hundred
years after An-sky's campaign to yoke folklore and ethnography to dilemmas of Jewish identity is how and why the idea of folklore has evolved
from a functional approach to the Jewish text/object rooted in place to one
of a socially and cognitively constructed frame of action. Both viewpoints
arose under similar circumstances: the perceived decline of religiosity and
isolation along with the supposed threat of secularism, assimilation, and
modernization. Yet with the creation of a national State of Israel and the
emergence of North America as a demographic and cultural center for
Jews, the role of folklore as a vehicle for romantic nationalism changed.
With a revision of the standard historiography of ethnographic continuity
from An-sky that I present here, one also has to question whether folklore
and the understanding of ethnopoetics still figure significantly in the conceptualization of Jewish sustainability in a fragmented, global Jewish culture. My purpose is to point out the continuities and disparities between
An-sky's foundation and the American edifice as it later arose toward the
theorizing of Jewish identity as tradition in response to modernization.
In this move of location and orientation, I argue, was an abandonment
of a nationalistic project to renew Jewish social and cultural solidarity
in favor of a model that guided Jews as individuals to navigate through a
world of strangers.

AN-SKY'S ETHNOPOETICS AND
CULTURAL NATIONALISM

An inquiry into the uses of folklore in a philosophy of Jewish cultural action can begin with an examination of An-sky's essay on ethnopoetics, originally published in 1908 in the Russian-language collection *Perezhitoe* (The past). Two epigraphs set the tone for the essay. The first comes from the pen of Ilya Orshansky (1846–1875), known more as a lawyer and historian than as an ethnographer. Orshansky's main legacy is as an activist for Jewish emancipation in Russia. The quote that An-sky used refers apparently to the limitations of history and the advantages of understanding identity through "a people's poetry," or folklore viewed as vernacular artistry: "A people's poetry depicts, vividly and in clear relief, the hidden inner world of national life, to which we are admitted neither by the pen of the diligent historian nor by the sharp eye of the chronicler."[9] The second epigraph is the Talmudic directive "Go out and see what the people do" (BT Eruvin 14b). The original context of the phrase is in regard to arguments among the rabbis on the width of a post in an *eruv*. The answer from one rabbi was to learn from the people's customs rather than dictate a rule. Yet An-sky implied that this knowledge was hard to come by when he stated, "One may boldly say that there is no other people who speak about themselves so much and know themselves so little as the Jews do."[10] An-sky contended that Jews could be revealed, or, that is to say, their "inner world of national life" could be imparted, through their customary expressions, or "people's poetry."

An-sky pointed out that the Jewish "intelligentsia," occupied with recognition in the fine arts and humanities, had not helped unveil this "inner world." Indeed, they appeared bent on separating from and hiding their cultural roots to achieve success. A new kind of study and student was necessary, he maintained, to expose "matters of Jewish ethnography and folklore, that treasury of folk art which provides the only way to discover the Jewish national character and to penetrate to the depths of the worldview of the Jewish people and its ethnographic-cultural and moral lineaments."[11] The meaning he wanted to convey is apparent in the rhetorical equivalence of lore and art, suggesting that attempts to restrict Jewish cultural production to the elite level of "civilization" in enlightenment discourse were misplaced. According to An-sky, this discourse impelled Jewish fine artists to abandon the richness of their traditions as a cultural resource and instead to build on an essentially foreign heritage. Jewish fine artists, he argued, were not being true to themselves.

Looking to scholars who previously worked with folklore, An-sky's models for action were nineteenth-century Russian ethnographers Vladimir Dal, Lev Shternberg, Moisei Krol, Vladimir Bogoraz, Pavel Schein, and Vladimir Jochelson.[12] But he complained that although many of them were of Jewish origin, they gave little attention to Jewish folklore or else devoted themselves to "savage and half-savage nomads" out in the remote Siberian tundra instead of the people of the western provinces of the Russian Empire. He also lamented that notwithstanding songs and proverbs collected in chronicles of Jewish folklore, "no attempt has even been made to collect and record the folktales, legends, parables, spells, superstitions, and so on" of the Jews. Taken together, these kinds of material could show the holistic fabric and interrelatedness of Jewish culture, he thought, rather than isolating a particular thread. He compared the urgency of collecting this disappearing folklore to losing a treasure trove of art. "Every year, and even every day," he wrote, "the most precious pearls of folk art are being lost. The older generation, that which preceded the cultural revolution, is departing this world and taking with it to the grave a millennia-old heritage of folk art."[13] The cultural revolution to which he referred dates to the late nineteenth century, when Russia felt pressure to modernize as its Western European neighbors had. The changes took the form of transitions from village life to industrialization and urbanization which were sustained by an ethos of progress and innovation, rather than tradition and social intimacy. An-sky feared that the imposition of the majority culture would destroy Jewish culture.

An-sky blared in the essay what can be read as a call to cultural arms: "Our task today is to organize without delay the systematic collection of the works of folk art, of the monuments of the Jewish past, and to describe Jewish lifestyles over the generations. This task is not partisan, but national and cultural, and the best forces of our people must be mobilized and unified for it. The time has come to create Jewish ethnography!"[14] An-sky's original definition of "folk art" was oral rather than visual: "tales, legends, songs, parables, superstitions, sayings, proverbs, and so on, produced by the people itself, as well as works that penetrated it and won great popularity."[15] He noted the common criticism that the Jews appeared "cultureless" because their folklore resembled the traditions of their host societies,[16] and he hypothesized that going to the people to see what they did would reveal "forms, character, and orientation" that were distinctively Jewish.[17] He called for the analysis of European literary "motifs" that were rendered in folk tales performed by Jews with a "different form and character." An example he gave was of the "hidden *tsadik*" or *nister* replacing the fool of European *Märchen*. Although Jewish and European narratives are structurally similar, the function of the character is different in Jewish culture, he declared. Although the *nister* is depicted as a simpleton, the apparent butt of many jokes, An-sky pointed out that "when the time is ripe—generally when Jews must be saved from peril— he is suddenly revealed and turns out to be wiser than all the greatest *tsadikim,* with total mastery not only of the entire Torah but also of the arcane lore that only angels achieve."[18] An-sky generalized that whereas in European folklore this and other motifs appear against the background of "material and physical might, in Jewish art they are shown against the background and in the domain of spiritual power only."[19] Suggesting a function of folklore not just as entertainment, but potentially as resistance to oppression and a parable of social reality, he commented that Jewish heroes fight with spiritual strength rather than physical power. They "act not with the sword but through word and the power of the spirit," he wrote.[20] An "ethnopoetics" thus serves to identify from a group's perspective its own "patterns, images, and terms," or, put another way, its folk aesthetics and native classifications as sources of power. An-sky's poetics is distinguished from those that look for universal and external—or what he calls "superficial"—similarities, and therefore emphasizes the uniformity of the culture of a particular historical experience. The "ethno" in ethnography and ethnopoetics indicates the distinctiveness of the group as conveyed in their artistic expressions, most vividly evident in the collective folklore of people close to the land.

An-sky's social cause apparently came to him late.[21] He claimed earlier in his Russian literary career to have harbored a "hatred and contempt" for Jewishness until he discovered in folklore "the beauty of the poetry that lies buried in the old historical foundations and traditions."[22] But Jewish

literary critic David G. Roskies wrote of this return to Jewish identity, "Far
from being a pious act of self-negation, Ansky's was a Western sensibility engaged in a highly self-conscious act of retrieval."[23] Seeking out the
original versions of "old historical" poetic texts surviving in the present
among peasants uncontaminated by modernization, An-sky offered that
his expedition would venture into a zone he recalled from his childhood
as "the thick of Jewish life."[24] Aware that some collectors in America such
as Leo Wiener and Yehudah Leib Cahan had recorded Yiddish folk songs
from Eastern Europe among Jewish immigrants in New York City, An-sky
insisted in a letter to Chaim Zhitlovsky that "Yiddish tales, legends, and
the like must be collected among old folks who carry the past with them in
unadulterated form."[25] That unadulterated form, he believed, could be re-
covered only from the cultural source area of the Pale, which presumably
contained homogeneous, tradition-centered communities of Orthodox
Jews. Roskies observed that in An-sky's emphasis on spiritual power in
folklore is a reckoning with, or remaking of, Judaism in his old age in the
midst of social and technological change. Roskies proclaimed that with
his expedition in 1912, An-sky "turned the disparate remains of Jewish
folklore and folk life into an all-embracing Oral Torah."[26] And so he established a paradigm for Jewish revitalization with a cultural rather than
religious turn. An-sky epitomized the folkloristic stance for the twentieth
century of the insider who turned observer to confront the sacrifices he or
she had made to assimilate and modernize. Jews needed to take responsibility for their own culture and use their studies of authentic folklore to
shape the future, he asserted, instead of anthropologically or sociologically focusing on the traditions of "savages and half-savages" far removed
from their experience, and leaving often antisemitic non-Jews to dictate
the narrative of the halted progress of the so-called Jewish race.

Dov Noy described the liminal folkloristic position of the Jewish ethnographer engaged in fieldwork of Jews in Hebrew terms of the *meshulah*,
or messenger-collector.[27] "A *meshulah*, unlike a *shaliah* (messenger)," Noy
wrote, "acts in total dedication to his mission, initiating original and individual steps and often displaying bizarre behavior, casting him in the
image of an outsider."[28] Noy noted how in An-sky's *Dybbuk*, the *meshulah*
yearned for the coming of the Messiah, but was paradoxically immersed in
the materialism of modern life, and Noy observed parallels with An-sky's

situation and that of many of his followers in the folkloristic field.[29] One weakness of this preoccupation with the spiritual, Noy claimed, was a relative neglect of visual tradition, although he pointed out An-sky's growing awareness of the material once out among the people on his expedition. Although not as comparative or visual as Noy would like for the future generation of Jewish folklorists working to preserve old identities as well as construct new ones, Noy asserted that An-sky holds "a distinguished place as a pioneer in folkloristics and ethnography."[30] For Noy's student Haya Bar-Itzhak, representing the next generation of Jewish folklorists into the twenty-first century, An-sky made too many sweeping generalizations and over-relied on textual evidence; nonetheless she recognized him as "the keystone of Jewish folklore studies to the present day."[31]

JEWISH ETHNOGRAPHY IN RELATION TO THE ETHNOGRAPHY OF JEWS

As important as An-sky was to the long-term project of collecting folklore and constructing a comprehensive ethnography of Jews, his influence did not significantly extend to North America.[32] Yet a central European scholar of Jewish background, Franz Boas, who arrived in the United States in 1884 at the age of twenty-six, established principles of cultural relativism and particularism in his folklore-based ethnography that were similar to An-sky's. From his teaching post in anthropology at Columbia University, Boas drew from African American and Native American folklore to encourage the replacement of the reigning paradigm of an evolutionary ladder of progress that all cultures climb from savagery to civilization. Cultural evolutionists placed modern industrialized societies, devoted to science rather than superstition, at the top of the ladder and relegated ethnic groups such as Jews to "barbaric" stages at the lower rungs; the old "superstitious" traditions associated with Judaism, they contended, had been displaced by progressive-minded Christianity. Boas proposed a flattened heterogeneous model of many cultures that were relative to one another instead of this hierarchical model based on notions of cultural superiority. Boas maintained that his relativist model countered a racist undertone in evolutionary thought that connected biological differences to a cultural hierarchy from dark to white peoples. Facing resistance to his ideas and antisemitism from colleagues in the American Anthropological Association, he used the American Folklore Society and the *Journal of American Folklore* (JAF), which he edited from 1908 to 1924 (and influenced through 1940 with his students Ruth Benedict and Gladys Reichard at the helm), to expand his vision of culture as holistic, relativistic, and pluralistic.[33]

Boas's explanation of cultural similarities in different parts of the globe followed the historical experience of Jews in the diaspora. He embraced folklore as primary cultural evidence that revealed the particular character of a group and the ways that cultural ideas move. Folklore for Boas comprised the tales and myths that revealed the specific values and history within a bounded group. Using folklore even more than linguistics or physical anthropology, he described cultures by their geographical spread and special conditions rather than by their level and type.[34] As editor of the JAF, he departed from An-sky's call for Jewish "insider" ethnographers by insisting on the anthropological stance of objectivity for ethnographers, who he thought should be outsiders to the cultures they observed. Thus he discouraged his Jewish students Paul Radin and Melville Herskovits from studying Jewish communities, but nonetheless published the folkloristic observations in 1916 and 1918 by Russian-born, Yiddish-speaking Jewish high school teacher Leah R. C. Yoffie (1884–1956) of Eastern European Yiddish-speaking Jewish immigrants. Although she noted in both articles that "the majority of their practices are common to the orthodox Jews in all the lands of the earth," she drew attention to the emergent lore of immigrants adapting to the particular conditions of urban St. Louis.[35] For example, she collected the Yiddish saying "Zie is azei dick wie die grobe blecherin" (She is as large as the tinner's fat wife) and commented that "this is a purely local St. Louis expression. About twenty years ago there lived on North Seventh Street a tinner whose wife was abnormally large. This simile is the result of that good woman's excessive girth, and is still used by Yiddish-speaking Jews in this city."[36] In contrast to An-sky's search for authentic lore of the remote past in isolated rural environs, Yoffie declared the urgency of going into the cities, where Jewish immigrants had settled, to collect their folklore and get a sense of their continuity and change. Echoing An-sky's rhetoric of "inner life" and a "lack of knowledge" of Jewish culture, she declared, "Very little is known

to most of us about the inner life of the people who have recently come to
this country from other lands. There is a promising field for the scholar in
the folk-lore of the immigrants in our large cities. This is especially true
of the legends and customs among the orthodox Jews in our country."[37]

Boas, like An-sky, was concerned for religious and ethnic identity in
a modernizing society associated with individual freedom, but Boas expressed more ambivalence toward the contribution of tradition to progress. Perhaps having in mind the tradition-centered Eastern European
Ostjuden in contrast to the "liberal" Jews of Germany, he announced, "My
whole outlook upon social life is determined by the question: how can
we recognize the shackles that tradition has laid upon us? For when we
recognize them, we are also able to break them."[38] Boas, then, was not calling for the preservation of tradition, as much as for using its knowledge to
enhance intellectual freedom. In a rare reference to his Jewish upbringing,
he used his father's example to make his point:

> My father had retained an emotional affection for the ceremonial of his
> parental home without allowing it to influence his intellectual freedom.
> Thus I was spared the struggle against religious dogma that besets the
> lives of so many young people.... As I remember it now, my first shock
> came when one of my student friends, a theologian, declared his belief in
> the authority of tradition and his conviction that one had not the right to
> doubt what the past had transmitted to us. The shock that this outright
> abandonment of freedom of thought gave me is one of the unforgettable
> moments of my life.[39]

For other public intellectuals, Boas's stands sounded revolutionary, and
indeed, Boas had publicly mentioned that he had been conditioned by "a
German home in which the ideals of the revolution of 1848 were a living
force," referring to unsuccessful protests of noble privilege and efforts to
guarantee civil liberties for Jews and other minorities.[40]

As a result of his social and political stands, Boas frequently suffered
antisemitic as well as ideological attacks in America. Working in the same
city as Boas, Brooklyn Museum curator Stewart Culin unleashed some
of the most vitriolic rhetoric against the Columbia professor. Embittered
in the 1920s by the decline of museum evolutionism and fired up over
the type of antisemitic rhetoric of *The International Jew,* Culin implied
that Boas's scholarship was a brand of Russian-inspired radical social-

ism spread by a conspiracy of international Jewry. He observed that at a
council meeting of the American Anthropological Association in Philadelphia, members "were aligned, divided into two parties, who separated
and seated themselves on opposite sides of the room. On one side were
the Jews and the converts and supporters, mostly students of Franz Boas
of Columbia University, and on the opposite side, their opponents. The
Jews stood for Internationalism, and so proclaimed themselves. They had
succeeded in securing possession of this important association and used
it for their personal and political ends."[41] Culin's friend Adolph F. A. Bandelier accused Boas of clannishly relying on Jewish ethnographers composed of "some blooming youngsters and . . . a Sheeny from Russia." He
viewed them as being culturally as well as academically ill-equipped because they did not live up to the standards of Christian modernism. These
"children of Abraham, Isaac and Jacob," he sarcastically wrote to Culin,
compose "the JEW speculating on the ignorance of others."[42]

Beyond ample evidence of ethnic prejudice by evolutionary anthropologists Culin and Bandelier against the very idea of Jewish ethnographers, there was an intellectual problem for them in the discourse on
evolution posed by the presence of supposedly "superstitious" Jews in
the advancement of rational science, indeed in the very persistence of ancient Judaism in modern industrial civilization. The progress and mobility
of Jews, indeed the recurring reference to an ascribed Jewish scientific
"genius," challenged the consistency of evolutionary racial doctrine based
upon the backwardness and ignorance of Jews stuck in a barbaric stage
of progress.[43] Joseph Jacobs, an Australian-born Jewish scholar known
for his diffusionist folklore studies, presented the results of an elaborate
social study defying evolutionary predictions of cultural backwardness.
In essays such as "The Comparative Distribution of Jewish Ability" (1886)
and later in his book *Jewish Contributions to Civilization* (1919), he found
that Jews had shown a higher rate of intellectual ability than evolutionary
doctrine predicted. In his prideful phrase, "'Tis a little people, but it has
done great things."[44]

Typical of the case for Jewish racial typology in cultural evolution is
John Sterling Kingsley, who in *The Standard Natural History* insisted on
Jews as a race at a "low stage of culture" characterized by ignorance, fanati-
cism, and superstition.[45] Yet if an evolutionary racial classification based

on English Christian superiority placed Jews at a primitive cultural rung, Kingsley had to explain the renown of highly regarded Jewish scientists, intellectuals, and leaders such as British prime minister Benjamin Disraeli, who was of Jewish heritage. "A Jew, it is true," Kingsley admitted, "can rise to be the premier of the British empire, but this is the exception noted; here there was contact with other people. To see the Jew in all his purity and the accompanying degradation, *we must visit those places, like southern Russia, where they form whole communities.*"[46] In contrast to this prevailing intellectual bias against Jewish life in the Pale of Settlement, An-sky's insistence on the vernacular artistry of the Russian communities and Boas's defiance of biological determinism bear the stamp of their concerns for Jewish emancipation resulting from an appreciation, and recasting, of the stigmatized Jewish vernacular as valuable art. Although they viewed Jewish folklore as material for a relativistic, liberating agenda, they were aware of the risk that Jewish folklore would be used for racist purposes as a sign of social backwardness. An-sky's response was to elevate and creatively adapt Jewish folklore as a national symbol. Boas's was to redirect Jewish concerns regarding racism and antisemitism to distinctive non-Jewish native artistry in exotic locales. Even if they had similar aims, it was Boas who ended up being more influential in creating a relativistic cultural awareness of ethnic tradition in modern life and in positing rational functions for the persistence of folklore.

Joseph Jacobs (who is notable in his dual roles as editor of the British journal *Folklore* as well as of *Jewish Social Studies*) was one Jewish folklorist of the era whose work dealt with Jewish-Christian relations as opposed to Jewish folklore in isolation. He openly ridiculed attempts by renowned British folklorists such as George Laurence Gomme and Andrew Lang to portray Judaism as a "savage" religion displaced by Christianity and therefore render Jews obsolete and necessarily "backward."[47] He mocked the Victorian folklorists by stating that if that was the case, then the Christian mass was barbaric because it involved eating the host. He connected Passover historically to Christian communion, but argued that Passover's meaning could not be narrowed historically to the original commemoration of Exodus, as the Victorians were wont to do. Ethnographically pointing to varieties of customs attached to Passover in different Jewish communities, he argued that folk practices should be observed to determine how they functioned differently according to the locale. He contended that rather than being a survival of the ritual eating of unleavened bread as a historical commemoration, the consumption of the communal wafer in the Christian mass functioned to create holiness through the belief in bodily transference. Years later, eminent folklorist Alan Dundes, who had a Jewish background, went one step further, with a psychoanalytic interpretation that hypothesized that the blood-libel legend was a "projective inversion" of Christian guilt over the cannibalism of eating the host. He maintained that this guilt was instead projected onto narratives of Jews killing the Christian child for blood to eat in a wafer-like matzo. It thus was a legend with the function of relieving Christian anxiety rather than an outgrowth of historical practices.[48]

Jacobs, who was known as a diffusionist, like Boas, made a major contribution to the use of folklore studies generally by recasting the meaning of "folk," arguably based upon his Jewish experience. Reflecting a concern about diasporization, Jacobs presented folklore not as an irrational survival of savage practices, but as a functional expression of tradition that spread with social movements, and that was capable of producing new forms emerging in contemporary situations.[49] Resisting racial stereotypes, Jacobs characterized the folk not as primitives, but as social segments of societies, "many-headed . . . and often many-minded."[50] Instead of portraying culture as a hierarchy with folk at the bottom and moderns at the top, Jacobs declared the relativist concept, "We are the Folk as well as the rustic, though their lore may be other than ours, as ours will be different from that of those that follow us."[51] In this conception, folk shifted from a noun for a remote group or lower level of culture to an adjective for a traditional process that marks, and indeed is needed by, all people. It could be collected in the city as well as the country, among the elite as well as the peasantry, and even more significantly could constitute individual agency of—rather than "shackles" on, as Boas lamented—one's identity.

THE RISE OF AMERICAN FUNCTIONALISM

With the devastation of the Holocaust in mind, and Jewish rediasporization renewing ethnographic urgency for collecting folklore in Israel and North America toward a revised picture of post-shtetl, modern Jewish cul-

ture, in 1977 a landmark meeting in Chicago titled the Regional Conference on Jewish Folklore, organized by the Association for Jewish Studies
(AJS) at the Spertus College of Judaica, sought to reflect on the progress
of Jewish folkloristic work and query whether it represented a unified
movement. The conference gave special attention to the problem of settling uprooted communities from Eastern Europe and North Africa in
new locales, particularly in the United States and Israel. The reference to
"regional" in the title in relation to the national AJS belies its global importance. The conference's driving force, Dov Noy, claimed it was the first
Jewish studies conference outside of Israel devoted explicitly to folklore,
and went on to view it historically as the "cornerstone in the development
of the academic study of Jewish culture as part of the field of Jewish Studies."[52] He implied that this interdisciplinary field was more hospitable than
anthropology, religious studies, or literature to Jewish folklore broadly
conceived and analyzed by Jews. In Israel, where folklore was a popular
subject, he pointed out, Jewish folklore studies had been narrowly defined
as a literary resource and its study was centered on origins of narratives in
ancient texts. In the United States, there was an opportunity to integrate
new developments beyond literature in Jewish studies and a greater acceptance in folklore studies than in Boasian anthropology of "fieldwork
at home."[53]

To be sure, Jewish folklore since the nineteenth century had been previously discussed in scholarly meetings, including those of the American
Folklore Society and the Association for Jewish Studies, but the Chicago
conference conspicuously pushed for folklore as a separate ethnographic
approach as well as a type of renewable, modern resource in Jewish studies. This concern for folklore as key evidence of a new interdisciplinary
Jewish studies aiming to uncover cultural relationships was especially
apparent seven years after the AJS conference in the organization of "Living Tradition: Jewish Folk Creativity and Cultural Survival," sponsored
by the Center for Jewish Studies of the City University of New York and
YIVO in New York City. The organizers of the New York City conference
boasted that because the AJS conference had been a regional one, "Living
Tradition" was appropriately "the first national conference devoted to Jewish folklore."[54] The conferences had many of the same speakers who were
visibly initiating courses on Jewish folklore at Indiana University, the Uni-

versity of Pennsylvania, Harvard University, UCLA, and other prominent
national universities. Folklore emerged as a large umbrella under which
to connect genres of narrative, music, and art as well as to confront big
ideas about ethnic identity, the interrelationship of tradition and modernity, and cultural massification and sustainability. Folklore studies also
seemed more hospitable to the idea of Jews studying other Jews, despite
the anthropological questions of objectivity. Yet folklore studies was the
product of scattered individuals rather than the kind of concentrated,
comprehensive team project represented by the An-sky expedition. Still
using fieldwork to recognize outstanding tradition-bearers and varied
cultural scenes, the participants in the conferences presented more of
Jacobs's picture of a many-headed and many-minded Jewish culture than
An-sky's ur-source of Jewishness in the shtetl.

These events of the 1970s and 1980s suggested to participants the beginnings of a revitalization as well as an intellectual movement. It was a
period of consolidation that led to a push for new ethnographic perspectives on contemporary Jewish culture countering the prevalent emphasis
on ancient literary and historical foundations of Jewish civilization. In
many ways, the movement took the An-sky expedition as its inspiration
for this effort, although it wanted to be sure to present new ethnography
not as a salvage operation but as an inquiry into the adaptation of traditional forms and the emergence of new ones. It also faced a lack of institutional support and contemplated whether such a movement could be
sustained with individual, rather than organized team, projects. Although
not driven by a singular project, the ethnographic perspective on the Jewish subject, I maintain, has cast the problem of Jewish culture as a paradox
of identity out of the conflict of tradition and modernity and has challenged conventional categorizations of Jewish studies.

No longer amassing poetic material for a case for cultural nationalism,
many conference participants observing Jews in the practice of traditions
that were not isolated in time and place and analyzing "urban villagers"
(such as the Hasidim in new modern settings) as folk societies problema-
tized the supposed primary function of group maintenance. More of the
issues at hand concerned the way that practices and performances of folklore constructed individual identities and projected anxieties about the
relation of Jewishness to a dominant Christian society. Rather than treat-

ing popular culture as sitting on an opposite pole from tradition, more questions arose about the hybridization of folk and popular culture into ethnic symbols.

In the major theoretical move from positing functions of Jewish practices to situating behavior within frames of communication, ethnographers of the Jewish subject redefined culture as a process of representation and subjective organization of experience.[55] This is an old story in social sciences but the narrative I propose that is new or revised is the uneasy alignment of folklore and ethnography in the emergence of Jewish studies. In the twenty-first century, I contend, a new period of reconfiguration has been recognizable in which Jewish folklore and ethnography, viewed in the context of popular culture, merged into Jewish cultural studies.

With the theoretical shift came a different historiography that emerged from the study of Jewish folklore in the modernized, heterogeneous societies of Central and Western Europe rather than the relatively isolated, homogeneous shtetls of Eastern Europe. For example, Noy, in narrating eighty years of ethnographic progress toward the creation of a Jewish folklore field at the Chicago conference, credited Prussian-born Max Grunwald rather than An-sky in Russia for setting the stage for later work.[56] Noy noted the instrumental use of "folklore" in the years that followed as an umbrella term to cover the spectrum of culture including (1) names and oral aspects, (2) poetry, (3) belief and legend, (4) customs and folkways, (5) augury, and (6) material culture. Notably absent was music, which had aligned largely with musicology, although Noy included presentations on the ballad and Yiddish music to draw attention to the possibilities of folkloristic perspectives on music and song, much as had been done for Anglo American folk music.[57]

Another factor in the integration of music into folklore studies came from the Yiddish world, where figures such as Vilna-born Yehudah Leib Cahan promoted the linkage of folk narrative and folk song studies as part of *folksshafung,* or folk creativity, and others worked with the broader concept of *folkloristik,* or the study of traditions.[58] Still, the predominant approach of mining historical texts for references to folklore was evident in books such as Angelo S. Rappoport's *The Folklore of the Jews* (1937), Joshua Trachtenberg's *Jewish Magic and Superstition* (1939), and

Theodor H. Gaster's *The Holy and The Profane: Evolution of Jewish Folkways* (1955), all of which appeared in the United States and Great Britain and were concerned with the origins of modern customs in pagan or ancient rituals. They owed much to Grunwald's stated aim of *Volkskunde:* to go back to the roots of humankind ("Rückwärtsschreiten zu den Wurzeln der Menschheit").[59]

Noy, who had been a Talmudic scholar, broke away from religious studies, literature, and anthropology by receiving a degree in folklore in 1954 from Indiana University, and viewed folklore in the Boasian sense as a mirror of culture. Together with the anthropologically oriented Raphael Patai and literary scholar Francis Lee Utley, Noy spearheaded a volume titled *Studies in Biblical and Jewish Folklore* (1960), published by Indiana University's Folklore Institute, to show new research by individuals calling themselves folklorists. Patai used the opportunity to reiterate a call he made in "Problems and Tasks of Jewish Folklore and Ethnology" in 1946 (in English; it appeared in Hebrew the year before) advocating that "the study of the folklore of *present-day* Jewish communities" receive "the highest priority within the general field of Jewish learning."[60] The folklorists were agitating for a shift from an emphasis on the historic relics or survivals of Jewish beliefs to an ethnographic project analyzing the contemporary functions of Jewish customs in everyday life. Sensitive to the charge that Judaism as an ancient religion was "superstitious" and therefore anachronistic, the folklorists wanted to show the rationale, indeed necessity, of Jewish folkloric production in the modern age. Richard Dorson, for example, posited the need of an assimilated American generation to deal with their immigrant legacy in the formation of Jewish American dialect stories, and Beatrice Weinreich closed *Studies in Biblical and Jewish Folklore* with a classic study of the Americanization of the Passover seder.[61] By the time the Chicago conference came together in 1977, the peripatetic Noy was especially sanguine about Jewish folklore as a key to unlocking puzzles of Jewish culture in multiple locations, and about its connection to mass culture within the new interdisciplinary construct of Jewish studies. The contemporaneousness of folklore was rhetorically conveyed by dropping "biblical" from the title of the publication of the conference, *Studies in Jewish Folklore,* and by its sponsorship by the Association for Jewish Studies.[62]

Raphael Patai laid the foundation for this realignment of practice with functionalism in a Jewish perspective with his assertion in *Studies in Biblical and Jewish Folklore* that "as an anthropologist, one agrees with the anthropological definition of folklore as 'dependent on oral transmission' and thus including 'myths, legends, tales, proverbs, riddles, the texts of ballads and other songs, and other forms of lesser importance, but not folk art, folk dance, folk music, folk costume, folk medicine, folk custom or folk belief.' But as a student of Jewish culture one knows that Jewish legends and tales can be studied only in the context of Jewish folk custom."[63] His emphasis on the significance of custom as a context for analysis suggests that in Jewish culture, the function of tradition matters most because it explains the persistence of a variety of traditional material in terms of the social and psychological benefits it provides rather than a backward, stubborn, or superstitious character of a group of people. Explaining Jewish cultural scenes as rational responses to diverse social and cultural contexts held an urgency for many mid-twentieth-century anthropologists and folklorists willing to study their own cultures. Yet it also carried over into analyses of other groups. In the lead essay of the Chicago conference, folklorist Roger Abrahams, who had Jewish roots and devoted most of his career to African American folklore, even asserted that "to the extent that we all study others that we may better understand ourselves, for me all folklore is, at least by refraction, Jewish."[64] For Abrahams, the concept of folklore as a key expression of culture shifted discussion of race to ethnicity and the capability of agency in the formation of identity.

SITUATING AND FRAMING JEWISH CULTURE

Discontent with functionalism arose across the social sciences during the 1980s because of skepticism about its capacity to serve as an explanation for cultural practice. According to Jewish folkloristic critics such as Elliott Oring, it often described unintended consequences of events rather than their causes. It also raised a psychological question of whether functions outside the awareness of participants constitute motivations by those participants to engage in cultural scenes. One could posit functions as factors contributing to the perception of an event rather than as a reason for behavior within the cultural scene. This criticism appeared to signal a general antipsychological turn in ethnographic work as fieldworkers strove to validate the experiences of participants as reasons for engagement with culture.[65] The criticism led to a frequent assertion of multiple meanings coming out of a single event, coupled with the charge that functionalism was reductionist because it typically relied on an observer's interpretation of a single reason for participation in a cultural scene. Decentering the ethnographer's viewpoint in an alternative to functionalism, there could be as many explanations as there are participants because they each bring individual perspectives to an event.

In historiography, one could speculate on the American connection to a decentered view of cultural analysis because of the popularity of performance or poststructural ideas in individualistic societies related to the critique of functionalism. Yet one might also note that Jewish folklore studies relied heavily on functionalist explanations of contemporary events.[66] In advancing the symbolist position coupled with functionalism that participants have motivations and impulses outside of their awareness, folklorist Alan Dundes especially advocated for psychological explanations of both Jewish religious ritual and popular myths and legends that circulated among non-Jews about Jews.[67]

One methodological adjustment to functionalism was to ground analysis in specific situations, many of which are not bounded in space but defined by individuals who form a cultural relationship. Such situations went by the terms "cultural scenes" or "frames." Sociologist Erving Goffman, whose book *Frame Analysis* (1974) is a benchmark for this kind of study, underscored the often unspoken negotiation of socially constructed frames by participants in a cultural "situation" when he wrote, "I assume that definitions of a situation are built up in accordance with principles of organization which govern events—at least social ones—and our subjective involvement in them."[68] Although credited with promoting frame analysis, undoubtedly influenced by his experience in a family of Ukrainian Jews migrating to Canada in the late nineteenth century, he did not draw examples from many Jewish situations.[69] Nonetheless Goffman's conception of socially constructed frames, according to those who knew him, was aroused by issues of his own Jewish identity and his negotiation of social interactions far from his Manitoba home. For instance, classmate Saul Mendlovitz, who shared a Jewish background with Goffman, remarked of their graduate school experience together at the University of Chicago, "Erving was a Jew, acting like a Canadian, acting like a Britisher. . . . He felt that he was Jewish yet didn't want to be Jewish. He wanted to be something else. He really wanted to be an English gentleman [in line with] the picture of him that he had in his head."[70] A central problem in Goffman's paradigm-changing approaches to social interaction was one of altering identity that could be appropriated and related through expressive acts by participants of gesture and talk in selected settings.

Goffman never wrote about his childhood but he was quoted as asserting that "being a Jew and a Russian Jew at that, explained a lot about me," which biographer Ronald Fernandez took to mean that "he was a perennial outsider, caught between his ancestry and the prejudices of the larger society."[71] Taking the analytical role of observer looking in on someone else's culture, Goffman sought to be an insider looking out, and developed theatrical metaphors for cultural behavior of stages and performances to describe variable social roles, much like those of touring actors who adapted to different physical settings and audiences. Mendlovitz indicated that Goffman "was very much into that observational stuff very early on," based on his concern for fitting into different social groups on campus as a Jew and as a Canadian. Mendlovitz, who also had a self-impression as an outsider in Chicago, recalls that as Jews, "Erving and I used to go to [ethnically mixed] parties and agree that we would exchange [thoughts on] what we had seen. He especially was interested in what we had seen and then he would take copious notes on that. . . . And we would then go over very carefully what the girl said to him, who was going off into another room, what was the content, how come there were no paintings on the wall, but it was a full range of ethnography and that kind of stuff."[72] In these settings, often populated by strangers, Goffman noticed that a standard part of dialogue would be the extraction of information such as birthplace, occupation, and ethnicity to figure out another person's identity and categorize what to expect socially from that person. Goffman was apparently concerned about what the label "Jew" meant to others and how that identity matched his own self-awareness. Even though Goffman was self-conscious about his Jewish background as a basis for frame analysis, as a professor he encouraged ethnographers, including his Jewish students, to avoid studying their own families or cultural groups so as to maintain an objective distance from the observed scenes.[73]

One can read a concern about the kinds of interaction between individuals who have a self-awareness of ethnic difference in Goffman's reference to "stereotype" in his groundbreaking study, *The Presentation of Self in Everyday Life* (1959): "If unacquainted with the individual, observers can glean clues from his conduct and appearance which allow them to apply their previous experience with individuals roughly similar to the one before them or, more important, to apply untested stereotypes to him. They can also assume from past experience that only individuals of a particular kind are likely to be found in a given social setting."[74] Before Goffman applied the terminology of the "frame," drawn from the work of English anthropologist Gregory Bateson, he used the looser terminology of "situation" to refer to a recognizable context, or at least recognizable by participants, that drives distinctive forms of expression, and impression, that people convey to one another. Goffman was interested in the attempts of participants to manage situations, often through symbolic communication in talk and action, to advance their own interests. A proposition he advanced that drew consideration in scholarly circles was the idea that in these situations boundaries as well as connections are established through symbolic communication, often embedded in artistic performances, including the use of proverbs, slang, and body language.

Goffman's microsociological approach attracted wide notice because of the implication that participants in social situations have agency in the formation of their cultural life rather than follow precedents of superorganic traditions or repeat fixed texts of lore in their expressive talk.[75] He outlined an ethnographic goal of analyzing through observation whether the expressive and often ethnically inflected communication that occurs within a situation is dictated by the setting, often outside the awareness of participants, or is strategically guided by one or more figures in the frame. Setting up a frame socially is an attempt by interacting participants to gain social order by emphasizing connections among one another and moving potential conflicts to the margins or edges of the frame. Goffman declared that this constant negotiation of different social settings is a function of modern everyday life in which identities are open to alteration in response to conditions of high mobility, social diversity, and extreme individualism. He conceptualized modern society as one in which people are strangers to one another and consequently create social frames constantly to establish familiarity and construct an identity appropriate to the situation.[76] In Goffman's view, identities are not shaped by family line or locality alone, but are flexible and overlapping. Modernity offers individuals choices about who they want to be or how they appear to other strangers, but with those choices comes the often difficult cultural work of formulating and managing their identities in various social relations on a daily basis. Forced into this role of presenting themselves, individuals become actors to one another and learn from culture the dimensions of acts they can ply variously to communicate with and impress others. More recently, other scholars have added historical and psychological inquiries into this sociological premise to more deeply analyze the experiences and drives that shape socially framed behavior, particularly in Jewish contexts where issues of stereotype, migration, boundary, and difference abound.[77]

To be sure, frame analysis is not a Jewish property. Yet I have observed a Jewish perspective of sorts through my editing of four volumes of the Jewish Cultural Studies series for the Littman Library of Jewish Civilization, in which ethnographic essays often refer to the mobility and constructiveness of Jewish expression and representation.[78] In such essays the psychology of Jewishness as a cultural quality appears to prevail over a static anthropology of Jews and Judaism. This approach is especially evident in confronting Jewish coding in digital communication, a medium that reduces ethnic affiliation on its surface but might also be harnessed to raise it.[79] Still, one could complain that although this view of Jewishness as a framed cultural quality is applicable to the Jewish subject, it has not been fully integrated into Jewish studies as a whole.[80] Ethnography and folklore gravitate toward a separate development of Jewish cultural studies that has arisen as a new hybrid, distinct from both Jewish studies and cultural studies.[81] Perhaps in reaction to the presumption that biblical and ancient sources dictate later behavior, this hybrid seeks sociological and psychological explanations that posit the *production* of tradition and culture prompted by individuals acting with agency.

The new configuration of Jewish cultural studies centered on ethnography and folklore declares analysis to be about what people think of as

Jewish, which may be distinct from the Jew or the things made by Jews. It is revealed in the expressions of culture—speech, folklore, literature, art, architecture, music, dance, ritual, film, theater—that blur boundaries between Jew and non-Jew, past and present, folk and popular, modern and traditional.[82] Although growing out of modern American conditions, the orientation has driven a return to Eastern Europe, still recovering a disappearing past, but more so in the twenty-first century at points of encounter and emergence such as touristic zones, museums, camps, festivals, and representations and adaptations of tradition betwixt and between national and ethnic identities.[83] These points often involve invocation of cultural memory suited to the occasion, and surrounding social and political conflicts, rather than exhibition of relict features of folklore as "unadulterated" artifacts. This shift compels a reassessment of historiography toward the fabric of Jewish cultural studies out of the twisted strands of folklore, literature, sociology, and history. In this historiography, one could expound on the transformation of the vessel of Jewish nationalism molded out of the cultural clay of the shtetl or community into what I call the "culturalism" of Jewish identity: occasions or frames for expression perceived as Jewish in a transnational, dispersed culture. This concept of culturalism locates the production of traditions that provide a sense of cultural identity in the absence or deterioration of institutions in a mass society devoted to handing down, and often imposing, values through folklore from one generation to the next.[84]

The search for texts and objects is less about distilling the "pure" strains of the folk than about interpreting the meaning of folk processes and behavior in the often murky and conflicted representations of Jewishness. This Jewishness is complicated in the framing of Jewish culture by considerations of overlapping or disruptive identities of gender, sexuality, age, family, region, body, and age. Less prone to digging in a secluded location for a remote settlement of Jews representing a bygone age, new ethnographers set their sights closer to home on everyday encounters and enactments of Jewishness, and have posed questions of continuity and adaptability frequently evident in a multicultural environment. As An-sky had reconstituted his religion with the folklore of the disappearing Russian shtetl, so have Goffman-inspired folklorists, cognizant of the foundation of ethnographic expedition to the cultural "homeland" (as a

contrast to the Holy Land), reframed Jewish identity as outcomes of mobile practices in contemporary culture. Although oriented to the process
of the many-headed and many-minded Jews in the myriad cultural scenes
of modern life, this development still builds on An-sky's invocation to "go
out and see what the people do."

NOTES

1. See Itzik Nakhmen Gottesman, *Defining the Yiddish Nation: The Jewish Folklorists
of Poland* (Detroit: Wayne State University Press, 2003), 75–110; Cecile E. Kuznitz, "An-
sky's Legacy: the Vilna Historic-Ethnographic Society and the Shaping of Modern Jewish
Culture," in *The Worlds of S. An-sky: A Russian Jewish Intellectual at the Turn of the Century*,
ed. Gabriella Safran and Steven J. Zipperstein (Stanford, CA: Stanford University Press,
2006), 320–345; Simon Rabinovitch, "Positivism, Populism and Politics: The Intellectual Foundations of Jewish Ethnography in Late Imperial Russia," *Ab Imperio* 3 (2005):
227–256; Nathaniel Deutsch, *The Jewish Dark Continent: Life and Death in the Russian Pale
of Settlement* (Cambridge, MA: Harvard University Press, 2011); Eugene M. Avrutin et al.,
eds., *Photographing the Jewish Nation: Pictures from S. An-sky's Ethnographic Expeditions*
(Waltham, MA: Brandeis University Press, 2014); Benjamin Lukin, "An-ski Ethnographic
Expedition and Museum," in *The YIVO Encyclopedia of Jews in Eastern Europe*, ed. Gershon
David Hundert (New Haven, CT: Yale University Press, 2008), 48–51.

2. Rivka Gonen, "An-Sky in Jerusalem," in *Back to the Shtetl: An-Sky and the Jewish
Ethnographic Expedition, 1912–1915*, ed. Rivka Gonen (Jerusalem: Israel Museum, 1994),
viii. It should be pointed out, however, that despite the celebration of An-sky in Jewish
folkloristic circles, he is rarely cited in histories of folklore studies in Europe. Giuseppe
Cocchiara's 703-page *The History of Folklore in Europe* (1971) omits any reference to him,
although it covers scholarship in Russia. Y. M. Sokolov has a chapter titled "Problems
and Historiography of Folklore" in *Russian Folklore* (1971), but it also makes no mention
of An-sky. No citations of An-sky appear in *The Study of Russian Folklore* (1975), edited by
Felix J. Oinas and Stephen Soudakoff, giving the impression that the study of Jews in Russia was separate from the study of Russian Christians.

3. Dov Noy, "An-Sky the Meshulah: Between the Verbal and the Visual in Jewish Folk
Culture," in Gonen, *Back to the Shtetl*, xvii.

4. Haya Bar-Itzhak, "S. An-ski (S.Z. Rappoport) the Ethnographer of the Jews and his
'Jewish Ethnopoetics,'" in *Pioneers of Jewish Ethnography and Folkloristics in Eastern Europe*,
ed. Haya Bar-Itzhak (Ljubljana: Scientific Research Centre of the Slovenian Academy of
Science and Arts, 2010), 28.

5. Gabriella Safran, *Wandering Soul: The Dybbuk's Creator, S. An-sky* (Cambridge, MA:
Belknap Press of Harvard University Press, 2010), 6.

6. See Giuseppe Cocchiara, *The History of Folklore in Europe*, trans. John N. McDaniel
(Philadelphia: Institute for the Study of Human Issues, 1971), 375–389; Richard M. Dorson, *The British Folklorists: A History* (Chicago: University of Chicago Press, 1968); Don
Yoder, "The Folklife Studies Movement," *Pennsylvania Folklife* 13 (July 1963): 43–56. An-
sky's expeditions and the study of Jewish folklore and ethnology are also absent from historiographies of Russian folklore: Y. M. Sokolov, *Russian Folklore*, trans. Catherine Ruth

Smith (Detroit: Folklore Associates, 1971); Felix J. Oinas and Stephen Soudakoff, eds., *The Study of Russian Folklore* (The Hague: Mouton, 1975). This omission appeared to affirm the role of Jews as outsiders to Russia. Although the historiographies of Russian folklore included other ethnic-religious groups, Jews were not viewed as an indigenous group, or they were considered not to constitute a living tradition.

7. See Simon J. Bronner, *Following Tradition: Folklore in the Discourse of American Culture* (Logan: Utah State University Press, 1998), 129–140. See also Jean Baumgarten and Céline Trautmann-Waller, *Rabbins et savants au village: L'étude des traditions populaires juives xix–xx siècles* (Paris: CNRS, 2014); Jonathan Boyarin, "Trickster's Children: Genealogies of Jewishness in Anthropology," in *Framing Jewish Culture: Boundaries and Representations*, ed. Simon J. Bronner (Oxford: Littman, 2014), 77–96; Barbara Kirshenblatt-Gimblett, "Exhibiting Jews," in *Destination Culture: Tourism, Museums, and Heritage* (Berkeley: University of California Press, 1998), 79–128; Simon J. Bronner, "Framing Jewish Culture," in Bronner, *Framing Jewish Culture,* 1–29.

8. See Jack Kugelmass, "The Father of Jewish Ethnography?," in Safran and Zipperstein, *The Worlds of S. An-sky,* 346–360; Mariëlla Beukers and Renée Waale, eds., *Tracing An-sky: Jewish Collections from the State Ethnographic Museum in St. Petersburg* (Amsterdam: Joods Historisch Museum, 1992).

9. S. An-ski, "Jewish Ethnopoetics," trans. Lenn Schramm, in Bar-Itzhak, *Pioneers of Jewish Ethnography and Folkloristics in Eastern Europe,* 34.

10. Ibid.

11. Ibid.

12. Ibid.

13. Ibid., 35.

14. Ibid.

15. Ibid., 40.

16. Boyarin, "Trickster's Children," 85–92.

17. An-ski, "Jewish Ethnopoetics," 51.

18. Ibid., 61.

19. Ibid., 51.

20. Ibid.

21. Benjamin Lukin, "From Folklore to Folk: An-Sky and Jewish Ethnography," in Gonen, *Back to the Shtetl,* xiv.

22. David G. Roskies, "S. Ansky and the Paradigm of Return," in *The Uses of Tradition: Jewish Continuity in the Modern Era,* ed. Jack Wertheimer (New York: Jewish Theological Seminary, 1992), 247.

23. Ibid.

24. Ibid.

25. Ibid., 257.

26. Ibid., 260.

27. Others refer to the position as "new class" consciousness. See Simon J. Bronner, "Plain Folk and Folk Society: John A. Hostetler's Legacy of the Little Community," in *Writing the Amish: The Worlds of John A. Hostetler,* ed. David L. Weaver-Zercher (University Park: Pennsylvania State University Press, 2005), 56–97; B. Bruce-Briggs, *The New Class?* (New York: McGraw-Hill, 1979); Jay Mechling, "Richard M. Dorson and the Emergence of the New Class in American Folk Studies," *Journal of Folklore Research* 26 (1989): 11–26.

28. Noy, "An-Sky the Meshulah," xvii.

29. Ibid.

30. Ibid.

31. Bar-Itzhak, "S. An-ski (S.Z. Rappoport)," 33.

32. Kugelmass, "The Father of Jewish Ethnography?," 346.

33. Julia Liss, "Boas, Franz," in *A Companion to American Thought,* ed. Richard Wightman Fox and James T. Kloppenberg (Oxford: Basil Blackwell, 1995), 81–83.

34. Gladys Reichard, "Franz Boas and Folklore," *Memoirs of the American Anthropological Association* 61 (1943): 52–57; Melville Jacobs, "Folklore," in *The Anthropology of Franz Boas: Essays on the Centennial of His Birth,* ed. Walter Goldschmidt (San Francisco: American Anthropological Association and Howard Chandler, 1959), 119–138.

35. Leah R. C. Yoffie, "Present-Day Survivals of Ancient Jewish Customs," *Journal of American Folklore* 29 (1916): 413.

36. Leah R. C. Yoffie, "Yiddish Proverbs, Sayings, Etc., in St. Louis, Mo.," *Journal of American Folklore* 33 (1918): 165.

37. Yoffie, "Present-Day Survivals," 413.

38. Franz Boas, "An Anthropologist's Credo," *The Nation,* August 27, 1938, 202.

39. Ibid., 201.

40. Ibid. See also Simon J. Bronner, *Following Tradition: Folklore in the Discourse of American Culture* (Logan: Utah State University Press, 1998), 129–134; Leonard B. Glick, "Types Distinct from Our Own: Franz Boas on Jewish Identity and Assimilation," *American Anthropologist* 84 (1982): 545–565.

41. Stewart Culin, "The International Jew," unpublished manuscript, n.d., Brooklyn Museum, Stewart Culin Papers. Quoted in Bronner, *Following Tradition,* 133.

42. Adolph F. A. Bandelier to Stewart Culin, January 16, 1912, Brooklyn Museum, Stewart Culin Papers. Quoted in Bronner, *Following Tradition,* 134.

43. See Sander Gilman, *Smart Jews: The Construction of the Image of Jewish Superior Intelligence* (Lincoln: University of Nebraska Press, 1996).

44. Quoted in ibid., 71.

45. John Sterling Kingsley, ed., *The Standard Natural History,* vol. 6, *The Natural History of Man* (Boston: S. E. Cassino, 1885), 472.

46. Ibid.; emphasis added.

47. Bronner, *Following Tradition,* 134–137; see also Dorson, *The British Folklorists.*

48. Alan Dundes, "The Ritual Murder or Blood Libel Legend: A Study of Anti-Semitic Victimization through Projective Inversion," in *The Meaning of Folklore: The Analytical Essays of Alan Dundes,* ed. Simon J. Bronner (Logan: Utah State University Press, 2007), 386–409.

49. Gary Alan Fine, "Joseph Jacobs: Sociological Folklorist," *Folklore* 98 (1987): 183–193.

50. Joseph Jacobs, "The Folk," *Folklore* 4 (1893): 234.

51. Ibid., 237.

52. Dov Noy, foreword to *Studies in Jewish Folklore,* ed. Frank Talmage (Cambridge: Association for Jewish Studies, 1980), xi.

53. Dov Noy, "Eighty Years of Jewish Folkloristics: Achievements and Tasks," in Talmage, *Studies in Jewish Folklore,* 1–12.

54. "Conferences and Meetings," *Jewish Folklore and Ethnology Newsletter* 6 (1983–1984): 5–6.

55. Bronner, "Framing Jewish Culture," 1–30; Robert Georges and Michael Owen Jones, *Folkloristics: An Introduction* (Bloomington: Indiana University Press, 1989), 289–293; Galit Hasan-Rokem, "Jewish Folklore and Ethnography," in *The Oxford Handbook of Jewish Studies*, ed. Martin Goodman (Oxford: Oxford University Press, 2002), 969–972; Barbara Kirshenblatt-Gimblett, *Destination Culture: Tourism, Museums, and Heritage* (Berkeley: University of California Press, 1998), 17–78.

56. See Max Grunwald, "Fünfundzwanzig Jahre jüdische Volkskunde," *Mitteilungen zur jüdischen Volkskunde* 25 (1923): 1–22; Christoph Daxelmüller, "Hundert Jahre jüdische Volkskunde—Dr. Max (Meïr) Grunwald und die 'Gesellschaft für jüdische Volkskunde,'" *Aschkenas: Zeitschrift für Geschichte und Kultur der Juden* 9 (1999): 133–144; Dov Noy, "Dr. Max Grunwald: The Founder of Jewish Folkloristics," *Folklore Research Center Studies* 6 (1982): ix–xiv; Dan Schrire and Galit Hasan-Rokem, "Folklore Studies in Israel," in *A Companion to Folklore*, ed. Regina F. Bendix and Galit Hasan-Rokem (Malden, MA: Wiley-Blackwell, 2012), 331–332.

57. Noy, "Eighty Years," 5–10.

58. Y. L. Cahan, *Shtudyes vegn yidisher folksshafung* (New York: YIVO, 1952); Barbara Kirshenblatt-Gimblett, "Di Folkloristik: A Good Yiddish Word," *Journal of American Folklore* 98 (1985): 331–334.

59. See Klaus Hödl, "The Viennese Jews' Search for Integration through the Jewish Museum in the Late 19th Century," *Yearbook of Jewish Studies at the Central European University* 3 (2002–2003): 56.

60. Raphael Patai, "Jewish Folklore and Jewish Tradition," in *Studies in Biblical and Jewish Folklore*, ed. Raphael Patai, Francis Lee Utley, and Dov Noy (Bloomington: Indiana University Press, 1960), 11; emphasis added.

61. Richard M. Dorson, "Jewish-American Dialect Stories on Tape," in Patai, Utley, and Noy, *Studies in Biblical and Jewish Folklore*, 111–176; Beatrice S. Weinreich, "The Americanization of Passover," in Patai, Utley, and Noy, *Studies in Biblical and Jewish Folklore*, 329–360.

62. Talmage, *Studies in Jewish Folklore.*

63. Patai, "Jewish Folklore and Jewish Tradition," 21. Patai cites the definition of folklore as "verbal art" from the work of American-born Africanist William Bascom (1912–1981); see William R. Bascom, "Verbal Art," *Journal of American Folklore* 68 (1955): 245–252. See also William Bascom, "Folklore, Verbal Art, and Culture," *Journal of American Folklore* 86 (1973): 374–381.

64. Roger D. Abrahams, "Folklore in the Definition of Ethnicity: An American and Jewish Perspective," in Talmage, *Studies in Jewish Folklore*, 14.

65. Alan Dundes, "Folkloristics in the Twenty-First Century (AFS Invited Presidential Plenary Address, 2004)," *Journal of American Folklore* 118 (2005): 385–408.

66. See the contents of *Jewish Folklore and Ethnology Review* through its run from 1977 to 2000.

67. Alan Dundes, *The Shabbat Elevator and Other Sabbath Subterfuges: An Unorthodox Essay on Circumventing Custom and Jewish Character* (Lanham, MD: Rowman & Littlefield, 2002); Dundes, "The Ritual Murder or Blood Libel Legend," 382–409; Alan Dundes and Galit Hasan-Rokem, *The Wandering Jew: Essays in the Interpretation of a Christian Legend* (Bloomington: Indiana University Press, 1986).

68. Erving Goffman, *Frame Analysis: An Essay on the Organization of Experience* (New York: Harper Colophon, 1974), 10–11.

69. John Murray Cuddihy, *The Ordeal of Civility: Freud, Marx, Lévi-Strauss, and the Jewish Struggle with Modernity* (Boston: Beacon, 1974), 68; Ronald Fernandez, *Mappers of Society: The Lives, Times, and Legacies of Great Sociologists* (Westport, CT: Greenwood, 2003), 206–207; Erving Goffman, *Stigma: Notes on the Management of Spoiled Identity* (Englewood Cliffs, NJ: Prentice-Hall, 1963), 60, 114.

70. Dmitri Shalin, "Saul Mendlovitz: Erving Was a Jew Acting like a Canadian Acting like a Britisher," *Remembering Erving Goffman*, July 28, 2009, http://cdclv.unlv.edu//archives /interactionism/goffman/mendlovitz_08.html.

71. Fernandez, *Mappers of Society*, 206–207.

72. Shalin, "Saul Mendlovitz."

73. Renowned ethnographer Gary Alan Fine, who has a Jewish background, recalled that Goffman emphatically told him with a Jewish inflection when Fine proposed to study a Jewish wedding that "anyone who studies their own family is a schmuck." He told this anecdote as part of his delivery of the Francis Lee Utley Memorial Lecture, "The Folklore of Small Things: Tiny Publics and Realms of Local Knowledge," at the Annual Meeting of the American Folklore Society, Nashville, October 2010.

74. Erving Goffman, *The Presentation of Self in Everyday Life* (New York: Anchor, 1959), 1.

75. Thomas Scheff, *Goffman Unbound: A New Paradigm for Social Science* (Boulder, CO: Paradigm, 2006).

76. See Kwang-Ki Kim, *Order and Agency in Modernity: Talcott Parsons, Erving Goffman, and Harold Garfinkel* (Albany: State University of New York Press, 2002); Vance Packard, *A Nation of Strangers* (New York: David McKay, 1972); Richard Sennett, *The Fall of Public Man* (New York: Vintage, 1977).

77. Ra'anan Boustan, Oren Kosansky, and Marina Rustow, *Jewish Studies at the Crossroads of Anthropology and History: Authority, Diaspora, Tradition* (Philadelphia: University of Pennsylvania Press, 2011); Jonathan Boyarin and Daniel Boyarin, eds., *Jews and Other Differences: The New Cultural Studies* (Minneapolis: University of Minnesota Press, 1997); Andrew Bush, *Jewish Studies: A Theoretical Introduction* (New Brunswick, NJ: Rutgers University Press, 2011), 57–67; Simon J. Bronner, "Jewish Naming Ceremonies for Girls: A Study in the Discourse of Tradition," in *Jewish Lifeworlds and Jewish Thought*, ed. Nathaniel Riemer (Wiesbaden, Germany: Harrassowitz Verlag, 2012), 211–220; Samuel Heilman, *Sliding to the Right: The Contest for the Future of American Jewish Orthodoxy* (Berkeley: University of California Press, 2006); Riv-Ellen Prell, *Prayer and Community: The Havurah in American Judaism* (Detroit: Wayne State University Press, 1989); Marshall Sklare, *Observing America's Jews* (Waltham, MA: Brandeis University Press, 1993).

78. See the Jewish Cultural Studies series website at http://littman.co.uk/jcs; and Simon J. Bronner, ed., *Jewishness: Expression, Identity, and Representation* (Oxford: Littman, 2008); Simon J. Bronner, ed., *Jews at Home: The Domestication of Identity* (Oxford: Littman, 2010); Simon J. Bronner, ed., *Revisioning Ritual: Jewish Traditions in Transition* (Oxford: Littman, 2011); and Bronner, *Framing Jewish Culture*.

79. See Simon J. Bronner, "The Jewish Joke Online: Framing and Symbolizing Humor in Analog and Digital Culture," in *Folk Culture in the Digital Age: The Emergent Dynamics of Human Interaction*, ed. Trevor J. Blank (Logan: Utah State University Press, 2012), 119–149; Andrea Lieber, "Domesticity and the Home (Page): Blogging and the Blurring of Public and Private among Orthodox Jewish Women," in Bronner, *Jews at Home*, 257–282.

80. For instance, *AJS Review,* the journal of the Association for Jewish Studies, categorizes articles by historical periods, and the mission statement of the Association for Jewish Studies refers to "Jewish Studies scholarship" rather than Jewish culture.

81. See Simon J. Bronner, "The Chutzpah of Jewish Cultural Studies," in Bronner, *Jewishness,* 1–28.

82. See Bronner, "Framing Jewish Culture," 1–29.

83. See Haya Bar-Itzhak, *Israeli Folk Narratives: Settlement, Immigration, Ethnicity* (Detroit: Wayne State University Press, 2005); Ruth Ellen Gruber, *Virtually Jewish: Reinventing Jewish Culture in Europe* (Berkeley: University of California Press, 2002); Erica T. Lehrer, *Jewish Poland Revisited: Heritage Tourism in Unquiet Places* (Bloomington: Indiana University Press, 2013).

84. Simon J. Bronner, *Explaining Traditions: Folk Behavior in Modern Culture* (Lexington: University Press of Kentucky, 2011), 261–266. See also Simon J. Bronner, "From *Landsmanshaften* to *Vinkln:* Mediating Community among Yiddish Speakers in America," *Jewish History* 15 (2001): 131–148; Simon J. Bronner, "The 'Handiness' of Tradition," in *Tradition in the Twenty-First Century: Locating the Role of the Past in the Present,* ed. Trevor J. Blank and Robert Glenn Howard (Logan: Utah State University Press, 2013), 186–218; Alanna E. Cooper, *Bukharan Jews and the Dynamics of Global Judaism* (Bloomington: Indiana University Press, 2012); Annette B. Fromm, *We Are Few: Folklore and Ethnic Identity of the Jewish Community of Ioannina, Greece* (Lanham, MD: Lexington Books, 2007).

CONTRIBUTORS

HAYA BAR-ITZHAK is Professor of Literature and Folklore at the University of Haifa, where she serves as Head of Folklore Studies and Director of the Israel Folktale Archives. The focus of her research is Jewish folk literature, with an emphasis on the ethnographic and poetic aspects. She has published extensively on settlement, immigration, and ethnicity in Israel, and on Jewish folk literature in Eastern Europe. She has published nine books, is editor of the *Encyclopedia of Jewish Folklore and Traditions*, and is a recipient of several awards, among them the American National Jewish Book Award and the Lerner Foundation for Yiddish Culture Award.

ELISSA BEMPORAD is the Jerry and William Ungar Chair in Eastern European Jewish History and the Holocaust and Assistant Professor of History at Queens College, City University of New York. She was trained at the University of Bologna and the Jewish Theological Seminary of America. She received a PhD in history from Stanford University and is most recently the author of *Becoming Soviet Jews: The Bolshevik Experiment in Minsk* (IUP, 2013), which received the Fraenkel Prize in Contemporary History and a National Jewish Book Award. She is currently working on a book on pogroms and ritual murder in the Soviet Union, for which she has received an NEH fellowship.

SIMON J. BRONNER is Distinguished University Professor of American Studies and Folklore and Chair of the American Studies Program at the Pennsylvania State University, Harrisburg, where he is also Director of

333

the Holocaust and Jewish Studies Center. The author and editor of over thirty books, including *Explaining Traditions: Folk Behavior in Modern Culture* and *American Folklore Studies: An Intellectual History,* he serves as editor of the Jewish Cultural Studies series for the Littman Library of Jewish Civilization.

NATHANIEL DEUTSCH is Professor of History and the Neufeld-Levin Endowed Chair of Holocaust Studies at the University of California, Santa Cruz, where he is Co-director of the Center for Jewish Studies and Director of the Institute for Humanities Research. Among his books are *The Maiden of Ludmir: A Jewish Holy Woman and Her World* and *The Jewish Dark Continent: Life and Death in the Russian Pale of Settlement,* for which he received a Guggenheim Fellowship.

LARISA FIALKOVA graduated from Kiev State Pedagogical Institute and received her PhD from the University of Tartu. She has lived in Israel since 1991, and teaches in the Department of Hebrew and Comparative Literature at the University of Haifa. Together with Maria Yelenevskaya, she is the co-author of more than twenty-five articles and the books *Ex-Soviets in Israel: From Personal Narratives to a Group Portrait* and *In Search of the Self: Reconciling the Past and the Present in Immigrants' Experience.* She also authored the book *Koly hory skhodiat'sia: Narysy z ukrains'ko-izrail's'kykh folklornykh vzaemyn* (When mountains meet: Essays in Ukrainian-Israeli Folklore Studies) (in Ukrainian).

DAVID E. FISHMAN is Professor of Jewish History at the Jewish Theological Seminary and Director of Project Judaica, a Jewish studies program based in Moscow that is sponsored jointly by JTS and the Russian State University for the Humanities. His books include *Russia's First Modern Jews* and *The Rise of Modern Yiddish Culture.*

HALINA GOLDBERG is Associate Professor of Musicology at the Jacobs School of Music and Affiliate Faculty of the Robert A. and Sandra S. Borns Jewish Studies Program and Russian and East European Institute at Indiana University Bloomington. She is author of *Music in Chopin's Warsaw* (2008) and co-designer of "In Mrs. Goldberg's Kitchen," the multimedia exhibit at the Central Museum of Textiles in Łódź about the Jewish quarter in pre–World War II Łódź.

SERGEI KAN is Professor of Anthropology and Native American Studies at Dartmouth College and Faculty Associate at the Davis Center for Russian and Eurasian Studies at Harvard University. His most recent books include *A Russian American Photographer in Tlingit Country: Vincent Soboleff in Alaska.*

MIKHAIL KRUTIKOV is Professor of Slavic and Judaic Studies at the University of Michigan and a cultural columnist for the *Yiddish Forward.* He is author of *Yiddish Fiction and the Crisis of Modernity, 1905–1914* and *From Kabbalah to Class Struggle: Expressionism, Marxism, and Yiddish Literature in the Life and Work of Meir Wiener.*

MARINA MOGILNER is Edward and Marianna Thaden Chair in Russian and East European Intellectual History at the University of Illinois at Chicago. She is also cofounder and coeditor of the *Ab Imperio* quarterly, which develops the field of new imperial history. Her most recent book, *Homo Imperii: A History of Physical Anthropology in Russia* (2013), offers a comprehensive history of race science in the Russian Empire.

ALEXANDRA POLYAN is a PhD candidate at the Institute of Linguistics at the Russian Academy of Sciences, Research Fellow in the Jewish Studies Department at the Institute of Asian and African Studies at Moscow State University, and a Yiddish instructor at the Russian State University for the Humanities and at Eshkolot Project. She is coauthor, with O. V. Budnitskii, of *Russian-Jewish Berlin, 1920–1941,* and has translated into Russian Zalmen Gradovskii's manuscript *V serdtsevine ada* (2010).

ASYA VAISMAN SCHULMAN is Director of the Yiddish Language Institute at the Yiddish Book Center in Amherst, Massachusetts, and Adjunct Assistant Professor at Hampshire College. She received her PhD in Yiddish language and culture from Harvard University. Her dissertation was titled "Being Heard: The Singing Voices of Contemporary Hasidic Women." She has published articles on topics related to her dissertation research, Hasidic children's literature, Yiddish folk songs, and Yiddish theater.

SEBASTIAN Z. SCHULMAN is a PhD candidate in Jewish history at Indiana University Bloomington and Director of Translation Programs at the Yiddish Book Center in Amherst, Massachusetts. He teaches Soviet and Jewish history at Hampshire College and Smith College.

JEFFREY VEIDLINGER is Joseph Brodsky Collegiate Professor of History and Judaic Studies and Director of the Frankel Center for Judaic Studies at the University of Michigan. He is author of *In the Shadow of the Shtetl: Small-Town Jewish Life in Soviet Ukraine* (IUP, 2013), *Jewish Public Culture in the Late Russian Empire* (IUP, 2009), and *The Moscow State Yiddish Theater: Jewish Culture on the Soviet Stage* (IUP, 2000).

DEBORAH YALEN is Associate Professor of History at Colorado State University–Fort Collins. Her publications explore the interaction of Jewish scholars with the Soviet state apparatus during the interwar period. Together with colleagues at the Center "Petersburg Judaica" at European University in St. Petersburg, Russia, she is authoring a volume dedicated to the legacy of Yehoshu'a (Isaiah Mendelevich) Pul'ner, director of the Jewish Section of the State Museum of Ethnography in Leningrad from 1937 to 1941.

MARIA YELENEVSKAYA received her PhD from the Leningrad State Pedagogical Institute. She has lived in Israel since 1990. She teaches courses on technical English and develops programs for computer-assisted language teaching. Together with Larisa Fialkova, she is the author of more than twenty-five articles and the books *Ex-Soviets in Israel: From Personal Narratives to a Group Portrait* and *In Search of the Self: Reconciling the Past and the Present in Immigrants' Experience*.

SARAH ELLEN ZARROW received her PhD from New York University in 2015. Her dissertation examines the social role of ethnographic documentation and museums for Jews in interwar Poland (1918–1939). She conducted the majority of the research for her chapter in this volume as a Research Fellow in Polish Jewish Studies at YIVO.

INDEX

Abbe, Dawid Wolf, 272, 280n17

Abrahams, Roger, 321

Abramovitch, Gershon, 167

Abramovitsh, Khayim-Zanvl. *See* Ribnitser Rebbe (Khayim-Zanvl Abramovitsh)

Abramovitsh, Sholem Yankev. *See* Moykher-Sforim, Mendele

absorption stories, 181; boundary setting, 189–190; food stories, 185–186; monster stories, 182–184

Adams, Tony E., 239

aggadah (fables from rabbinic literature), 6

agricultural organizations, Jewish, 130–131

Aleichem, Sholem, 148, 196

Aliyah Senior Citizens' Center (Venice Beach), 27, 35–36

all-Union folklore conference (1936), 106

American Anthropological Association, 312, 314

American Folklore Society, 312, 317

American Jewish Joint Distribution Committee (JDC), 229, 231, 242

Amitin-Shapiro, Zalmen, 125

analytical paradigm, 240–241

ancient national spirit, 177

Anders, Władysław, 189

Anderson, Leon, 240, 245

An-sky, S., 1–7, 11–12, 20; ethnopoetics, 304, 307–311; Jewish ethnography

and ethnography of Jews, 311–316; life cycle questionnaires, 30–31, 149–150; Marxist-Leninist teaching and, 103, 104, 109; "Mentsh" program, 74; not cited by folklorists, 304–305; "Oral Torah," 137, 310; Pale of Jewish Settlement as "primitive," 29, 31–32; past, view of, 31, 305–306, 308; as populist, 70–71; as "priest," 41–42; religiosity of Jewish folklore, 34, 114, 128; return to Jewish identity, 309–310; *Works: The Dybbuk*, 7, 33, 37–38, 310–311; "Jewish Folk Creativity," 1–2, 29; *Perezhitoe* essay, 30, 307–311. *See also* Jewish Ethnographic Expedition

"Anthropological Studies of Jews Written in the Course of the Past Ten Years" (El'kind), 48

anthropometric data, 48–49, 54, 57, 68

"anticosmopolitan" campaign, 120

antipsychological turn, 321–322

antireligious campaigns, 74, 80, 103, 127, 205–207

antisemitism, 75–76, 97, 313–315

Antokolsky, Mark, 167

Anuchin, Dimitri, 48–49, 52

Aptekman, O. V., 3–4

Arabs, 188–189

Archives of Historical and Ethnographic Yiddish Memories (AHEYM), 17–18, 208

CPSIA information can be obtained
at www.ICGtesting.com
Printed in the USA
LVOW04s2320160816

500630LV00012B/109/P

9 780253 019141